An Attachment-Based Model of Parental Alienation: Foundations

C.A. Childress, Psy.D.

An Attachment-Based Model of Parental Alienation: Foundations

Oaksong Press. Claremont, California

Printed in the United States of America

ISBN 978-0-9961145-0-9

Contents

Introduction

PARADIGM SHIFT

The Current Paradigm

The term "parental alienation" is used in discussions by mental health and legal professionals to characterize a set of family dynamics in which a child is influenced by one parent into rejecting a relationship with the other parent, who is otherwise a normal-range and affectionally available parent. This type of negative parental influence on the child typically occurs following a divorce, although the processes of the child's "alienation" can begin while the family is still intact and before the actual divorce occurs. "Parental alienation" is often alleged in high-conflict custody disputes in which the parents can battle for years over custody issues surrounding the children, co-parenting, and visitation. However, despite the term "parental alienation" being used in professional contexts, the actual construct lacks a defined meaning within clinical psychology.

The construct of "parental alienation" was popularized in the 1980's by a psychiatrist, Richard Gardner, who proposed a set of eight anecdotal clinical indicators for recognizing "parental alienation," such as a campaign of denigration by the child directed against the targeted parent for reasons that are considered weak and frivolous, child criticisms of the targeted parent using "borrowed scenarios" provided by the alienating parent, or the child staunchly maintaining that the child's animosity and rejection of the targeted parent were authentic to the child's experience and were not being created by the negative influence of the allied and favored parent, a characteristic that Gardner referred to as the "independent thinker" phenomenon for the child.

Unfortunately, none of these proposed indicators of "parental alienation" have any basis in established psychological principles or constructs within professional psychology. They were all developed by Gardner as uniquely representing what he claimed was a new psychological syndrome, which he termed "Parental Alienation Syndrome" (PAS). According to Gardner and the supporters of the PAS model, these eight diagnostic indicators may or may not be present in any individual case of PAS and the degree of "alienation" could range along a continuum from mild, to moderate, to severe, although it is unclear by what criteria placement along this continuum can be established. As a result, it is unclear what features of the PAS model constitute mild "alienation" versus moderate "alienation" versus severe "alienation," so that making this determination of whether PAS is present and at what severity appears to be a matter of clinical judgment.

The methods by which one parent induces a child to reject a relationship with the other parent were also not adequately clarified by Gardner. As a result, the vague and non-clinical term of "brainwashing" is often applied to describe the processes by which the child is induced into rejecting a relationship with the other parent. This has led in the past to supposed treatments that were designed to "deprogram" the child. Since the symptom induction process is unclear, the required treatment for PAS remains equally unclear. This has resulted in situations where "parental alienation" is established as being responsible for the child's rejection of a normal-range and affectionally available parent, yet the court nevertheless remains reluctant to separate the child from the alienating parent out of concern for the possibly detrimental impact on the child of severing the child's seemingly bonded relationship with the allied and supposedly favored alienating parent.

While the clinical phenomenon identified by Gardner is valid, the PAS model he proposed is not based in any established or accepted psychological principles or constructs. None of the symptoms proposed for PAS represent defined constructs in clinical psychology, nor are the concepts of "brainwashing" and "deprogramming" defined and accepted constructs in clinical psychology. The PAS model proposed by Gardner was therefore met with considerable skepticism within many factions of professional psychology and the legal system because it lacked sufficient theoretical foundation for the proposal of a new "syndrome" defined by anecdotal indicators, arbitrarily identified by Gardner, that were unrelated to any established psychological principles or constructs.

To further compound the controversy surrounding PAS, Gardner also proposed that the presence of PAS, despite being a vaguely defined theoretical construct, was often associated with false allegations of sexual abuse made by mothers against fathers in custody disputes. Gardner proposed that mothers used these false allegations of sexual abuse as manipulative tools to gain advantage in the post-divorce custody proceedings. According to Gardner, when PAS is present then allegations of sexual abuse against the father should be met with skepticism and could be discounted if PAS is present. This proposal by Gardner regarding false allegations of sexual abuse made by mothers in divorce proceedings against fathers because of PAS drew considerable criticism and generated considerable controversy.

Both sides in this controversy are correct. The clinical phenomenon of "parental alienation" is authentic, but Gardner's description of the construct is inadequate. As a result of both sides being correct, the field of professional psychology became polarized into proponents and opponents of the PAS construct. The proposal for a new diagnosis of Parental Alienation Syndrome in professional psychology immediately drew supporters who advocated for the existence of this clinical phenomenon. Yet the inadequate theoretical foundations provided by Gardner for this new syndrome also created detractors as well, who staunchly argued that the PAS model lacked sufficient theoretical substance, and the phrase "junk science" was coined to describe the lack of scientific support for the PAS model. The authenticity of the clinical phenomenon combined with Gardner's inadequate definition of the construct split professional psychology into polarized camps with regard to "parental alienation." The controversy generated in professional psychology was then transferred into the legal arena as the proponents of PAS as a legitimate mental health construct tried to have it introduced into divorce and custody proceedings, while the opponents of PAS challenged the use of the construct in a legal setting as not having a sufficient scientific basis.

Over the decades since Gardner first proposed the PAS model, proponents for the construct of "parental alienation" have tried to establish a research-based foundation for the validity of the anecdotal clinical indicators identified by Gardner, and they have tried repeatedly, but without success, to have the construct of "parental alienation" included as a recognized diagnostic entity within the DSM diagnostic system of the American Psychiatric Association. Gradually, through the persistent efforts of the proponents for a PAS model, the mental health and legal systems have grudgingly recognized the existence of "parental alienation," although the construct remains poorly defined. With the increased recognition for the construct by professional mental health, the existence of "parental alienation" has also been granted some recognition in the legal setting as well.

However, within clinical psychology the construct of "parental alienation" still lacks a clearly defined meaning, which limits its usefulness as a clinical construct for diagnosis and treatment. Yet within clinical psychology the component family dynamics and psychological processes that have traditionally been called "parental alienation" in the general popular culture have already been defined in established and accepted psychological principles and constructs. It is simply that these established psychological principles and constructs have not been applied to define the construct of "parental alienation." At some level, this theoretical failure is understandable given the complexity of the psychological and interpersonal processes, yet at the same time this failure is puzzling given that the processes involved in "parental alienation" are clearly recognized mental health constructs.

From the perspective of clinical psychology, there is absolutely nothing new or unique about the construct of "parental alienation" except the name. The component psychological and family processes within clinical psychology that define the clinical phenomenon of "parental alienation" are all standard and well established psychological principles and constructs, but these established principles and constructs of professional psychology were simply not applied by Gardner within the PAS model, or subsequently by his supporters. Gardner was correct in identifying an authentic clinical phenomenon, yet he too quickly abandoned the professional rigor necessary for defining "parental alienation" within established psychological principles and constructs. The subsequent supporters of the PAS model have likewise failed to accept the constructive criticism offered by establishment mental health which would have led them to develop a more substantial theoretical foundation for defining the construct of "parental alienation." Instead, both sides in the debate have maintained polarized positions of argument and counter-argument without recognizing the validity of the other position and without seeking a synthesis of views that would better serve the needs of targeted parents and their children.

Syndrome

From the perspective of an attachment-based reconceptualization and redefinition for the construct of "parental alienation," there is nothing new about the psychological or family processes involved. All of the component processes that comprise an attachment-based model for the construct of "parental alienation" are established and accepted psychological principles and constructs. Yet the psychological and interpersonal processes are complex, at least on first pass, so that it is helpful to have a label by which the complex dynamics can be efficiently labeled in discussion.

My approach has been to continue using the label "parental alienation" but to place this term in quotes to indicate that the construct itself does not have a defined clinical meaning, but is instead comprised of component processes that are defined within clinical psychology. In order to differentiate this new definition for the construct of "parental alienation" from Gardner's inadequate PAS model, I have applied the additional phrase "attachment-based" ahead of the term "parental alienation" to indicate that I am not discussing the Gardnerian PAS model, and also to emphasize the importance of the attachment system in understanding the dynamics surrounding the clinical phenomenon traditionally described as "parental alienation."

Does the construct of "parental alienation" warrant the designation as a syndrome? The definition of a syndrome according to the Merriam-Webster Dictionary (2015) is:

1. a group of signs and symptoms that occur together and characterize a particular abnormality or condition

2. a set of concurrent things (as emotions or actions) that usually form an identifiable pattern

An attachment-based reconceptualization for the construct of "parental alienation" seemingly meets the definitional criteria as a syndrome, although the theoretical foundations for an attachment-based model of "parental alienation" bear no resemblance to the anecdotal definition of the Gardnerian PAS model. In order to avoid any confusion between the attachment-based model of "parental alienation" and the Gardnerian PAS model, I am going to refrain from using the term "syndrome" in my discussions of "parental alienation." But eventually, once the paradigm has shifted away from the Gardnerian PAS definition to an attachment-based reconceptualization, then the re-application of the term "syndrome" would seemingly be appropriate for the complex and interwoven family systems, personality disorder, and attachment system processes evidenced in an attachment-based model for the construct of "parental alienation."

In the professional and legal debate that has surrounded the construct of "parental alienation" for nearly three decades, both sides are correct. There is a valid clinical phenomenon that is manifested in an identifiable pattern of symptoms that occur together (i.e., a syndrome) involving a child's induced rejection of a relationship with a normal-range and affectionally available parent as a product of the distorting parental influence on the child by the allied and supposedly favored parent, AND the PAS model for defining this phenomenon lacks sufficiently established scientific foundation. The definition of "parental alienation" proposed by the PAS model is professionally inadequate. The critics of the PAS model are absolutely correct in their assertion that the PAS model lacks scientifically supported theoretical grounding. This does not mean, however, that Gardner was incorrect in identifying the existence of a valid clinical phenomenon, only that his initial effort at defining this phenomenon lacked sufficient professional precision.

An attachment-based model of "parental alienation" returns to the roots of the clinical phenomenon identified by Gardner and redefines the construct of "parental alienation" from entirely within standard and established psychological principles and constructs of the attachment system, personality disorder characteristics, and family systems constructs. By applying the necessary professional rigor needed to redefine the construct of "parental alienation" from entirely within standard and established psychological principles and constructs, an attachment-based model of "parental alienation" represents a complete break with the earlier PAS model proposed by Gardner. An attachment-based model for the construct of "parental alienation" represents an entirely different paradigm for understanding and defining the clinical phenomenon traditionally referred to as "parental alienation."

Pathogenic Parenting

As noted earlier, throughout this book and in my other writings I always place the term "parental alienation" in quotes. I do this because, in my view as a clinical psychologist, the construct of "parental alienation" is not a defined clinical construct. From the perspective of clinical psychology the more accurate clinical term for "parental alienation" is "pathogenic parenting" (patho=pathological; genic=genesis, creation). Pathogenic parenting refers to parenting practices that are so aberrant and distorted that they produce significant psychopathology in the child. In professional psychology, the term "pathogenic parenting" is most often used in the context of distortions to the child's attachment system, since the attachment system does not spontaneously or independently dysfunction, but only becomes dysfunctional in response to problematic and "pathogenic parenting" practices.

The correct clinical term for what has traditionally been referred to as "parental alienation" is pathogenic parenting involving a parentally induced suppression of the child's attachment bonding motivations toward a normal-range and affectionally available parent. Going forward, I would encourage mental health professionals to gradually transition to the more accurate clinical term of "pathogenic parenting" in describing the pathology associated with an attachment-based model of "parental alienation." As a label for the complex pathology of attachment-based "parental alienation," mental health professionals may wish to link the terms "pathogenic parenting" and "parental alienation" in order to specify the associated type of pathogenic parenting, thereby creating the combined phrase of "pathogenic parenting associated with attachment-based "parental alienation" as a more accurate label for the pathology.

The reason for the recommended shift in phrasing within mental health is to achieve greater clarity and accuracy in diagnosis and treatment. Shifting to the term "pathogenic parenting" subtly shifts the conceptual focus of mental health professionals from diagnosing the distorted parenting practices of the alienating parent to a more direct clinical focus on the impact of these distorted parenting practices on the child, who is developing and expressing symptoms of great clinical concern.

An Attachment-Based Model

In the descriptions to follow, an attachment-based model for the construct of "parental alienation" will be elaborated. The component clinical constructs that make up the complex family dynamics will be described through three levels of analysis that comprise an integrated model; first at the level of the family system dynamics, then at the level of the personality disorder processes of the narcissistic/(borderline) parent, and then finally at the underlying substrate of the attachment system level. The clinical phenomenon of "parental alienation" is comprised of these three component psychological levels, so that an overall clinical description of "parental alienation" incorporates all three levels of analysis.

Clinical Definition of "Parental Alienation"

The construct of "parental alienation" represents the child's triangulation into the spousal conflict through the formation of a cross-generational coalition with a narcissistic/(borderline) parent. This cross-generational coalition of the narcissistic/(borderline) parent with the child is directed against the other parent, causing a breach in the child's relationship with the targeted parent. In this cross-generational coalition, the child is being used by the narcissistic/(borderline) parent in a role-reversal relationship as a "regulatory object" for the regulation of excessive parental anxiety triggered by the divorce.

The anxiety experienced by the narcissistic/(borderline) parent that is being regulated through the child's induced symptomatic rejection of the targeted parent originates from three interrelated sources:

1) **Narcissistic Anxiety:** The threatened collapse of the parent's narcissistic defenses against the experience of primal self-inadequacy;

2) **Borderline Anxiety:** A borderline personality dynamic surrounding an intense fear of abandonment;

3) **Trauma Anxiety:** The re-experiencing by the parent of childhood attachment trauma (called "complex trauma" or "developmental trauma") that was responsible for creating the narcissistic and borderline personality processes that are driving the "parental alienation."

The developmental trauma experienced by the narcissistic/(borderline) parent during childhood is contained in the internal working models of the narcissistic/(borderline) parent's attachment networks in the representational pattern of "abusive parent"/"victimized child"/"protective parent." These attachment trauma patterns (as well as the additional role of "bystander") from the childhood attachment trauma of the narcissistic/(borderline) parent are being reenacted in current relationships with the current child and targeted parent as a means for the narcissistic/(borderline) parent to regulate the reactivated anxiety from the childhood trauma. In the trauma reenactment narrative, the current child is assigned the attachment trauma role as the "victimized child," the targeted parent is assigned the role as the "abusive parent" in the trauma reenactment, and the narcissistic/(borderline) parent adopts the coveted role as the "protective parent" in the trauma reenactment narrative. Through the reenactment of childhood attachment trauma into the current family relationships the narcissistic/(borderline) parent is able to obtain psychological mastery over the childhood trauma experience, and over the associated trauma-related anxiety that is embedded in this parent's attachment networks.

But this clinical definition becomes a very long and complicated description to repeatedly say each time we wish to reference the clinical phenomenon, so it would benefit us to have a shorter label to represent this underlying clinical phenomenon. We could call it "trauma reenactment alienation," or "induced child rejection through role-reversal," or "parentally induced child alienation," or any of a variety of other labels. However, the label used over the past thirty years within the mainstream culture for this clinical phenomenon has been "parental alienation." Therefore, I have decided to continue in this tradition, but I have placed the phrase "parental alienation" in quotes to indicate that it is not, in itself, a defined clinical construct, but is instead defined by a set of component clinical constructs that have defined meanings within the scientific literature. In addition, to differentiate this new model for the construct of "parental alienation" from the prior PAS model of Gardner, I have added the phrase "attachment-based" in front of the popularized term of "parental alienation" to indicate the reference to this new model rather than the older Gardnerian PAS model.

Paradigm Shift

The attachment-based redefinition for the construct of "parental alienation" that is based entirely within standard and established psychological principles and constructs as a replacement for the earlier laudable but professionally inadequate PAS model proposed by Gardner represents a fundamental paradigm shift for how the construct of "parental alienation" is defined. The attachment-based model described here is completely separate from and has no association with the earlier PAS model proposed by Gardner, except that they both use the term "parental alienation" (although I place this term in quotes to indicate that it is not, in itself, a defined clinical term) and both paradigms address a similar, but not necessarily identical, clinical phenomenon.

While the Gardnerian PAS model and the attachment-based model for the construct of "parental alienation" share some overlap in the identified clinical phenomenon, there is nevertheless some variation in the actual clinical phenomenon being addressed by the attachment-based model as compared to the PAS model. The attachment-based redefinition for the construct of "parental alienation" is dichotomous rather than the dimensional definition of Gardnerian PAS, meaning that attachment-based parental alienation is diagnostically either present or absent, whereas the Gardnerian PAS model allows mild, moderate, and severe forms (although it does not specify clear criteria for differentiating various degrees of "alienation"). In an attachment-based model of "parental alienation," there are no mild or moderate cases. Attachment-based "parental alienation" is **always** a manifestation of severe psychopathology within the family that is either present or absent.

The diagnostic indicators for the presence (or absence) of attachment-based "parental alienation" are also entirely different from the anecdotal diagnostic signs proposed by Gardner for PAS. Gardner proposed a set of eight anecdotal clinical indicators that may or may not be present in any given case, and the nature of these clinical signs had no relationship to established psychological constructs or symptoms but were unique to the Gardnerian diagnosis of PAS. An attachment-based model, on the other hand, relies instead on a theoretical formulation of the pathology to identify a specific set of three diagnostic indicators based in both the theory of attachment-based "parental alienation" and in standard clinical symptom indicators. This set of three diagnostic indicators for attachment-based parental alienation must all be present in order for the clinical diagnosis of attachment-based "parental alienation" to be made, and the application of these three diagnostic indicators yields a dichotomous diagnosis of attachment-based "parental alienation" as being either present or absent in any specific case.

In addition, the means by which the child's symptoms are induced are conceptually different, or perhaps simply more elaborated within an attachment-based model of "parental alienation." The attachment-based model of "parental alienation" does not rely on the poorly defined construct of "brainwashing" the child or inducing the child's symptoms through direct parental denigration of the targeted parent by the allied and supposedly favored alienating parent. Instead, an attachment-based model of "parental alienation" turns to the sophisticated scientific evidence from parent-child communication research, and relies on a more thorough understanding regarding the functioning of the attachment system during childhood for explaining how the child's rejection of a relationship with the targeted parent is induced. This description of the symptom induction process involves a more fully considered understanding for the reenactment of trauma to then describe the subtle and complex means of interpersonal influence on the child that leads to the suppression of the child's attachment-bonding motivations toward a normal-range and affectionally available parent and that induces the child's specific symptom display.

Finally, since an attachment-based model of "parental alienation" is based in established and accepted psychological principles and constructs, it leads directly to more definitive treatment recommendations than does the earlier PAS model. An attachment-based model identifies four interrelated phases for the treatment of the distortions to the functioning of the child's attachment system that are created by the child's role-reversal relationship with the narcissistic/(borderline) parent. The initial phase of treatment for the severe pathology being expressed in attachment-based "parental alienation" requires a child protection response during the active phase of the child's treatment and recovery stabilization period. Once the child is protected from the ongoing and relentless pathogenic influence of the narcissistic/(borderline) parent, then the treatment involves two interrelated phases of recovering the child's authenticity from the role-reversal relationship with the narcissistic/(borderline) parent and the restoration of an affectionally bonded relationship with the normal-range targeted parent. The final phase of treatment involves the monitored reintroduction of the pathology of the narcissistic/(borderline) parent which allows the child to establish healthy attachment bonds to both parents.

The attachment-based model for "parental alienation" and the Gardnerian PAS model are distinctly different. They represent two separate paradigms for conceptualizing the construct of "parental alienation." After 30 years of the PAS model as representing the dominant paradigm for describing the clinical phenomenon of "parental alienation," the Gardnerian model of PAS has failed to produce a solution to the family tragedy of "parental alienation." The Gardnerian PAS model represents a failed paradigm across a range of considerations and it needs to be replaced by a more scientifically grounded model for the construct of "parental alienation." After 30 years as the dominant paradigm, the PAS model of Gardner is a failed theoretical paradigm, it is a failed diagnostic paradigm, it is a failed legal paradigm, and it is a failed treatment paradigm.

PAS as a Failed Theoretical Paradigm

In defining the construct of PAS, Gardner too quickly abandoned the professional rigor required to define his proposed construct of "parental alienation" within scientifically established and professionally accepted psychological principles and constructs. Instead, he proposed a new "syndrome" that was not based in any established psychological principles or constructs, and was defined solely though anecdotal clinical indicators. When we build any structure, we start by first laying a firm foundation that can support the structure we build. By proposing a new "syndrome" that is not anchored in any established psychological principles or constructs, Gardner too quickly abandoned the necessary professional rigor required to first lay a solid theoretical foundation for the construct of "parental alienation."

Instead, Gardner built the theoretical structure for the construct of PAS on the shifting sands of anecdotal clinical signs, rather than on the theoretical bedrock of established psychological principles and constructs.

As a result, when targeted parents and the legal profession then tried to leverage the PAS model of "parental alienation" to achieve a solution to the family pathology, the shifting sands of its theoretical foundation shifted beneath their feet and the theoretical structure of PAS collapsed. In the 30 years since its introduction, the PAS model has failed to provide and actualized solution to the family tragedy of "parental alienation."

An attachment-based model for the construct of "parental alienation" returns to the core bedrock of the theoretical foundations on which the construct of "parental alienation" is based. An attachment-based model of "parental alienation" is established on the solid bedrock of standard and established psychological principles and constructs. This opens the door to a wealth of scientifically grounded research literature, which then allows the mental health and legal professions to leverage an attachment-based model of "parental alienation" into an actualizable solution for the family. When the theoretical foundations for an attachment-based model of "parental alienation" are relied on to achieve a solution, our feet will be firmly grounded on the bedrock of scientifically established psychological principles and constructs.

PAS as a Failed Diagnostic Paradigm

The eight anecdotal diagnostic signs of PAS proposed by Gardner are too vague and ill-defined to be useful in clinical practice. The diagnostic indicators may or may not be present in any individual case, with no established guidelines for how many diagnostic indicators are necessary for either the diagnosis in any individual case or for establishing the level of severity of "parental alienation" in any individual case. This has led to a great deal of debate surrounding the relative contribution of the targeted parent to the child's symptom display even when highly distorted parenting practices by the allied and supposedly favored parent have been identified.

Since the PAS diagnostic model is dimensional, it allows cases of "parental alienation" to be placed along a continuum from mild, to moderate, to severe. This dimensional diagnostic structure for the PAS model permits mental health professionals to divide parental responsibility for the child's symptoms between the alienating parent and the targeted parent. Dividing responsibility for the creation of the child's severe symptomatology fails to recognize the actual truth behind the child's symptoms; i.e., that they are the sole result of severely distorted parenting practices by a narcissistic/(borderline) parent. The dimensional quality of the Gardnerian PAS model undermines the clarity of diagnosis. Even when highly distorted parenting practices by the alienating parent are identified and acknowledged by mental health professionals, these professionals are often reluctant to absolve the targeted parent of responsibility for having at least some role in the child's symptomatic rejection displayed toward the targeted parent. This, in turn, leads to treatment efforts that are misguided because they fail to fully comprehend the nature of the severe psychopathology being expressed in the family processes.

The diagnostic structure for an attachment-based model of "parental alienation," on the other hand, is dichotomous. This means that the use of the diagnostic indicators for an attachment-based model of "parental alienation" will provide a definitive diagnostic identification of "parental alienation" as being either present or absent, and as being the sole causative agent for the child's symptomatic rejection of a relationship with the normal-range and affectionally available targeted parent. Furthermore, the diagnostic indicators for an attachment-based model of "parental alienation" are derived from the underlying theoretical constructs that form the foundational bedrock of the model, rather than from anecdotally suggestive clinical indicators, so that the foundations for the diagnostic indicators are professionally sound and definitive.

PAS as a Failed Legal Paradigm

The PAS model requires that targeted parents prove "parental alienation" in court in order to obtain legal remedies for their problems in shared custody, and for their child's symptomatic displays of rejection. However, proving "parental alienation" in court is far too long and protracted a process, allowing the child's symptomatic state to go unresolved for years. Proving "parental alienation" in court is also far too expensive for most targeted parents to achieve. In most cases, proving "parental alienation" in court is financially beyond the reach of the targeted-rejected parent.

In addition, only the most egregious cases of "parental alienation" can typically meet the standards of evidence required for proof in legal proceedings. The complex psychological manipulation and exploitation involved in "parental alienation" is too subtle and difficult to describe for the court during trial. The role-reversal processes by which the narcissistic/(borderline) parent induces the child's symptomatic rejection of the targeted parent are extremely subtle and insidious, and do not provide the exposed evidence necessary for proof of distorted parenting in a legal context. As a result, the pathology of "parental alienation" often goes unrecognized within the legal context.

Furthermore, proving "parental alienation" in court can become an excessively long and drawn out effort, often requiring years of repeated litigation that never resolves the problem, and this extensive and repeated litigation disproportionately clogs and over-burdens the family law courts. Of considerable concern is that throughout the years of unproductive litigation the child and targeted parent lose precious time from their affectionally bonded relationship during important developmental periods of childhood. Once lost, these periods of child development and lost relationship can never be recaptured. The requirement imposed by the PAS model that targeted parents prove "parental alienation" in court does not provide targeted parents and their children with a realistic and actualizable solution for the pathology being expressed within the family.

An attachment-based model of "parental alienation" takes the diagnosis of mental health pathology out of the courtroom and returns it to the mental health profession. By analogy, the diagnosis of a patient with schizophrenia or bipolar disorder does not require years of protracted litigation in the legal system to prove the patient has the diagnosed disorder. Unusual cases regarding diagnosis may sometimes enter the legal system, yet even in these rare cases the legal system tends to rely more fully on professional diagnosis rather than litigating the applicability of diagnostic criteria for a mental health disorder.

By returning to established and accepted psychological principles and constructs for the definition of "parental alienation," an attachment-based model allows the mental health profession to bring to a close its unnecessary and destructive internal polarization regarding the validity of the construct of "parental alienation." Once the mental health profession becomes unified in recognizing and describing the nature of the pathology, a united mental health profession can provide the legal system with clear and unambiguous identification of the family pathology, and with clear and definitive recommendations for the treatment remedy necessary for restoring healthy and normal-range child development and family relationships. When mental health speaks with a single united voice then the legal system will be able to act with the decisive clarity necessary to solve the family processes of attachment-based "parental alienation." Once mental health achieves clarity regarding the nature of the pathology, the legal system will be able to rely on the professional diagnosis of the pathology and on the recommendations for needed treatment, resulting in greater efficiency and clarity in court decisions and substantially reduced financial cost and time required for litigating family conflict.

PAS as a Failed Treatment Paradigm

Since Gardner's PAS model lacks theoretical foundations in established psychological principles and constructs, it cannot offer guidelines regarding treatment recommendations. Any treatment recommendations derived from the PAS model are only speculative since the PAS model is not defined or explained within any linking theoretical structure for understanding the processes involved.

An attachment-based model of "parental alienation," on the other hand, defines the construct of "parental alienation" through its underlying dynamics. These dynamics are based in established psychological principles and constructs which then lead directly to the required treatment interventions that are necessary for resolving the identified psychological pathology being expressed within the family. We cannot understand how to treat a disorder until we first understand what that disorder entails. By defining the core pathology of "parental alienation," an attachment-based model for the construct of "parental alienation" leads to identifiable and clearly defined treatment recommendations.

An attachment-based model of "parental alienation" represents a paradigm shift in which the prior Gardnerian model for the construct is retired and is replaced by a more robust and scientifically grounded attachment-based model for the construct of "parental alienation." By returning to the foundational definition that describes the construct of "parental alienation," an attachment-based model recognizes the actuality of the clinical phenomenon while correcting the fundamental weakness of the PAS model in defining the nature of this clinical phenomenon. This change in paradigms provides targeted parents and their children with immediately actualizable solutions for the pathology, and courts will be able to rely on the unified voice of mental health for clarity in identifying the diagnosis and treatment needs of the child.

While the laudable early conceptual work of Gardner should be appreciated for highlighting the presence of an authentic and important clinical phenomenon, it is long-past overdue to shift toward a more scientifically and professionally grounded definition for the construct of "parental alienation." The professional definition for the construct of "parental alienation" needs to be based in established and accepted psychological principles and constructs that can be used to define the theoretical foundations, the diagnostic indicators, and the treatment structure for the construct of "parental alienation."

Theoretical Overview

The psychological processes involved in attachment-based "parental alienation" are complex, but they become increasingly self-evident with familiarity. The primary reason for the initial apparent complexity of the dynamics is that they involve the psychological expressions within family relationship patterns of a narcissistic/(borderline) personality structure that has its origins in early attachment trauma from the childhood of the parent which is influencing, and in fact driving, the patterns of relationship interactions currently being expressed within the family. The inner psychological processes of the narcissistic/(borderline) mind are inherently complex and swirling, and linking these distorted personality processes into the functioning of the underlying attachment system adds another level of complexity. However, the nature of the pathology is stable across cases of "parental alienation," so that this consistency in the pathology provides ever increasing clarity of understanding from increasing familiarity for the concepts.

Fully understanding these seemingly complex psychological and family factors requires an integrated recognition of the psychological and interpersonal dynamics across three interrelated levels of clinical analysis, 1) the family systems level, 2) the personality disorder level, and 3) the attachment system level. Each of these levels individually provides a coherent explanatory model for the dynamics being expressed in "parental alienation," and yet each individual level is also an interconnected expression of the pathology contained at the other two levels of analysis as well, so that a complete recognition of the psychopathology being expressed as "parental alienation" requires a conceptual understanding of the process across all three distinctly different, yet interconnected, levels of analysis.

The family systems processes involve the family's inability to successfully transition from an intact family structure that is united by the marital relationship to a separated family structure that is united by the continuing parental roles with the child. The difficulty in the family's ability to transition from an intact family structure to a separated family structure is manifesting in the child's triangulation into the spousal conflict through the formation of a cross-generational coalition with one parent (the allied and supposedly favored parent) against the other parent (the targeted-rejected parent). These principles are standard and established family systems constructs that are extensively discussed and described by preeminent family systems theorists, such as Salvador Minuchin and Jay Haley.

The problems occurring at the family systems level of analysis have their origin in the narcissistic/(borderline) personality dynamics of the allied and supposedly favored parent. The personality pathology of the narcissistic/(borderline) parent is creating a distorted emotional and psychological response in this parent to the psychological stresses associated with the interpersonal rejection and perceived abandonment surrounding the divorce. The inherent interpersonal rejection associated with divorce triggers specific psychological vulnerabilities for the narcissistic/(borderline) parent, who then responds in characteristic but pathological ways that adversely influence the child's relationship with the other parent.

The characteristic psychopathology of the narcissistic/(borderline) parent draws the child into a role-reversal relationship with the parent in which the child is used by the narcissistic/(borderline) parent as an external "regulatory object" to help the narcissistic/(borderline) parent regulate three separate but interrelated sources of intense anxiety that were triggered by the divorce,

1) **Narcissistic Anxiety:** The threatened collapse of the parent's narcissistic defenses against an experience of core-self inadequacy that is being activated by the interpersonal rejection associated with the divorce;

2) **Borderline Anxiety:** The triggering of severe abandonment fears as a result of the divorce and dissolution of the intact family structure;

3) **Trauma Anxiety:** The activation and re-experiencing of excessive anxiety embedded in attachment trauma networks from the childhood of the narcissistic/(borderline) parent that become active when the attachment system of the narcissistic/(borderline) parent activates in order to mediate the loss experience associated with the divorce.

At the core level of the psychological and family dynamics that are traditionally described as "parental alienation" is the attachment trauma of the narcissistic/(borderline) parent that is being triggered and then reenacted in current family relationships. It is this childhood attachment trauma of the narcissistic/(borderline) parent that is responsible for creating the narcissistic and borderline pathology of this personality. The childhood attachment trauma experienced by the narcissistic/(borderline) parent subsequently coalesced during this parent's adolescence and young adulthood into the narcissistic and borderline personality structures that are driving the distorted relationship dynamics associated with the "parental alienation." The childhood attachment trauma (i.e., a disorganized attachment) creates the narcissistic and borderline personality structures that then distort the family's transition from an intact family structure to a separated family structure.

At the foundational core for triggering this integrated psychological and interpersonal dynamic is the reactivation by the divorce of attachment trauma networks from the childhood of the narcissistic/(borderline) parent that are contained within the internal working models of this parent's attachment system. The representational schemas for this childhood attachment trauma are in the pattern of "victimized child"/"abusive parent"/"protective parent," and it is this trauma pattern from the childhood of the "alienating" narcissistic/(borderline) parent that is being reenacted in the current family relationships.

The childhood trauma patterns for role-relationships contained within the internal working models of the narcissistic/(borderline) parent's attachment system are being reenacted in current family relationships. The current child is adopting the trauma reenactment role as the "victimized child." The child's role as the "victimized child" then imposes the reenactment role of the "abusive parent" onto the targeted parent, and the coveted role in the trauma reenactment narrative of the all-wonderful "protective parent" is being adopted and conspicuously displayed by the narcissistic/(borderline) parent to the "bystanders" in the trauma reenactment. The "bystanders" in the trauma reenactment are represented by the various therapists, parenting coordinators, custody evaluators, attorneys, and judges. Their role in the trauma reenactment is to endorse the "authenticity" of the reenactment narrative. These "bystanders" also serve the function of providing the narcissistic/(borderline) parent with the "narcissistic supply" of social approval for the presentation by the narcissistic/(borderline) parent as being the idealized and all-wonderful "protective parent."

At its foundational core, "parental alienation" represents the reenactment of a false drama of abuse and victimization from the childhood of a narcissistic/(borderline) parent that is embedded in the internal working models of the "alienating" parent's attachment networks. This false drama of the reenactment narrative is created by the psychopathology of a narcissistic/(borderline) parent in response to the psychological stresses of the divorce and the reactivation of attachment trauma networks as a consequence of the divorce experience. In actual truth, there is no victimized child, there is no abusive parent, and there is no protective parent. It is a false drama, an echo of a childhood trauma from long ago, brought into the present by the pathological consequences of the childhood trauma in creating the distorting narcissistic/(borderline) personality structures of the alienating parent.

The child, for his or her part, is caught within this reenactment narrative by the distorting psychopathology and invalidating communications of the narcissistic/(borderline) parent that nullify the child's own authentic self-experience in favor of the child becoming a narcissistic reflection for the parent. Under the distorting pathogenic influence of the narcissistic/(borderline) parent, the child is led into misinterpreting the child's authentic grief and sadness at the loss of the intact family, and later at the loss of an affectionally bonded relationship with the targeted parent, as representing something "bad" that the targeted parent must be doing to create the child's hurt (i.e., the child's grief and sadness). The (influenced) misinterpretation by the child for an authentic experience of grief and loss is then further inflamed by distorted communications from the narcissistic/(borderline) that transform the child's authentic sadness into an experience of anger and resentment toward the targeted parent who (supposedly) caused the divorce and who (supposedly) is causing the child's continuing emotional pain (i.e., the child's misunderstood and misinterpreted feelings of grief and sadness).

Through a process of distorted parental communications by the narcissistic/(borderline) parent, the child is led into adopting the "victimized child" role within the trauma reenactment narrative. Once the child adopts the "victimized child" role within the trauma reenactment narrative, this "victimized child" role automatically imposes upon the targeted parent the role as the "abusive parent," and then the combined role definitions of the "abusive parent" and "victimized child" that are created the moment the child adopts the "victimized child" role allows the narcissistic/(borderline) parent to adopt the coveted trauma reenactment role as the all-wonderful nurturing and "protective parent," which will then be so conspicuously displayed to the "bystanders" for their validation and "narcissistic supply."

The description of an attachment-based model for the construct of "parental alienation" will uncover the layers of pathology, beginning with the surface level of the family systems dynamics involving the family's difficulty in making the transition from an intact family structure to a separated family structure. The description will then move into the personality disorder level to describe how the pathological characteristics of the narcissistic/(borderline) personality structures become expressed in the family relationship dynamics, particularly surrounding the formation of the role-reversal relationship of the narcissistic/(borderline) parent with the child in which the child is used (exploited) as a "regulatory other" for the psychopathology and anxiety regulation of the narcissistic/(borderline) parent. Finally, the origins of the "parental alienation" process in the attachment trauma networks of the narcissistic/(borderline) parent will be examined, with a particular focus on the induced suppression of the child's attachment bonding motivations and the formation and expression of the trauma reenactment narrative.

Following this discussion of the theoretical foundations for an attachment-based model of "parental alienation," a broad overview of the diagnostic considerations emanating from an attachment-based model of "parental alienation" will be discussed, and three definitive diagnostic indicators for identifying attachment-based "parental alienation" will be described. A descriptive framework for a model of reunification therapy will also be presented which will be based on the theoretical underpinnings for an attachment-based model of the "parental alienation." Finally, a discussion of the domains of knowledge necessary for professional competence in diagnosing and treating this special population of children and families will be identified.

PART I: Family Systems Level

Chapter 1

FAMILY TRANSITIONS

The Family Context

Family systems theory establishes that children's behavior is both created and expressed within a relationship context of the family, so that understanding and altering the behavior of children requires a corresponding understanding for how change occurs within the surrounding family context that is both creating and supporting the child's behavior. A foundational construct within family systems theory is of the interrelated balance maintained within family processes that creates stability in family relationship patterns. The balanced stability achieved in family structures and relationship patterns is called "homeostasis" (homeo=same; stasis=static, stable state). In dysfunctional families, the child's symptoms act to stabilize the dysfunctional relationship patterns that are being threatened with collapse from an overwhelming challenge that the family is unable to navigate. The child's symptoms are acting to restore the "homeostatic" balance within the family's relationships.

In adaptive family structures the relationships are flexible enough to allow appropriate levels of intimacy to develop, while still providing sufficient structure and boundaries between individuals to allow for the development of individual self-autonomy within the family as well. If psychological boundaries among family members are too rigid and inflexible then relationships become disengaged and psychologically distant. If, on the other hand, psychological boundaries between family members are too porous and diffuse, then a fusion of psychological states develops among family members, called "psychological enmeshment," which hampers the development of individual autonomy within the family members.

Family Transitions

Over the developmental course of the family's lifespan, the relationship structures among the family members must adapt to a variety of transitions that occur within the family. Family relationships must adapt and accommodate to changes occurring in the family in order retain the family's effective functioning in response to the normal transitions that occur as family members mature and change. Each developmental transition encountered by the family poses a new set of challenges for the family's adaptive structures. Meeting these challenges requires that new relationship patterns emerge to resolve the demands imposed by the developmental transition.

The initial challenge faced by the family is the formation of an adaptive and stable marital bond. The marital unit serves as the structural core for the family. The initial marital unit, prior to the addition of children, represents a proto-family stage in the family's development. At this stage, if a functional marital unit fails to form, so that the marriage collapses prior to having children, then the proto-family created by the marital couple dissolves back into its pre-family stage of two separate individuals with no family ties to each other.

The fully formed family unit is created with the birth of the first child. From that point on, if the marital couple dissolves through divorce the family structure nevertheless remains through the continuing parental roles that the father and mother have with the child. With the addition of the first child the full family structure is formed. If a divorce occurs after the birth of the child, the family must then navigate the developmental transition from an intact family structure that is united by the marital bond to a separated family structure that is united by the continuing parental roles and attachment bonds to the child.

The birth of the first child represents a significant developmental transition for the family that presents a variety of stresses and challenges to the marital unit that must be adaptively met. In addition to the marital roles of husband and wife, new parental roles of father and mother emerge and must be negotiated relative to the martial roles. The demands of child rearing place additional stresses on the marital relationship that require adaptations within family relationships. Problems in the formation of the marital unit will become amplified and highlighted by the new adaptations required by the addition of children.

Once the family navigates these initial developmental transitions of forming the marital unit and integrating the roles of father and mother into the marriage, a new set of developmental challenges emerge from the child's maturation into school-age development. Emerging demands for school achievement and homework place additional stresses on the family. The addition of the child's extracurricular activities, of early formations of peer social relationships, and increased child defiance and assertion of independence, all place further stresses on the family's relationships and adaptive functioning. The possible birth of a second or third child will create additional sibling relationship patterns and add further stresses and challenges to the adaptive functioning of the family, and for the marital unit at the core of the family's structure.

Once the family's relationship structures stabilize into these new developmental challenges that are created by children's maturation into school-age development, the eldest child then matures into adolescence and the family must adapt to a whole new set of developmental challenges associated with puberty and the child's increasing proto-adult psychological independence. The developmental transition into adolescence is then followed by the transition into launching each young adult child in turn out from the family of origin and into their own independent adulthoods, ultimately creating the "empty nest" experience for the parents. The parents now return to the original marital couple without children present which potentially creates new challenges for the marriage. The parents must then adapt to their new roles of grandparents as their children form their own family units.

These are natural developmental transitions that all families must navigate. If the family relationship structures are able to successfully adapt to each of these developmental transitions in turn, then the family will display healthy interpersonal relationships that promote the emotional and psychological growth and development of the children. If, on the other hand, the family's relationship structures are not able to successfully navigate these family transitions, then maladaptive family relationship patterns will develop and will create symptoms that are expressed by the children. When the family is having difficulty successfully navigating a developmental transition, the symptoms created in children by the family's unsuccessful transition act in characteristic ways to stabilize the dysfunctional family relationship patterns and restore the "homeostatic" stability to the family's relationships. Within the established family systems construct of homeostasis, the child's symptoms serve to stabilize family functioning in response to dysfunctional family adaptation to a developmental challenge.

Divorce

Divorce represents the end of the marital unit, but it is not the end of the family. When there are children, the family unit remains even after the divorce because of the continuing parental roles of mother and father that remain, even though the spousal roles of husband and wife have ended. Divorce presents the family with a significant developmental transition from an **intact family structure** that is united by the marital unit to a **separated family structure** that is united by the child. The child acts as an ongoing unifying force within the family through the continuing parental roles and affectional bonds that each parent shares with the child. This represents a significant realignment of role-relationships within the family. In an intact family structure the marital unit forms the core of the family structure. In a separated family structure the parental bonds form the core structure of the family.

In divorce, the forces of separation within the marital unit can place strains on the newly emerging unifying function of the children's roles within the family. The less intense the separating forces are within the marital unit, expressed through marital discord, the less stress will be placed on the children in their emerging roles as being continuing unifying forces within the family. Conversely, the greater the degree of overt spousal discord surrounding the divorce, the greater the psychological and developmental stresses will be placed on the children in their newly emerging unifying role within the family.

Child symptoms can emerge either prior to the divorce as a means to prevent the collapse of the marital unit, or following the divorce in response to the problematic transition of the family's relationship patterns from their pre-divorce intact family role-relationships to their post-divorce separated family role-relationships. In both cases, the risk is that the child will become "triangulated" into the spousal conflict as a means to stabilize one or both parents' response to the failing marital relationship.

During the divorce process, if the family's communication and role-relationships are functional and adaptive then the family will be able to successfully meet the challenges of transitioning from an intact family structure united by the marriage to a new separated family structure united by the child (through the continuing parent-child role-relationships of "mother" and "father," and through the continuing shared parent-child attachment bonds). A functional and successful transition to a separated family structure places minimal additional stresses on the children. If, however, the family's prior relationship structures are problematic then the family will have difficulty adapting to the new developmental challenges posed by the dissolution of the marital unit and the family's transition into a new separated family structure. Problems in the family's transition to the new role-relationships in a separated family structure will lead to the emergence of child symptoms as an expression of the family's inability to adaptively adjust to the new challenges posed by the transition.

Treating Child Symptoms

Family systems theory describes the patterns of symptom development in response to dysfunctional relationship structures within the family. When family role-relationships are unable to successfully adapt to a developmental challenge, the child will develop symptomatic behaviors that serve to stabilize the dysfunctional family relationship structures that are threatened with collapse as a result of the family's inability to adaptively cope with the new challenges posed by the transition. The child's symptomatic behavior keeps the family's dysfunctional role relationships in a stable "homeostatic balance" through the function served by the child's symptoms. The stabilizing role of the child's symptoms within the family means that treatment efforts designed to eliminate the child's symptomatic behavior that do not also alter the surrounding context of the dysfunctional and maladaptive relationship patterns within the family that are creating the child's symptoms will be met with resistance by the family's dysfunctional relationship patterns. The function of the child's symptoms within the family of stabilizing the homeostatic balance in dysfunctional family relationships will undermine treatment efforts designed to alter the child's symptoms unless the underlying dysfunctional relationship patterns are also resolved.

In order to change the child's symptoms, family systems therapy recognizes the need to alter the dysfunctional relationship patterns in the surrounding family context that are both creating and maintaining the child's symptoms through the function the child's symptoms are serving for the family. If therapy does not first release the child for change by altering the surrounding family relationship context that is both creating and maintaining the child's symptoms, then treatment efforts will be resisted and will be unsuccessful because of the countervailing force of the homeostatic stability created in the family relationships by the child's symptoms. The methods for altering the surrounding family systems context that is creating and maintaining the child's symptoms represent the central principles and core constructs for family systems therapy.

Triangulation

One of the central constructs of family therapy is the principle of the child's "triangulation" into the spousal conflict through the actions of one or both parents. When the source of the problematic relationship patterns is located in the spousal relationship, as is often the case prior to and surrounding divorce, the child can become incorporated into the spousal conflict as a third party to the marital conflict in order to stabilize the dysfunctional marital relationship. This process is referred to as the child's "triangulation" into the spousal conflict, in which the two-person spousal conflict is expanded into a three-person, parent-child-parent, triangulated conflict. The child is placed into the middle of the spousal conflict and becomes a participant in the spousal conflict through the actions of one or both parents.

The child's triangulation into the marital conflict can take two different forms that serve different functions within the family. In the first type of child triangulation the two parents form a **coalition** against the child. In this type of triangulation, the child develops a problematic display of symptoms and both parents become united in their shared concern over the child's symptoms. This type of **same-generational** parent-parent coalition against the child often occurs prior to the divorce, and the child's symptoms are serving the homeostatic function of stabilizing the threatened collapse of the marital unit by bringing the spouses together over their shared parental concern for the child.

The child in this first type of triangulation becomes the "identified patient" who is expressing the symptom for the dysfunctional marital relationship in order to distract the parents from their own marital problems and relieve stresses within their marriage. In this type of triangulation, the child's symptoms are serving to stabilize the family's functioning by diverting potential spousal conflict onto the child in order to prevent the possible collapse of the marriage in divorce. Efforts to alter the child's symptoms without also creating increased stability within the marital unit will be resisted by the family's relationship patterns because of the homeostatic function being served by the child's symptoms in stabilizing the marital core of the family structure.

In the second type of child triangulation one parent forms a **cross-generational** parent-child coalition with the child against the other parent. This type of cross-generational coalition typically develops as a means to divert the expression of the allied parent's anger at the other spouse through the child's covertly elicited and supported expressions of anger or defiance toward the targeted parent. In this type of triangulation, the child's anger toward the targeted parent is an expression of **"spousal anger"** rather than parent-child anger that is authentic to the child's actual relationship to the targeted parent. This type of cross-generational redirection of spousal anger through the child is typically the result of the allied parent's feelings of powerlessness in being able to effectively influence the other spouse directly. The allied parent is able to increase his or her **power** relative to the other spouse by triangulating the child into the spousal conflict through a cross-generational coalition. By diverting the spousal anger of the allied parent through the child, the allied parent is able to express this parent's anger toward the other spouse in a way that may not be possible to express directly.

In this second type of triangulation, in which one parent forms a cross-generational coalition with the child against the other parent, the child is covertly induced and seduced through a combination of subtly manipulative parental control tactics and the granting of material and affectionate indulgences, into forming a cross-generational coalition of the child with the allied parent against the other parent. This pattern of triangulation will be evidenced by a distinct imbalance in the child's relationship between the two parents. As a result of the child's inappropriate coalition with one parent, the child becomes over-empowered in the family hierarchy to a status above that occupied by the other parent. The child's inappropriate elevation in the family hierarchy allows the child to become empowered to judge and defy the authority of the targeted parent.

Meanwhile, the child's relationship with the allied parent will appear to be relatively free of conflict, and the child and allied parent will seemingly have a wonderfully bonded relationship of mutual understanding. The response of the allied parent to the child's hostility expressed toward the targeted parent will be to offer the child sympathetic "understanding" for the child's anger, which tacitly supports the child's position in the conflict with the other parent. The tacit support of the allied parent for the child's position in the child's conflict with the other parent over-empowers the child in the family hierarchy to a position above that occupied by the targeted parent. As a result of the cross-generational coalition, the child is elevated to a position of entitlement and judgment regarding the other parent through the covert support the child is receiving from the allied parent in the coalition.

In structural family systems theory this is referred to as an "inverted" family hierarchy, in which the child sits in judgment of the parent. In a normal and healthy family hierarchy, the parent judges the child's behavior as appropriate or inappropriate and delivers parental guidance or discipline based on the parent's judgment of the child's behavior. In an inverted family hierarchy created by a cross-generational coalition of the child with one parent against the other parent, it is the child who judges the parent, and the child delivers punishment to the parent for the parent's supposed misdeeds.

The inverted parent-child hierarchy created by the cross-generational coalition is tacitly supported by the allied parent, who may offer superficial expressions of concern regarding the child's behavior but who then offers additional rationalizations that justify the child's hostility and disrespect for the other parent. In a healthy parent-child relationship the child is expected to show appropriate behavior and respect for both parents, and for all adults, including teachers, coaches, and store clerks. In a cross-generational coalition, however, the allied parent tacitly accepts and rationalizes the child's anger, defiance, and disrespect toward the targeted parent as being "understandable" and justified by the supposedly bad parenting practices of the other parent. Of note, however, is that the allied parent does not similarly accept and justify the child's anger, defiance, and disrespect toward teachers, coaches, or other adults, even if the child judged these other adults to deserve the child's disrespect. The rationalizations of the allied parent for the child's disrespect is limited to just the child's acting out behavior directed toward the targeted parent. By isolating the child's misbehavior to only the targeted parent, a narrative is created that the child's misbehavior is the result of problematic parenting by the targeted parent rather than the child's inherent defiance

The overt display of conflict in this type of family pathology will be evidenced between the child and the targeted parent, but the source of the conflict will be in the child's triangulated relationship with the allied and supposedly favored parent. In this type of triangulation pattern, the child's anger toward the targeted parent is actually "spousal anger" whose origin is in the allied and supposedly favored parent. The spousal anger of the allied parent is being redirected through the child by means of the child's coalition with the allied parent against the other parent.

The child's triangulation into the spousal conflict through the formation of a cross-generational parent-child coalition with one parent against the other parent is a standard and well-described relationship pattern that occurs within families in response to dysfunctional family adaptation to developmental transitions, and it is this type of family relationship pattern that is being expressed in attachment-based "parental alienation." Jay Haley, one of the premier family systems theorists, refers to the cross-generational coalition as a "perverse triangle," and Salvador Minuchin, another premier family systems theorist, refers to it as a form of "rigid triangle." Haley (1977), provides a clinical definition for the child's triangulation into the spousal conflict through a cross-generational coalition of the child with one parent against the other parent,

> "The people responding to each other in the triangle are not peers, but one of them is of a different generation from the other two... In the process of their interaction together, the person of one generation forms a coalition with the person of the other

> generation against his peer. By 'coalition' is meant a process of joint action which is against the third person... The coalition between the two persons is denied. That is, there is certain behavior which indicates a coalition which, when it is queried, will be denied as a coalition... In essence, the perverse triangle is one in which the separation of generations is breached in a covert way. When this occurs as a repetitive pattern, the system will be pathological" (p. 37).

Haley describes the cross-generational parent-child coalition as "perverse" because the coalition violates generational boundaries. Boundary violations across generations are of significant clinical concern. Kerig (2005), for example, identifies the violation of generational boundaries as a being a significant risk factor in parental emotional abuse of the child,

> "The breakdown of appropriate generational boundaries between parents and children significantly increases the risk for emotional abuse... When parent-child boundaries are violated, the implications for developmental psychopathology are significant. Poor boundaries interfere with the child's capacity to progress through development which, as Anna Freud suggested, is the defining feature of childhood psychopathology" (pp. 6-7).

Haley's characterization of the cross-generational coalition of the child with one parent against the other parent as being a "perverse triangle" captures the clinically disturbing features of this type of parent-child boundary violation.

Another preeminent family systems theorist, Salvador Minuchin, also defines the cross-generational coalition as occurring when "one of the parents joins the child in a rigidly bounded cross-generational coalition against the other parent" (Minuchin, 1974, p. 102), and he describes an illustrating example for the formation and impact of the cross-generational coalition,

> "An inappropriately rigid cross-generational subsystem of mother and son versus father appears, and the boundary around this coalition of mother and son excludes the father. A cross-generational dysfunctional transactional pattern has developed" (Minuchin, 1974, pp. 61-62).

Minuchin also describes the impact on family relationships of this cross-generational coalition,

> "The parents were divorced six months earlier and the father is now living alone... Two of the children who were very attached to their father, now refuse any contact with him. The younger children visit their father but express great unhappiness with the situation" (Minuchin, 1974, p. 101).

It is the formation of exactly this type of "perverse triangle" involving a pathological cross-generational parent-child coalition, which is described extensively in the family systems literature, that is being manifested in the construct otherwise called "parental alienation." The construct traditionally termed "parental alienation" is not a new syndrome, it is an established and fully described construct within the family systems literature. The construct commonly referred to as "parental alienation" represents the *triangulation* of the child into the spousal conflict by one parent (the allied and supposedly favored parent) through the formation of a *cross-generational coalition* of the parent with the child against the other parent. The triangulation of the child into the spousal conflict by the allied and supposedly favored parent represents the symptomatic expression of the parent's inability to adapt to the family's transition from an intact family structure united by the marriage to a separated family structure united by the continuing parental roles with the children.

In the family processes surrounding an attachment-based model of "parental alienation," the source of the allied and supposedly favored parent's difficulties in adapting to the family's transition from an intact family structure to a separated family structure lay in two underlying narcissistic and borderline personality vulnerabilities:

1) The characterological inability to process sadness and grief;

2) The splitting dynamic characteristic of narcissistic and borderline personality processes.

In attachment-based "parental alienation," the child's symptoms are being produced as a result of the child's triangulation into the spousal conflict. The child's symptoms are serving the homeostatic function of stabilizing the fragile psychological organization of the narcissistic/(borderline) parent which is being threatened with collapse because of the psychological challenges presented by the divorce. The narcissistic injury and rejection/abandonment inherent to the divorce are overwhelming the fragile coping ability of the narcissistic/(borderline) personality. The child is being triangulated into the spousal conflict by the narcissistic/(borderline) parent as a means to stabilize the fragile psychological structure of the parent.

What has come to be called "parental alienation" by the general public is fully identified and described within the family systems literature using established family systems constructs. The child is being triangulated into the spousal conflict through the formation of a pathological cross-generational coalition with the narcissistic/(borderline) parent against the other parent, called a "perverse triangle" by Haley and a "rigid triangle" by Minuchin. The child's triangulation into the spousal conflict is the product of the dysfunctional adaptation of the allied and supposedly favored narcissistic/(borderline) parent in navigating the developmental transition from an intact family structure united by the marriage to a separated family structure that is now united by the ongoing parental roles and attachment bonds with the child.

The primary variation to the typical cross-generational coalition described in the family systems literature and the type evidenced in attachment-based "parental alienation" is the addition to the cross-generational coalition of the prominent narcissistic and borderline personality psychopathology of the allied and supposedly favored parent. The narcissistic and borderline psychopathology of the parent transforms the pathology of the cross-generational coalition into a particularly malignant and virulent form that seeks to entirely terminate the targeted parent's relationship with the child. Within the pathological personality structure of the narcissistic/(borderline) parent, the transmuting psychopathology is the characterological inability of the narcissistic/(borderline) personality structure to adequately process sadness and grief, and the splitting dynamic associated with narcissistic and borderline psychopathology that polarizes relationships into extremes of idealization and devaluation. Within the splitting dynamic of the narcissistic/(borderline) personality structure, ambiguity is impossible. The ex-spouse must also become an ex-parent as well.

At a deeper level, the parental narcissistic/(borderline) personality pathology is the product of an attachment trauma history (i.e., disorganized attachment) during the childhood of the narcissistic/(borderline) parent that significantly damaged the self-structure development of this parent. The underlying patterns of disorganized attachment during early childhood subsequently coalesced during adolescence and young adulthood into a stable, but pathological, narcissistic and borderline personality organization. This pathology in the personality structure of the narcissistic/(borderline) parent is preventing the family's successful transition from an intact family structure into a separated family structure. Instead, the narcissistic/(borderline) parent is enlisting the child into a cross-generational coalition in order to stabilize the fragile personality structure of narcissistic/(borderline) parent that is threatened with collapse in response to the narcissistic injury and rejection/abandonment of the divorce.

Both the personality pathology of the narcissistic/(borderline) parent and the attachment trauma history that created the personality pathology are being expressed through the child's symptoms created in the cross-generational coalition of the child with the narcissistic/(borderline) parent. The family systems pathology of the cross-generational coalition is the product of an underlying substrate of narcissistic and borderline psychopathology, which in turn is based on a deeper underlying substrate of disorganized attachment pathology.

Severity of the Pathology

At the family systems level, the family processes traditionally described as "parental alienation" represent the manifestation of the child's triangulation into the spousal conflict through the formation of a cross-generational coalition with one parent against the other parent, as defined within family systems theory by both Haley and Minuchin. The traditionally described range of mild to moderate "parental alienation" within the Gardnerian PAS model simply represents the clinically typical range of mild to moderate negative parental influence on the child that can occur in the cross-generational coalition of the child with one parent against the other parent. The severe form of "parental alienation" within the Gardnerian PAS model represents the addition of parental narcissistic/(borderline) pathology to the standard family systems construct of a cross-generational parent-child coalition. The addition of narcissistic/(borderline) parental psychopathology (i.e., severe underlying pathology in the attachment system) creates a particularly malignant form of the "perverse triangle" described by Haley that completely terminates the parent-child attachment bond with the targeted parent.

Mild and moderate cases of Gardnerian PAS are best described and addressed using standard family systems models for the child's triangulation into the spousal conflict through the formation of a cross-generational parent-child coalition against the other parent. The construct of "parental alienation" should be reserved for the more severely malignant and virulent form of "perverse triangle" that occurs with the addition of parental narcissistic and borderline psychopathology. An attachment-based model for the construct of "parental alienation" represents a multi-layered description for the more severely malignant form of the cross-generational parent-child coalition that occurs with the addition of parental narcissistic/(borderline) pathology, and for the origins of this pathology within the underlying dynamics of the attachment system.

The parental narcissistic/(borderline) pathology, and the subsequent distortions to the child's functioning that are created by this parental pathology, have their foundational origins in distortions to the attachment networks of the narcissistic/(borderline) parent caused by early childhood relationship trauma. The foundational origins of the parental narcissistic/(borderline) pathology in childhood developmental trauma to the attachment system leads to the specific symptomatic expression of the current "parental alienation" pathology as a severe disruption to the child's normal-range attachment bonding motivations toward a parent. At its core, the current symptoms of "parental alienation" that are being expressed by the child represent the trans-generational transmission and manifestation of attachment trauma from the childhood of the narcissistic/(borderline) parent into the current relationships. The central pathology in "parental alienation" is in the attachment system of the narcissistic/(borderline) parent. This foundational attachment pathology is reflected in both the formation of the parent's narcissistic/(borderline) pathology itself, and in the primary symptomatic expression of this core attachment pathology through the distortions created to the child's attachment bonding motivations toward the targeted parent.

In less severe forms of pathological cross-generational coalitions, the child's symptomatic expressions toward the targeted parent are reflected in the child's increased displays of hostility, contempt, argumentativeness, and defiance directed toward the targeted parent. But in these less severe forms of cross-generational coalition the child's attachment bonding motivations remain relatively intact. The child does not seek to entirely sever the parent-child bond in milder forms of the cross-generational parent-child coalition. In these less severe forms of the cross-generational coalition, the child's induced symptomatic hostility toward the targeted parent is serving the homeostatic function of redirecting through the child the expression of the allied parent's "spousal anger" toward the other spouse.

The addition of parental narcissistic and borderline psychopathology into the cross-generational parent-child coalition, however, transforms the inherent pathology of the cross-generational coalition into a particularly malignant form of pathology that seeks to completely terminate the child's relationship with the other parent. The malignancy created by the addition of parental narcissistic/(borderline) dynamics stems from the severity of the parental personality and attachment psychopathology, and characteristic features of this parental pathology are evidenced in child's induced symptom display.

Chapter 2

BARRERS TO FAMLY TRANSITIONS

Equivalence of Narcissistic/Borderline Pathology

Both the narcissistic and borderline personalities represent the coalesced product of disorganized attachment patterns from childhood. Disorganized attachment is one of the three primary categories of insecure attachment, the other two being anxious-ambivalent attachment, sometimes referred to as "preoccupied" attachment, and anxious-avoidant attachment, in which the person minimizes the importance of relationships. Of the three types of insecure attachment, disorganized attachment is considered the most severely pathological.

During childhood, the attachment system forms internal working models for attachment expectations regarding self- and other-in-relationship. Narcissistic and borderline personalities have the same underlying core expectations for self- and other-in-relationship, which creates an identical underlying core pathology for these two personality pathologies. For both the narcissistic and borderline personality organizations, the expectations are:

Self-in-relationship: "I am fundamentally inadequate."

Other-in-relationship: "The other person will reject and abandon me because of my fundamental inadequacy."

The difference between the outward manifestation of these identical core beliefs held by both the narcissistic and borderline personality is in the defensive structure surrounding these primary vulnerabilities. The borderline-style personality lacks an established defensive structure needed to ward off the continual self-experience of these core beliefs. For the borderline-style personality, the underlying core beliefs in primal self-inadequacy and impending abandonment by the attachment figure are ever-present threats and repeated self-experiences.

The borderline-style personality seeks to find a stable psychological organization in the perfectly attuned and perfectly responsive other. For the borderline-style personality, the attachment figure is the idealized perfectly regulating "parent" to the vulnerable infantile personality structure of the borderline-style personality. However, when the attachment figure fails to provide perfectly attuned and continually available regulation for the borderline-style personality, then the borderline personality organization collapses into its core beliefs of primal self-inadequacy and fears of abandonment. The borderline-style personality responds to the collapse in self-structure organization with intense anger in an effort to maintain a semblance of psychological self-cohesion. The response of the borderline-style personality toward the attachment figure of the spouse alternates between devaluing the attachment figure as fundamentally inadequate for failing to keep the borderline personality in a regulated state, and self-denigration originating from the core belief in primal self-inadequacy that is triggered by the abandonment of the attachment figure ("You don't love me because I am inherently unlovable").

In contrast, the narcissistic-style personality has been able to form a rudimentary defensive structure of narcissistic self-inflation that provides a modicum of stable continuity in psychological functioning as long as the fragile narcissistic defense is maintained. However, if this fragile narcissistic veneer is punctured by criticism or rejection from others, then the narcissistic personality structure will also collapse into the chaotic disorganization of its underlying borderline dynamics. When the psychological organization of the narcissistic-style personality collapses into its borderline core, the narcissistic-style personality will seek to reestablish the fragile narcissistic defense of self-inflation by denigrating the attachment figure as completely worthless and inadequate ("I'm the wonderful person, you're the inadequate person. I'm rejecting you because you're worthless, you're not rejecting me because I'm worthless. I'm wonderful, you're inadequate").

One of the leading figures in narcissistic and borderline personality processes, Otto Kernberg, describes the underlying similarities in the core organizations for both the narcissistic and borderline personalities. In his description of narcissistic and borderline processes, he identified the narcissistic personality as representing a subgroup of a more foundational borderline personality organization,

> "One subgroup of borderline patients, namely the narcissistic personalities... seem to have a defensive organization similar to borderline conditions, and yet many of them function on a much better psychosocial level" (Kernberg, 1977, p. xiii).

The Borderline Style Personality Organization

The borderline-style personality has no internal structural defense against the continual experience of the core vulnerabilities of primal self-inadequacy and fear of abandonment. The borderline personality structure is therefore continually seeking an external "regulatory object" (also called a "regulatory other") who will provide scaffolding support to the fragile borderline personality organization. The borderline-style personality seeks a "perfect" idealized love from the attachment figure in order to fill the void of primal self-inadequacy that is at the core of the borderline personality organization. To quiet the abandonment fears of the borderline personality, the attachment figure must provide the borderline personality with the perfectly attuned constant availability that creates the idealized "perfect" security of never being abandoned by the attachment figure. So central is this stabilizing role provided by the other person in the relationship, who is acting as an external "regulatory object" for the instability of the borderline personality organization, that any empathic failure by the relationship partner in their role as the external "regulatory object" for the unstable borderline personality structure will result in the complete collapse of the borderline personality organization into chaotic rages and intensely experienced fears of abandonment.

The fragile borderline personality structure needs the attachment figure to be completely dedicated to their role as the external "regulatory object" for the stabilization of the borderline personality organization, much in the same way as a parent is totally dedicated to regulating the psychological state of an infant. When the other person in the relationship does not meet the needs of the borderline personality for a perfectly attuned and regulating other, then the borderline personality lashes out in infantile rage against the failure of the "regulatory object" of the attachment figure. The borderline personality will accuse the relationship partner of providing insufficient love and devotion, and of failing to be completely devoted to the borderline personality (as a parent would be to regulating an infant's emotional state). These accusations regarding the other person's inadequacy are mixed with collapses into the alternate pole of self-devaluation, in which the borderline personality expresses self-loathing as being a horrible and unlovable person. The chaotic organization of the borderline personality lunges between these alternate poles of critical assaults devaluing the other person as inadequate, and collapses into tearful tirades of self-devaluation and victimization.

The underlying disorganized attachment of the borderline personality structure means that the person has developed no organized approach to restoring relationships once they are ruptured. The borderline-style personality therefore needs to remain in a constant state of psychological fusion with the other person in order to prevent unrepairable breaches to the relationship. Any breach in the relationship with the attachment figure triggers a complete collapse of the borderline-style personality structure into chaotic and disorganized responses from the disorganized patterns of attachment.

The fundamentally disorganized attachment of the borderline-style personality also evidences anxious-ambivalent overtones. The anxious-ambivalent overtones mean that the borderline-style personality continues to strive to form an attachment relationship, but will be unable to form a coherent strategy for creating a stable attachment bond because of the underlying disorganized attachment patterns. As a result of the fundamentally disorganized attachment of the borderline-style personality, any rupture to the perfectly fused relationship with the attachment figure will result in a complete collapse of the borderline personality structure into disorganization. The disorganized attachment system with anxious-ambivalent overtones of the borderline-style parent will present a conflicting display of chaotically organized approach and avoidance motivations. This results in the characteristic display of swirling "drama" surrounding the borderline-style personality, in which the borderline personality alternately seeks an intense bonding of perfectly attuned and idealized love, followed by a collapse into rages, critical onslaughts, and accusations of perceived abandonment, real or imagined.

One of the primary differences between the narcissistic and borderline variations for the identical underlying core beliefs of personal inadequacy and anticipated abandonment is in the pattern of attachment overtones to their shared foundation of disorganized attachment. The borderline-style personality displays anxious-ambivalent overtones to a foundationally disorganized attachment that continues to motivate the borderline-style personality to seek an emotionally bonded relationship of "perfect love" with the idealized "regulatory other" of the attachment figure. The narcissistic-style personality, on the other hand, has anxious-avoidant attachment overtones to the core disorganized attachment of the narcissistic personality. The dismissive anxious-avoidant overtones to narcissistic-style personality's attachment style create an alternate strategy for coping with the core beliefs of primal self-inadequacy and fears of rejection that involves dismissing and devaluing the importance of emotionally bonded relationships. By devaluing the attachment relationship, the narcissistic-style personality achieves a relative self-inflation over the attachment figure that protects against the primal fears of self-inadequacy, and by diminishing the importance of attachment figures the narcissistic-style personality protects himself or herself against fears of rejection and abandonment.

The Narcissistic Style Personality Organization

Instead of the "perfect love" sought by the borderline-style personality, the narcissistic-style personality seeks the perfectly adoring other, who maintains the narcissistic defense by providing continuing "narcissistic supply" of adoration. Once the other person ceases to provide adequate "narcissistic supply" to feed the narcissistic defense of self-inflation, the other person is discarded. For the narcissistic personality, the other person has no intrinsic value other than the "narcissistic supply" they provide. This represents a narcissistic-style defense against the experience of primal self-inadequacy and fears of rejection by the attachment figure. By devaluing the importance of the attachment figure the narcissistic personality creates a psychological defense of narcissistic self-inflation by comparison to the devalued attachment figure, and the narcissist rejects the attachment figure for inadequacy before the attachment figure can reject the narcissist for inadequacy.

The narcissistic defense psychologically expels the experience of core self-inadequacy by projecting it onto others. The core belief of the narcissistic personality is that the other person is inadequate, while the narcissist remains ideal and perfect. This projection of inadequacy onto others in order to maintain the self-image of ideal narcissistic perfection results in the externalization of blame and responsibility characteristic of the narcissistic personality. It is the other person who is a failure, who is inadequate, not the narcissistic personality. The fears of rejection and abandonment are avoided by minimizing the importance of others to the narcissistic personality. For the narcissistic personality style, relationships are shallow and superficial and people are easily discarded when they stop providing "narcissistic supply."

The fragile structural stability provided by the narcissistic defense keeps the underlying borderline organization of "I am inadequate"/"I'm going to be abandoned" at bay. This allows for a higher level of organized and functional behavior for the narcissist than is displayed by the more overtly borderline personality which is continually being exposed to collapse into disorganized fragmentation. However, if the narcissistic veneer is punctured through criticism or rejection of the idealized narcissistic self-image, this inflicts a "narcissistic injury" that penetrates the narcissistic defense and collapses the narcissistic personality structure into its core borderline personality organization. The collapse of the narcissistic defense results in onslaughts of rageful anger in which the narcissist degrades the other person in the relationship in order to reestablish the narcissistic defense of grandiose perfection by diminishing the value of the other person.

The narcissistic defense is maintained by devaluing the importance of others and by exploiting others as a source of continual "narcissistic supply." The foundationally disorganized attachment means that the narcissistic person has no organized strategy for restoring relationships once they are breached. In response to relationship breaches, the primitive narcissistic defense simply tries to dominate the other person through onslaughts of degradation back into a submissive role as the external "regulatory object" for the narcissistic personality organization. The role of the other person in the relationship is simply to provide continual "narcissistic supply" of adoration to support the narcissistic defense against the experience of primal self-inadequacy.

In attachment-based "parental alienation," differences in parental narcissistic and borderline personality styles will be reflected in minor differences in the outward manifestations of the family relationship dynamics, but the underlying core dynamics will be the same. Both the narcissistic and borderline personality structures share the same underlying attachment system pathology with differing outward manifestations. The underlying similarity of the narcissistic and borderline personality structures will become evident when the attachment system level of analysis is discussed, since both personality styles are embedded in the same underlying attachment system dynamics.

Metabolizing Sadness

The narcissistic personality is characterologically unable to process the emotion of sadness and grief. According to Kernberg,

> "They [narcissists] are especially deficient in genuine feelings of sadness and mournful longing; their incapacity for feeling depressive reactions is a basic feature of their personalities. When abandoned or disappointed by other people they may show what on the surface looks like depression, but which on further examination emerges as anger and resentment, loaded with revengeful wishes, rather than real sadness for the loss of a person who they appreciated" (Kernberg, 1977, p. 229).

The loss of the intact family structure will be grieved by all family members, even if the marriage was conflicted and unsustainable. The loss of attachment mediated relationships, such as the spousal and parent-child relationships, will invariably produce feelings of grief and sadness. The narcissistic personality, however, is characterologically incapable of processing the emotions of grief and sadness, and instead converts the experience of sadness into "anger and resentment, loaded with revengeful wishes."

This characterological inability to process sadness as an emotion prevents the narcissistic/(borderline) parent from processing and resolving the sadness and grief triggered by the loss of the marital relationship through the divorce. Instead of processing and resolving the sadness and grief associated with the loss of the marital relationship, the narcissistic/(borderline) parent translates this sadness into "anger and resentment" toward the other spouse (the other parent). This anger of the narcissistic/(borderline) parent is also "loaded with revengeful wishes," which will ultimately find expression through the pain inflicted on the targeted parent by the child's rejection.

Because of the divorce, the narcissistic/(borderline) parent is powerless to influence or directly retaliate against the attachment figure of the other spouse for causing the "narcissistic injury" of rejecting the narcissistic/(borderline) personality. However, by triangulating the child into the spousal conflict through the formation of a cross-generational coalition with the child, the narcissistic/(borderline) parent is able to redirect the "spousal anger" through the child, creating suffering in the targeted parent. The parental coalition with the child increases the power available to the narcissistic/(borderline) parent within the family system, and acts to stabilize the functioning of the narcissistic/(borderline) parent relative to the processing of "sadness and mournful longing" as "anger and resentment, loaded with revengeful wishes."

However, by triangulating the child into the spousal conflict as a pathological means of processing sadness and anger, the family is prevented from making a successful transition from an intact family structure united by the marriage to a separated family structure united by the continuing parental roles with the child. Instead of achieving a stable bi-focal separated family structure in which the child's continuing role-relationship and affectional bonding with each parent serves a unifying function within this new separated family structure, the child's unifying function is distorted into a separating role consistent with the separation occurring in the spousal unit. As a consequence of the character pathology of the narcissistic/(borderline) parent which is unable to successfully process and resolve the emotion of sadness associated with the loss of the intact family structure and the spousal relationship, the family is prevented from successfully transitioning to a separated family structure.

The triangulation of the child into the spousal conflict through the formation of a cross-generational coalition with the narcissistic/(borderline) parent against the targeted parent is the product of the narcissistic/(borderline) parent's inability to process the sadness and grief associated with the dissolution of the marriage and the loss of the intact family. When a family is unable to successfully navigate a developmental transition, symptoms emerge to stabilize the family relationships that are threatened with collapse. In the case of attachment-based "parental alienation," the threatened collapse within the family represents the inherent vulnerability of the narcissistic/(borderline) parent's fragile personality structure that is triggered by the interpersonal rejection inherent to the divorce. This prompts the narcissistic/(borderline) parent to triangulate the child into the spousal conflict in a cross-generational coalition against the other parent in which the child's hostility and rejection toward the targeted parent acts to stabilize the dysfunctional psychological processes of the narcissistic/(borderline) parent.

If the narcissistic/(borderline) parent can be assisted in processing the sadness and grief associated with the loss of the marriage and intact family structure, rather than converting the experience of "sadness and mournful longing" into "anger and resentment, loaded with revengeful wishes," then the narcissistic/(borderline) parent would no longer need to triangulate the child into the spousal conflict as a means of stabilizing the narcissistic/(borderline) parent's dysfunctional personality structure that is being threatened with collapse by the challenges inherent to the divorce and the family's transition to a separated family structure. Unfortunately, the primitive and immaturely developed structure of the narcissistic/(borderline) personality lacks the capacity for self-insight. Instead, both the narcissistic and borderline styles of personality organization externalize blame and responsibility by projecting their own fears of self-inadequacy onto others; it is the other person who is wrong, who is a failure.

The characterological inability of the narcissistic/(borderline) personality organization to process the emotion of sadness will almost inevitably lead to the child being triangulated into the spousal conflict by the narcissistic/(borderline) parent. The child will be both induced and seduced by the narcissistic/(borderline) parent into forming a cross-generational coalition with the narcissistic/(borderline) parent against the other parent. The narcissistic/(borderline) parent then uses the cross-generational coalition with the child and the child's rejection of the other parent to stabilize the fragile personality organization of the narcissistic/(borderline) parent which is being threatened with collapse into disorganization by the inherent rejection associated with divorce.

Splitting

One of the primary features of both narcissistic and borderline pathology is a defensive process called "splitting," in which the other person in the relationship is perceived in polarized extremes of being either entirely perfect and idealized, or as being entirely bad and devalued. The origins of this characteristic personality trait for both the narcissistic and borderline styles of personality organization is found in the underlying structures of the attachment system.

Narcissistic and borderline personality dynamics represent the coalesced product of underlying patterns of attachment expectations. The particular type of attachment pattern that results in the formation of a narcissistic/(borderline) personality organization is called a disorganized attachment. In this type of attachment the child cannot develop a coherent strategy for forming an attachment bond to the parent. A variety of distorted parenting practices can give rise to a disorganized attachment in the child. Among the causal origins of a disorganized attachment is a frightening parent who is simultaneously both a source of threat to the child and a source of parental protection. Beck et al. (2004) describe the research findings on this association of borderline personality development and childhood disorganized attachment,

> "Various studies have found that patients with BPD [borderline personality disorder] are characterized by disorganized attachment representations. Such attachment representations appear to be typical for persons with unresolved childhood traumas, especially when parental figures were involved, with direct, frightening behavior by the parent. Disorganized attachment is considered to result from an unresolvable situation for the child when "the parent is at the same time the source of fright as well as the potential haven of safety" (van Izendoorn, Schuengel, & Bakermans-Kranberg, 1999, p. 226.)" (p. 191).

When a child is presented with a threat, the attachment system motivates the child to flee from the threat and seek the protection of the parent. However, when the parent is at the same time the source of the threat and the source of protection from threat, this presents an unresolvable conflict for the child. When the parent is both the threat and the "haven of safety" from threat, the child's motivating systems for both attachment bonding and avoidance are simultaneously activated. The child is simultaneously motivated both to flee from the parent who poses the threat, and to seek protective bonding with the parent, who is simultaneously the source of the threat.

This creates intense yet incompatible motivational directives both to flee from the parent and to seek attachment bonding with the same parental figure, who is also the source of threat. Chronic exposure to this unresolvable form of motivational conflict toward the parent creates a disorganized attachment to the parent in which the child is unable to develop any coherent strategy for forming a viable attachment bond to the parent. This underlying disorganized attachment pattern then coalesces during adolescence and early adulthood into stable, albeit pathological, narcissistic and borderline personality dynamics.

The splitting defense of polarized extremes of judgment regarding relationships develops as a means of resolving the intense motivational conflict created by a parent who is simultaneously a source of threat and of protection. In order to resolve this unresolvable conflict, the brain neurologically "splits" these two motivational systems into completely separate networks, one entirely dedicated to avoidance and one entirely dedicated to attachment bonding. This is accomplished by completely cross-inhibiting the activity of these networks, so that only one or the other motivational network can be active at any one time. When the attachment bonding motivating system is active, the avoidance motivating system is completely inhibited, it is completely shut off. Alternatively, when the avoidance motivating system is active, it entirely inhibits the attachment bonding motivating system. Only one or the other of these two systems can be active at a time. This resolves the conflict in motivational directives.

However, the splitting of these two networks into separate systems (i.e., entirely cross-inhibiting the activity of these systems), also leads to extreme polarization in the perceptions of relationships. When the motivating systems for attachment bonding and avoidance have been "split," only one or the other of these two motivating systems, either for attachment bonding or for avoidance, can be active at any one time. As a result, perceptions of other people become polarized into extremes. Other people are seen as being either entirely good (i.e., the attachment bonding system is active and the avoidance system is entirely shut down;

neurologically inhibited) or entirely bad (i.e., the avoidance motivating system is active and the attachment bonding system is entirely shut down; neurologically inhibited). As a result of splitting the child is able to resolve the psychological conflict of simultaneously incompatible motivations and achieve a single motivational directive, but at the cost of nuanced and blended interpretations of relationships.

The process of splitting occurs at the neurological level of the brain. The splitting of these two motivational networks is achieved through a complete neural cross-inhibition of the attachment bonding and avoidance motivating systems. When one motivating system is on, the other motivating system is entirely turned off (inhibited). In normal development, both the attachment bonding and avoidance motivational systems can be on simultaneously, with only a slight inhibition from one motivational network on the activity of the other. This simultaneous activation of the attachment bonding and avoidance motivating systems allows us to experience blended perceptions of other people as possessing both positive (attachment bonding motivation) and negative (avoidance motivation) qualities at the same time. There is a slight cross-inhibition of these systems, so that if we like someone (i.e., an attachment bonding motivation) we are more likely to notice positive traits of the person and minimize negative qualities (called a "positive halo" effect). On the other hand, if we dislike someone (i.e., an avoidance motivation) then we are more likely to notice and highlight the person's negative qualities and minimize their positive traits (called a "negative halo" effect). Despite this slight cross-inhibition of the attachment bonding and avoidance motivational systems, in normal-range psychological development both systems can be active at the same time, which allows us to have nuanced and blended perceptions of other people.

However, as a result of the intense simultaneous activation of both attachment bonding and avoidance motivating systems associated with the formation of disorganized attachment in early childhood (which in turn, leads to the formation of narcissistic and borderline personality traits during later adolescences and early adulthood), the intensity of the simultaneous activation of these incompatible motivational systems for bonding and avoidance leads to a psychological splitting in the functioning of these systems. This involves their complete neurological cross-inhibition, so that only one or the other of these two motivational systems can be active at any one time.

The child's exposure to a simultaneously threatening and protective parent creates both the child's disorganized attachment and the neuropsychological process of splitting. The disorganized attachment coalesces during adolescence and young adulthood into stable narcissistic and borderline personality characteristics, which is why splitting into polarized extremes of perception is a characteristic of both narcissistic and borderline personality structures. Both the personality pathology and the splitting dynamic have their origins in the same parent-child attachment trauma that produced a disorganized attachment.

At the neuro-biological level, splitting represents the complete neurological separation of the motivations for attachment bonding with the "protective parent" from the avoidance motivations to flee from the threatening, dangerous, and "abusive parent." As a result of splitting, the child's internalized representational networks for the parent becomes "split" into two components; representations for the all-good nurturing and "protective parent" who triggers the activation of the child's attachment bonding motivational system, and representational networks for an all-bad, dangerous and "abusive parent," who represents the activation of the child's avoidance motivating system.

In order to create a coherent and consistent motivational directive toward the parent, the internalized representation for the all-good, nurturing and "protective parent" (and its associated attachment bonding motivation) cannot be active at the same time as the child's internalized representation for the all-bad, dangerous and "abusive parent" (and its associated avoidance motivation). Only one or the other of these motivational systems, and its associated internalized representation for the parent as either the all-good "protective parent" or the all-bad "abusive parent," can be active at any one time. This is achieved by a complete neurological cross-inhibition of these motivational systems and the complete separation of the representational networks for the all-good "protective parent" from the all-bad "abusive parent."

While this resolves the psychological conflict created by incompatible motivational directives, it comes at the cost of having blended and nuanced perceptions of others. Perceptions of the relationship partner (i.e., the attachment figure) become polarized into extremes of the other person being either the all-good and idealized relationship partner, or the all-bad and entirely devalued relationship partner. For the more borderline-style personality organization, the all-good polarity represents an idealized "perfect love," in which the other person represents the completely attuned, perfectly empathic, and totally dedicated other. When the relationship partner fails to live up to this idealized standard, the neurological networks within the brain switch entirely to the avoidance motivation system in which the relationship partner (i.e., the attachment figure) becomes completely devalued as the embodiment of malevolence and "abusive" evil.

For the narcissistic-style personality, the idealized extreme in this polarized perception of others is the adoring other who is a perfect narcissistic reflection of the grandiose self-perception of the narcissistic personality. The other person in the relationship is of no intrinsic value, but is only of value for the "narcissistic supply" of reflective adoration they provide to the narcissistic personality. Unlike the borderline-style personality, the narcissistic-style personality is not seeking "perfect love." Instead, the narcissistic-style personality is seeking the perfectly adoring self-reflection of the narcissistic personality, which provides continual "narcissistic supply" to the fragile narcissistic defense against the core belief regarding the narcissist's fundamental self-inadequacy. If the relationship partner fails to provide this source of continual "narcissistic supply," then the avoidance motivating system is triggered and other person becomes the object of dismissive contempt and angry onslaughts.

The splitting dynamic characteristic of narcissistic and borderline psychological processes creates dichotomous black-and-white thinking in which other people are perceived as either all-good and idealized, or as all-bad and are entirely devalued. Ambivalence is an impossibility within the complete neurological cross-inhibition of the attachment bonding and avoidance motivational systems associated with narcissistic and borderline processes. This is important to understand regarding the manifestation of attachment-based "parental alienation;" psychological ambivalence is a neurological impossibility for the narcissistic/(borderline) personality.

When the family transitions from an intact family structure united by the marital couple to a separated family structure united by the child, the spouse becomes an ex-spouse (i.e., activation of the avoidance motivating system), but remains a current parent (i.e., the attachment bonding system). This represents a transition in the family from a fundamental consistency in both the spousal and parental role-relationships (i.e., attachment-bonding motivational systems for both roles) to one of disparate spousal and parental role-relationships (the spouse becomes an ex-spouse, but remains a bonded parent). In the intact family, the husband is also the father, and the wife is also the mother. However, in a separated family structure the former spouse has become an ex-husband or an ex-wife, yet remains an active and affectionally bonded father or mother for the child. The ex-husband does not also become an ex-father, nor does the ex-wife become and ex-mother. With the divorce, the spousal and parental role relationships are no longer consistent.

This inconsistency in role-relationships is not a problem for normal brains in which both the attachment bonding and avoidance motivating systems can be active simultaneously. In a normal brain, the activation of the avoidance motivating system relative to the ex-spouse still allows for the attachment bonding motivating system to be active, so that the role of the ex-spouse as a continuing bonded mother or father to the child can still be recognized. The ex-spouse (i.e., the avoidance motivating system) can still be recognized as a currently bonded parent to the child (i.e., the attachment motivating system).

However, within the black-and-white dichotomous splitting processes of the narcissistic/(borderline) parent this type of inconsistency in relationships cannot be perceived because of the complete neurological cross-inhibition of the attachment bonding motivational system from the avoidance motivational system. The complete cross-inhibition of the attachment bonding and avoidance motivational networks prevents, at a neurological level, the ability to perceive blended and nuanced role-relationships. Either one or the other of these motivational systems can be active, but not both. Perception is completely polarized. When the avoidance motivating system is activated relative to the spouse becoming an ex-spouse, this entirely inhibits the activation of the attachment bonding motivating system. The narcissistic/(borderline) personality cannot ***perceive*** the continuing parental attachment bond of the targeted parent to the children. With the divorce, when the husband becomes an ex-husband, he must also become an ex-father; when the wife becomes an ex-wife she must also become an ex-mother as well. Within the neuro-biological process of splitting, ambiguity in role relationships is a neurological impossibility.

Furthermore, when the husband or wife is no longer the source of narcissistic or borderline supply as the "regulatory object" totally dedicated to the regulation of the emotional and psychological state of the narcissistic/(borderline) parent, then the husband or wife becomes entirely devalued as being an all-bad, evil and "abusive" person. In the brain of the narcissistic/(borderline) personality, the ex-spouse switches from the attachment bonding motivational system to the complete activation of the avoidance motivating system. Since the neurological substrate of splitting cannot accommodate to inconsistency, the all-bad, evil and "abusive" ex-husband or ex-wife also becomes the all-bad, evil and "abusive" ex-father or ex-mother as well. By its very nature, the intense neural cross-inhibition of attachment bonding and avoidance motivational networks inherent to the splitting dynamic are designed to eliminate inconsistency and ambiguity at the neurological level by creating a single certainty, either bonding or avoidance, but never both simultaneously.

The neurological substrate of the spitting dynamic requires that the ex-husband become an ex-father; that the ex-wife become an ex-mother. It is a neurologically imposed imperative that accepts no other alternative. This is why adding narcissistic and borderline pathology to a cross-generational coalition transmutes the already pathological cross-generational coalition into a particularly malignant and virulent form that seeks to entirely terminate the other parent's relationship with the child. The neurological imperative imposed by the splitting dynamic makes attachment-based "parental alienation" fundamentally different from other forms of problematic parenting. Cross-generational parent-child coalitions that do not include parental narcissistic or borderline pathology are still highly problematic family dynamics, and will result in mild to moderate cases of negative parental influence that create increased parent-child conflict between the child and the targeted parent. However, the addition of narcissistic and borderline psychopathology, particularly the addition of the splitting dynamic, transforms an already pathological cross-generational coalition into a particularly malignant and virulent form of pathology that is lethal to the other parent's relationship with the child.

The developmental challenge of the family surrounding divorce is to transition from an intact family structure united by the marital unit to a separated family structure united by the child, and by the continuing parental roles as mother and father with the child. However, the neurological imperative for consistency imposed by the splitting dynamic of the narcissistic/(borderline) parent prevents the family from making this transition. The continuing parental role of the targeted parent with the child cannot be perceived by the narcissistic/(borderline) parent because the attachment bonding system that would be necessary to recognize the targeted parent's continuing parental role with the child is being entirely cross-inhibited by the activation of the avoidance motivating system in the brain of the narcissistic/(borderline) parent.

The narcissistic/(borderline) parent will, with near certainty, triangulate the child into the spousal conflict through the formation of a cross-generational coalition with the child against the other parent In order to stabilize the fragile personality structure of the narcissistic/(borderline) parent that is threatened with collapse as a consequence of the divorce. The addition of parental narcissistic and borderline pathology to the cross-generational coalition, particularly surrounding the splitting dynamic, will transmute the pathology of the cross-generational coalition into a particularly malignant and virulent form that seeks to entirely terminate the other parent's relationship with the child (i.e., to make the ex-husband an ex-father; the ex-wife an ex-mother). The neurological substrate of the splitting dynamic that is inherent to the pathology of both the narcissistic and borderline personality structure will tolerate no other alternative.

PART II: Personality Disorder Level

Chapter 3

PERSONALITY AND ATTACHMENT

Attachment Origins of Personality Traits

The attachment system contains our fundamental expectations for self- and other-in-relationship. The characteristics of narcissistic and borderline personality styles are expressions of these underlying relationship expectations that are contained in the internal working models of the attachment system. The internal working models of attachment expectations develop across childhood through multiple relationships, but primarily through the child's early relationship experiences with the parents. These internal working models for attachment provide the template for the child's expectations of self- and other-in-relationship. The internalized patterns of relationship expectations formed during childhood, and embedded in the attachment system, then guide both the future formation of emotionally close relationships as well as the approaches used for repairing breaches in the attachment bond when they occur. The internal working models embedded in the attachment system mediate the formation, as well as the loss, of closely bonded attachment relationships throughout the lifespan. According to John Bowlby, who first described the functioning of the attachment system,

> "No variables, it is held, have more far-reaching effects on personality development than have a child's experiences within his family: for, starting during the first months of his relations with his mother figure, and extending through the years of childhood and adolescence in his relations with both parents, he builds up working

models of how attachment figures are likely to behave towards him in any of a variety of situations; and on those models are based all his expectations, and therefore all his plans for the rest of his life" (Bowlby, 1973, p. 369).

During adolescence and young adulthood, the internalized working models of attachment coalesce into stable personality traits that express the relationship expectation patterns within the person's attachment system regarding the formation and loss of closely bonded emotional relationships. When the internal working models of attachment are distorted and pathological, then the subsequent formation of personality characteristics regarding the expectations and responses of self- and other-in-relationship will be equally distorted.

The origins of the highly distorted relationship patterns expressed as narcissistic and borderline personality traits arise from childhood attachment trauma that form severely problematic internal working models of attachment organization regarding expectations of both self- and other-in-relationship. At the level of the attachment system, narcissistic and borderline personality structures share the same basic internal working models of attachment, and so have similar core organizing structures. The difference between the overt manifestation of narcissistic and borderline personalities is in the overlay of defensive processes, not in their underlying core structure. In his analysis of narcissistic and borderline personality structures, Kernberg (1975) described how narcissistic personalities "present an underlying borderline personality organization" (p. 16) leading him to classify the narcissistic personality structure as a "subgroup of borderline patients" (p. xiii).

Within the internal working models of the attachment system, narcissistic and borderline personality organizations share the same expectations for self-in-relationship as being fundamentally inadequate and unworthy of being loved ("Because I am fundamentally inadequate as a person, I am inherently unlovable"). Both the narcissistic and borderline personalities expect to be rejected/abandoned by the other person in the relationship because of the fundamental inadequacy of the narcissistic/(borderline) personality ("I will be rejected and abandoned by the other person (by the attachment figure) because I am fundamentally inadequate and unlovable"). The difference in the external presentation of the narcissistic and borderline personality is simply the result of the defensive organization surrounding these identical core beliefs, not in the core beliefs themselves.

The borderline personality is a fragile personality structure with minimal to no internalized defensive organization to prevent the continual direct experience of these emotionally destabilizing core beliefs regarding primal self-inadequacy and expectations of being abandoned by the attachment figure. This results in the borderline personality directly and continually experiencing the emotional and psychological impact of these destabilizing core beliefs. The absence of internalized psychological defenses creates intense emotional instability for the borderline personality, who seeks externalized solutions to regulate these intensely painful core beliefs of the attachment system. The borderline personality organization is continually threatened with collapse without the constant external regulatory support provided by the other person.

The expression of the borderline-style of personality organization seeks an idealized love of perfect fusion with the attachment figure that will provide the fragile borderline personality structure with an externalized defense against the direct experience of the core beliefs of the attachment system. The borderline personality seeks constant demonstrations of the "perfect love" of the attachment figure to fill the borderline personality's void of self-experience as being fundamentally unlovable. The continual demonstrations of the attachment figure's complete devotion to the borderline personality's regulation keeps at bay the borderline personality's primal fear of being unloved and abandoned by the attachment figure.

For the borderline personality, the desired demonstration of idealized love represents a psychological enmeshment with the attachment figure in which there is a complete fusion of psychological states. The underlying disorganized attachment structure of the narcissistic/(borderline) personality organization does not possess a coherent strategy for repairing breaches to the relationship with the attachment figure. Ruptures in the psychological relationship with the attachment figure withdraw the external regulatory support of the attachment figure for the fragile personality structure of the narcissistic/(borderline) parent and result in a complete collapse of the underlying personality structure. The borderline personality's ability to maintain an organized psychological state is entirely dependent on the continual external regulatory support provided by the fused, perfectly attuned and reflective psychological relationship with the "regulatory other" of the attachment figure.

The borderline personality organization lacks the capacity for internal self-regulation. In order to maintain a regulated emotional and psychological state, the borderline personality structure relies entirely on the external regulatory support provided by the fused psychological state with the attachment figure. If there is a breach in this fused psychological state with the attachment figure, the organization of the borderline personality completely collapses into the intense and unprotected experience of intense abandonment fears and the emptiness of the self-experience as being fundamentally unlovable. So painful is this collapse into primal psychological disorganization that the borderline personality becomes obsessively focused on demanding that the attachment figure maintain a continual focus on regulating the psychological state of the borderline personality.

However, perfect and continual psychological fusion with the attachment figure is neither healthy nor possible. Normal-range and healthy relationships involve reciprocal exchanges between separate individuals, and minor failures of empathy are both expectable and developmentally healthy relationship experiences (Kohut, 1971; Tronick, 2003). Within healthy relationships, the two relationship partners seek to maintain a more-or-less coordinated psychological state with each other by making adjustments to their responses based on cues provided by the other person. This leads to broadly synchronous and coordinated psychological states of shared mutuality, with intermittent minor "breach-and-repair" sequences that develop from and correct dissynchronies in the relationship.

Maintaining a continually fused psychological state is impossible to achieve for two independently autonomous individuals in relationship. Since a relationship involves two separate psychological integrities, minor breaches in their shared psychological state arising from normal-range empathic failures will occur. In response to these ruptures in the shared psychological state, the partners engage in a series of more-or-less effective communications and "relational moves" to first try to maintain their coordinated state, or then to repair a breach in their shared psychological state when this occurs. The approach by which the relationship partners seek to repair minor breaches to their relationship is dependent upon their internal working models of attachment.

The formation of closely bonded emotional relationships and the repair of minor breaches to these attached relationships have been extensively studied in early childhood mental health because this is the period in which the initial internalized patterns for attachment bonding are created. The subtle rhythms of mutual relationship coordination and repair are also more clearly displayed during early childhood attachment bonding. Edward Tronick, a preeminent investigator of relationship processes, describes the interpersonal relationship dance that leads to the formation of a shared psychological state between parent and child,

> "In response to their partner's relational moves each individual attempts to adjust their behavior to maintain a coordinated dyadic state or to repair a mismatch. When mutual regulation is particularly successful, that is when the age-appropriate forms of meaning (e.g., affects, relational intentions, representations) from one individual's state of consciousness are coordinated with the meanings of another's state of consciousness... a dyadic state of consciousness emerges" (Tronick, 2003, p. 475)

The formation of a shared psychological state, described by Tronick as a "dyadic state of consciousness," is more generally referred to as an "intersubjective" psychological state in the research literature, and as psychological "intimacy" in the general population. The formation of this shared psychological state stabilizes the psychological functioning of both people in the relationship, particularly of the child in the parent-child relationship. According to Tronick,

> "A dyadic state of consciousness has dynamic effects. It increases the coherence of the infant's state of consciousness and expands the infant's (and the partner's) state of consciousness. Thus, dyadic states of consciousness are critical, perhaps even necessary for development" (Tronick, 2003, p. 475).

But maintaining the coordinated rhythm of a shared state of consciousness over extended periods of time is not possible for two separate psychological integrities. Inevitable empathic failures occur, creating breaches in this shared psychological state (Kohut, 1971; Trevarthen, 2001; Tronick, 2003). These minor breaches in the shared psychological state of the relationship partners establish psychological boundaries that are inherent to the separate psychological integrity of two separate individuals. Minor breach-and-repair sequences are critical relationship experiences in the formation and maintenance of healthy relationships. In repairing these inevitable breaches to the shared psychological state, the two relationship partners communicate self-authenticity within the relationship and simultaneously develop approaches for repairing the relationship in response to inevitably empathic failures. Tronick describes the importance of these relationship breaches to the development of healthy relationships,

> "Unlike many other accounts of relational processes which see interactive 'misses' (e.g., mismatches, misattunements, dissynchronies, miscoodinations) as indicating something wrong with an interaction, these 'misses' are the interactive and affective 'stuff' from which co-creative reparations generate new ways of being together. Instead there are only relationships that are inherently sloppy, messy and ragged, and individuals in relationships that are better able, or less able, to co-create new ways of sloppily being together… Out of the recurrence of reparations the infant and another person come to share the implicit knowledge that 'we can move into mutual positive states even when we have been in a mutual negative state.' Or 'we can transform negative into positive affect" (Tronick, 2003, p. 477-478).

However, the attachment patterns of the narcissistic and borderline personality organization are fundamentally unable to repair breaches that occur in the relationship. The early childhood attachment experiences that should have led to an understanding for how "we can move into mutual positive states even when we have been in a mutual negative state" were absent from the formative experiences of the narcissistic/(borderline) personality. When breaches occur in the "intersubjective" state of shared psychological understanding, the narcissistic and borderline personality structure collapses into primal disorganization. In the formative processes of creating a disorganized attachment in the childhood of the narcissistic and borderline personality, the parenting practices experienced by the narcissistic/(borderline) personality as a child were so confusing, disorienting, and frightening that the child was unable to develop a coherent strategy for forming an attachment bond to the parent, and for repairing breaches to the relationship when they occurred. The narcissistic and borderline personality is unable to "transform negative into positive affect."

Because the narcissistic/(borderline) personality cannot repair relationship breaches when they occur, the narcissistic/(borderline) personality therefore seeks to maintain a continually fused "dyadic state of consciousness" with the attachment figure. The internal working models of relationship contained in the attachment networks of the narcissistic/(borderline) personality structure are unable to repair breaches to the coordinated dyadic state when they occur. For the narcissistic/(borderline) personality, relationship breaches with the attachment figure result in an immensely painful collapse of the narcissistic/(borderline) personality's self-structure organization into a highly disorganized and dysregulated state. The internal models of the narcissistic/(borderline) personality's attachment system that guide relationship responses for the formation and repair of attachment-mediated relationships do not contain patterns for how "to move into mutual positive states when we have been in a mutual negative state." This means that when a breach in the fused psychological state occurs, the narcissistic/(borderline) personality does not possess the internal resources necessary to repair the lost relationship coordination with the attachment figure, leading to a complete collapse of personality organization.

It is therefore essential to the psychological state regulation of the narcissistic/(borderline) personality that a continually fused "dyadic state of consciousness" with the attachment figure be maintained in order to keep the narcissistic/(borderline) personality in a regulated state. The borderline-style personality seeks this continual fusion of psychological states with the attachment figure through an idealized perception of perfect love with a perfectly empathic and attuned relationship partner. The narcissistic-style personality seeks this continual fusion of psychological states with the attachment figure through the perfectly reflective adoration of narcissistic self-reflection (called "narcissistic supply") provided by the attachment figure.

When the inevitable failure of empathy by the attachment figure occurs, the narcissistic/(borderline) personality then collapses into a dysregulated and disorganized emotional and psychological state. The intensity of anger displayed by the narcissistic/(borderline) personality in the collapse into disorganization is a means of trying to maintain self-cohesion in response to the collapse of psychological structure. The emotion of anger imposes a cohesive integration to self-organization during the period of anger. The intense displays of anger by the narcissistic/(borderline) personality in response to empathic failures by the attachment figure imposes a degree of affective self-cohesion onto the collapsing narcissistic/(borderline) personality structure.

The narcissistic personality structure has the same underlying core beliefs as the borderline personality organization regarding fundamental self-inadequacy and ultimate rejection by the attachment figure. The difference is that the narcissistic-style personality has been able to form a very rudimentary internalized psychological defense against the direct and continual experience of primal self-inadequacy and fears of rejection/abandonment. This primitive narcissistic defense acts to stabilize the functioning of the narcissistic personality in relationships. As a result, the narcissistic-style personality is not as prone to the wildly chaotic emotional and relationship displays evidenced by the borderline-style personality, as long as the narcissistic defense is not threatened. If, however, the narcissistic defense is challenged (referred to as a "narcissistic injury") then the narcissistic personality will also collapse into displays of rage and psychological disorganization that are characteristic of the underlying borderline personality structure.

The narcissistic defense of grandiose self-inflation protects the narcissistic personality against the direct experience of fundamental self-inadequacy and fears of abandonment. These core beliefs of self-inadequacy and fears of rejection are expelled by the narcissistic-style personality onto the other person. The narcissistic-style personality sits in judgment of the other person who is deemed to be inferior, thereby creating the narcissistic defense of self-inflation by comparison to the inadequate other. The narcissistic defense expels the experience of primal self-inadequacy and fundamental unlovability at the core of the narcissistic/(borderline) personality onto the other person ("I'm not the inadequate one, you are").

By devaluing the other person, the narcissistic personality dismisses the importance of relationships with others because the other person is unworthy. In dismissing and devaluing relationships with the other (inadequate) person, the narcissistic defense is able to diminish fears of rejection and abandonment, since relationships with others are of no inherent value ("You're not rejecting me, I'm rejecting you"). As a result of the narcissistic defense, the core beliefs of the attachment system that "I am fundamentally inadequate and will be rejected by the other person because of my inadequacy" are psychologically expelled though their projection onto others; "You are inadequate, and I'm rejecting you because of your inadequacy."

The modicum of structural support provided by this narcissistic defense against the continual and direct experience of the underlying borderline personality organization of primal self-inadequacy and impending rejection by the attachment figure provides the narcissistic personality with sufficient self-stabilization for adequate social functioning. The social presentation of the narcissistic defense of seemingly confident superiority and arrogant self-assertion can even be successful in some domains of work and in superficial social relationships. However, the fragility of the narcissistic defense, and the deeper hidden pathology of the underlying borderline personality organization, becomes highly problematic in intimate relationships where the internal working models of attachment expectations become unable to modulate the inevitable processes of repairing breaches to the relationship.

Since the narcissistic personality is not founded on attachment structures of authentic self-esteem (i.e., core schemas for self- and other-in-relationship of "I am valuable, and I will be loved and nurtured by the other because of my inherent value"), the narcissistic personality needs continual external validation from others for his or her value, referred to as "narcissistic supply." For the narcissistic-style personality, the role of other people is simply to provide this continual "narcissistic supply" of admiration to support the fragile narcissistic defense. This leads to the characteristic display of the narcissistic personality as exploitative in relationships with others. The sole role of the other person in a relationship with the narcissistic personality is to provide a perfectly fused reflection of the narcissistic personality's own idealized self-perception, rather than forming a reciprocal relationship of appreciation and mutual regulation.

The borderline personality shows this same exploitation of others in relationship, except for the borderline-style personality the exploitation of others is labeled as being "manipulative." The uniting feature of narcissistic "exploitation" and borderline "manipulation" is their use of the other person as a means to meet the emotional and psychological needs of the narcissistic/(borderline) personality. The other person's sole role in the relationship is to serve as an external "regulatory object" for the emotional and psychological state of the narcissistic/(borderline) personality.

Since the underlying attachment structure of the narcissistic/(borderline) personality is unable to repair breaches in relationship, the narcissistic/(borderline) personality seeks to maintain a continually fused psychological state with the attachment figure. The other person is exploited by the narcissistic/(borderline) personality as an external "regulatory object" to serve as a narcissistic reflection of the narcissistic/(borderline) personality. The approaches of the narcissistic-style and borderline-style personalities differ in how they use the other person as a "regulatory object," but both require that the other person in the relationship remain in a completely fused psychological state with the narcissistic/(borderline) personality.

The borderline-style personality requires that the other person remains in a continually fused psychological state through perfectly attuned and constantly devoted attention to the moment-to-moment state regulation of the borderline personality. To achieve this continually fused psychological state, the borderline-style personality seeks to seduce the other person into an idealized image of "perfect love" in order to achieve a continual and perfectly fused psychological state with the attachment figure. The narcissistic-style personality, on the other hand, adopts a style of superiority that seeks to dominate the other person into a submissive state in which the separate autonomy of the other person is nullified and made subordinate to the psychological state of the narcissistic personality. The personality styles differ, but the goal is the same. The borderline-style personality seeks to seduce the other person into a continually fused psychological state, while the narcissistic-style personality seeks to control and dominate the other person into a submissive psychological surrender to the psychological state of the narcissist. In dominating and controlling the relationship partner, the narcissistic-style personality achieves the same perfectly fused psychological state as the borderline-style personality in which the other person acts as the "regulating other" for the narcissistic/(borderline) personality organization.

In a relationship with either a narcissistic or borderline personality, there is only one person present in the relationship; the narcissistic or borderline personality. The independent authenticity of the other person disappears from the relationship in order to meet the emotional and psychological needs of the narcissistic/(borderline) person for a fused psychological state totally dedicated to regulating the emotional and psychological needs of the narcissistic/(borderline) personality. If the attachment figure fails to be the perfectly attuned, perfectly reflective, "regulatory other" for the needs of the narcissistic/(borderline) personality, the result is a collapse of the narcissistic/(borderline) personality structure into disorganized tirades of vitriolic rage, chaotic and irrational accusations, and exhibitions of supposed victimization.

The chaotically angry intensity of these collapses of personality regulation by the narcissistic/(borderline) personality lead the other person in the relationship into trying to respond in ways that avoid the collapse of the narcissistic/(borderline) personality into dysregulation. In an effort to avoid the dysregulation of the narcissistic/(borderline) personality, the other person surrenders into becoming the external "regulatory other" for the psychological and emotional state of the narcissistic/(borderline) personality. In response to the unpredictable and volatile tirades of the narcissistic/(borderline) personality, the other person in the relationship becomes highly motivated to remain empathically attuned to the internal emotional and psychological state of the narcissistic/(borderline) personality in order to respond in ways that keep the narcissistic/(borderline) personality in a regulated state. The chaotic collapse of the narcissistic/(borderline) personality structure into complete dysregulation thereby achieves the goal of acquiring a perfectly attuned and empathic attachment figure who is continually striving to avoid relationship breaches.

Rappoport (2005) identifies the person who is in a relationship with the narcissist as being "co-narcissistic." The co-narcissistic relationship partner essentially disappears in the relationship. According to Rappoport, "there is, psychologically, only one person present. The co-narcissist disappears for both people, and only the narcissistic person's experience is important" (p. 3). The other person in relationship with the narcissistic/(borderline) personality is required to be a mere reflection of the psychological state narcissistic/(borderline) personality. Both personality styles reflect the use of the other person as an externalized "regulatory object" to support the inadequate self-regulation of the underlying borderline personality organization. In the case of the narcissistic-style personality, the use of the other person as a "regulatory object" is characterized as "exploitation," while for the borderline-style personality it is described as "manipulation,"

This process of using the other person as a "regulatory object" for the emotional and psychological state of the narcissistic/(borderline) personality organization becomes directly applicable to understanding the pathology in the parent-child relationship being expressed in attachment-based "parental alienation." The narcissistic/(borderline) parent forms a cross-generational coalition with the child against the other parent as a means to use (exploit; manipulate) the child's induced symptomatic rejection of the other parent to regulate the core vulnerabilities of the narcissistic/(borderline) personality of primal self-inadequacy and abandonment fears that were activated through the divorce.

The child is being used as a "regulatory object" by the narcissistic/(borderline) parent to expel from the narcissistic/(borderline) parent the primal self-inadequacy and abandonment fears onto the other parent, who, by means of the child's rejection, becomes the "inadequate" parent/(person) who is the one being rejected and abandoned because of the fundamental inadequacy of this parent as a person. The child is being used as a "regulatory object" by the narcissistic/(borderline) parent through the formation of a cross-generational coalition in which the child is induced into rejecting the targeted parent.

Chapter 4

THE DRIVING ENGINE OF ALIENATION

The Divorce

The divorce represents the precipitating trigger for the collapse of the narcissistic/(borderline) personality into disorganization, and the subsequent efforts to reestablish and maintain organized self-regulation create the family patterns traditionally referred to as "parental alienation." The response of the narcissistic/(borderline) personality to the psychological challenges created by the rejection inherent to the divorce process, and the subsequent efforts of the narcissistic/(borderline) parent to cope with these psychological challenges, represents the driving engine for the "alienation" process in the family.

The divorce represents a fundamental rejection of the narcissistic/(borderline) personality parent due to his or her inadequacies in the spousal relationship. This public rejection of the narcissistic/(borderline) parent as a spouse triggers the core personality vulnerabilities of primal self-inadequacy and the fear of being abandoned by the attachment figure. The narcissistic-style personality and the borderline-style personality, while sharing underlying core beliefs, will process this rejection and exposure of fundamental inadequacy in different ways as they strive to reestablish and maintain their self-organization in response to the psychological challenges for the personality structures created by the divorce.

The Narcissistic Style Response to Divorce

The narcissistic defense provides a more complete defense against the experience of abandonment fears than it does against the experience of core self-inadequacy. For the narcissistic style parent, relationships are superficial and can be easily discarded once the other person no longer provides "narcissistic supply." This does not mean that the fear of abandonment is absent, only that the narcissistic defense of devaluing others offers a more complete defense against the experience of abandonment fears than it does against the experience of self-inadequacy.

In fact, the more complete defense against abandonment fears offered by the narcissistic self-inflation potentially makes the narcissistic personality even more exposed to assaults on self-inadequacy. The narcissistic defense is extremely fragile. Criticisms and rejections can easily collapse this defense into the experience of primal self-inadequacy. In response to criticism and rejection, the narcissistic personality responds with extreme anger and aggressive psychological onslaughts of degradation directed against the other person (referred to as "narcissistic rage"). The narcissist's hyper-aggressive response to rejection, however, is not from triggering a fear of abandonment as it is with the more borderline-style personality, but instead reflects the inherent exposure of self-inadequacy that the rejection entails. The other person is rejecting the narcissist because of the inadequacy of the narcissist as a person, and it is this public exposure of inadequacy that produces the vitriol of the narcissistic response.

For the narcissistic style parent, the interpersonal rejection inherent to divorce threatens to collapse the fragile psychological defense of narcissistic self-inflation that the narcissistic parent maintains against the experience of primal self-inadequacy. The divorce is a public exposure of the spousal inadequacy of the narcissistic parent and represents a rejection by the attachment figure that triggers the attachment vulnerabilities of being rejected and abandoned by the attachment figure because of the fundamental inadequacy of the narcissistic parent. Divorce represents a direct hit on the core vulnerabilities of the narcissistic parent that provokes two related sources of tremendous anxiety for the narcissistic parent, 1) the threatened exposure of primal self-inadequacy at the core of the narcissistic self-experience, and 2) a tremendous anxiety related to profound abandonment fears.

While superficially the narcissistic personality appears to present as confident and self-assured, this presentation is merely a fragile defensive veneer against the experience of fundamental self-inadequacy that exists at the core of the narcissistic self-structure. Additionally, the fear of abandonment is so profound that the only defense available is to entirely dismiss the importance of others and banish from awareness all desire to form an attachment bond to others. Underneath the defensive presentation of arrogant self-inflation, the narcissistic-style personality is extremely vulnerable.

The divorce strikes at both of these primal vulnerabilities of the narcissistic personality. The interpersonal rejection by the other spouse that is inherent to the divorce represents a public exposure of the inadequacy of the narcissist as a spouse, and the narcissist is being publicly rejected for this fundamental inadequacy. The rejection punctures the defensive veneer of narcissistic self-inflation and publicly exposes the inadequacy at the core of the narcissistic personality. The threatened collapse of the narcissistic defense resulting from this public exposure of inadequacy triggers a tremendous anxiety for the narcissistic personality. The inherent rejection of the divorce and the collapse of the narcissistic defense threatens to plunge the narcissistic personality into the depths of the disorganized attachment that is at the foundational core of the narcissistic personality structure. The rejection of the narcissistic parent by the attachment figure of the other spouse also strikes at the core attachment expectation that the attachment figure will abandon the narcissistic personality because of the fundamental personal inadequacy of the narcissistic personality. This primal attachment fear is exactly what is occurring during the divorce.

While the narcissistic personality presents as dismissive of others, this dismissive stance represents a defensive response to keep at bay the fear of the attachment figure's potential abandonment of the narcissistic personality. By dismissing the importance of attachment bonds, the narcissistic-style personality is seeking to manage the tremendous anxiety surrounding primal fears of being abandoned by the attachment figure. The rejection of the divorce bypasses this narcissistic defense and strikes directly at the underlying vulnerability by creating the feared rejection and abandonment by the attachment figure. This activates a second related source of tremendous anxiety for the narcissistic personality from the threatened breakthrough into the awareness of the narcissistic personality of the primal fears of being abandoned by the attachment figure.

The divorce places pressure on both aspects of the narcissistic defense. It triggers a public exposure of the narcissist's primal self-inadequacy and awakens the experience of the deep abandonment fears at the core of the narcissistic personality structure. The inherent rejection of the divorce experience threatens to collapse the narcissistic defense, which triggers two separate but interrelated sources of tremendous anxiety. The tremendous anxiety experienced by the narcissistic personality creates a psychological imperative for the narcissistic personality to reestablish the fragile and threatened narcissistic defense.

The narcissistic defense is predicated on psychologically expelling the experience of self-inadequacy by projecting this rejected quality of the narcissistic personality onto others. With the narcissistic defense, it is the other person who is made inadequate. This projective expulsion of core self-inadequacy onto the other person allows the narcissistic personality to retain the self-image of idealized perfection essential to the narcissistic defense. Similarly, the fear of being rejected by the other person, by the attachment figure, is also psychologically expelled from the narcissistic personality by its projective displacement onto others. Through the narcissistic defense, the other person, the attachment figure, is dismissively rejected by the narcissistic personality as being expendable and unimportant. The importance of the attachment figure is only for the "narcissistic supply" that this other person can provide. For the narcissistic personality, relationships are shallow and superficial, and once the other person no longer provides "narcissistic supply" then the other person becomes expendable and is discarded. As a result of the narcissistic defense, it is the other person who is being rejected and abandoned by the narcissist (before the attachment figure can reject and abandon the narcissistic personality for his or her inherent inadequacy).

The divorce is threatening to collapse this fragile narcissistic defense. In order to restore the narcissistic defense that is being challenged by the public exposure of the narcissist as inadequate and rejected, the narcissistic personality must reestablish the projective expulsion of these qualities onto the other person. The other person must once more be made to be the inadequate and rejected person. Yet the divorce precludes this from occurring within the spousal relationship, since the divorce separates the marital bond and already defines the narcissistic personality as the inadequate spouse who is being rejected for this spousal inadequacy. So in order to reestablish the narcissistic defense, the narcissistic parent triangulates the child into the spousal conflict through the formation of a cross-generational coalition against the other parent. The narcissistic/(borderline) parent then uses this cross-generational coalition with the child to induce the child into rejecting the other parent. Through the child's rejection of the targeted parent for alleged parental inadequacy, the narcissistic personality is able to once again expel through projective displacement onto the other parent (the other spouse) the narcissist's own primal self-inadequacy and abandonment fears that are at the core of the narcissistic personality.

Through the child's rejection of the targeted parent, it becomes the targeted parent who is being publicly exposed as the inadequate parent. It is the targeted parent who is being rejected and abandoned by the child for the fundamental inadequacy of the targeted parent, as both a parent and as a person. The narcissistic/(borderline) parent is using the child's rejection of the targeted parent to publicly expose the targeted parent's supposed fundamental inadequacy and abandonment, which re-establishes the narcissistic defense by projecting these primal vulnerabilities onto the other person. The pubic definition of the other spouse, of the other parent, as the inadequate and rejected parent (person) reestablishes for the narcissistic spouse the projective expulsion of the self-inadequacy and abandonment fears that are at the core of the narcissistic personality structure.

Reestablishing the narcissistic defense directly through the spousal relationship is impossible because in the spousal relationship it is the narcissistic personality that is being exposed as the inadequate person (spouse) who is being rejected for this fundamental inadequacy. However, the narcissistic defense can be reestablished by triangulating the child into the spousal conflict and then using the child's rejection of the targeted parent to define the targeted parent as the inadequate and rejected person.

The triangulation of the child into the spousal conflict to define the targeted parent as the fundamentally inadequate parent (person) who is being rejected for supposed parental inadequacy allows the narcissistic parent to then also reestablish the narcissistic self-ideal as being the all-wonderful and perfect parent (person), and to publicly display this narcissistic self-ideal to therapists and the court. By reestablishing the narcissistic self-ideal, the reparation of the narcissistic defense is complete. Through the child's rejection of the targeted parent and the child's expressed desire to be with the narcissistic/(borderline) parent, the targeted parent is defined as being the inadequate and rejected person and the narcissistic/(borderline) parent is defined as being the wonderful and perfect parent (person). The reparation of the narcissistic defense is enacted through the triangulation of the child into the spousal conflict through the formation of a cross-generational coalition with the child in which the child is induced into rejecting the other parent.

Another important regulatory role for the child is as the external symbol of narcissistic superiority and victory. Possession of the child represents a symbol of narcissistic superiority and the victory of the narcissistic parent over the targeted parent. The possession of the idealized child who is totally dedicated to the narcissistic parent also provides the narcissistic parent with a source of "narcissistic supply" from the child's elicited adoration and dedication to the narcissistic parent. Kernberg notes this quality of the narcissistic parent,

> "The need to control the idealized objects, to use them in attempts to manipulate and exploit the environment and to "destroy potential enemies," is linked with inordinate pride in the 'possession' of these perfect objects totally dedicated to the patient" (Kernberg, 1977, p. 33).

By possessing the child, the narcissistic personality is also able to exact a retaliatory revenge on the other spouse. The narcissistic personality has what the targeted parent wants; the child. By completely possessing the child who is desired by the targeted parent, and by withholding the coveted child from the targeted parent, the narcissistic parent is able to exact a cruel revenge on the other spouse (the abandoning attachment figure) for failing to appreciate the self-inflated magnificence of the narcissistic personality and for abandoning the fragile narcissistic personality.

> "If others fail to satisfy the narcissist's 'needs,' including the need to look good, or be free from inconvenience, then others 'deserve to be punished'... Even when punishing others out of intolerance or entitlement, the narcissist sees this as 'a lesson they need, for their own good" (Beck et al., 2004, p. 252).

In the mind of the narcissistic personality, the other parent (spouse) "deserves to be punished," and the narcissistic parent takes satisfaction in the "justice" of the targeted parent's immense suffering. This attitude of the narcissistic parent is then acquired by the child toward the targeted parent through the influence of the narcissistic parent on the child. In attachment-based "parental alienation," the child will display a similar attitude toward the targeted-rejected parent; i.e., that the targeted parent "deserves" to be rejected and deserves to suffer for the supposed parental inadequacies of this parent. The attitude of the child that the targeted parent "deserves" to be rejected and "deserves" to suffer is a direct transfer to the child of this identical attitude held by the narcissistic parent. Appropriate clinical interviewing can usually expose this attitude in the narcissistic parent along with a complete absence of empathy for the suffering of the targeted parent that are then transferred to the child's attitudes toward the targeted-rejected parent.

The child's triangulation into the spousal conflict reestablishes the homeostatic balance of the narcissistic defense needed to maintain the fragile self-structure organization of the narcissistic personality that is being challenged by the interpersonal rejection inherent to the divorce and the family's transition to a separated family structure. By triangulating the child into the spousal conflict, and then inducing the child's rejection of the other parent, the narcissistic parent is able to restore the narcissistic defense that is being threatened with collapse within the spousal relationship from the public exposure of the narcissist's fundamental inadequacy and rejection inherent to the divorce experience. Through the formation of a cross-generational coalition with the child against the other parent (as described in the family systems literature by Haley and Minuchin), the child's induced rejection of the targeted parent serves to publicly define the targeted parent as being the inadequate parent (person) who is the one being rejected. The child's hyper-bonding to the narcissistic parent and rejection of the targeted parent also serves to publicly display and reestablish the definition of the narcissistic parent as a being the all-wonderful and perfect parent (person), thereby reestablishing the self-inflation of the narcissistic defense that is being challenged within the spousal relationship by the public rejection of the narcissistic personality as a spouse. Obtaining full possession of the "narcissistic object" represented by the child also serves as a symbol of the narcissistic/(borderline) parent's superiority and victory over the targeted parent, and complete possession and withholding of the child acts as a retaliatory weapon to exact emotional revenge on the targeted parent for the narcissistic injury of the divorce.

The Borderline-Style Response to Divorce

The same underlying dynamics apply to the borderline-style personality, but the outward manifestation will be somewhat different because of the absence of the narcissistic defense of grandiose self-inflation afforded to the narcissistic personality. For the narcissistic-style personality, the anxious-avoidant attachment overtones to the fundamentally disorganized attachment, in which attachment needs are devalued and dismissed, provides the narcissistic personality with a stronger defense against the direct experience of the core abandonment fears. As a result of devaluing relationships with others, the narcissistic defense is afforded a somewhat stronger psychological protection from fears of abandonment. On the other hand, by engaging a protective veneer of narcissistic self-expansion the narcissistic defense becomes more vulnerable to the exposure of the primal self-inadequacy vulnerabilities that reside at the core of the narcissistic self-structure.

The borderline personality, on the other hand, lacks the overtly narcissistic defensive structure and so is more directly exposed to the experience of abandonment fears. The borderline personality seeks to allay the experience of self-inadequacy and abandonment fears by seeking continual psychological protection within an idealized "perfect love" of constant attention and devotion by the attachment figure. For the borderline-style personality, the other person is expected (and is required) to remain entirely dedicated to the regulation of the borderline personality's emotional and psychological state. This is reflective of the infantile state of the borderline personality structure in which the attachment figure represents the idealized "perfect parent" who is entirely devoted and completely dedicated to the regulation of the infant's emotional and psychological state. The borderline personality style seeks the idealized "regulatory other" of the perfectly attuned and completely dedicated attachment figure for the infantile self-structure of the borderline personality.

So while the narcissistic personality style uses grandiose self-inflation to devalue attachment to the relationship partner, the borderline personality style over-values attachment to the other person in an effort to avoid abandonment. The narcissistic personality style is inherently more vulnerable to threats to self-inadequacy, whereas the borderline personality style is inherently more vulnerable to threats of abandonment. For the borderline-style personality structure, the primary threat posed by the divorce is the abandonment of the borderline personality by the attachment figure of the spouse. The borderline-style personality therefore develops the compensatory defensive response of preventing abandonment by replacing the loss of the perfectly adoring "regulatory other" of the spouse with the possession of the perfectly adoring "regulatory other" of the child. For the narcissistic personality style, complete possession of the "narcissistic object" of the child represents an external symbol of the superiority of the narcissistic personality over the targeted-rejected parent, whereas for the borderline-style personality the complete possession of the child represents a defense against abandonment fears.

The borderline personality style engages the child into a hyper-bonded emotional relationship in which the child becomes the embodiment of the perfect "regulatory object" who will "never abandon" the borderline parent (unlike the attachment figure of the ex-spouse). This theme of abandonment will be presented to the child by the borderline-style parent in the form of accusing the other parent of having abandoned the borderline-style parent, and by implication the child ("Your father left *us* for a new girlfriend"). By presenting this theme of abandonment to the child, the borderline-style parent elicits reassurances from the child that the child will remain committed to the borderline-style parent and will never abandon this parent (like the other, bad parent did). Abandonment themes, as well as themes of an idealized "perfect love" supposedly shared between the child and borderline-style parent will be prominent characteristics in the borderline-style presentation of attachment-based "parental alienation."

For the borderline-style parent, the possession of the child who is of value to the targeted parent also acts to prevent the abandonment of the borderline personality parent by the ex-spouse. As long as the borderline parent has possession of the child, the ex-spouse will remain continually involved with the borderline parent's emotional regulation. The ongoing drama surrounding custody and visitation, and the continual intrusion of the borderline parent into the home life of the targeted parent that is afforded by the shared relationship with the child, are manifestations of the borderline personality's efforts to maintain the relationship with the attachment figure of the other spouse, thereby avoiding abandonment by the ex-spouse. If the borderline-style parent allowed the family to transition successfully into a separated family structure then the bond between the other spouse and the borderline-style parent would actually be severed. By maintaining conflict over the child, and particularly by possessing the coveted child, the borderline-style parent is able to keep the ex-spouse continually focused on the emotional and psychological state of the borderline parent. In a separated family structure, the minimal spousal bond that exists is through the continuing parental roles with the child. By making the child an issue of ongoing contention, the borderline parent maximizes the required involvement of the ex-spouse with the borderline parent.

The greater relevance of abandonment fears for the more borderline-style parent can also reveal itself in the timing of "parental alienation." In some cases, the active "alienation" of the child may not begin at the point of the divorce since the other spouse may still be involved with the borderline parent surrounding co-parenting issues with the child. The active "alienation," however, may begin in earnest when the targeted parent remarries, which more fully separates the former spousal unit of the borderline parent with the targeted parent. With the more borderline-style parent, it is often the remarriage of the targeted parent that acts as the trigger for the borderline parent's abandonment fears, which then triggers the enactment of attachment-based "parental alienation."

When it is the remarriage (or potential remarriage) of the targeted parent that is triggering attachment-based "parental alienation" through the activation of the borderline-style parent's abandonment fears, this feature may be expressed by the child who objects to the new step-parent and makes complaints that the targeted parent is not spending enough "special time" with just the child. In this variant of attachment-based "parental alienation," the child seeks to entirely terminate a relationship with the targeted parent for reasons surrounding the targeted parent's new spouse. This rationale for the child's rejection of the targeted parent has absolutely no logical coherence – "I want more time with you so I'm never going to see you again" – but it is commonly offered as a justification for the child's rejection of the targeted parent following remarriage.

The actual underlying process behind this child symptom is an effort to disrupt the targeted parent's new marriage by using the child's objections to interfere in this new marital relationship. The form of the child's complaints are typically that the targeted parent does not spend enough one-on-one time with the child. This complaint is with the subliminal purpose of separating the targeted parent from the new spouse. Special one-on-one time with a parent can be valuable, but it is not a reason for a child wanting to entirely sever the parent-child bond. When it is offered as a reason for the child's rejection of the targeted parent, it is essentially being offered as blackmail. The child's demand is forcing the targeted parent to choose between the child and the new spouse. If the targeted parent chooses the attachment bond with the child, then the bond to the new spouse is severed. If, on the other hand, the targeted parent chooses to remain attached to the new spouse, then the targeted parent loses the relationship with the child. The borderline-style parent is using the child's (induced) demand for exclusive "one-on-one" time with the targeted parent to disrupt the targeted parent's new spousal relationship. In normal-range post-divorce family relationships, children adjust to and incorporate the new spouses of their parents.

The borderline-style parent can also use continual conflicts over scheduling custody and visitation transfers to intrude into and disrupt the relationship of the targeted parent with the new spouse. By continually creating turmoil and drama surrounding custody and visitation with the child, the borderline-style parent requires that the targeted parent maintains an ongoing focus on the former spouse, on the borderline parent, which then intrudes into and disrupts the serenity of bonding in the new marital relationship with the new spouse. The borderline-style parent is essentially using the child to sow discord and conflict in the targeted parent's new marital relationship. By using the shared parental bond to the child to create conflict, the borderline-style parent becomes an active participant-by-proxy in the targeted parent's new marital relationship.

Stylistic Differences

Both the narcissistic and borderline personality styles share the same underlying core expectations regarding self- and other-in-relationship that are embedded in the internal working models of the attachment system. The overt differences in the manifestation of these underlying core beliefs merely represent the presence afforded to the narcissistic parent of some structural support to self-regulation provided by the narcissistic defense of grandiose self-inflation and devaluing of relationships with others.

From the perspective of the attachment system, both personality styles represent disorganized forms of attachment in which the internal working models of attachment do not provide the narcissistic/(borderline) parent with any organized strategy for repairing relationship breaches when they occur. This results in a complete breakdown of the organized self-coherence of the narcissistic/(borderline) parent whenever attachment bonds are breached. The loss of the attachment-mediated spousal relationship as the result of the divorce produces a complete collapse of the narcissistic/(borderline) parent's capacity for organized self-regulation, leading to the triangulation of the child into the spousal conflict in order to stabilize the fragile self-structure organization of the narcissistic/(borderline) parent.

The stylistic differences between the narcissistic and borderline approaches to forming relationships, and repairing relationship breaches when they occur, represent differences in the attachment overtones to the underlying disorganized attachment. The narcissistic-style personality has a fundamentally disorganized attachment with anxious-avoidant overtones in which the importance of relationships are devalued. The more borderline-style personality, on the other hand, has a fundamentally disorganized attachment with anxious-ambivalent overtones, in which attachment bonds are sought through displays of highly demanding protest and needy attention seeking behaviors that elicit the continual involvement of the attachment figure.

The anxious-avoidant overtones to the disorganized attachment allow the narcissistic-style personality to develop the narcissistic defense of devaluing others as a means to psychologically expel the core beliefs of self-inadequacy and fear of abandonment onto the other person.

Through the narcissistic defense, the other person becomes the inadequate and rejected psychological container for holding the core psychological vulnerabilities of the narcissistic/(borderline) personality ("I'm not inadequate; you are. I'm not rejected and abandoned; you are"). The ability to develop even a primitive narcissistic defense provides the narcissistic-style personality with at least some degree of underlying structure to the fundamentally disorganized attachment networks, which provides the narcissistic-style personality with somewhat greater stability.

The rudimentary defensive structure of the narcissistic defense also provides the narcissistic personality with a limited approach to restoring breached relationships. In response to breaches in the attached relationship, the narcissistic-style personality uses vitriolic onslaughts to dominate the other person back into a submissive role as the "regulatory object" for the narcissistic personality. While this represents a proto-organized strategy for repair of breaches to the relationship, more advanced approaches to restoring breaches to the relationship through negotiated cooperation remain beyond the ability of the disorganized attachment networks at the core of the narcissistic personality.

The interpersonally dominating approach of the narcissistic-style personality makes the development of a cooperative co-parenting relationship impossible. The sense of entitlement and disregard for the value of the other person in the relationship will lead the narcissistic-style parent to entirely disregard the rights and interests of the targeted parent. The narcissistic-style parent will exercise an unrestricted freedom of impulse originating from the underlying lack of organized structure. The narcissistic-style parent will take whatever action is needed to regulate the internal emotional and psychological state of the narcissistic personality, without regard for the rights or needs of the targeted parent, or for existing court orders.

> "Narcissistic individuals also use power and entitlement as evidence of superiority... As a means of demonstrating their power, narcissists may alter boundaries, make unilateral decisions, control others, and determine exceptions to rules that apply to other, ordinary people... Out of their vehement certainty of judgment, boundary violations of all sorts may occur, as narcissists are quite comfortable taking control and dictating orders ('I know what's

right for them') but quite uncomfortable accepting influence from others" (Beck et al., 2004, p. 215).

While the narcissistic-style personality has anxious-avoidant overtones to the fundamentally disorganized attachment patterns, the borderline-style personality displays anxious-ambivalent overtones to the underlying disorganized attachment. The central strategy of an anxious-ambivalent attachment for restoring relationship breaches is to acquire the involvement of the attachment figure through attention seeking displays of either protest or neediness. This means that the borderline-style parent will respond to breaches in the relationship with the attachment figure through increased displays of protest behavior designed to elicit the involvement of the attachment figure. These protest displays will either be in the form of angry dysregulated tantrums or intense displays of needy attention seeking vulnerability.

Both the angry tantrum and the needy-vulnerable displays are designed to control the attachment figure. Both the narcissistic and the borderline personality pathology seeks to control the attachment figure, but their styles of interpersonal control differ. The narcissistic-style personality seeks to control the attachment figure through domination. The borderline-style personality seeks to control the attachment figure through manipulation. The chaotic displays of angry tantrums in response to breaches in the relationship are highly aversive for the attachment figure. Over time, the aversive nature of these angry tantrums motivates the attachment figure to respond to the borderline-style personality in ways that limit the collapse of the borderline personality into these angry tantrums. The attachment figure is thus being controlled by the display of these tantrums.

The needy displays of supposed vulnerability seek to manipulatively control the attachment figure by requiring that the attachment figure provide continual nurturing support for the supposed neediness of the borderline personality. The emotional display by the borderline-style personality of needy vulnerability seeks to bind the attachment figure into a caretaking role, thereby limiting the independent autonomy of the attachment figure. Both the display of angry protest and the display of needy vulnerability are manipulative efforts of the borderline-style personality to control the attachment figure and prevent abandonment by engaging the continual focus of the attachment figure.

The anxious-ambivalent overtones to the fundamentally disorganized attachment of the borderline-style personality means that the more borderline-style parent will present an intensely chaotic mixture of angry, demanding, and needy displays designed to make the borderline-style parent the continual center of attention and involvement. This chaotic attention-seeking approach to relationship will make it exceedingly hard, if not impossible, to develop a stable co-parenting relationship with the borderline-style personality. The psychological goal of the borderline-style personality is not to cooperate on the tasks of co-parenting, the goal is to become and remain the center of attention through displays of angry protest and needy vulnerability that continually creates chaos, which keeps the borderline personality at the center of everyone's attention.

The more borderline-style parent will also make greater use of emotionally seductive approaches to relationship formation, evidenced in a more emotionally hyper-bonded relationship with the child, than will be displayed by the narcissistic-style parent. The narcissistic style parent is more likely to use power and dominance assertion control tactics that include granting the child narcissistic indulgences of special privileges and gifts to induce the child's surrender to the will of the narcissistic parent. Whereas the borderline-style parent will tend to rely more on emotionally seductive tactics of hyper-affectionate and emotionally needy displays to seduce the child's surrender to the role of the external "regulatory object" for the borderline parent.

The borderline-style parent will also be more prone to display a hyper-anxious fearfulness regarding the child's supposed safety while in the care of the targeted parent. The hyper-anxious fearfulness for the child's safety is a product of the borderline-style personality's reliance on needy displays of vulnerability to achieve control of others. By presenting as hyper-fearful for the child's safety, the borderline-style parent justifies a variety of highly intrusive parenting practices that disrupt the child's ability to form a normal-range attached relationship with the targeted parent. The borderline-style parent manipulatively uses parental over-anxious concern for child's supposed safety to justify frequent intrusions into the child's time and relationship with the targeted parent. These intrusions are justified by the borderline-style parent as necessary to check on and monitor the child's well-being and safety when the child is with the targeted parent. Alternatively, the borderline-style parent will sometimes frame the child as being needy of continual nurturing contact with the borderline parent, so that it is the child who is framed as needing the frequent reassurance of the borderline parent when the child is with the targeted parent. In this role-reversal presentation, it is the child who is supposedly fearful of the targeted parent. The child is made to become the externalized regulatory "holder" of the borderline-style parent's anxious fearfulness.

The child's symptoms created by the borderline-style parent, while still prone to angry and hostile rejection toward the targeted parent, may also evidence a more pronounced display of anxious fearfulness toward the targeted parent. When the child's rejection of the targeted parent is created by a borderline-style parent, the child's offered reasons for rejecting the targeted parent may have a more prominent tone of hyper-anxious fearfulness. Whereas, when the child's rejection of the targeted parent is created by a narcissistic-style parent, the child may tend to display a stronger symptom presentation of contemptuous judgement that the targeted parent "deserves" to be punished for parental inadequacies.

Attachment-based "parental alienation" created by a borderline-style parent tends to present with:

- **Emotionally Seductive:** The borderline-style parent tends to create stronger characteristics of seductive hyper-emotional bonding between the child and the borderline parent.

- **Separation Anxiety:** The borderline-style parent tends to create a surrounding symptom context of more intensive separation anxiety displays, reflecting the borderline personality's fear of abandonment.

- **Hyper-Anxious Fearfulness:** The borderline-style personality tends to produce a symptom context of more pronounced hyper-anxious fearfulness for the child's safety regarding the care provided by the targeted parent.

Attachment-based "parental alienation" created by a narcissistic-style parent tends to present with:

- **Contemptuous Judgment:** The narcissistic-style personality tends to produce a surrounding symptom context marked by greater contemptuous judgment of the targeted parent, by both the child and narcissistic parent.

- **Theme of "Deserving" Rejection:** The narcissistic-style parent tends to create a stronger presentation in the child's rejection of the targeted parent that the targeted parent "deserves" to be rejected as justified punishment for the supposed character failure or past actions of the targeted parent.

- **Narcissistic Indulgences:** The narcissistic-style parent relies less on hyper-affectionate displays with the child and instead uses narcissistic indulgences of granting adult-like privileges to the child and providing gifts of material items.

However, these stylistic characteristics between the narcissistic-style or borderline-style parent exist along a continuum, with considerable overlap between the two personality styles being possible. The foundational organization for both the narcissistic and borderline style personalities is the same. Both personality styles represent superficially different manifestations of underlying core beliefs in self-inadequacy and fears of abandonment by the attachment figure. An overlap between narcissistic and borderline characteristics, which reflects the shared underlying disorganized attachment of both the narcissistic and borderline personality structures, is more the norm than the exception.

The presentation of attachment-based "parental alienation" can also be influenced by the addition of other parental personality disorder traits in the personality structure of the narcissistic/(borderline) parent. For example, the addition of antisocial personality traits in a parent can create a more hostile-aggressive tone to the child's rejection of the targeted parent. When parental antisocial personality traits are also present, the family processes take on a more pronounced "domestic violence" feel to the "alienation," in which the child is more prominently used by the narcissistic/antisocial parent as a weapon to inflict suffering on the targeted parent. The addition of parental obsessive-compulsive personality traits can produce a more moralistic and judgmental presentation to the "alienation," with possible religious overtones evidenced in the moral condemnation directed toward the targeted parent. A stronger presentation of paranoid personality traits in the narcissistic/(borderline) parent can lead to more pronounced parental fears for the child's safety, while histrionic personality traits with the narcissistic/(borderline) parent can lead to a greater display of using the child's symptoms as a means for the parent to become the center of attention.

Chapter 5

THE ROLE-REVERSAL CORE

The "Regulatory Other"

Of central importance to understanding the core personality processes creating attachment-based "parental alienation" is the child's role-reversal relationship with the narcissistic/(borderline) parent in which the child is used by the parent as a "regulatory other" (also referred to as a "regulatory object") to regulate the emotional and psychological state of the parent. The construct of regulation has become an important part of the child development literature and is central to understanding the formative processes of childhood, so a brief departure into explaining the nature of regulation, the "regulatory other," and the development of self-regulation is necessary to understanding the core personality pathology of attachment-based "parental alienation."

The concept of regulation can best be understood by analogy to the functioning of a thermostat in regulating the temperature of a room. If the room temperature becomes too hot or too cold, then the thermostat registers the fluctuation in temperature and turns on either the air conditioner or heater to bring the room temperature back into a comfortable mid-range. The thermostat regulates the room's temperature to ensure that the temperature remains in a comfortable mid-range. The brain has a variety of regulatory systems to ensure that our emotions, behavior, and social relationships remain in an organized and adaptive mid-range of functioning, with neither too much nor too little of the regulated quality. When we become too stressed, too anxious, or too sad, for example, various regulatory systems act to help us regain an organized and regulated emotional state.

Development of the internalized capacity for self-regulation of emotional, behavioral, and social expression develops gradually across the period of childhood. Infants possess almost no capacity for self-regulation and are almost entirely dependent on the parent for external regulation of the child's physical, emotional, and psychological state. The parent acts as an external "regulatory other" for the child in helping the child both to maintain and regain organized and regulated emotional and psychological states. As the child begins to become dysregulated, the parent responds in attuned and sensitive ways to ensure that the child remains in an emotionally and psychologically organized and regulated state, and if the child does become dysregulated, the parent responds in attuned and sensitive ways that help the child regain an organized and regulated state. Through both anticipatory and responsive regulatory support provided by the parent, the child's own brain networks responsible for independent self-regulation gradually become stronger and more integrated through "use-dependent" neural growth and development.

Brain networks grow and develop based on the principle of "we build what we use." The renowned neuroscientist, Donald Hebb, referred to use-dependent neural development as "neurons that fire together, wire together." Every time we use a brain pathway or network, the connections within this network become stronger, more sensitive, and more efficient through use-dependent neurodevelopmental processes. The process of use-dependent development of brain networks is called "canalization" (like building "canals" or channels within the brain networks). When the attuned and responsive parent provides the child with "scaffolding" support for helping the child remain in a regulated state, or to regain an organized and regulated emotional and psychological state when the child becomes overwhelmed by challenges the child cannot independently master, the parent helps build the child's own brain networks for self-regulation (through use-dependent "canalization" of these networks).

In early infancy, the child becomes easily overwhelmed by emotional and environmental stimuli, leading to frequent episodes of emotional and behavioral disorganization and dysregulation. Even the smallest of challenges, like being overly tired or hungry, can lead to the collapse of the child's organized and regulated state into tantrums of tears and protest behavior. By helping the young infant repeatedly regain an organized and well-regulated state, the child's parents help to scaffold the use-dependent development ("canalization") in the child's brain of the networks and pathways that the child will ultimately use in "self-regulation."

In providing this regulatory support for the child, the parent takes on the interactive role with the child as an external "regulatory object" (or "regulatory other") for the child's emotional and psychological state-regulation. The role of the parent as an external "regulatory object" for the child is to help the child maintain a well-organized and well-regulated state through attuned and responsive parental caregiving. The parent essentially becomes an external part of the child's own internal regulatory system, helping to build these internal regulatory networks by scaffolding the use-dependent neurodevelopment of the various brain pathways used in the child's maintaining and regaining organized and well-regulated emotional and psychological states.

As the child matures, the child begins to encounter increasingly complex developmental challenges such as the need to delay gratification of immediate desires, to control impulses, and to tolerate increasing levels of frustration. As the child encounters increasingly complex challenges, and in the context of the child's increasing capacity for independent self-regulation, the scaffolding support provided by the "regulatory other" of the parent becomes increasingly more sophisticated and nuanced. By repeatedly providing the child with responsive and sensitive scaffolding support for the child's transitions from disorganized and dysregulated emotional states back into organized and well-regulated states, the "regulatory other" of the parent helps build the neural networks in the child's brain that will ultimately develop into the child's own capacity for self-regulation. Gradually, by the child repeatedly using the scaffolding support offered by the "regulatory other" of the parent, the child's brain develops the internal networks needed to make these state transitions from disorganized and dysregulated states back into organized and well-regulated states independently from the external regulatory support provided by the parent. This process is called the child's development of self-regulation, and the organized capacity for self-regulation is an integral part of the child's development of "self-structure."

One of the leading researchers in child development, Alan Sroufe, describes this process of parental scaffolding support for the development of the child's own internalized capacity for self-regulation,

> "In the typical course of events, caregivers quickly learn to 'read' the infant and to provide care that keeps distress and arousal within reasonable limits. And they do more. By effectively engaging the infant and leading him or her to ever longer bouts of emotionally charged, but organized behavior, they provide the infant with critical training in regulation. If they do become threatened or distressed, the caregiver will help them regain equilibrium. Such confident expectations are precisely what is meant by attachment security. They are secure in their attachment. It is this security that supports confident exploration of the environment and ease of settling when distressed"
>
> "The movement toward self-regulation continues throughout the childhood years, as does a vital, though changing, role for caregivers. During the toddler period, the child acquires beginning capacities for self-control, tolerance of moderate frustration, and a widening range of emotional reactions, including shame and, ultimately, pride and guilt. Practicing self-regulation in a supportive context is crucial. Emerging capacities are easily overwhelmed. The caregiver must both allow the child to master those circumstances within their capacity and yet anticipate circumstances beyond the child's ability, and help to restore equilibrium when the child is over-taxed. Such 'guided self-regulation' is the foundation for the genuine regulation that will follow" (Sroufe, 2000, p. 71).

Initially, the parent acts as an external "regulatory other" for the child's internal emotional and psychological state. Eventually, the child's neural networks for making these state transitions become sufficiently developed ("canalized") through the scaffolding support provided by the external "regulatory other" of the parent that the child is able to independently make these state-transitions, and is able to independently maintain an organized and well-regulated state in response to stresses, without the need for the scaffolding support from the parent. When the child is able to independently maintain a regulated emotional and behavioral state, the child is said to have acquired the capacity for self-regulation. This progressive development of self-regulatory capacities creates an organized "self-structure" that is capable of independently managing a variety of emotional and psychological stresses without collapsing into emotional or psychological disorganization and dysregulation.

The Role-Reversal Relationship

In healthy child development, the child uses the parent as an external "regulatory other" for the child's emotional and psychological state as the child increasingly develops the capacity for internalized self-regulation through the use-dependent scaffolding support provided by the "regulatory other" of the parent. The child uses the parent to meet the child's emotional and psychological needs.

However, pathological parent-child relationships arise when the parent inverts this healthy development, and instead uses the child in a role-reversal relationship as a "regulator object" to meet the parent's emotional and psychological needs. Role-reversal relationships develop when the parent's own self-structure development and capacity for self-regulation is significantly compromised. The parent needs external regulatory support for the regulation of the parent's own emotional and psychological state. Instead of providing regulatory support for the child, the parent instead uses the child as a "regulatory object" for the parent's own inadequate self-regulation of emotional and psychological states. This results in a role-reversal relationship in which the roles of the parent and child are inverted, so that it is the child who becomes the "regulatory other" for the parent.

- In healthy parent-child relationships, the child uses the parent as a "regulatory other" to regulate the child's internal emotional and psychological state.

- In a role-reversal relationship the parent uses the child as a "regulatory other" to regulate the parent's internal emotional and psychological state.

A role-reversal relationship is extremely pathological and is a characteristic of the parenting in a disorganized attachment. Essentially, the parent's own childhood development of regulatory self-structure was robbed of parental scaffolding support by the disorganized attachment to the parent, so that now, as an adult, this person has compromised self-structure development that is unable to provide adequate internalized self-regulation. A parent who is incapable of regulating his or her own emotional and psychological state cannot provide the child with regulatory support. Instead, the parent uses the child as an external "regulatory object" to regulate the parent's emotional and psychological state.

The inadequate self-structure development of the narcissistic/(borderline) parent requires the constant external regulatory support of the relationship partner (i.e., of the attachment figure) to remain in an organized and regulated state. The narcissistic-style personality seeks a continually fused psychological state with the attachment figure who provides a narcissistic reflection for the idealized grandiosity of the narcissistic personality. The regulatory function of the attachment figure for the narcissistic-style personality is to provide a continual source of "narcissistic supply" for the self-inflation of the narcissistic defense. Failure of the "regulatory other" to provide the perfectly attuned reflection of the narcissistic personality's own self-inflated grandiosity leads to a breakdown in the regulation of the narcissistic self-structure into angry and hostile attacks on the inadequate "regulatory object." These attacks on the inadequate "regulatory object" of the attachment figure represent an effort to dominate and return the relationship partner to their role as the perfectly reflective "regulatory object" for the psychological state of the narcissistic personality. The angry vitriol of the narcissistic collapse into dysregulation essentially represents a childlike emotional-behavioral tantrum that tries to compel an attuned regulatory response from the regulatory attachment figure in order to return the toddler-like narcissistic personality structure to an organized and regulated state.

The borderline-style personality also seeks a fused psychological state with the attachment figure. The borderline-style personality requires the attachment figure to provide a perfectly empathic and attuned state of monitoring the ever-shifting inner emotional and psychological needs of the borderline personality. The "regulatory object" for the borderline-style personality is responsible for maintaining the moment-to-moment state regulation of the borderline personality. The role of the attachment figure is to be totally dedicated to the infantile borderline personality structure, constantly monitoring and regulating the borderline personality's emotional and psychological state to ensure that the borderline personality will not collapse into painful psychological disorganization. This is essentially the role of the parent with an infant, to be completely dedicated to monitoring and regulating the inner state of the infant.

Any empathic failure by the external "regulatory object" of the attachment figure will result in the complete collapse of the borderline personality's state regulation into chaotic displays of angry assaults directed toward the inadequate "regulatory other." For the borderline-style personality, these angry assaults are mixed with tearful displays of self-devaluation. The infantile level of the borderline-style personality organization is essentially displaying anxious-ambivalent attachment patterns of angry protest and presentations of needy vulnerability, seeking the attuned regulating response of the "parental" attachment figure.

The degree of complete dedication and perfectly attuned regulatory support demanded by the borderline-style personality represents an infantile need for the complete state regulation of the borderline personality structure. The borderline-style personality requires a continual and perfectly attuned external "regulatory other" in order to prevent the collapse of the infantile self-structure of the borderline personality into the chaotic experience of complete emotional and psychological disorganization. The infantile level of self-structure development and self-regulation expressed by the borderline personality is consistent with a disorganized attachment in early childhood that significantly undermined the formation of stable self-structure organization capable of internalized self-regulation.

In the marital relationship, the narcissistic/(borderline) personality expects the primary attachment figure of the other spouse to perform this "parental" role as the external "regulatory object" for the stabilization of the inadequately developed narcissistic/(borderline) personality self-structure. Following the divorce and the loss of the spouse as a "regulatory object," the narcissistic/(borderline) parent turns to the child as the primary attachment figure to perform this role as the externalized "regulatory object" for maintaining the fragile emotional and psychological state of the narcissistic/(borderline) parent. The narcissistic/(borderline) parent then forms a role-reversal relationship with the child in which the child is used by the parent as a "regulatory object" to provide the parent with the attuned and empathic responses needed to maintain the state-regulation of the narcissistic/(borderline) parent.

The formation of a pathological role-reversal relationship with the child essentially reflects the narcissistic/(borderline) parent's transferring the psychological damage from his or her own childhood development into the current parent-child relationship. The narcissistic/(borderline) parent's damaged self-structure is feeding off of the child's healthy development in order to support the damaged self-structure and inadequate self-regulation of the narcissistic/(borderline) parent. In feeding off of the child's healthy development through a role-reversal relationship, in which the child is being used to meet the emotional and psychological needs of the parent, the narcissistic/(borderline) parent is robbing the child of healthy development. In healthy child development, the child would be using the parent as a "regulatory other" for the child's emotional and psychological experience. Instead, in a role-reversal relationship, the narcissistic/(borderline) parent is using the child to regulate the parent's emotional and psychological state.

Despite the severe pathology of the role-reversal relationship, the outward superficial appearance will be one of a highly bonded parent-child relationship. But this outward appearance is highly misleading. The appearance of a bonded parent-child relationship is a reflection of an extremely pathological "psychological feeding" of the narcissistic/(borderline) parent's damaged and inadequate self-structure off of the child's own healthy self-structure development. The metaphorical image to conjure is of the empty life-force of a vampire feeding off of the still vital life-force of its victim in order to fill the inherent vacancy of essential life within the vampire. The victim of this feeding surrenders psychologically to the feeding process, to the role as the "regulatory object" to meet the parent's needs, and the child enters a state of shared psychological fusion with the feeding parent.

A role-reversal is extremely pathological, yet superficially the psychological surrender of the child to the psychopathology of the narcissistic/(borderline) parent appears to be one of bonding. Instead, the pathology of the role-reversal relationship represents the child's surrender of self-authenticity to the role of being the "regulatory object" for the parent. The child's surrender and psychological submission to the parent's psychopathology is in no way a sign of a healthy parent-child relationship. The role-reversal relationship is an extremely unhealthy and highly pathological parent-child bond.

The role-reversal relationship is referred to as a psychological "boundary violation." The parent in the role-reversal relationship is violating the psychological integrity of the child in order to use the child to meet the parent's emotional and psychological needs. Boundary violations are extremely pathological and damaging to the child's development. In the Journal of Emotional Abuse, Kerig (2005) describes the damaging effects of boundary violations on the emotional and psychological development of children,

> "Examination of the theoretical and empirical literatures suggests that there are four distinguishable dimensions to the phenomenon of boundary dissolution: role reversal, intrusiveness, enmeshment, and spousification" (p. 8).

> "The breakdown of appropriate generational boundaries between parents and children significantly increases the risk for emotional abuse... In the throes of their own insecurity, troubled parents may rely on the child to meet the parent's emotional needs, turning to the child to provide the parent with support, nurturance, or comforting. Ultimately, preoccupation with the parents' needs threatens to interfere with the child's ability to develop autonomy, initiative, self-reliance, and a secure internal working model of the self and others" (p. 6).

> "When parent-child boundaries are violated, the implications for developmental psychopathology are significant. Poor boundaries interfere with the child's capacity to progress through development which, as Anna Freud suggested, is the defining feature of childhood psychopathology" (p. 7).

> "There is evidence for the intergenerational transmission of boundary dissolution within the family. Adults who experienced boundary dissolution in their relationships with their own parents are more likely to violate boundaries with their children" (p. 22).

Creating the Role-Reversal Relationship

Inducing the relationship partner, either the spouse or the child, into becoming the external "regulatory object" for the unstable emotional and psychological functioning of the narcissistic/(borderline) parent is relatively easy to accomplish. A classic display of inducing the relationship partner into becoming a "regulatory object" is in William Shakespeare's play, the Taming of the Shrew. In this play, the protagonist, Petruchio, continually presents his betrothed, Kate, with chaotic and dysregulated behavior until she finally surrenders to his will. In the climactic scene of Kate's psychological surrender to Petruchio, Kate distorts reality by calling the sun the moon and an old man a maid in an effort to keep Petruchio in an organized and regulated state.

In a relationship with a psychologically dangerous narcissistic/(borderline) personality, when the spouse or child fails to respond in ways that provide the narcissistic/(borderline) personality with adequate regulatory support, then the regulation of the narcissistic/(borderline) personality collapses into chaotic onslaughts of anger and emotional dysregulation. The hostile unpredictable chaos of these collapses into dysregulation by the narcissistic/(borderline) personality are extremely stressful and aversive experiences for the relationship partner. The responses of the relationship partner are quickly shaped by the onslaughts of hostile-aggressive dysregulation into seeking to respond in ways that keep the narcissistic/(borderline) personality in a calm, organized, and regulated state.

When the relationship partner carefully monitors the inner state and psychological needs of the narcissistic/(borderline) parent and is then successful in responding in ways that stabilize the functioning of the narcissistic/(borderline) personality, the relationship partner escapes the painful consequences of the psychological collapse of the narcissistic/(borderline) parent into emotional and psychological dysregulation. The relationship partner, either the spouse or the child, of a narcissistic/(borderline) personality is easily induced into the assuming the role as the external "regulatory other" for the narcissistic/(borderline) personality through the painful consequences experienced for failing to regulate the narcissistic/(borderline) spouse or parent, and by the corresponding rewarding consequences of avoiding a collapse of the narcissistic/(borderline) personality into dysregulation when the relationship partner is successful in keeping the narcissistic/(borderline) personality in an organized and regulated state.

Cognitive Dysregulation

The profound dysregulation of the narcissistic/(borderline) personality is across all levels of psychological functioning, including the dysregulation of the organized cognitive functioning necessary for an accurate perception of reality. The self-structure of the narcissistic-borderline personality is at a nearly infantile level of development. When the fragile regulation of the narcissistic/(borderline) personality organization is lost, the collapse into psychological disorganization is nearly complete, including the cognitive structures needed to interpret reality.

When the psychological structure of the narcissistic/(borderline) personality collapses into chaotic disorganization, the thought processes of the narcissistic/(borderline) personality become equally disorganized and dysregulated. If the narcissistic/(borderline) personality needs to distort truth or reality in an effort to regain an organized and regulated state, then truth and reality are readily sacrificed. The limiting constraints imposed on the narcissistic/(borderline) personality by truth and reality become secondary considerations as the self-structure organization of the narcissistic/(borderline) personality collapses into chaotic disorganization. In the chaotically swirling emotional experience of the narcissistic/(borderline) personality's collapse into disorganization, truth and reality become fluid and subjectively defined constructs, capable of being bent, distorted, and fabricated to meet the emotional and psychological needs of the moment. For the narcissistic/(borderline) personality, maintaining or regaining an organized and regulated psychological state takes precedence over all other considerations, including the restrictions imposed by truth and reality. If truth and reality need to be altered or distorted in order for the narcissistic/(borderline) personality to maintain or regain an organized and regulated state, then truth and reality become redefined to meet the needs of the narcissistic/(borderline) personality.

The label "borderline" was placed on this personality style because it was believed that the underlying organization of these personalities was on the "borderline" between neurotic and psychotic. Similarly, Theodore

Millon, one of the leading authorities on personality disorders, describes the collapse of the narcissistic personality into psychotic delusions under stress,

> "Under conditions of unrelieved adversity and failure, narcissists may decompensate into paranoid disorders. Owing to their excessive use of fantasy mechanisms, they are disposed to misinterpret events and to construct delusional beliefs. Unwilling to accept constraints on their independence and unable to accept the viewpoints of others, narcissists may isolate themselves from the corrective effects of shared thinking. Alone, they may ruminate and weave their beliefs into a network of fanciful and totally invalid suspicions. Among narcissists, delusions often take form after a serious challenge or setback has upset their image of superiority and omnipotence. They tend to exhibit compensatory grandiosity and jealousy delusions in which they reconstruct reality to match the image they are unable or unwilling to give up."
>
> "Delusional systems may also develop as a result of having felt betrayed and humiliated. Here we may see the rapid unfolding of persecutory delusions and an arrogant grandiosity characterized by verbal attacks and bombast. Rarely physically abusive, anger among narcissists usually takes the form of oral vituperation and argumentativeness. This may be seen in a flow of irrational and caustic comments in which others are upbraided and denounced as stupid and beneath contempt. These onslaughts usually have little objective justification, are often colored by delusions, and may be directed in a wild, hit-or-miss fashion in which the narcissist lashes out at those who have failed to acknowledge the exalted status in which he or she demands to be seen" (Millon, 2011, pp. 407-408).

The self-structure organization of the narcissistic/(borderline) personality is at the infantile level. When the structure for the infantile self-organization of the narcissistic/(borderline) personality collapses into disorganization and dysregulation, the collapse is total. Even the structures inherent to cognitive processes that recognize and define reality will collapse into dysregulation, making the basic core of cognitive structures pliable to the emotional and psychological needs of the narcissistic/(borderline) personality. If the narcissistic/(borderline) personality needs to alter truth and reality to regain an emotionally and psychologically regulated state, then the accurate perception of truth and reality will be sacrificed to meet the emotional and psychological needs of the narcissistic/(borderline) personality. For the narcissistic/(borderline) personality, "Truth and reality are what I assert them to be." If the narcissistic/(borderline) personality needs the sky to be red in order to regulate their emotional and psychological state, then they simply assert that the sky is red. If, ten minutes later, they now need the sky to be yellow in order to regulate their emotional and psychological state, then they simply assert that the sky is yellow, with no apparent awareness of either their inherent self-contradiction or the actual reality that the sky is blue. For the narcissistic/(borderline) personality, "Truth and reality are what I assert them to be."

In this world of chaotic emotional dysregulation and ever-shifting truth and reality, the relationship partner of the narcissistic/(borderline) personality cannot even rely on objectively verifiable truth and reality as a defense against the onslaughts of emotional dysregulation from narcissistic/(borderline) personality. In the face of the ever-changing subjectively defined truth and reality asserted by the narcissistic/(borderline) parent, even grown adults can begin to question the accuracy of their own perceptions and interpretations of events. For the developing self-experience of the child who is in a relationship with the pathology of the narcissistic/(borderline) parent, maintaining a grasp on self-authenticity and objective reality is even more challenging.

When the child is subjected to onslaughts of emotional dysregulation from the narcissistic/(borderline) parent, the child is unable to rely on truth or reality as a defense. Truth and reality are defined by the needs of the narcissistic/(borderline) parent at the moment, and the definition of truth and reality may change later. If the relationship partner of the narcissistic/(borderline) parent tries to offer a defense of truth and accuracy, the narcissistic/(borderline) personality will launch into a counter accusation of "Don't try to put words in my mouth" or may simply offer a flat denial of reality, "That's not true, I never said that." If cornered by objective truth and reality, the narcissistic/(borderline) personality will then launch into a counterattack of rapid accusations, often involving wild assertions of subjective reality and distorted characterizations of truth, which creates a chaotic communication context in which linear clarity is entirely lost.

The infantile structure of the narcissistic/(borderline) personality leads to very primitive attempts at self-regulation. The narcissistic/(borderline) personality can only regulate their psychological disorganization by altering reality to meet their emotional and psychological needs. For the infantile self-structure of the narcissistic/(borderline) personality, containing their psychological disorganization within the restrictions imposed by truth, accuracy, and reality is impossible. In order for the fragile narcissistic/(borderline) self-structure to maintain its organized regulation, truth, accuracy, and reality need to be sacrificed. Achieving freedom from the external restrictions imposed by truth and reality is best accomplished in an atmosphere of communication and relationship chaos. Clarity and linear rational reasoning restrict the freedom of the narcissistic/(borderline) to distort reality to the degree necessary to maintain their psychological organization. In chaotic communication and the absence of clarity, the narcissistic/(borderline) personality can more easily create the "truth" and "reality" as they need it to be.

Efforts to contain the disorganized cognitive processes of the narcissistic/(borderline) parent within the confines of objective truth, reality, and linear rationality will be experienced by the narcissistic/(borderline) personality as being efforts at preventing the regulation of psychological collapse, and as "forcing" the narcissistic/(borderline) parent to experience the painful collapse into disorganization. As a result, efforts to contain the narcissistic/(borderline) parent within the confines of objective truth and reality will often lead to accusations that the other person is being "abusive" in trying to constrain the primitive regulation efforts of the borderline-style personality.

"Abusive" Others

The borderline-style personality experiences the regulatory failures by the relationship partner as being responsible for the collapse of the borderline personality structure into painful disorganization. The painful collapse of psychological self-structure created by the regulatory failure of the relationship partner leads the borderline-style parent to characterize the other person's treatment as being "abusive," because these empathic failures by the attachment figure lead to and create the collapse of the borderline personality structure into disorganization. In the mind of the borderline-style parent, the role of the attachment figure is to be the perfectly attuned and completely available "regulatory other," much in the same way that an infant needs the parent to provide external regulatory support to the infant's ongoing state regulation. When the relationship partner fails to provide this complete and total regulatory support to the infantile self-structure of the borderline personality, then the subsequent collapse of the borderline personality structure into disorganization is blamed on the failure of the "regulatory other" to perform the function of being the perfectly attuned "regulatory other" needed by the inadequately formed and infantile borderline personality self-structure.

The primitive venting of hostility and chaotic emotionality by the borderline-style personality is an expression of the borderline personality's painful collapse into disorganization, and is neuro-biologically similar to how an infant will collapse into a tantrum expressing primitive "catastrophic emotions" in response to dysregulation. If the relationship partner then tries to limit and constrain the venting of emotional dysregulation by the borderline-style personality, this too will be perceived by the borderline-style personality as being "emotionally abusive" because these efforts to constrain the emotional venting of the borderline personality in response to dysregulation limits the capacity of the borderline-style parent to regain an organized and re-regulated state through the unrestrained venting of emotions.

For the borderline personality, if truth and reality need to be sacrificed in order to regain an emotionally and psychologically re-regulated and organized state, then truth and reality will be distorted in whatever fashion is necessary to meet the regulatory needs of the borderline personality. Within the confines of their psychological disorganization, truth, accuracy, and reality become secondary considerations to relieving the pain of emotional and psychological disorganization. The distortion of truth and reality, however, can be extremely frustrating for the relationship partner of the borderline-style personality. The relationship partner is being blamed in tirades of vitriol as being responsible for the dysregulation of the borderline personality structure based on distorted assertions of truth and false characterizations of reality. Yet when the relationship partner then tries to constrain the accusations of the borderline personality within the limits of truth, accuracy, and reality, this effort is perceived as trying to "force" the borderline personality to remain in a psychologically painful disorganized and dysregulated state, leading the borderline-style personality to accuse the relationship partner of being emotionally "abusive" on two counts. First, for having caused the collapse into dysregulation by failing to be the perfectly attuned "regulatory other," and second, for then trying to keep the borderline-style parent in a painful state of dysregulation by attempting to constrain the borderline parent into limitations based on truth and accuracy.

Any efforts by the relationship partner to impose constraints on the borderline personality's distortions to truth and reality are perceived by the borderline personality as being "abusive" because these efforts hinder the emotional and psychological coping required by the borderline personality to regain an organized and re-regulated state. Efforts to limit the borderline personality to objective truth, accuracy, and reality are experienced by the borderline personality as trying to keep the borderline personality in a disorganized state of emotional pain, leading to accusations that the other person is being "abusive."

The borderline-style personality perceives the other person to be responsible for the painful collapse of the borderline personality into disorganization as well as trying to keep the borderline personality in this state of disorganization by "forcing" the borderline personality to accept an imposed truth and reality. This perception of the borderline-style personality leads to accusations that the other person is being "abusive." Allegations that other people are being "abusive" become a common description used by the borderline-style personality to characterize the actions of other people. So characteristic is the use of the terms "abuse" and "abusive" by the borderline-style personality to describe other people, that whenever any person uses the terms "abuse" and "abusive" in describing another person, two differential diagnoses should immediately be considered:

1) Authentic abuse by the other person,

2) A borderline personality structure of the person who is using the term "abusive."

Normal-range people use words like "mean," "rude," "cruel," "insensitive," and "inconsiderate," but rarely the term "abusive," except in cases of authentic abuse. Normal-range people understand that the word "abusive" represents an extreme and very serious allegation and so are appropriately circumspect in using this term, limiting its use only to authentic cases of abuse and using less hyperbolically exaggerated terminology for less severe forms of interpersonal insensitivity.

Borderline personalities, on the other hand, lack internal regulatory controls and they experience intensely painful emotions during their psychological collapse. As a result, borderline-style personalities will regularly use the specific words "abuse" and "abusive" to describe their relationships with other people because that is an authentic characterization of the internal experience of the borderline-style personality. The other person is not being abusive, but the subjective internal experience of the borderline-style personality is one of extremely painful psychological fragmentation and disorganization. In the mind of the borderline-style personality, the other person is supposed to be the perfectly attuned and responsive "regulatory other" for the borderline personality structure. The collapse of the borderline personality's capacity to maintain a regulated state is therefore attributed to the failure of the other person to be the perfectly attuned "regulatory object" for the emotional and psychological state of the borderline style personality structure. In the mind of the borderline-personality, the other person is creating the emotional and psychological pain experienced by the borderline-style personality, leading to the allegation that the other person is being "abusive."

Allegations of abuse should never be summarily discounted under any circumstances, and should always receive a full and complete assessment. Child and spousal protection are of paramount concern, and the differential diagnosis of authentic abuse is always present whenever someone makes the allegation of abuse. In addition, the use of the specific terms "abuse" and "abusive" are so characteristic of a borderline-style personality organization that whenever a person uses the descriptive terms "abuse" and "abusive" to describe the actions of other people, an additional differential diagnosis of borderline personality processes should also be considered.

The Child as the "Regulatory Other"

Attachment-based "parental alienation" involves the role-reversal use of the child by a narcissistic/(borderline) parent as a "regulatory other" to meet the emotional and psychological needs of the parent.

Creating this role-reversal relationship is relatively easy to accomplish. In the world of shifting and subjectively defined truth and reality surrounding the narcissistic/(borderline) personality, the child is unable to rely on any objectively established truth or reality to create meaning, and the child is unable to establish a ground in personal self-experience and self-authenticity by which the child can define truth and reality. In this world of shifting and subjectively defined reality, when the child comes under psychological assault from the narcissistic/(borderline) parent the child is unable to rely on a defense of truth or reality since these constructs are not objectively defined but are dependent on the momentary needs of the narcissistic/(borderline) parent. Since the child cannot rely on objective truth or reality as a defense, the child becomes entirely exposed to the variable moods and shifting needs of the narcissistic/(borderline) parent.

Prior to the divorce, the child at least had the availability of the normal-range targeted parent who could protect the child from the pathology of the narcissistic/(borderline) parent. While the family was still together, the moderating influence and psychological protection available from the normal-range parent could limit the child's exposure to the pathology of the narcissistic/(borderline) parent. In addition, prior to the divorce the pathology of the narcissistic/(borderline) parent was primarily directed toward the attachment figure of the other spouse, not directly toward the child, which further limited the child's direct exposure to the pathology of the narcissistic/(borderline) parent.

Once the parents divorce, however, custody of the child is shared separately between the parents. The normal-range targeted parent is no longer available when the child is with the pathology of the narcissistic/(borderline) parent. As a result of the divorce, the child becomes isolated and more fully exposed to the pathology of the narcissistic/(borderline) parent. Gone is the protective and modulating influence of the targeted parent when the child is with the narcissistic/(borderline) parent. The child is psychologically alone and exposed, and the pathology of the narcissistic/(borderline) parent becomes more fully directed toward establishing the role-reversal relationship with the attachment figure of the child, rather than the prior focus on the attachment figure of the other spouse.

The narcissistic/(borderline) parent has lost the "regulatory object" of the other spouse, and the personality structure of the narcissistic/(borderline) parent is threatened with collapse by the public exposure of primal self-inadequacy and abandonment surrounding the rejection inherent to the divorce. In order to re-regulate the impending psychological collapse of the narcissistic/(borderline) personality structure into primal self-inadequacy and fears of abandonment, the narcissistic/(borderline) parent needs to reestablish the narcissistic defense by psychologically expelling the primal self-inadequacy and abandonment fears by projecting them onto the other spouse. However, the narcissistic/(borderline) parent cannot directly accomplish this projective displacement of inadequacy and abandonment fears onto the other spouse since the martial relationship has dissolved through the divorce. So the child is enlisted in a role-reversal relationship to regulate the emotional and psychological state of the narcissistic/(borderline) parent through the formation of a cross-generational coalition against the other parent.

After the divorce, the only avenue available to the narcissistic/(borderline) parent to psychologically expel the primal self-inadequacy and abandonment fears onto the other spouse is through their continuing role relationships as parents to the child. By triangulating the child into the "spousal" conflict through a cross-generational coalition against the other parent, the narcissistic/(borderline) parent uses the child as a "regulatory object" to expel the parent's inadequacy and abandonment fears onto the targeted parent by defining the targeted parent as being an inadequate parent who is being rejected and abandoned by the child. The child's (induced) rejection of the targeted parent publicly defines the targeted parent as the inadequate and abandoned parent (person), and simultaneously defines the narcissistic/(borderline) parent as the idealized "perfect" parent, thereby restoring the narcissistic defense.

The divorce represents a public exposure of the inadequacy and abandonment of the narcissistic/(borderline) spouse. In the child's public display of rejection for the targeted parent, the narcissistic/(borderline) parent is then allowed to make an equally public display of the targeted parent's inadequacy and abandonment by the child, and of the narcissistic/(borderline) parent's idealized perfection. This public display of the targeted parent's inadequacy and rejection, and of the narcissistic/(borderline) parent's perfection as a parent, counteracts the prior public exposure of the inadequacy and rejection of the narcissistic/(borderline) parent as a spouse that was created by the divorce.

The emotional and psychological instability of the narcissistic/(borderline) parent, in which truth and reality are subjectively defined constructs, elicits the child's hyper-vigilant monitoring of the emotional and psychological state of the narcissistic/(borderline) parent. By closely monitoring the emotional and psychological state of the narcissistic/(borderline) parent, the child is able to provide responses that maintain the parent's regulated state. In order to keep the narcissistic/(borderline) parent in a regulated emotional and psychological state, the child is required to become a narcissistic reflection of the parent's inner state and needs. As long as the child remains in a perfectly attuned state of psychological fusion with the narcissistic/(borderline) parent, the parent remains in an organized and regulated emotional and psychological state.

This means that the child must surrender self-authenticity to the narcissistic/(borderline) parent in order to serve as the "regulatory other" for the emotional and psychological state of the narcissistic/(borderline) parent. Only one person is present in a relationship with a narcissistic/(borderline) personality, and the authentic child is lost to becoming a narcissistic reflection for the needs of the narcissistic/(borderline) parent. Even the child's truth and authentic reality are surrendered to the narcissistic/(borderline) parent. Since truth and reality are shifting constructs that are solely defined by the changing needs of the narcissistic/(borderline) parent, the child must also surrender the definition of truth and reality to the narcissistic/(borderline) parent as well. In order to keep the narcissistic/(borderline) parent in an organized and regulated state, the child can no longer independently define truth and reality but must instead socially reference the attitudes and beliefs of the narcissistic/(borderline) parent for the definition of truth and reality. Whether the sky is red, or green, or yellow depends on how it is defined by the narcissistic/(borderline) parent. The child can no longer simply look up to the sky and independently define the sky as blue. The child's independent self-authenticity is surrendered to the narcissistic/(borderline) parent in the child's role-reversal as the "regulatory object" for the parent.

Within this relationship context, the child becomes the perfectly attuned "regulatory other" for the maintenance of the emotional and psychological state of the narcissistic/(borderline) parent. Once the child becomes the "regulatory object" for the emotional and psychological state of the parent, and has surrendered self-authentic definitions of truth and reality to the definition of realty provided by the narcissistic/(borderline) parent, all the narcissistic/(borderline) parent needs to do to create the child's rejection of the targeted parent is to provide the child with signals as to what responses from the child are needed to keep the narcissistic/(borderline) parent in an emotionally and psychologically regulated state.

Initially, all that's required is for the child to accept the role as being the "victimized child" relative to the child's relationship with the other parent. The narcissistic/(borderline) parent begins to co-create with the child a narrative of the child's victimization by the supposedly "abusive" parenting practices of the targeted parent. Criticisms of the targeted parent are elicited from the child by the motivated and directive questioning of the narcissistic/(borderline) parent. Over time, this initial "victimized child" role is further shaped by the distorted parental responses of the narcissistic/(borderline) parent into the child's more overt rejection of the targeted parent, which serves to projectively displace onto the targeted parent the self-inadequacy and abandonment fears of the narcissistic/(borderline) parent.

In the shared custody of the child following the divorce, the child becomes psychologically exposed to the pathology of the narcissistic/(borderline) parent. The psychological safety of the child is dependent on the child meeting the emotional and psychological needs of the narcissistic/(borderline) parent. The child's psychological safety with the narcissistic/(borderline) parent requires that the child provide the responses that are needed to keep the narcissistic/(borderline) parent in a regulated emotional and psychological state. In order to keep the narcissistic/(borderline) parent in a regulated state, the child must become a reflection of the narcissistic/(borderline) parent's attitudes and beliefs, particularly surrounding the targeted parent.

The stability of the child's attachment bond to the narcissistic/(borderline) parent is contingent upon the child's becoming the perfectly empathic and reflective "regulatory other" for the narcissistic/(borderline) parent. For the child, this means that the parental love of the narcissistic/(borderline) parent is contingent upon the child meeting the needs of the narcissistic/(borderline) parent. This contingent parental love creates an insecure-preoccupied attachment to the narcissistic/(borderline) parent in which the child must continually monitor and meet the emotional and psychological needs of the narcissistic/(borderline) parent. When the child surrenders independent self-autonomy to the narcissistic/(borderline) parent to become a perfectly attuned reflective-other for the narcissistic/(borderline) parent, the child can achieve relief from the anxiety of being in relationship with an emotionally and psychologically unstable parent by stabilizing the security of the attachment bond to the narcissistic/(borderline) parent.

Kerig (2005) describes the process of the parent's psychological control of the child's inner experience and the child's surrender to the needs of the parent:

> "Rather than telling the child directly what to do or think, as does the behaviorally controlling parent, the psychologically controlling parent uses indirect hints and responds with guilt induction or withdrawal of love if the child refuses to comply. In short, an intrusive parent strives to manipulate the child's thoughts and feelings in such a way that the child's psyche will conform to the parent's wishes" (p. 12)

> "In order to carve out an island of safety and responsivity in an unpredictable, harsh, and depriving parent-child relationship, children of highly maladaptive parents may become precocious caretakers who are adept at reading the cues and meeting the needs of those around them. The ensuing preoccupied attachment with the parent interferes with the child's development of important ego functions, such as self-organization, affect regulation, and emotional object constancy. (p. 14).

Being continually aware of the emotional state and psychological needs of the parent alleviates the child's anxiety regarding the potentially dangerous emotional unpredictability of the narcissistic/(borderline) parent. If the parent begins to dysregulate into a hostile-threatening state, the child's awareness of this impending parental dysregulation allows the child to provide attuned responses that prevent the parent's collapse into emotional and psychological dysregulation. If the collapse cannot be prevented, then the child's monitoring of the parent's state may allow the child to take protective steps to avoid the parent prior to the regulatory collapse, and perhaps to escape the onslaught of parent's impending collapse into emotional dysregulation.

Not being aware of the emotional and psychological state of the narcissistic/(borderline) parent would be a source of tremendous stress and anxiety for the child. Being unaware of the psychological state of the narcissistic/(borderline) parent would expose the child to unpredictable rages and tirades from the parent. The child might inadvertently say or do something that provokes the collapse of the narcissistic/(borderline) parent, and the tirades of the narcissistic/(borderline) parent would be unanticipated and would catch the child by surprise. Unless the child remains constantly aware of the emotional and psychological state of the narcissistic/(borderline) parent the child is unable to take the preventative steps necessary to keep the parent in a regulated state or the protective steps necessary to avoid the narcissistic/(borderline) parent who is collapsing into dysregulation. Being unaware of the emotional and psychological state of the narcissistic/(borderline) parent is anxiety provoking for the child, yet maintaining a constant vigilance regarding the state of the parent is stressful.

The child can be released from the tremendous anxiety surrounding the need to continually monitor the state of the narcissistic/(borderline) parent by surrendering self-authenticity to the narcissistic/(borderline) parent. Surrendering self-authenticity to the needs of the parent frees the child from the stress and anxiety of continually having to monitor the parent's state. Once the child surrenders self-authenticity, then the child simply follows the lead of the narcissistic/(borderline) parent to become whatever the parent needs. By remaining in a constantly fused state of psychological reflection for attitudes and beliefs of the narcissistic/(borderline) parent, the child no longer needs to worry about causing a breach to the relationship because the child's self-authenticity and self-autonomy have been surrendered to the narcissistic/(borderline) parent. The child simply becomes a reflection of whatever the parent needs.

The child's surrender of self-authenticity to the needs of the narcissistic/(borderline) parent coincides with the infantile psychological needs of this parent to have a perfectly attuned "regulatory other" who is entirely dedicated to maintaining the emotional and psychological regulation of the narcissistic/(borderline) personality structure. The underlying disorganized attachment of the narcissistic/(borderline) personality means that the narcissistic/(borderline) personality cannot organize a coherent approach to restoring breaches to the relationship with the attachment figure when they occur, so the "regulatory other" must respond in ways that maintain a continually fused psychological state with the narcissistic/(borderline) parent.

Narcissistic/(Borderline) Parent: "The sky is red"

Child: "No its not, the sky is blue."

N/(B) Parent: "How dare you say that! Don't ever say the sky is blue again, do you hear me! It's not blue, it's red. I don't ever want to hear you call the sky blue again. The sky is red."

<later> **N/(B) Parent:** "The sky is yellow"

Child: "I thought you said the sky was red?"

N/(B) Parent: "I never said the sky was red! Don't put words in my mouth! I never said that! The sky is yellow, not red."

<later> **N/(B) Parent:** "What color is the sky?"

What should the child say? Saying the sky is blue clearly is the wrong response and will provoke the collapse of the narcissistic/(borderline) parent. Maybe the sky is yellow. But it might be red. What's the child to do?

Child: "What color do you think it is?"

N/(B) Parent: "I think it's green."

Child: "Yeah, me too. It looks green to me too."

The child learns to read the cues of the parent in order to remain in a continually fused reflective state with the parent. As long as the child surrenders self-authenticity to the parent, then the child is relieved of the stress surrounding triggering a potential collapse of the narcissistic/(borderline) parent. If the inner reality of the narcissistic/(borderline) parent changes, the child simply flows with the change.

N/(B) Parent: "Or maybe the sky is red."

Child: "Yeah, it kind of looks red."

N/(B) Parent: "No, I think the sky is green. Don't you think the sky is green?"

Child: "Yeah, it looks green to me too."

The child avoids the stress and anxiety of continually monitoring the parent by simply surrendering self-authenticity to the parent.

The Expulsion Demand

The surrender of self-authenticity to the narcissistic/(borderline) parent is the source of an odd but often characteristic feature of attachment-based "parental alienation" in which the child demands that the targeted parent no longer attend the child's events, such as music recitals, sporting events, or school ceremonies. The child reports that when the targeted parent attends these events it makes the child stressed.

In actuality, it's not the targeted parent that is making the child anxious and stressed, it is having to monitor the state of the narcissistic/(borderline) parent. When the targeted parent attends the child's events, the narcissistic/(borderline) parent becomes upset. The child's role as the "regulatory object" for the narcissistic/(borderline) parent is to keep this parent in an organized and regulated state by reflecting the state of the parent.

The potential collapse of the narcissistic/(borderline) parent into dysregulation draws the focus of the "regulatory other" child, distracting the child from the activity of the music recital, sporting event, or school activity. The child is no longer able to relax and simply enjoy the event because the child becomes preoccupied with regulating the distraught narcissistic/(borderline) parent. The child is stressed, not by the targeted parent's presence, but by the effect the targeted parent's presence has on the narcissistic/(borderline) parent, whose job it is for the child to keep in an organized and regulated state.

The child has learned that to keep the narcissistic/(borderline) parent in a regulated state, the child must surrender to becoming a reflective mirror for the state of the parent. The child has learned to read the cues emitted by the parent, whether the sky is red, or green, or yellow, and to then reflect this state back to the parent. The narcissistic/(borderline) parent dislikes the presence of the targeted parent at the child's events, so the child adopts the same reflective state of not wanting the targeted parent to attend events.

This demand by the child that the targeted parent stop coming to the child's events is based in the child's authentic experience of increased anxiety and stress created by the presence of the targeted parent. But it is not the targeted parent per se who is creating this increased anxiety and stress, it is the reaction of the narcissistic/(borderline) parent that that child must then regulate that is anxiety provoking and stressful for the child.

But what about the child's authentic joy and happiness at having a parent attend the child's event? The child cannot allow the self-experience of authentic happiness at the targeted parent attending the child's event. Self-authentic experience is dangerous because it might inadvertently cause a breach in the fused relationship with the narcissistic/(borderline) parent. The child has surrendered self-authenticity to be free of the anxiety and stress of continually monitoring the state of the narcissistic/(borderline) parent. The child can no longer simply look at the sky and say it's blue.

One of the leading figures in borderline personality processes, Marsha Linehan, refers to the nullification of self-authenticity as the "invalidating environment," which she describes as,

> "A defining characteristic of the invalidating environment is the tendency of the family to respond erratically or inappropriately to private experience and, in particular, to be insensitive (i.e., nonresponsive) to private experience... Invalidating environments contribute to emotional dysregulation by: 1) failing to teach the child to label and modulate arousal, 2) failing to teach the child to tolerate stress, 3) failing to teach the child to trust his or her own emotional responses as valid interpretations of events, and 4) actively teaching the child to invalidate his or her own experiences by making it necessary for the child to scan the environment for

> cues about how to act and feel." (Linehan & Koerner, 1993, p. 111-112)

Fruzetti, Shenk, and Hoffman (2005) describe the loss of self-authenticity and psychological fusion that occurs as a result of the invalidating environment,

> "In extremely invalidating environments, parents or caregivers do not teach children to discriminate effectively between what they feel and what the caregivers feel, what the child wants and what the caregiver wants (or wants the child to want), what the child thinks and what the caregiver thinks." (p. 1021)

For the more borderline-style parent, this psychological fusion with the child represents an idealized interpretation of "love," in which the attachment figure meets an infantile desire for a perfectly attuned and empathic "regulatory other." For the narcissistic-style parent, this fused psychological state is achieved when the relationship partner provides the perfect narcissistic reflection for the self-grandiosity of the narcissistic personality. This continually fused psychological state is not healthy. In an authentically healthy loving relationship, the two relationship partners are separate autonomous individuals who are bonded in a shared state of mutual affection that nevertheless has clearly established psychological boundaries which acknowledge and respect the psychological integrity and psychological separateness of the other person. The perfect and idealized "love" sought by the borderline-style personality and the perfectly reflecting narcissistic object sought by the narcissistic personality represent extremely pathological relationship structures involving unhealthy boundary violations of the psychological integrity of the child as a separate and autonomous person.

Granting Affectionate and Material Indulgences

In return for the child's psychological surrender to the borderline-style parent, the child is provided with hyper-affectional displays from the borderline-style parent of idealized and supposedly perfect "love." The shared psychological state of the child's perfect reflection of the emotional and psychological needs of the parent is offered as evidence of their supposedly "perfect love" for each other. However, these hyper-affectional displays between the parent and the child actually represent the borderline parent's need for continual reassurances from the child that the borderline parent will not be abandoned by the child. This hyper-affectional bonding between the child and the borderline-style parent is not healthy and will severely undermine the child's development of separate psychological autonomy. In normal-range and healthy parent-child relationships, affectional displays between the parent and child are less overt and intense, although their shared love is deep and abiding.

For the more narcissistic style parent, the psychological fusion with the child represents the child's psychological surrender to being a perfectly reflective narcissistic object for the parent. The child's role is to provide the parent with continual "narcissistic supply" of adoration and narcissistic reflection for the parent in order to maintain the parent's narcissistic defense. The separate authenticity of the child must be surrendered so that the child can serve as the perfectly reflecting mirror for the narcissistic parent. In return for the child's psychological surrender to the narcissistic parent, the child is granted narcissistic indulgences of adult-like privileges and material gifts. The granting of these narcissistic indulgences actually represents a form of parental disengagement and neglect. In granting the child narcissistic indulgences of material items and adult-like privileges, the narcissistic parent is avoiding the stress of parenting obligations by simply gratifying the child's superficial wishes.

Authentic and False Empathy

In a healthy parent-child relationship in which the parent acts as the "regulatory other" for the child, *the parent* must be empathically attuned to the child's inner emotional and psychological state in order to respond in ways that *organize and regulate the child's state*. A prominent researcher in the neuro-development of the brain during childhood, Allan Shore, describes the necessary parental attunement to the child' inner needs in a supportive parent-child relationship,

> "The mother must monitor the infant's state as well as her own and then resonate not with the child's overt behavior but with certain qualities of its internal state, such as contour, intensity, and temporal features" (Shore, 1997, p. 600).

The parent in a developmentally healthy parent-child relationship recognizes the psychological separateness of the child. This allows the parent to temporarily put aside the parent's own psychological state and adopt the separate and alternate psychological frame of reference of the child. Fonagy (2011) refers to this as the parent's capacity for "mentalization" of the child's separate psychological experience, in which the parent recognizes and co-creates the child's inner psychological state. Recognizing the child's autonomous psychological state allows the parent to respond to the child's authentic emotional and psychological needs, even if these needs might be different from the parent's. In authentic parental empathy, the parent's understanding of the child's inner experience is based on the child's frame of reference.

In a role-reversal reversal relationship, the parent is unable to recognize the separate authenticity of the child. The child becomes a regulatory object for the parent. The child's function is to meet the emotional and psychological needs of the parent. In a role-reversal relationship, it is the child who must "mentalize" and reflect back to the parent the inner psychological state of the parent. Under these conditions, authentic parental empathy for the separate experience of the child is impossible. Instead, "empathy" for the narcissistic/(borderline) parent represents the child's fusion with and reflection of the parent's own psychological state.

The narcissistic/(borderline) parent is incapable of authentic empathy. The experience of empathy for the narcissistic/(borderline) parent represents the projection of the parent's own wants and needs onto and into the child. In the process, the parent obliterates the child's separateness and imposes on the child the parent's own wants and needs for what the child supposedly feels and desires. The separate authenticity of the child is not recognized by the narcissistic/(borderline) parent, and when the parent cannot see and respond to the child's separate psychological experience, the child's psychological authenticity atrophies. The inability of the narcissistic/(borderline) parent to "mentalize" the child's separate authenticity invalidates and eventually nullifies the child's separate self-authenticity.

Empathy for the narcissistic/(borderline) parent represents the parent imposing onto and into the child the parent's own experience, wants, and needs. In the role as a "regulatory object" for the emotional and psychological state of the parent, the child dutifully adopts these imposed needs of the parent as the child's own. Failure to meet the needs of the parent can result in the collapse of the narcissistic/(borderline) personality into angry onslaughts of emotional dysregulation. If the parent needs the sky to be red, the child agrees that the sky is red. In Shakespeare, when Petruchio needs the sun to be the moon, Kate surrenders her self-authenticity and complies. In order to keep the parent in a regulated state, the child becomes the perfect reflection of the moment-to-moment psychological state of narcissistic/(borderline) parent.

The narcissistic/(borderline) parent will adopt a presentation to others as being the ideal and perfect parent who is perfectly attuned and responsive to the child's needs. This presentation as the ideal parent often includes assertions of a "perfect empathy" for what the child feels and needs. Coincidentally, the child's supposed feelings and needs just happen to coincide exactly with the needs and desires of the narcissistic/(borderline) parent. The narcissistic/(borderline) parent uses this perfect alignment of the child's expressed views with those of the narcissistic/(borderline) parent as evidence for the accuracy of their shared views. In truth, there is only one set of beliefs and perceptions, those of the narcissistic/(borderline) parent. The child's self-authenticity is no longer present.

Since the child is merely a reflection of the parent's needs and desires, the narcissistic/(borderline) parent can hide behind the child. The child is placed out front to express the wants and needs of the narcissistic/(borderline) parent, who takes a secondary position of supporting the child. The child becomes the manipulated puppet, the narcissistic/(borderline) parent the controlling ventriloquist, and the audience responds to the puppet rather than the skillful ventriloquist. In this way, the narcissistic/(borderline) parent is able to exploit the child's role-reversal reflection of the narcissistic/(borderline) to achieve the goals desired by the parent. The narcissistic/(borderline) parent hides his or her own agenda behind the child's supposed wants and needs;

- It's not the narcissistic/(borderline) parent who wants to terminate the targeted parent's visitations with the child; it's the child who wants to terminate these visitations.

- It's not the narcissistic/(borderline) parent who wants to exclude the targeted parent from the child's activities; it's the child who wants to exclude the targeted parent.

- It's not the narcissistic/(borderline) parent who is encouraging the child to be mean and disrespectful to the targeted parent, it is the child who has formed an "independent" attitude toward the targeted parent.

The mantra for the narcissistic/(borderline) parent becomes empowering the child:

- "We need to listen to what the child wants."
- "The child should be allowed to decide."
- "The child shouldn't be forced to do what the child doesn't want to do."
- "The child should be allowed to tell the judge what the child wants."

All of this reflects the pathology of the role-reversal relationship in which the child's self-authenticity has been nullified and surrendered in order to meet the emotional and psychological needs of the narcissistic/(borderline) parent. Unfortunately, far too many mental health professionals believe this false presentation by the child because these professionals lack a foundational professional understanding for normal child psychology and child development. Because these mental health professionals do not understand authentic child development and authentic parent-child conflict, they cannot recognize the inauthentic presentation of the child and inauthentic parent-child conflict. It all looks the same to these mental health professionals. The ignorance of these mental health professionals allows the narcissistic/(borderline) parent to effectively exploit the child as a means to manipulate these mental health professionals into becoming allies of the narcissistic/(borderline) parent in support of the child's induced psychopathology.

Chapter 6

INDUCING SYMPTOMS

Methods of Symptom Induction

There is a general misconception that the child's rejection of a relationship with the targeted parent is produced as a consequence of the child hearing bad things said about the targeted parent by the allied and supposedly favored parent. This is not exactly accurate. If this were the case, why wouldn't the child's authentic relationship experiences with the targeted parent counteract and override the distorted criticisms of the targeted parent being provided by the "alienating" parent? Why wouldn't a child instead believe the relationship evidence from the child's actual interactions with the targeted parent? How could the child be induced to develop seemingly motivated distortions regarding the targeted parent as being somehow a bad and malevolent parent rather than rely on the child's own authentic experience with the targeted parent?

It is these unexplained processes that are sometimes used as criticisms for the construct of "parental alienation," and which lead to the counter-proposal that there must be some actual basis for the child's criticism of the targeted parent that serve as a foundation for the child's beliefs. In an effort to explain how the child's authentic experiences with the targeted parent can be nullified by the untrue criticisms leveled against the targeted parent by the "alienating" parent, supporters for the Gardnerian PAS model have sometimes invoked the constructs of "brainwashing" and "indoctrination" of the child. From the perspective of clinical psychology, these constructs are dubious at best. A more substantial understanding is needed for how the child overrides authentic self-experience and acquires the distorted beliefs of the narcissistic/(borderline) parent regarding the targeted parent.

The actual induction process is much more subtle and insidious than the "alienating" parent simply criticizing the other parent. The process of symptom induction involves an integrated set of pathological communication processes initiated by the narcissistic/(borderline) parent that act to nullify and invalidate the child's self-orientation to authentic self-experience and reality in favor of surrendering to and adopting the distorted belief system of the narcissistic/(borderline) parent.

The two primary processes of symptom induction involve:

1) **Establishing a Role-Reversal Relationship:** The first primary component process of inducing the child's symptomatic rejection of the targeted parent is inducing the child into forming a role-reversal relationship with the narcissistic/(borderline) parent in which the child becomes a "regulatory other" for the emotional and psychological state of the narcissistic/(borderline) parent.

2) **Inducing the "Victimized Child" Role:** Once the role-reversal relationship is established, the second primary component process is to then induce the child into accepting the "victimized child" role in the trauma reenactment narrative, described more fully in the Attachment System Level of analysis, in which the child accepts and displays a false belief that the child is being somehow victimized by the supposedly "abusive" parenting practices of the targeted parent. Inducing the child into adopting the "victimized child" role relative to the targeted parent involves eliciting from the child a criticism of the targeted parent. This initial elicited criticism is then enlarged, distorted, and inflamed by the parental responses that this elicited criticism receives from the narcissistic/(borderline) parent into supposed evidence of the abusively inadequate parental treatment the child is receiving from the targeted parent.

Over the repeated course of systematically distorted parent-child interactions with the narcissistic/(borderline) parent, in which the child is acting as a "regulatory other" for the emotional and psychological state of the narcissistic/(borderline) parent, the child's own self-evaluations are suppressed and nullified in favor of surrendering to the fused psychological state of the child's complete dedication to regulating the emotional and psychological state of the narcissistic/(borderline) parent.

Once the two primary relationship processes are in place, the child's role-reversal relationship with the narcissistic/(borderline) parent and the child's acceptance of the "victimized child" role in the trauma reenactment narrative, then secondary communication processes are added to enhance and expand the child's acquisition of distorted beliefs regarding the parenting practices of the targeted parent. These secondary processes include:

- **Themes of Criticism:** The narcissistic/(borderline) parent provides subtle but clear verbal indications to the child regarding the acceptable themes that can be used by the child in criticizing the other parent.

- **Parental Emotional Signaling:** Emotional signals provided to the child by the narcissistic/(borderline) parent can convey two types of information, 1) parental anxiety regarding the parenting practices of the targeted parent that communicate to the child that the other parent presents some form of threat to the child, and 2) emotional signals from the parent that convey to the child whether the child provided the proper, parentally desired, response to the narcissistic/(borderline) parent, or whether the child provided a non-desired response which then signals the potential impending collapse of the narcissistic/(borderline) parent into emotional dysregulation as a result of the non-desired child response.

- **Parental Attunement and Misattunement:** The child's behavior and internal psychological state can be parentally shaped by differential parental attunement or misattunement to the child by the narcissistic/(borderline) parent. Differential parental attunement and misattunement to desired and non-desired child responses and child psychological states, such as attuned parental responses for child expressions of anxiety and hostility toward the other parent and misattuned parental responses for child expressions of acceptance and affection for the other parent, will amplify and dampen the child's own self-experience, gradually shaping the child's self-experience into the form desired by the parent.

Through the combined distorting influence of primary and secondary pathological communication processes, the narcissistic/(borderline) parent can completely nullify the child's own authentic self-experience and establish a role-reversal relationship with the child in which the child expresses attitudes and behaviors as a "regulatory other" for the emotional and psychological needs of the narcissistic/(borderline) parent. Within this context of the child's role as a "regulatory other" for the emotional and psychological state of the parent, the narcissistic/(borderline) parent simply needs to communicate to the child through subtle non-verbal cues that the parent needs the child to adopt the role of the "victimized child" relative to the supposedly "abusive" parenting of the other parent in order to keep the narcissistic/(borderline) parent in a regulated emotional and psychological state. As a "regulatory object" for the parent, the child will readily and fully comply with this parental desire to become a "victimized child" in order to keep the narcissistic/(borderline) parent in an organized and regulated state.

This communication dynamic is so subtle and covert that even the child is unaware it is occurring. From the child's perspective, it is the child who is criticizing the other parent and the narcissistic/(borderline) parent is simply being understanding and supportive of the child. In the hidden subtlety of this distorted parent-child communication process, the child actually comes to believe that rejecting the other parent represents the child's authentic experience and that the narcissistic/(borderline) parent is simply being an understanding and supportive parent.

Establishing the Role-Reversal Relationship

As noted earlier, establishing the role-reversal relationship in which the child becomes the "regulatory other" for the emotional and psychological state of the narcissistic/(borderline) parent is relatively easy. When the child fails to provide the narcissistic/(borderline) parent with the parentally desired responses needed to keep the parent in an organized and regulated state, the narcissistic/(borderline) parent collapses into emotional and psychological dysregulation in which truth and reality offer no defense for the child. On the other hand, whenever the child provides the narcissistic/(borderline) parent with the response desired by the parent then the child avoids the regulatory collapse of the narcissistic/(borderline) parent and is granted displays of hyper-affectionate bonding from the borderline-style parent and narcissistic indulgences from the narcissistic-style parent.

In the swirling world of subjectively defined truth and reality created by the narcissistic/(borderline) personality, the child soon surrenders self-authenticity to the definitions of truth and reality that are constructed by the narcissistic/(borderline) parent. The child, anxious to avoid the collapse of the narcissistic/(borderline) parent, readily provides the responses desired by the pathology of the narcissistic/(borderline) parent. Initially, these child responses simply involve providing the narcissistic/(borderline) parent with criticisms of the other parent. Later, as the pathology takes hold and progresses, the child will more actively engage in providing the narcissistic/(borderline) parent with elaborated criticisms and more dramatic demonstrations of rejection for the targeted parent.

Inducing the "Victimized Child" Role

While the unconscious goal of the narcissistic/(borderline) parent is to attain the child's rejection of the other parent in order to projectively displace onto the other parent (spouse) the narcissistic/(borderline) parent's own self-inadequacy and abandonment fears, the efforts of the narcissistic/(borderline) parent to induce the child's rejection of the other parent do not directly target the child's attitude of rejection. For the pathology of the narcissistic/(borderline) parent, it is not enough for the child simply to reject the targeted parent because the child is an ally of the narcissistic/(borderline) parent, the child must "independently" reject the parent. By seeming to "independently" reject the targeted parent, the narcissistic/(borderline) parent can exploit and hide behind the child's induced symptom display.

In addition, the child's "independent" rejection of the targeted parent defines the targeted parent as being the inadequate and abandoned parent. This child-imposed definition of the targeted parent allows the narcissistic/(borderline) parent to projectively displace onto the targeted parent the self-inadequacy and abandonment fears of the narcissistic/(borderline) parent. The targeted parent must not simply be rejected. The targeted parent must be "independently" defined by the child as being an inadequate parent (person), who is being rejected (abandoned) by the child because of this fundamental parental (personal) inadequacy. The child must appear to be "independently" rejecting the targeted parent for the supposed inadequacy of this parent as a person in order to enact the child's role-reversal regulatory function for the narcissistic/(borderline) parent.

This goal of creating the child's "independent" rejection of the targeted parent is accomplished by first inducing the child into accepting and adopting the role as the "victimized child" relative to the parenting practices of the other parent. This "victimized child" role has a central function within the trauma reenactment narrative described in the next section regarding the Attachment System Level of analysis. Once the child accepts and adopts the role as the "victimized child," this immediately imposes on the targeted parent the role of the "abusive parent" in the trauma reenactment narrative created by the narcissistic/(borderline) parent. The combined roles of "victimized child" and "abusive parent" then allow the narcissistic/(borderline) parent to adopt and conspicuously display the coveted role as the "protective parent" in the trauma reenactment narrative. The central importance of the trauma reenactment narrative within attachment-based "parental alienation" will be more fully described in the next section.

The difference between inducing the child into rejecting the targeted parent and inducing the child into accepting and adopting the "victimized child" role is subtle but extremely important. If the narcissistic/(borderline) parent tried to directly convince the child to reject the other parent by overtly making denigrating comments regarding the other parent, this could produce a backlash of motivating the child to defend the targeted parent. A frontal assault on the targeted parent through overt parental criticism levied by the narcissistic/(borderline) parent would also be directly contrary to the child's authentic experience with the targeted parent, and so could be rejected by the child as an inaccurate portrayal of the targeted parent. The psychological manipulation and control of the child by the pathology of the narcissistic/(borderline) parent is vastly more subtle and insidious. Narcissistic and borderline personality styles are exquisite masters at exploitation and manipulation, and their skills at exploitation and manipulation are on full display in attachment-based "parental alienation."

This is not to say that the narcissistic/(borderline) parent never directly criticizes or denigrates the targeted parent. Such criticism of the targeted parent occurs with regularity. But these criticisms from the narcissistic/(borderline) parent only occur AFTER the narcissistic/(borderline) parent first elicits an initial criticism of the targeted parent from the child. Superficially, it will appear as though the criticism is coming "independently" from the child and that the narcissistic/(borderline) parent is simply being a "supportive" and "understanding" parent for the child's supposedly "independent" judgements of the targeted parent's fundamental inadequacy.

> **Narcissistic/(Borderline) Parent:** "I'm simply listening to the child. It's the child who is criticizing the other parent, not me. You should ask the child. Just listen to the child. I tell the child that they should love their mother/(father) no matter how bad the other parent is. But what can I do? I can't force the child to love the other parent. And I know just what the child is complaining about. The other parent acted just like that with me during our marriage."

The description offered for the manipulative parental tactics used by the narcissistic/(borderline) parent in attachment-based "parental alienation" is not meant to discount cases of severe domestic violence in which the child is influenced by an abusive spouse who continually denigrates and degrades the other spouse, which then leads the child to adopt a similarly denigrating and degrading attitude toward the victimized spouse. Cases of domestic violence in which the child identifies with and models the aggressive parent occur. However, in attachment-based "parental alienation" the manipulative and exploitative tactics used by the narcissistic/(borderline) parent can be much more sophisticated and subtle. In some cases, a history of domestic violence and subsequent attachment-based "parental alienation" can co-occur.

In attachment-based "parental alienation," the narcissistic/(borderline) parent projectively displaces his or her own self-inadequacy and abandonment fears onto the targeted parent through the child's rejection of the targeted parent. To accomplish this requires that the child appear to "independently" reject the targeted parent. The child must not appear to be influenced by the narcissistic/(borderline) parent because then the targeted parent would not be identified as representing the "abusive parent" and would instead become the victim of the narcissistic/(borderline) parent and child. So it is crucial that the child appear to "independently" judge and then reject the targeted parent.

In addition, by "independently" rejecting the targeted parent the child then allows the narcissistic/(borderline) parent to adopt and conspicuously display to others the coveted role as the all-wonderful, understanding, and nurturing "protective parent." This is a crucial role for the narcissistic/(borderline) parent, as described more fully in the Attachment System Level of analysis. Part of the child's role as the "regulatory object" for the narcissistic/(borderline) parent is for the child to play the role as the "victimized child" in order to allow the narcissistic/(borderline) parent to become and display to others the role as the all-wonderful, nurturing and "protective parent." If the narcissistic/(borderline) parent and child simply align against the targeted parent then the child is not "victimized" and is therefore not in need of "protection." The induction of the child's rejection of the targeted parent therefore becomes subtle, and requires that the child appear to be making an "independent" decision to reject the targeted parent because of the child's supposed "victimization."

This narrative construction of the "victimized child"/"abusive parent"/"protective parent" is easily accomplished if the child is first induced into adopting the "victimized child" role rather than directly seeking to elicit the child's rejection of the other parent. The moment the child adopts the role as the "victimized child" the other two roles in the trauma reenactment narrative, of the "abusive parent" and "protective parent," are immediately created for the targeted parent and narcissistic/(borderline) parent. Once the child adopts the role of the "victimized child," then the child's rejection of the targeted parent is easily created by extending the narrative of the child's "victimization" to include the "abusive parent" role for the targeted parent.

The narrative construction that the child's rejection of the targeted parent is the product of the child's "victimization" gives the superficial appearance of the child's supposed "independence" in rejecting the targeted parent. The storyline for this narrative is plausible and it does not directly expose the influence of the narcissistic/(borderline) parent on the child, either to other people or to the self-awareness of the narcissistic/(borderline) personality. In the mind of the narcissistic/(borderline) parent, the trauma reenactment narrative of "abusive parent"/"victimized child"/"protective parent" is entirely true with absolute certainty.

The Trauma Reenactment Narrative

The role of the "victimized child" is at the center of the pathology in attachment-based "parental alienation." A deeper level core understanding for the child's symptomatic rejection of the targeted parent is found in the trans-generational transmission of attachment trauma from the childhood of the narcissistic/(borderline) parent into the current relationships. This childhood trauma of the narcissistic/(borderline) parent is being expressed through a trauma reenactment narrative, which is being mediated by the narcissistic and borderline psychological pathology of the "alienating" parent.

There are three key roles in the trauma reenactment narrative of the narcissistic/(borderline) parent; the "victimized child" role, the "abusive parent" role, and the role of the all-wonderful "protective parent." The lynchpin to creating the trauma reenactment is the "victimized child" role. Once the child adopts the role as the "victimized child" this immediately imposes the role of the "abusive parent" onto the targeted parent, and the "victimized child" role allows the narcissistic/(borderline) parent to adopt the coveted role as the nurturing "protective parent." When the child accepts and adopts the "victimized child" role, this automatically defines the targeted parent as being "abusive" irrespective of the actual parenting practices of the targeted parent. This represents a masterful display of manipulative exploitation. The child's induced symptoms automatically define the targeted parent, regardless of what the actual parenting practices of the targeted parent are.

The targeted parent is immediately placed on the defensive and must continually prove a negative, i.e., that the targeted parent is <u>not</u> abusive. By adopting the "victimized child" role the assumption of guilt is immediately and irrevocably placed on the targeted parent. This imposes the burden of proof on the targeted parent for continually proving a negative; that he or she is not abusive. While at the same time this distracts attention away from the pathogenic parenting practices of the narcissistic/(borderline) parent. All of the clinical focus of mental health professionals is directed toward the allegations of "abusive parenting" made by the child's role as the "victimized child," and the extreme pathology of the narcissistic/(borderline) flies entirely under the clinical radar of mental health professionals.

What a masterful display of fully integrated manipulative exploitation. The "abusive parent" role is imposed on the targeted parent irrespective of the parenting practices of the targeted parent, the burden of proof is immediately placed on the targeted parent to continually prove a negative, which is nearly impossible, and the focus of clinical attention is diverted away from the psychopathology of the narcissistic/(borderline) parent onto the normal-range targeted parent, while the narcissistic/(borderline) parent is allowed to present as the all-wonderful, perfect and idealized parent. This is truly a masterful display of fully integrated manipulative exploitation.

Of prominent professional concern is that the extreme severity of this pathology often goes entirely unrecognized within mental health, resulting in mental health professionals who are actively colluding with the psychopathology to the ultimate destruction of the child's normal-range healthy development, and to the tragic grief of the targeted parent that results from a lost relationship with their beloved child. There is no excuse. Mental health professionals should know better. If they don't, then they may be practicing beyond the boundaries of their professional competence in violation of professional practice standards.

The two trauma reenactment roles of "victimized child" and "abusive parent" that are created the moment the child adopts the role of the "victimized child" allow the narcissistic/(borderline) parent to then adopt and conspicuously display to others the coveted role as the all-wonderful "protective parent." Through this trauma reenactment narrative, the targeted parent is being defined as the "abusively" inadequate parent who is being rejected by the child because of this fundamental parental inadequacy, thereby projectively displacing onto the targeted-rejected parent the primal self-inadequacy and abandonment fears of the narcissistic/(borderline) parent. This then also allows the narcissistic/(borderline) to adopt and publicly present to others the coveted role within the trauma reenactment narrative as the all-wonderful, idealized and nurturing, "protective parent." The key to creating the trauma reenactment narrative is inducing the child into accepting and adopting the "victimized child" role.

It is not at all difficult to induce the child into accepting the role as a "victimized child" of the other parent's supposedly insensitive and emotionally "abusive" parenting, given the pathology of the role-reversal relationship in which the child is actively monitoring the psychological and emotional state of the narcissistic/(borderline) parent in order to respond in ways that keep the narcissist/(borderline) parent in a regulated state. All the narcissistic/(borderline) parent needs to do is gradually shape the child's regulatory responses that are offered to the narcissistic/(borderline) parent into the parentally desired form of the child's accepting the "victimized child" role relative to the parenting practices of the other parent. Given that the child's role-reversal regulatory function is to psychologically surrender self-authenticity to the narcissistic/(borderline) parent in order to maintain a fused and reflective psychological state in the ever-shifting reality defined by the narcissistic/(borderline) parent, shaping the child's responses into adopting the "victimized child" role relative to the other parent is immensely easy to accomplish. The narcissistic/(borderline) parent simply needs to subtly signal the child that the response required from the child to maintain the organized and regulated state of the narcissistic/(borderline) parent is for the child to accept the role as being "victimized" by the supposedly insensitive and "abusive" parenting of the other parent.

Initially, the "victimized child" role does not involve rejecting the targeted parent. The child must simply provide the narcissistic/(borderline) parent with criticisms of the targeted parent. These criticisms are elicited from the child through the motivated and directive questioning of the child by the narcissistic/(borderline) parent. Once the child provides the narcissistic/(borderline) parent with a criticism of the targeted parent, the narcissistic/(borderline) parent sets about distorting, enlarging, and inflaming this initial criticism offered by the child into supposed evidence of the targeted parent's insensitive, inadequate, and "abusive" parenting. The narcissistic/(borderline) parent responds as if the child is being "victimized," and the child eventually comes to believe this is true. After all, the sky is red if the narcissistic/(borderline) parent says it is.

When the child psychologically surrenders into adopting the "victimized child" role, the child is rewarded with hyper-affectionate displays of nurturing comfort from the borderline-style parent, and with narcissistic indulgences of special adult-like privileges and gifts from the narcissistic-style parent. The divorce has left the child alone with the narcissistic/(borderline) parent, fully exposed to the complex and sophisticated manipulation of the narcissistic/(borderline) personality. The targeted parent is not present to protect the child, or balance the child's perceptions. Through the formation of the "victimized child" narrative and the granting of borderline and narcissistic indulgences, the child is led to believe that the targeted parent is bad, abusive, and deserves to be punished, while the narcissistic/(borderline) parent is a nurturing, understanding, and wonderful parent. Gradually, the trauma reenactment narrative of the narcissistic/(borderline) pathology is constructed, with the current family members playing roles in the past childhood trauma of the narcissistic/(borderline) psychopathology.

Once the child is induced into accepting and adopting the "victimized child" role in the trauma reenactment, creating the child's overt rejection of a relationship with the now supposedly "abusive parent" flows naturally from the various roles assigned and adopted in the reenactment narrative. A false narrative of "abuse," "victimization," and "protection" is created by the pathology and pathogenic parenting of the narcissistic/(borderline) parent. The various participants are simply enacting their assigned roles in this false drama. The psychological origins for this false drama are found in the childhood attachment trauma of the narcissistic/(borderline) parent that created the narcissistic/(borderline) pathology in the first place. All that is necessary to create the trauma reenactment narrative from the childhood of the narcissistic/(borderline) parent is to induce the child into accepting the defining role as the "victimized child" in the false drama.

Once the trauma reenactment is engaged, it moves inexorably toward its final conclusion of the child's complete rejection of a relationship with a normal-range and affectionally available parent, and it becomes nearly impossible for the targeted parent to escape the imposed false role as the "abusive parent" within the trauma reenactment narrative without the active support from mental health professionals who recognize and respond appropriately to the nature and severity of the involved psychopathology. The targeted parent and child need mental health professionals as an ally to negate the role-reversal psychopathology and dismantle the false trauma reenactment narrative being constructed by the pathology of the narcissistic/(borderline) parent.

Instead, professional ignorance too often becomes an ally of the narcissistic/(borderline) psychopathology, **colluding with the psychopathology** rather than healing the psychopathology.

Trapping the Targeted Parent

In the face of both the "victimized child" role being adopted and displayed by the child and the "protective parent" role being adopted and displayed by the narcissistic/(borderline) parent, the targeted parent is placed in a position of continually being required by therapists and the court to prove a negative, that he or she is <u>not</u> an abusive parent. On the other hand, the standards placed on the child and narcissistic/(borderline) parent to prove the positive, i.e., that the targeted parent is actually "abusive" and that the child's symptoms are an authentic response to the parenting practices of the targeted parent, are usually quite low. As long as the child maintains the "victimized child" role (which is being actively supported by the views of the narcissistic/(borderline) parent in the role as the all-wonderful "protective parent") many "bystanders" of therapists, attorneys, custody evaluators, school personnel, judges, and parenting coordinators will accept the child's presentation of "victimization" as being seemingly reasonable evidence for the potentially problematic parenting of the targeted-rejected parent.

In an effort to escape the defensive stance of continually trying to prove a negative, the targeted parent may sometimes try to switch from proving a negative to instead trying to prove a positive, that the child's rejection of the targeted parent represents the induced symptoms of distorted parenting practices from the narcissistic/(borderline) parent. In an effort to prove the positive, the targeted parent may then allege that "parental alienation" is the source of the child's rejection. However, these allegations of "parental alienation" are oftentimes met with counter-accusations that the targeted parent is simply trying to avoid taking responsibility for his or her own bad parenting practices by shifting the blame onto the favored parent.

The targeted parent is thereby trapped into forever being on the defensive by the "victimized child" role adopted by the child, either by having to prove the negative that he or she is not an "abusive" parent, or by having to prove the negative that he or she is not trying to avoid responsibility for bad parenting by accusing the other parent of inducing the child's rejection of the targeted parent. Either way, the targeted parent must prove a negative. There is no escape. This feature of being trapped without being able to escape is a characteristic feature of trauma reenactment, and is another example of the masterful manipulation of the situation by the narcissistic/(borderline) personality through the exploitation of the child's symptoms.

In mental health, it is rare to encounter a reenactment narrative of childhood trauma. Much more common in professional experience are authentic parent-child conflicts, so that the vast majority of child-oriented mental health professionals are already pre-primed to accept parent-child conflict as being authentic. Since a delusional reenactment of childhood trauma is so rarely encountered, whereas treating the aftermath of child abuse is much more common in the experience of mental health professionals, the storyline offered by the trauma reenactment narrative of "abusive parent"/"victimized child"/"protective parent" fits more comfortably with the pre-established expectations of mental health professionals.

In addition, most child therapists and legal professionals are not experienced with the complex dynamics of narcissistic and borderline personality disorder presentations. Narcissistic and borderline personalities can be quite adept at hiding the severity of their pathology. At the attachment core of both the narcissistic and borderline personality styles is a fundamental sense of self-inadequacy and a fear of being rejected and abandoned by the attachment figure. As a result, both the narcissistic and borderline personalities have developed sophisticated social presentations designed to obtain the favor of other people.

The narcissistic-style personality can be quite charming, and presents as calm, confident, and self-assured. Consistent with the underlying needs of the narcissistic defense for self-inflation, the social presentation of the narcissistic-style personality tends to elicit admiration from others who then seek the approval of the narcissistic personality. The borderline-style personality also presents well initially. The superficial presentation of the borderline-style personality is socially charming and gregarious, with an undercurrent of emotional seduction. A common feature of the borderline-style presentation is exposing emotional vulnerability that acquires a nurturing response from others. The borderline-style personality often presents as being the helpless victim of abuse inflicted by others. The social presentation of the borderline-style personality tends to elicit a response of nurturing protection for the socially charming and vulnerable presentation by the borderline-style personality. Both personality styles are quite adept at eliciting other people as allies. It is only when the attachment system of the narcissistic and borderline personality is engaged in an emotionally bonded relationship that the full extent of their pathology becomes evident.

In addition, the psychological and interpersonal dynamics of attachment-based "parental alienation" involve the delusional collapse of the narcissistic/(borderline) personality structure. Truth, accuracy, and reality are being prominently distorted by the narcissistic/(borderline) pathology. Yet most child therapists and legal professionals are completely unfamiliar with the psychological decompensation of personality structures into delusional beliefs. Delusional beliefs are not commonly encountered, even by mental health professionals. In most encounters we assume that the other person has at least a basic anchor to a shared perception of reality. However, in the case of narcissistic and borderline decompensation, truth and reality will become highly distorted by self-serving motivations to present themselves as wonderful and as being victimized, and to present the other person as malevolent, inadequate, and "abusive."

Most child therapists and children's attorneys do not typically suspect that the initial presentation of the seemingly wonderful, charming, and "protective" parent actually represents a narcissistic or borderline-style personality presentation, even though in high-conflict divorce, particularly when a child is rejecting a relationship with a parent, a strong suspicion of parental narcissistic or borderline personality processes would be extremely prudent. As a consequence of their unwarranted trust in the superficial social presentation of the narcissistic/(borderline) parent, most child therapists simply do not typically assess for a psychotic level of distortion to the reporting of this parent regarding family processes.

Central to the pathology of attachment-based "parental alienation" is a role-reversal relationship in which the child is surrendering self-authenticity to the pathology of a narcissistic/(borderline) parent. Accurate assessment and treatment therefore requires advanced professional competence in recognizing the pathology and implications of a role-reversal relationship. Also central to the pathology of attachment-based "parental alienation" is the decompensation of a narcissistic/(borderline) personality into delusional beliefs. Accurate assessment and treatment therefore requires advanced professional competence in recognizing the pathology and implications of narcissistic and borderline personality processes. A further construct central to the pathology of attachment-based "parental alienation" is a severe disruption to the normal-range functioning of the child's attachment system. Accurate assessment and treatment therefore requires advanced professional competence regarding the attachment system and the recognition of authentic and inauthentic displays of the attachment system during childhood.

Greater professional expertise is needed in both the mental health and legal professions regarding the nature and features of narcissistic and borderline pathology as reflected in parenting practices, so that the reasonable efforts of targeted parents to escape the psychotic pathology of the trauma reenactment narrative being imposed on them by the psychopathology of a narcissistic/(borderline) parent will meet with an adequate response from mental health and legal professionals. Currently, when targeted parents try to switch from the nearly impossible task of proving the negative (i.e., that they are not abusive of the child despite the child's protestations, which are supported by the seemingly nurturing and bonded "favored" parent) to proving a positive (i.e., that the child's rejection is a symptom of "parental alienation" by the seemingly wonderful and apparently bonded parent) they are often met with general professional skepticism arising from the controversial history of Gardner's PAS model. Many mental health professionals and courts may then cavalierly dismiss the assertions of the targeted parent that the child's symptom display of rejection could possibly be the induced product of "parental alienation" without providing the concerns of the targeted parent with the proper assessment and consideration.

When the pathology of attachment-based "parental alienation" is dismissed by mental health and legal professionals, they wind up colluding with the severely pathological role-reversal use of the child by a narcissistic/(borderline) parent in which significant psychopathology is being induced in the child through the pathogenic parenting practices of the narcissistic/(borderline) parent. The narcissistic/(borderline) parent is using the child as a "regulatory object" for the inadequate self-structure development of the parent. As the "regulatory object" for the parent, the child is surrendering self-authenticity in order to remain in a continually fused psychological state with the parent in order to keep the narcissistic/(borderline) parent in a regulated emotional and psychological state. The seemingly "bonded" relationship of the child with the narcissistic/(borderline) parent is in no way an indicator of a healthy parent-child relationship. Instead, it is a symptomatic feature of extreme psychopathology, and essentially represents the parent feeding off of the child's healthy psychological development to support the inadequate self-structure of the narcissistic/(borderline) parent. In the process of feeding off of the child's healthy development, the pathology of the narcissistic/(borderline) parent is impoverishing the child's development of self-autonomy and independent self-structure.

The child's induced role as the "victimized child" which is supported by the "protective parent" role being adopted and conspicuously displayed by the narcissistic/(borderline) parent, effectively imposes onto the targeted parent the false role as the "abusive parent" in the trauma reenactment narrative of the narcissistic/(borderline) parent. The imposed "abusive parent" role is nearly impossible for the targeted parent to escape. The only escape for the targeted parent from the false role as an "abusive parent" comes from educated mental health and legal professionals who can recognize the severity of the pathology being enacted, and who can then take the steps necessary to restore the child's healthy development.

Eliciting the Criticism

Inducing the child into adopting the "victimized child" role in the trauma reenactment narrative of the narcissistic/(borderline) parent is accomplished by first eliciting a criticism of the other parent from the child through the motivated and directive questioning of the child by the narcissistic/(borderline) parent. This elicited child criticism, however small, is then exaggerated, distorted, and inflamed by the narcissistic/(borderline) parent into supposed evidence of the child's "victimization" from "abusively" inadequate parenting practices of the targeted parent. This process of first eliciting from the child a criticism of the targeted parent places the child in the leadership position of criticizing the targeted parent as being inadequate and "abusive." The child's leadership then allows the narcissistic/(borderline) parent to follow behind the child in presenting as the all-wonderful, nurturing and "protective parent." It is a kabuki theater presentation of predetermined roles which is being produced and directed by the psychopathology of the narcissistic/(borderline) parent.

This distorting communication exchange typically begins with the narcissistic/(borderline) parent subtly inviting the child's criticism of the other parent. If the child does not initially offer a criticism of the other parent then continued directive and motivated questioning by the narcissistic/(borderline) parent can usually communicate to the "regulatory other" of the child that the emotional and psychological regulation of the narcissistic/(borderline) parent requires receiving a child-initiated criticism of the other parent.

If the child still fails to recognize and respond to the desires of the narcissistic/(borderline) parent for a child-initiated criticism of the other parent, then the narcissistic/(borderline) parent will present to the child an emotional signal of impending dysregulation, such as an angry emotional tone and turning away from the child in a show of rejection for the child. If the child still does not self-correct into being an attuned and reflective "regulatory object" for the narcissistic/(borderline) parent by providing a criticism of the targeted parent, then the emotional regulation of the narcissistic/(borderline) parent will collapse into an onslaught of anger and rejection about any of a variety of unrelated issues.

The hostile emotional tirade of the narcissistic/(borderline) parent will be disconnected to any actual truth or reality based foundation, and may not necessarily be overtly connected to the child's relationship with the other parent. Still the message to the child will be clear, that the narcissistic/(borderline) expects the child to provide a criticism of the other parent. For example, if the child fails to provide the desired criticism of the targeted parent then the narcissistic/(borderline) parent might provoke a conflict with the child about an unrelated issue, such as the child's school performance or room tidiness, and then unleash a hostile-aggressive verbal assault on the child surrounding the provoked conflict that has no foundation in actual truth or in an accurate assessment of reality. Truth and reality provide no defense for the child from the retaliatory onslaughts of the narcissistic/(borderline) parent.

However, based on the child's prior experience with the narcissistic/(borderline) parent's emotional dysregulation, the child is fully aware of the negative consequences for failing to regulate the emotional and psychological state of the unpredictable and interpersonally dangerous narcissistic/(borderline) parent. As a result of the child's prior experience, the child rarely reaches the point of being the recipient of the emotional tirades of the narcissistic/(borderline) parent. Instead, the child surrenders psychologically to his or her role of reflecting a fused psychological state with the narcissistic/(borderline) parent in order to stabilize and maintain this parent's emotional regulation and avoid the onslaught of hostile-aggressive emotional tirades directed at the child for failing to provide the proper regulatory response.

In the child's active monitoring of the narcissistic/(borderline) parent, the child requires only subtle parental cues in order to self-correct into providing the parentally desired response. As the "regulatory object" for the psychological and emotional state of the narcissistic/(borderline) parent, the child must continually monitor the needs and wishes of the parent in order for the child to provide an attuned regulatory response to the needs of the parent. As a result, all the child needs is a subtle parental cue inviting the child's criticism of the targeted parent for the child to then supply the parentally desired criticism of the other parent.

Early in the process of inducing the child's symptomatic rejection of the targeted parent, the child's criticisms of the other parent will maintain a marginal connection to actual truth. However, over time and through repeated exposures to distorting communication exchanges with the narcissistic/(borderline) parent, the child eventually surrenders into adopting the parentally-desired role in these communication exchanges of offering full-throated and embellished criticisms of the other parent. The child learns that the more extreme the criticism offered, the more favorable the response the child will receive from the narcissistic/(borderline) parent.

Eventually, the child begins to actively participate in providing the narcissistic/(borderline) parent with the fully embellished criticisms of the targeted parent that are desired by the narcissistic/(borderline) parent. Normal-range restrictions imposed by truth and reality gradually begin to become less relevant, and the child's criticisms gradually evolve to more fully reflect the subjective assertion of truth and reality associated with narcissistic and borderline personality processes. External and verifiable truth and reality are not relevant considerations in these child criticisms of the targeted parent because for both the narcissistic/(borderline) parent and now for the child, "Truth and reality are what I assert them to be."

Narcissistic/(Borderline) Parent: <to the child returning from a visitation with his mother> "How were things at your mother's house? Did everything go okay?"

This represents the parental invitation for the child's criticism of the targeted parent. Superficially, the inquiry by the narcissistic/(borderline) parent seems innocuous. The parent is simply showing a seemingly normal-range interest in the child's experiences, and for a normal-range personality parent this question might indeed be innocuous. However, even for a normal-range parent this line of questions invites a child criticism of the other parent, and so potentially invites the child's triangulation into the spousal conflict. This is especially true with the subtle communicative prompt provided by the narcissistic/(borderline) parent of "Did everything go okay?" The child in a role-reversal relationship with a parent only needs a subtle communication as to whether the sky is red or green. This subtle communicative prompt offered by the narcissistic/(borderline) parent modifies the initial question about the child's experiences with his mother to indicate that the parent is seeking to identify problems in the child's relationship with the mother.

Child: "Yeah, everything was fine. It was okay."

The child ignores the invitation to provide a criticism of the targeted parent; the child is trying to remain neutral in the spousal conflict. Instead of accepting the parental invitation to criticize the other parent, the child is seeking to avoid being triangulated into the spousal conflict by offering an authentic but neutral response.

N/(B) Parent: "Really? Everything went okay? You and your mom got along okay and you guys didn't argue about anything?"

The response of surprise – "Really" – communicates that the narcissistic/(borderline) does not accept this child response and is instead seeking a different response from the child. A normal-range personality parent would respond, "That's great. I'm glad you two got along." The narcissistic/(borderline) parent, however, is seeking through directive and motivated questioning a child criticism of the other parent. The second and third questions provide the child with communicative cues about what the narcissistic/(borderline) parent is seeking, i.e., that everything didn't go okay and that the child and his mother argued about something. For a child who has surrendered to the role as the "regulatory other" for the narcissistic/(borderline) parent, this parental signaling would be sufficient cueing for the child to offer the parentally desired criticism of the other parent.

> **Child:** "Well, she got annoyed at me yesterday for leaving my stuff in the living room."

Recognizing the desires of the narcissistic/(borderline) parent, the child offers a relatively mild criticism of the other parent. At this early phase of the "alienation" process the child's criticism is anchored in truth and reality, the child did leave a mess in the living room and this did annoy his mother. As the distorted communication exchanges with the narcissistic/(borderline) parent become more firmly established, the child will begin to embellish and distort these criticisms to more fully meet the desires of the narcissistic/(borderline) parent.

> **N/(B) Parent:** "Oh my God, she got mad at you for that? Like you're only a guest at her house and you don't actually live there too? I can't believe her. Things always have to be her way or she gets so angry, and about little things too. If you don't do everything the way she wants she'll fly into one of her rages. Well, I'm sorry you have to put up with that, I wish she wouldn't do that."

The child's criticism doesn't need to be much in order for the narcissistic/(borderline) parent to then exaggerate and distort it into supposed evidence of the child's "victimization" by the "abusive" parenting practices of the other parent. In the initial response of – "Oh my God, she got mad at you for that" - the narcissistic/(borderline) parent communicates a sense of the child's entitlement. Based on the response of the narcissistic/(borderline) parent, the child is supposedly "entitled" to leave a mess around the house and shouldn't be chastised by the targeted parent for leaving a mess. And in framing this sense of child entitlement, the narcissistic/(borderline) parent implies that the mother was actually rejecting the child from belonging at her house. The actual truth of the episode is that the child left a mess in the living room and the mother became annoyed and asked the child to pick up the mess; this is an entirely normal-range and healthy parent-child interaction.

The sense of parental outrage conveyed by the narcissistic/(borderline) parent also emotionally communicates to the child that the other parent's response to the child was excessive and undeserved by the child, i.e., that the child is being "victimized" by the excessively restrictive and "abusive" parenting practices of the other parent. The child's report that the other parent was "annoyed" is also inflamed into her being "mad."

The father then provides the child with appropriate themes for criticizing the other parent; that the mother "always has to have things her way or she gets so angry," and that she gets angry over "the littlest things." In the future, these themes will be incorporated by the child into descriptions of his mother's supposedly problematic parenting.

The father's next response amplifies the theme of the mother's supposedly inappropriate anger with the statement, "If you don't do everything the way she wants she'll fly into one of her rages." The father first inflames the child's initial description of the mother as being "annoyed" into her being "mad." He then further inflames the criticism into her being "angry," and then into her supposed "rages." This distortion of truth and accuracy communicates to the child that these types of exaggerated distortions to accuracy are acceptable and desired. The next time the child offers a criticism of the mother the child will use these themes provided by the narcissistic father to describe his mother as "flying into one of her rages," when in truth she may have been just mildly irritated with the child's behavior (and most likely she will be justifiably irritated with the child, as it is completely typical and entirely normal-range for parents to sometimes become irritated with their children's behavior).

The father concludes this parent-child exchange by apologizing for the mother's behavior. Apologizing for the other parent subtly but clearly diminishes the mother and elevates the child to a position above the mother in the family hierarchy. By apologizing to the child for the mother's behavior, the father communicates that the child is entitled to judge the mother as a parent. When one parent apologizes to the child for the behavior of the other parent, this represents a subtle but highly manipulative parental response that undermines the authority of the other parent and gives permission to the child to sit in judgment of the other parent.

Yet, in this distorted communication exchange the father never overtly initiates the criticism of the mother. Instead the father acts as if he is just being an understanding and nurturing parent. To all outward appearances, it is the child who is criticizing the mother. But clearly the initial criticism of the mother was elicited from the child by the motivated and directive questioning of the child by the parent, and the initial child criticism was relatively mild. All of the subsequent distorting elaborations of the child's elicited criticism were the sole product of the narcissistic/(borderline) parent. However, if the child is asked, "does your father ever speak badly about your mother in front of you?" the child will respond, "No," since the child believes that it is the child who is criticizing the other parent, and that the narcissistic/(borderline) parent is simply being "understanding" and "supportive" of the child.

In the psychopathology of the narcissistic/(borderline) parent, the parent hides behind the role-reversal relationship with the child by placing the child into the leadership position of criticizing and rejecting the other parent. The child's leadership position then allows the narcissistic/(borderline) parent to exploit the child by hiding the parental influence of the child behind the child's supposedly "independent" assertions.

It is also psychologically imperative for the narcissistic/(borderline) parent not to be seen as overtly inducing the child's rejection of the other parent, because then the child would simply be an ally of the parent in the emotional retaliation against the other parent rather than a "victim" of the other parent's "abusive" parenting. As described in the Attachment System Level of analysis, the reenactment in current family relationships of the attachment trauma from the childhood of the narcissistic/(borderline) parent is an essential component for the regulation of the narcissistic/(borderline) parent's activated attachment trauma anxiety. It is not enough that the child simply rejects a relationship with the targeted parent; the child must fulfill the trauma reenactment role as the "victimized child" of the "abusive" parenting of the targeted parent. The child's supposed "victimization" allows the narcissistic/(borderline) parent to then adopt the coveted role as the "protective parent" for the child, which is an essential role in regulating the reactivated trauma anxiety. The foundational origin for the family dynamics being displayed in attachment-based "parental alienation" is in the reenactment of attachment trauma from the childhood of the narcissistic/(borderline) parent into current family relationships, and the child's role as the "victimized child" is central to this trauma reenactment process.

Secondary Communication Dynamics

While establishing a role-reversal relationship and inducing the child into adopting the "victimized child" role are the two primary means of inducing the child's symptomatic rejection of the other parent, three secondary communication processes also play an important role in creating the child's symptoms and are important in understanding the distorted communication processes by which attachment-based "parental alienation" is induced.

Communicating Themes for Criticism

The pathological influence of the narcissistic/(borderline) parent hides behind the child's induced rejection of the other parent. This is accomplished by first eliciting a criticism of the other parent from the child which the narcissistic/(borderline) parent then distorts and inflames into supposed evidence of the other parent's inadequate and "abusive" parenting. During the distorting exaggeration of the child's elicited criticism of the other parent, the narcissistic/(borderline) parent is able to convey to the child the acceptable themes for criticizing the other parent. The communication of these themes for criticizing the other parent are contained in the content of the distortions provided to the child by the narcissistic/(borderline) parent. As the narcissistic/(borderline) parent elaborates on the child's criticism, themes for criticizing the targeted parent are provided to the child.

N/(B) Parent: "Did everything go okay with your dad?"

Child: "It was kind of boring, we didn't do much."

N/(B) Parent: "I can't believe he didn't have anything planned for you guys to do together. He's just so inconsiderate of other people's feelings. It's like he's the only person that matters, and what other people want just doesn't matter to him."

While the initial criticism was offered by the child in response to the parental invitation, the elaboration offered by the narcissistic/(borderline) parent of this relatively mild child criticism of the targeted parent acts to distort and exaggerate the seriousness of the child's criticism into a fundamental personality failure of the other parent. In the elaborations offered by the narcissistic/(borderline) parent, the child is provided with themes that can be used in future criticisms of the other parent; i.e., that the other parent is self-centered and inconsiderate of other people's wishes.

> **N/(B) Parent:** "So, did you and your dad get along okay?"

Not satisfied with the initial child criticism, the motivated and directive questioning of the narcissistic/(borderline) parent seeks an additional criticism of the other parent from the child. The content of the parental question about the potential for parent-child conflict provides the child with a subtle cue about what type of criticism the child should offer.

> **Child:** "Well, on Saturday he got mad at me and said I was being rude, but I wasn't."

Actually, this parent-child conflict was provoked by the child using a disrespectful tone of voice toward his father. In response to the child's disrespectful tone, the father mildly rebuked the child with "Watch your tone of voice, young man. It's not okay to talk to me disrespectfully. I treat you with respect and I expect you to treat me the same way." This exchange between the father and child was entirely normal-range and appropriate, yet it was the only incident of conflict that occurred with his father so the child offers it to his mother when she seeks a report on an argument he had with his father.

> **N/(B) Parent:** "I can't believe him! You're not rude. I can't believe he called you rude. He's the one with the anger management problems. He just can't control his temper sometimes. He'll get mad at the littlest things."

Again, the initial criticism appears to be offered by the child yet is actually in response to the subtly directive parental questioning of the child by the narcissistic/(borderline) parent and the child's role as a "regulating other" for the narcissistic/(borderline) parent) in which the child offers responses that keep the parent in an organized and regulated state. In the elaborations and distortions to the elicited child criticism the narcissistic/(borderline) parent provides the child with the themes that can be used by the child in future criticisms of the other parent. In this case the themes are that the father has anger management problems and gets angry over trivial things. In the future, after repeated exposure to this type of distorted communication process, the child will return from visitations with his father with a litany of well-rehearsed complaints.

N/(B) Parent: "How were things with your dad?"

Child: "Awful. I hate it over there. He's just so self-centered and inconsiderate. All he ever thinks about is what he wants. He never considers what I want - and he gets so mad over the littlest things."

Through repetition, the child comes to understand that his or her role in the communication exchange is to provide the narcissistic/(borderline) parent with a criticism of the other parent in line with the acceptable themes. The child also learns that the more extreme the child is in displays of hostility and rejection of the targeted parent, the greater the approval the child receives from the narcissistic/(borderline) parent. Once this process is underway, the child will return from visits with the father primed and ready to offer the narcissistic/(borderline) parent a full litany of parentally desired child hostility directed toward the other parent. Normal-range visits with his father will soon be described as "horrible," and that the child supposedly "hates being with him."

Managing Guilt

However, the child's rejection of the targeted parent will also trigger guilt in the child for betraying his beloved-but-now-rejected parent. The child will ultimately need to manage the feelings of guilt regarding the child's betrayal of the targeted parent. The child can regulate this guilt by distorting his or her perception of the beloved-but-now-rejected parent so that the targeted parent somehow deserves the child's rejection. As long as the child can maintain a belief that the targeted parent "deserves" the child's rejection, then the child won't feel guilty. By remaining in a constant state of anger toward the targeted-rejected parent, the child can maintain the false belief that the targeted parent "deserves" to be rejected. This need to remain in a chronic state of inflamed anger ultimately transforms the child's anger into hatred.

Managing Truth

In the example, the child follows-up the general expression of hostility and rejection for the targeted parent by offering the approved themes for criticism, that the father is self-centered and overly angry. Once the child begins using these "acceptable themes" for criticizing the other parent, then the child no longer needs to create and report on specific incidents. This can greatly reduce the child's stress by eliminating the need to actually identify (or fabricate) specific incidents to report to the narcissistic/(borderline) parent. Instead the child can simply rely on generalized standard themes for the criticisms.

If needed, the child can always distort or fabricate a specific incident, or can provoke one while he is with his father so that the child has something negative to report to the mother in their standard "criticize the father" exchanges. But in general, once the child shifts to using the acceptable themes for criticizing the other parent that are provided by the narcissistic/(borderline) parent in earlier communication exchanges, the child becomes freed from the difficult task of developing specific reasons for "hating" the targeted parent.

If the child is then asked in therapy to describe a specific incident justifying the child's allegations that the father is self-centered or overly angry, the child often has difficulty doing so and may initially appear disoriented, since specific incidents were not necessary in reporting these criticisms to the narcissistic/(borderline) parent. When reported to the narcissistic/(borderline) parent, these general criticisms were simply accepted as valid reasons for why the child hates being with the targeted parent. Based on these repeated experiences of the child in reporting to the narcissistic/(borderline) parent, the child simply assumes that the therapist will also similarly accept the child's general assertions without the need for specifics, and indeed many therapists will do just that and simply accept the child's reporting on generalized themes as sufficient to justify the child's anger and hostility toward the targeted parent.

When the therapist does not simply accept the generalized theme and probes more deeply for specifics, the child will have difficulty identifying actual specific incidents that account for the child's hostility and rejection toward the targeted parent. In trying to generate specifics the child's proffered reasons for anger toward the targeted parent will appear weak and superficial. Faced with the challenge of identifying actual reasons for the child's hostility and rejection of the targeted parent, since none actually exist, the child may seek to avoid specifics by returning to one or two past incidents of supposed wrongs done to the child by the targeted parent as justifications for the child's continuing rejection of the parent. When asked the reason for the child's hostility and rejection, the child will repeatedly return to identifying these one or two past incidents of supposed injustice inflicted on the child by the targeted parent as representing "unforgivable" events for the child that justify both the current and all future child hostility and rejection toward the targeted parent.

In authentic parent-child conflict the child's anger is triggered by specific incidents and the anger dissipates once the specific incident passes. In the induced parent-child conflict of attachment-based "parental alienation," the parent-child conflict is the supposed product of the fundamental parental inadequacy of the targeted parent as a person, rather than about specific incidents. When asked for details about the reasons for rejecting the targeted parent, the child tends to offer general themes of parental inadequacy rather than specific incidents.

- "My mother is so selfish, she always has to have things her way."
- "My father has anger management problems, he gets so angry about the littlest things."
- "It's just something about the way my mother says things, it's just so annoying."
- "My father never spent enough time with me in the past, so now I don't want to spend time with him."

If specific incidents are reported on during therapy, these incidents will seem relatively trivial and innocuous because, in truth, these supposedly "justifying incidents" were actually minor incidents and were relatively innocuous. It is only through the distorted and exaggerating responses provided by the narcissistic/(borderline) parent that these trivial incidents become inflamed into the supposed evidence of "abusive" parenting practices by the targeted parent. The child, who is exposed to only the distorting exaggerations of the narcissistic/(borderline) parent, comes to believe that these incidents actually do represent "abusive" parenting by the other parent. Based on the child's experience in reporting these criticisms to the narcissistic/(borderline) parent the child fully expects that the therapist will be equally as outraged as the narcissistic/(borderline) parent was when the child first reported these incidents to this parent. But when reported in therapy, without the motivated distortions provided by the narcissistic/(borderline) parent, these incidents will return to their normal-range insubstantial truth.

However, if the therapist fails to appreciate the supposedly "abusive" parenting evidenced in these seemingly trivial and insubstantial incidents, then the child will report to the narcissistic/(borderline) parent and other "bystander" mental health and legal professionals that the therapist "doesn't understand." The child and allied narcissistic/(borderline) parent will then set about seeking a new therapist who is more "understanding" of the child, preferably a therapist who works from a humanistic model of child therapy in which "validating the child's feelings" is central to the therapy process. With a humanistic "child-centered" therapist, the need for specifics will not be as important as "validating the child's feelings." Therapists who work from a humanistic client-centered approach to child therapy will more readily accept as valid the child's generalized themes for rejecting the targeted parent that were provided to the child by the narcissistic/(borderline) parent early in the alienation process. The "bystander" role in the trauma reenactment narrative is to validate the legitimacy of the reenactment narrative. If the therapist does not enter this assigned "bystander" role then a change in therapists will be sought to one who accepts uncritically the legitimacy of the reenactment narrative.

<u>Co-Creating Distortions</u>

When the child offers the parentally desired criticism of the targeted parent, the narcissistic/(borderline) parent will provide the child with indulgences of affection, privileges, and gifts as a reward for the child's surrender to the narcissistic/(borderline) parent.

> **N/(B) Parent:** "Oh you poor thing. I know just what you're going through. Your father was just like that in our marriage. He's just so selfish and self-centered. It always has to be his way or else he gets so angry and controlling. I'm so sorry you have to put up with the way he is. I wish he wasn't like that. You poor thing. How about a bowl of ice cream to help make you feel better. Would you like that? Would that help make you feel better?"

The narcissistic/(borderline) parent places the child into a position of leadership in criticizing the other parent through a combination of motivated and subtly directive parental questioning and the role-reversal use of the child as a "regulatory other" for the emotional and psychological state of the parent. Once the child takes the lead in criticizing the targeted parent, the narcissistic/(borderline) parent responds by adopting the coveted role as the all-wonderful, nurturing and understanding parent. The borderline-style parent will provide a richer display of nurturing affectionate support for the child, and will more prominently display the "protective parent" role. The narcissistic-style parent will tend to show greater contempt and judgment toward the targeted parent's inadequacy as a parent.

In the example above, the mother's comparison of the child's relationship with his father to the mother's own spousal experience with the father during their marriage reflects the boundary dissolution between the mother's psychological experience and the child's. The child's criticism of the father is the same as the mother's because the child is acting as a narcissistic reflection of the mother's attitudes and beliefs from the child's role-reversal use by the mother as a "regulatory object" for the mother's own emotional and psychological state. As the external "regulatory object" for the mother's state, the child is required to provide the parent with a continually fused psychological reflection of the mother's own self-experience. The child's criticism of the father is being derived from the mother's experience with the father, so of course the two share a common experience of the father. However, the mother then uses this reflection of her own state by the child as evidence of her supposed "empathy" with the child, in which she and the child completely understand each other in the "perfection" of their shared love (i.e., "I know just what you're going through").

The mother also uses the similarity of their criticism themes as supposed evidence for the validity of the child's criticism. By presenting their shared criticisms back to the child, the mother highlights their "shared victimization" by the supposedly "abusive" perpetrator of the father. In bonding with the child around their shared experience of the father as "abusive" of them, the mother creates a "shared enemy" that defines an "in-group" and "out-group" within the family. The mother's highlighting for the child of their "shared victimization" creates an "in-group" bond between her and child ("us-versus-him").

This bond of "shared victimization" between the mother and the child can be further embellished if the mother somehow communicates to the child that it was the father who is responsible for the breakup of the family, such as,

> **N/(B) Parent:** "Your father decided to leave our family to start a new life for himself without us."

This type of statement blaming the father for the breakup of the family accomplishes two manipulative goals. First, blaming the father for the breakup of the family can be used to inflame the child' anger toward the father. Second, the mother defines the father as having left "our" family to start a life "without us," which carries the meaning that the father is outside the current family. The subtle use of the term "our" family implies that the other parent is no longer part of "our" family; because he left "us."

The father, in this example, is placed on the outside of the family unit by this manipulative statement that can be embedded in a variety of conversations. This type of manipulative statement that subtly includes the narcissistic/(borderline) parent and child in a shared "us" who are being rejected and abandoned by the other parent can take a variety of forms,

> **N/(B) Parent:** "Your mother decided to leave us because she doesn't care about our family anymore."

> **N/(B) Parent:** "Your father left us to start a new family with his new girlfriend."

By using plural pronouns that subtly exclude the targeted parent from the family, the alliance of the child with the narcissistic/(borderline) parent through their shared victimization creates an "in-group" solidarity with the narcissistic/(borderline) parent of "us-versus-him" (or "us-versus-her") which is amplified by subtle communications to the child that the targeted parent has abandoned the child and family and is now on the outside of the family unit.

In the prior example, the mother then presents to the child a set of themes that are acceptable for criticizing the father. These themes are introduced with a communication of the shared experience of the mother and child ("Your father was just like that in our marriage"). The mother then extends the child's criticism with the themes that the father is "selfish and self-centered" and is "angry and controlling." These themes provided by the mother are supposedly offered as displays of supportive nurturance in response to the child's criticism of the targeted parent, but they actually extend and elaborate on the child's initial criticism, and in doing so they subtly provide the child with parentally endorsed themes for later child criticisms of the targeted parent.

The mother then apologizes for the father's supposed inadequacy. By apologizing to the child for the actions of the father, the mother diminishes the father's status and elevates the child in the family hierarchy to a position above the father, in which the child feels empowered to judge the father's adequacy as a parent. Again, this statement by the mother is seemingly offered as being supportive and nurturing of the child, but it clearly communicates to the child that the father's parenting is wrong, and is so bad that the child "deserves an apology" (is "entitled" to an apology) from the father for the father's "abusive" treatment of the child.

In the final statement, the mother offers the child a narcissistic indulgence, a food treat. This narcissistic indulgence is more than a reward, it is a communication of parental approval. By offering the child a narcissistic indulgence, the parent communicates that the child did well in providing the mother with such rich criticisms of the father, and it signals parental approval for the child's participation in the criticism of the father's parenting. The mother is pleased, which communicates to the child that the child has been successful in the role as the "regulatory other" for the parent's emotional and psychological state.

Once the child has psychologically surrendered to the role-reversal relationship with the narcissistic/(borderline) parent, in which the child serves as the external "regulatory other" for the psychological and emotional state of the narcissistic/(borderline) parent, all the narcissistic/(borderline) parent needs to do in order to create the child's rejection of the targeted parent is to subtly signal to the child the type of parentally desired responses the child is to provide that will keep the parent in an organized and regulated sate. Once the child offers a criticism of the targeted parent, the narcissistic/(borderline) parent can then embellish and inflame the elicited child criticisms into supposed evidence of the "abusive" parental inadequacy of the targeted parent.

During this embellishment of the child's elicited criticism, the narcissistic/(borderline) parent subtly but clearly communicates to the child the acceptable themes for criticizing the targeted parent, which the child can then use in future criticisms.

As a "regulatory other" for the narcissistic/(borderline) parent, the child's criticisms of the targeted parent simply become a reflection of the attitudes held by the narcissistic/(borderline) parent. In highlighting for the child their shared experience of the targeted parent as inadequate and "abusive" of them, the narcissistic/(borderline) parent creates a bond of "shared victimization" with the child, supposedly perpetrated by the "abusive" inadequacy of the targeted parent. All the while, a superficial appearance is maintained to the child (and to the self-experience of the narcissistic/(borderline) parent) that it is the child who is "independently" criticizing the targeted parent, and that the narcissistic/(borderline) parent is simply responding as a concerned, understanding, and nurturing "protective parent" for the poor child who is being "victimized" by the "abusive" parenting of the other parent.

Parental Emotional Signaling

The explicit meaning contained in language is only one aspect of communicating meaning to the child. The meaning of a communication is also conveyed in the emotional tone and relationship context that surrounds the verbal communication. The attachment system of children is especially sensitive to registering parental emotional signals of anxiety and fear, as these parental emotions communicate the presence of a danger that could represent a survival risk for the child.

The importance of parental emotional signaling of anxiety was demonstrated in research by Mineka, Davidson, Cook, and Keir (1984) that examined how young monkeys acquired their fear of snakes. The researchers first placed a baby monkey in a cage alone with a snake. The baby monkey showed no fear of the snake. The investigators then placed the baby monkey and its mother into the cage with the snake. The mother monkey immediately displayed an intense fear of the snake, climbing the side of the cage and making distress calls. The baby monkey was again placed alone in the cage with a snake. This time the baby monkey displayed the same intense fear of the snake as it had previously witnessed from its mother. The young monkey had acquired a fear of snakes through the emotional signaling provided by the mother.

It is easy to understand how a parent's emotional signaling of anxiety would provide children with a significant survival advantage. By socially referencing the parent's perception of threat the child would learn which aspects of the environment are dangerous and represent a threat to the child's survival. Children who attended to their parent's emotional signals of anxiety and concern would survive at higher rates than children who disregarded their parents' emotional signals of anxiety and concern.

From an evolutionary perspective, predation represents one of the primary threats to children. Predators selectively target the old, the weak, and the young. Children are prey animals. The attachment system motivating children's bonding to parents evolved in response to the selective predation of children. Children who registered and responded to parental emotional signals of anxiety would avoid predation at higher rates than children who disregarded their parents' emotional signals of anxiety. The attachment system is therefore highly sensitized to registering parental signals of anxiety and threat perception.

The attachment system is a primary motivational system that strongly promotes children's bonding to parents. The attachment system developed in response to the selective predation of children. Children who formed affectional attachment bonds to parents would receive parental protection from predators. As a result, genes promoting children's attachment bonding to parents increased in the collective gene pool. On the other hand, children who bonded less strongly to their parents received less parental protection from predators and so fell prey to predators at higher rates, so that genes promoting weak, or even moderate attachment bonding to parents were selectively removed from the collective gene pool.

As a consequence of the selective predation of children, a primary motivational system developed that strongly promotes children's attachment bonding to their parents, particularly when the parent displays emotional signals of heightened anxiety and threat perception. The mother monkey in the Mineka et al. study did not need to directly instruct the child in the dangers posed by the snake. The child naturally acquired a fear of snakes by "socially referencing" the emotional signals of anxiety and fear displayed by the mother. Because of the significant survival advantage conferred to children from socially referencing and responding to parental displays of anxiety, the attachment system of children is neuro-biologically sensitized to register parental emotional signals of anxiety.

Heightened parental anxiety is conveyed both directly, through over-anxious indicators of heightened parental concern, and indirectly, through parental "retrieval behaviors" in which the parent seeks out the child and intrudes on the child's exploratory behavior in order to keep the child close to the parent for protection. While parents respond with retrieval behaviors surrounding a variety of environmental threats to the child, parental retrieval behaviors are a particularly characteristic parental response to the presence of a predator in the child's environment. Children's attachment system is therefore particularly sensitized to registering the parental communication of threat through parental retrieval behavior of preventing the child's separation and seeking to keep the child close to the parent.

Communicating Parental Anxiety

In attachment-based "parental alienation," there are a variety of ways that the narcissistic/(borderline) parent signals anxiety to the child regarding the supposed risk being posed to the child by the parenting practices of the targeted parent. One of the primary ways is through the over-anxious questioning of the child by the narcissistic/(borderline) parent following visitations with the other parent. The over-anxious and over-concerned questioning of the child by the narcissistic/(borderline) parent regarding what occurred at the other parent's house represents a clear communication to the child of heightened parental anxiety concerning the child's safety and well-being when the child is with the other parent. This hyper-vigilant monitoring of the child's well-being whenever the child is with the other parent communicates to the child that the anxious narcissistic/(borderline) parent perceives the parenting practices of the other parent to represent some type of threat to the child.

Parental anxiety can be communicated to the child through both the animated and concerned emotional tone of the narcissistic/(borderline) parent during the questioning of the child, much as the mother monkey's emotional tone communicated to the young monkey the threat posed by the snake, and through the content of parental questions that have as their implied premise that the parenting practices of the other parent present a threat to the child, such as:

- "Was everything okay at your father's house?"
- "Did you and your mother have any problems?"
- "Did anything bad happen while you were with your father?"

The content of these types of questions all contain the implication that the narcissistic/(borderline) parent expects that there might be some type of problem for the child when the child is in the care of the other parent. The parent asking these types of anxiety-signaling questions will justify them as simply showing natural parental concern for the child's well-being. However, the anxiety-based premise of these types of questions subtly but clearly communicates to the child the parent's concern and expectation that the parenting practices of the other parent represent some form of threat to the child. The neurobiology of the attachment system is highly sensitized by evolutionary pressures to recognize parental emotional signals of anxiety. These types of anxiety laden questions will be registered by the child's attachment system. The heightened anxiety of the "protective" narcissistic/(borderline) parent will then activate the child's attachment networks to respond in characteristic ways to parental signals of a threat to the child.

Anxiety-signaling parental questioning of the child regarding visitation experiences with the other parent will also triangulate the child into any existing "spousal" conflict by inviting the child to offer criticisms of the other parent. These parentally elicited child criticisms of the other parent will then be used to triangulate the child into any existing conflict within the spousal relationship. Child criticisms of one parent offered to the other parent can be used to induce the child into forming a cross-generational coalition with one parent, who becomes the favored and allied parent, against the other parent, who becomes the criticized and rejected parent.

In healthy and successful post-divorce families, where the parents get along and cooperate with each other, questions about the child's experience with the other parent pose less of a risk for triangulating the child into spousal conflicts because there is less post-divorce spousal conflict, and what spousal conflict does exist is successfully contained within the post-divorce spousal relationship. However, in post-divorce families where there is a high degree of active and unresolved inter-spousal conflict, asking the child about experiences with the other parent runs a considerable risk of being used to triangulate the child into the active and unresolved spousal conflict.

These types of anxiety-signaling questions contrast with parental questions that convey a more neutral or positive parental expectation, such as,

- "So, did you have fun at your dad's house?"
- "How were things at your mom's, did you guys do anything fun together?"
- "So, what did you do at your dad's house?"

These neutral or positively toned questions do not convey the parental expectation that bad things happened at the other parent's house, and these questions may actually indicate that the questioning parent anticipates that the child enjoys spending time with the other parent. Still, asking the child about experiences with the other parent always runs the risk of triangulating the child into spousal conflicts, even with positively toned or neutral questions.

A second primary means of emotionally communicating parental anxiety to the child is indirectly, through parental "retrieval behaviors." From an evolutionary perspective, when a parent saw a predator or other threat to the child, the parent would seek out the child and pull the child close, interrupting the child's exploratory behavior and preventing the child's separation from the protection afforded by the parent. This parental display is referred to as "retrieval behavior" by the parent. Parental retrieval behavior communicates to the child that the parent perceives a threat to the child in the environment. By communicating a parental perception of threat, parental retrieval behaviors activate the child's own attachment bonding system, thereby motivating corresponding attachment behaviors from the child that motivate the child to remain close to the protective parent and which terminate the child's motivations for exploratory behavior away from the protective parent who is displaying the retrieval behavior.

Parental retrieval behaviors work in tandem with the child's own attachment behaviors. The parent is motivated to seek out the child and to keep the child close for protection, and the attachment system of the child responds to the parental signal of retrieval behaviors by terminating the child's motivations for independent exploratory behavior away from the parent and motivating the child to remain close to the protective parent. This set of mutually coordinated parent and child attachment behaviors acts to provide the child with parental protection from threats, particularly the threat of predation.

From the perspective of evolution, children whose motivation for remaining close to the protective parent activated in response to parental retrieval behaviors more effectively avoided risks. These children survived at higher rates than children who disregarded the parental signals of threat perception contained in the display of parental retrieval behaviors. Children who disregarded the signaled parental perception of threat conveyed by parental retrieval behaviors were more likely to fall prey to predators and other environmental dangers that were recognized by the parent but were unrecognized by the child. As a result of the selective survival advantage provided to children who responded to parental retrieval behaviors with decreased motivation for exploratory behavior away from the parent and increased motivation to remain closely bonded to the protective parent, a set of characteristic child responses to parental retrieval behaviors became embedded in the neurological networks of the child's attachment system.

Parental emotional signals of heightened anxiety combined with a display of parental retrieval behaviors clearly communicates to the child's attachment system that the "protective parent" perceives a threat to the child in the environment. Together, emotional signals of parental anxiety and displays of parental retrieval behaviors will subconsciously activate the child's attachment system, which will then terminate the child's motivation for exploratory behavior away from the proximity of the protective parent, and simultaneously motivate the child to remain in the continual physical proximity of the protective parent who is the source of the anxiety signals.

These are exactly the behaviors seen in attachment-based "parental alienation," in which the child's motivations for exploration of an independent relationship with the targeted parent are terminated and the child seeks to remain in the continual "protective" proximity of the narcissistic/(borderline) parent. Of significant note in the creation of attachment-based "parental alienation" is how the narcissistic/(borderline) parent both conveys to the child a sense of threat posed to the child by the targeted parent, and also how the narcissistic/(borderline) parent adopts and prominently displays to the child the role as the "protective parent." It is the tandem of these two parental roles, the communication of parental threat perception and the role as the "protective parent," that fully triggers the activation of the child's neurologically embedded attachment system response to parental signals of threat perception.

Protest Behavior at Visitation Transfer

When the child is being transferred to the care of the other parent for visitation, the narcissistic/(borderline) parent can elicit child protest behavior at visitation transfers through subtle parental communications to the child in the child's role as a "regulatory other" for the parent. The narcissistic/(borderline) parent subtly communicates to the child a parental desire for the child to protest transfer to the other parent. The child is sensitized to registering and responding to the wants and needs of the narcissistic/(borderline) parent through the child's role as the "regulatory object" for parent. Subtle communications to the child by the narcissistic/(borderline) parent that the parent wants and would welcome child protest behavior surrounding the transfer of custody to the targeted parent can elicit protest from the child regarding the transfer of custody over to the other parent. Parental signals contained in verbal communications to the child might include:

> **N/(B) Parent:** "I know you don't want to go, but the court says you have to. It will only be for a few days, and then you'll be able to come home."

> **N/(B) Parent:** "Try not to worry or get too upset. If anything bad happens you have my phone number and you can call me."

In the first communication, the statement "I know you don't want to go..." gives the child in a role-reversal relationship clear instructions for what the child is supposed to want, or in this case not want. In a role-reversal relationship the child becomes a narcissistic reflection for the wants and needs of the parent in order to keep the parent in an organized and regulated state. The parental statement, "I know you don't want to go…" communicates to the child in a role-reversal relationship that this is the state the parent wants the child to adopt, i.e., that the child doesn't want to be separated from the narcissistic/(borderline) parent and go be with the targeted parent.

In a "call-and-response" fashion, this parental statement then elicits the called for response from the child of,

> **Child:** "But I don't want to go. I hate it over there. Don't make me go."

In addition to the verbal protest of the child, the child may then emit an escalation of protest at being transferred to the care of the targeted parent, such as refusing to get into the car of targeted parent. The narcissistic/(borderline) parent responds to the child's protest behavior either with non-action, communicating tacit support for the child's protest behavior, or with active sympathetic nurture for the child's supposed distress that communicates to the child that the child's protest is somehow justified and understandable, and that the child's protest behavior is the correct behavior to meet the emotional and psychological needs of the narcissistic/(borderline) parent.

The next statement by the narcissistic/(borderline) parent in the example, that "the court says you have to" go on visitations with the targeted parent, holds the implied extension, "but if it was up to me you wouldn't have to go be with the other parent." This implied extension statement carries a very subtle communication in the role-reversal relationship. The narcissistic/(borderline) parent is subtly communicating to the child that the parent doesn't want the child to go on visitations with the other parent (i.e., "if it was up to me you wouldn't go"). For a child in a role-reversal relationship, this carries the instructions as to what the narcissistic/(borderline) parent needs from the child in order for the parent to remain in an organized and regulated emotional and psychological state.

The most diabolical of the communications made to the child in the first example is, "It will only be for a few days, and then you'll get to come home." This carries two profound implications. First, that there actually is something bad about being with the other parent that must be tolerated by the child. Second, that the child's true home is with the narcissistic/(borderline) parent. This second communication defines the targeted parent as an outsider; that the child does not belong to the targeted parent. The targeted parent is not part of the family. The child's "true home" is with the narcissistic/(borderline) parent.

In the second example of eliciting the child's protest behavior at visitation transfer, the opening statement of "Try not to worry or get too upset" gives the child clear instructions regarding the parentally desired behavior; i.e., that the child should become anxious and upset about the visitation transfer to the targeted parent. This parental directive to the child can be confirmed by the child through the parental response the child receives from the narcissistic/(borderline) parent when the child becomes anxious and upset at the visitation transfer. If the child receives parental shows of comfort and support for the child's anxiety and protest, then the child has confirmation that the "try not to" part of the parental instruction was an irrelevant parental message, and that the true message was the parent's desire for the child to "become worried and upset."

When the child then displays anxiety and emotional upset at the transfer of care to the targeted parent, the narcissistic/(borderline) parent provides the child with expressions of parental understanding and concern for the supposed suffering of the child, such as:

N/(B) Parent: "I know you hate going over there, honey. I'm so sorry you have to go. I wish you didn't have to go. I'm so sorry."

These parental statements of supposed support and understanding communicate to the child that the child's distress and fear of being with the other parent is actually justified and warranted. These supposed offers of parental "understanding and support" for the child's supposed distress are clear parental communications to the child by the narcissistic/(borderline) parent that the parenting of the targeted parent is extremely bad and "abusive" of the child. Yet despite the clarity of these communications made to the child regarding the supposedly "abusive' parenting of the targeted parent, when the child is asked,

Custody Evaluator: "Does your parent ever say bad things about the other parent in front of you?"

the child responds,

Child: "No."

Technically this is true, if the question concerns verbal statements made by the narcissistic/(borderline) parent. However, if we consider non-verbally conveyed meaning, the narcissistic/(borderline) parent clearly and continually communicates to the child:

1. **Abusive Inadequacy:** That the parenting practices of the targeted parent are inadequate and "abusive" of the child.
2. **Desired Rejection:** That a required response of the child for the continued emotional and psychological regulation of the narcissistic/(borderline) parent is that the child reject being with the targeted parent.

These communications are simply made to the child by the narcissistic/(borderline) parent in powerful non-verbal channels, rather than though more overtly identifiable verbal channels of communication. As far as the child is aware, the narcissistic/(borderline) parent is simply being understanding and supportive of the child.

As time progresses and the pathology becomes more entrenched, the child may begin to emit more overt protests and resistance behavior at the transfer of visitation to the targeted parent. In response to these increased signs of protest from the child, the narcissistic/(borderline) parent will typically become passive in ensuring the successful transfer of the child ("What am I supposed to do? I can't force the child to go with the other parent").

A fundamental parental obligation is to ensure correct behavior of their children. What the narcissistic/(borderline) parent is essentially saying in this overt abdication of parental responsibility is that the narcissistic/(borderline) parent is declining to exercise appropriate parenting with the child.

In a role-reversal relationship with the child, communications of instructions to the child often take a reversal form.

N/(B) Parent: "Try not to become upset" communicates "Become upset."

N/(B) Parent: "Try to get along with your mom" communicates "Don't get along with your mom."

N/(B) Parent: "If anything bad happens, you can call me" communicates "Make something bad happen and call me."

The child can always confirm the meaning of these parental reversal communications by the response the child receives from the narcissistic/(borderline) parent for following the reversal instructions. If the child receives a nurturing and supportive response from the narcissistic/(borderline) parent for following the reversal instructions, then the child's interpretation is confirmed. If the child receives an angry and hostile response from the narcissistic/(borderline) parent, then the child did the wrong thing. So when the child responds to the parental reversal instruction of, "Try not to become upset" by becoming upset, if the child receives a parental response of nurture and comforting from the narcissistic/(borderline) parent then the child has confirmed that the narcissistic/(borderline) parent did indeed want the child to become upset. If the narcissistic/(borderline) parent responds with anger and hostility to the child becoming upset, then the child realizes that the overt verbal communication was the true communication. When the narcissistic/(borderline) parent tells the child, "If anything bad happens you have my phone number and you can call me," this communicates instructions to the child to manufacture something bad with the targeted parent and then to call the narcissistic/(borderline) parent about it. When the narcissistic/(borderline) parent responds to the child's text message, email, or phone call with understanding support for the child's supposed distress, this communicates to the child that the child correctly interpreted the parent's message, and that narcissistic/(borderline) parents seeks these exchanges to maintain the emotional and psychological regulation of the parent.

All of these parental communications are covert, but their meaning to the child in the role-reversal relationship is clear. However, the narcissistic/(borderline) parent maintains at least superficial deniability. The narcissistic/(borderline) parent will frame these statements as simply being supportive, understanding, and nurturing of the child's (supposedly justified) distress about having to spend time with the ("abusive") targeted parent.

This display of child protest behavior and parental understanding and nurture also acts to present the narcissistic/(borderline) parent to the child as being the concerned "protective parent," thereby further cementing their bond. The three primary roles in the trauma reenactment narrative are the "abusive parent," the "victimized child," and the "protective parent." By eliciting the child's supposed "victimization" by the "abusive" targeted parent, the narcissistic/(borderline) parent is allowed to adopt and then conspicuously display to the child and to "bystanders" the role of the "protective parent." In the presence of a parentally identified threat, the neurological networks of the child's attachment system motivate the child to flee from the parentally identified threat and seek bonding protection from the "protective parent," which is the role being conspicuously displayed to the child by the narcissistic/(borderline) parent.

The activation of the child's attachment system response to parentally signaled threat perception creates a characteristic pattern of child behavior at visitation transfers in which the child makes hyper-dramatic and ostentatious displays of protest at being transferred to the care of the other parent. The child may cry and plead not to be "forced" to go on the visitation with the targeted parent, and the child may either refuse to get out of the car of the narcissistic/(borderline) parent or refuse to get into the car of the targeted parent. Younger children may make a great display of clinging behavior with the narcissistic/(borderline) parent. In some cases the young child may need to be physically pried away from the narcissistic/(borderline) parent in order to make the transfer to the other parent.

The excessive displays of child anxiety at visitation transfer is typically created by the abandonment fears of the borderline-style personality. The primal fear of the borderline-style parent is that if the child is allowed to develop a bonded relationship with the targeted parent, then the child will also abandon the borderline parent just like the other spouse did. In the splitting dynamic of the borderline personality process, ambiguity is impossible. Within the splitting dynamic, the ex-spouse must also become the ex-parent. Within the mind of the narcissistic/(borderline) parent, whoever has possession of the child becomes the parent, and the other person becomes an ex-parent/ex-spouse. The splitting dynamic does not allow ambiguity and mixed roles. The splitting dynamic neurologically imposes polarized perceptions.

For the narcissistic/(borderline) parent, if the child is allowed to bond to the targeted parent then this means that the narcissistic/(borderline) parent will be abandoned by the child. The fear contained within the attachment schemas of the narcissistic/(borderline) parent is of being abandoned and rejected by the attachment figure. The fear of the narcissistic/(borderline) parent is that if the child is allowed to bond to the targeted parent then the targeted parent will take possession of the child and they will both abandon the narcissistic/(borderline) parent.

The potential for the child's abandonment of the narcissistic/(borderline) parent triggers an excessive anxiety for the parent. By making ostentatious displays of not wanting to be separated from the narcissistic/(borderline) parent, the child is serving as the "regulatory object" for stabilizing the abandonment fears of narcissistic/(borderline) personality structure. When the child is separated from the narcissistic/(borderline) parent during visitations with the targeted parent, then the regulatory function of the child is not available to the narcissistic/(borderline) parent and the personality structure of the narcissistic/(borderline) parent is threatened with collapse into disorganization and dysregulation. The potential abandonment of the narcissistic/(borderline) parent by the "regulatory object" of the child creates excessive parental anxiety surrounding separation from the child that could lead to the child's bonding with the other parent.

The experience of intense anxiety surrounding the parent's abandonment fears which is triggered by separations from the "regulatory object" of the child is misinterpreted by the narcissistic/(borderline) parent as representing an authentic emotional signal that the targeted parent represents some form of threat. This supposed threat posed by the child's transfer to the targeted parent is then identified as being a threat posed to the child by the "abusive" parenting of the targeted parent. The actual threat is from the impending collapse of narcissistic/(borderline) parent's fragile self-regulation which will occur if the child is allowed to form an attached bond to the other parent. However, the narcissistic/(borderline) parent lacks sufficient self-insight to make an accurate interpretation of an authentic experience of anxiety. Instead, the narcissistic/(borderline) parent interprets the excessive anxiety created by the child's potential bonding to the other parent as incorrectly indicating that the other parent presents some form of threat to the child, which then requires the "protective" response of the narcissistic/(borderline) parent. In the pathology of the narcissistic/(borderline) parent, the child requires "protection" from the threat posed to the child by the targeted parent.

This excessive anxiety and distorted threat perception of the narcissistic/(borderline) parent is then transferred to the child who, in the role-reversal as a "regulatory object" for the parent, adopts a reflective psychological state to that of the narcissistic/(borderline) parent. The child adopts an anxiety response to the targeted parent that then invites the narcissistic/(borderline) parent to "protect the child" by keeping the child away from the targeted parent. The child's display of excessive anxiety about forming a relationship with the targeted parent is serving a regulatory function for the emotional and psychological state of the narcissistic/(borderline) parent. This is the essence of a role-reversal relationship in which the child is used as an external "regulatory object" for the emotional and psychological state of the parent.

The parental display of anxiety by the narcissistic/(borderline) parent also triggers the child's attachment system response to threat, which motivates the child to remain in the continual physical proximity to the "protective parent" who is emitting the anxiety signal. This also creates the child's protest behavior at visitation. The child's attachment system does not want to be separated from the "protective parent." The motivational press of the attachment system is a predator-driven response. As such, it is extremely strong. The child's protest display at separation created by the activation of the child's attachment system can be exceedingly strong and demonstrative.

The child's protest behavior then receives displays of parental nurture and overt shows of parental reassurance from the narcissistic/(borderline) parent.

> **N/(B) Parent:** "Don't worry, it will only be for a few days, and I'm just a phone call away. I know you're scared. I am too. But it will be okay."

These parental displays of nurture and reassurance are ostensibly offered to comfort the child's distress, but they actually communicate that the child's fears are justified and carry the meaning that the targeted parent actually does represent some form of threat to the child which requires the reassurance and comfort of the "protective" narcissistic/(borderline) parent.

Despite the child's protests at visitation transfers, once the child's transfer to the targeted parent is finally achieved the child's display of protest behavior will oftentimes subside and the child will resume a normal-range relationship with the targeted parent (although the longer the "alienation" continues the more entrenched and longer lasting the child's symptoms will become). This restoration of the child's normal-range response to the targeted parent following visitation transfer occurs once the child is no longer being actively exposed to the parental signals of anxiety from the narcissistic/(borderline) parent. In the absence of parental signals of anxiety, the child's attachment system response to parental signals of threat disengages, allowing the child to recover normal-range motivations for affectional bonding with the targeted parent. In addition, parental signals of anxiety and threat perception turn off the child's motivations for exploratory behavior. Once the child is no longer directly exposed to the parental anxiety signals emanating from the narcissistic/(borderline) parent, the child recovers normal-range motivations for exploratory behavior in forming a relationship with the targeted parent.

However, the longer the pathology of the narcissistic/(borderline) parent is allowed to influence the child's attachment bonding motivations toward the targeted parent, the more entrenched the child's pathological responses to the targeted parent will become, and the child will gradually begin to display increasingly diminished recovery following visitation transfers. The child will begin to avoid interacting with the targeted parent while in the care of this parent, the child will begin to show a diminished interest in exploratory behavior with the targeted parent of going on outings and doing activities with this parent, and the child will display an increasingly obsessive fixation on restoring contact with the (supposedly) "protective" narcissistic/(borderline) parent through excessive texting, emails, and phone calls to the narcissistic/(borderline) parent while the child is in the care of the targeted parent.

Excessive displays by the child of emotional distress at visitation transfers also become increasingly stressful for the child to endure. Over time, the child will begin to dread the impending over-emotionality of these transfer events, and the child will begin to experience anticipatory stress prior to the visitation transfer centering on the impending distress at the transfer. The emotional distress created for the child by transfers of custody to the targeted parent eventually begins to produce avoidance behavior in which the child seeks to avoid the emotional distress of custody transfers by seeking to remain the continual care of the "protective" narcissistic/(borderline) parent.

Under the distorting influence of the narcissistic/(borderline) parent the child will misinterpret the anticipatory stress as being a fearfulness of being with the targeted parent. Expressions of anticipatory stress and anxiety will receive nurturing and comforting responses from the narcissistic/(borderline) parent, who will begin to support the child by insisting that the child not be "forced" to go on visitations with the targeted parent. However, it is not being with the targeted parent that is actually producing the child's stress and anticipatory anxiety, it is the pathology of the narcissistic/(borderline) parent.

Eventually, the child's anticipatory anxiety surrounding custody transfers that is creating a stressful visitation transfer to the targeted parent can result in the child evidencing a generalized phobic anxiety surrounding the targeted parent, in which the child expresses fear of the targeted parent and seeks to avoid transfer to the care of the targeted parent. Mental health professionals who are unfamiliar with how the child's anxiety symptoms have been created by the pathology of the narcissistic/(borderline) parent may misinterpret the child's phobic anxiety symptoms as indicating that the parenting practices of the targeted parent represent some form of authentic threat to the child. The child's anxiety symptoms thereby place the targeted parent in a position of continually having to prove a negative; i.e., that the parenting practices of the targeted parent are not "abusive" of the child and are not responsible for the child's phobic symptoms.

Two pathogenic factors in the child's relationship with the narcissistic/(borderline) parent are responsible for these displays of excessive child protest behavior at visitation transfer:

1. The child's role as a "regulatory object" for the emotional and psychological state of the narcissistic/(borderline) parent;

2. The natural response of the child's attachment system to parental signals of threat.

The Child's Role as a "Regulatory Object"

The child is being used by the narcissistic/(borderline) parent as a "regulatory other" for maintaining the emotional and psychological regulation of the narcissistic/(borderline) parent. The child's displays of anxiety and protest at visitations are for the benefit of regulating the parent's emotional and psychological state. The child's protest behavior at visitation transfers reassures the fears of the narcissistic/(borderline) parent regarding abandonment and potential bonding of the child with the targeted parent, and allows the narcissistic/(borderline) parent to adopt the coveted role as the nurturing "protective parent." The child's protest behavior also confers power to the narcissistic/(borderline) parent to deny visitations to the targeted parent. The narcissistic/(borderline) parent is able to exploit the child's protest behavior to nullify the parental rights of the targeted parent to shared joint custody, including the nullification of court orders for shared visitation and custody (e.g., "What can I do? The child doesn't want to go on visitations with the other parent. I can't force the child go.").

In the face of intensive and excessive child protest behavior, courts may become reluctant to enforce orders for shared custody and visitation. Instead, the court will often defer to mental health in evaluating and treating the child's intensive protest behavior toward visitation transfers to the targeted parent. Mental health professionals who are unfamiliar with the complex dynamics of attachment-based parental alienation may not accurately diagnose and interpret the child's symptom display, and so may wind up colluding with the pathology of attachment-based "parental alienation.

Attachment Response to Threat

A second prominent factor contributing to the child's protest behavior at visitation transfers is the subliminal activation of the child's attachment system response to a parental signal of threat to the child. The narcissistic/(borderline) parent is communicating to the child a parental perception of threat through emotional signals of parental anxiety and parental retrieval behaviors that seek to terminate the child's exploratory behavior away from the parent and keep the child in close proximity to the "protective parent."

The child's attachment system response to parental signals of threat perception is to terminate the child's motivation for independent exploratory behavior away from the "protective parent." As a result, the child's natural motivations to be with the targeted parent are turned off. Instead, the response of the child's attachment system to parental emotional signals of anxiety and threat perception is to motivate the child to avoid (flee from) the parentally identified threat and to remain close to the "protective parent" in order to receive parental "protection" from the danger (e.g., from the predator).

The role as the "protective parent" is being adopted and conspicuously displayed to the child by the narcissistic/(borderline) parent through parental signals of anxious over-concern and through nurturing caregiving responses offered to the child in response to the child's (elicited) displays of distress. By providing the child with nurturing support for the child's reluctance to go on visitations with the targeted parent, the narcissistic/(borderline) parent is also providing a signal of parental retrieval behavior by the "protective parent" who is seeking to keep the child close and prevent the child's exploratory behavior that would separate the child from the "protective parent."

Role-Reversal Displays of Parental Sadness

Displays of parental anxiety are not the only way the narcissistic/(borderline) parent can elicit the child's protest behavior at visitation transfers. The child's protest behaviors can also be elicited by conspicuous parental displays of immense sadness at being separated from the child. The child is motivated through his or her role as a "regulatory object" for the narcissistic/(borderline) to respond in ways that keep the parent in a regulated emotional and psychological state. Parental displays of sadness at separation activate the child's desire to reassure and soothe the parent's emotional distress as the "regulatory object" for the emotional and psychological state of the parent. A parental display of over-sadness at separation elicits from the child a corresponding regulatory response of seeking to reassure the parent ("Don't worry, I won't leave you").

By offering the sad parent reassurance and nurture, the child is fulfilling the child's role-reversal function within the parent-child relationship to be the external "regulatory object" for the parent to keep the parent in an emotionally and psychologically regulated state. The child's verbal and behavioral reassurances provided to the parent (that communicate, "Don't worry, I'll never leave you") represent a regulatory response to the narcissistic/(borderline) personality's fear of abandonment. Central to the pathology of attachment-based "parental alienation" is the role-reversal relationship in which the child is being used by the parent as a "regulatory object" to meet the emotional and psychological needs of the parent. By displaying great sadness at being separated from the child, the narcissistic/(borderline) parent elicits from the child the complementary response of nurturing reassurance for the parent that the child will not leave (will not abandon) the narcissistic/(borderline) parent.

Borderline-style personalities in particular are quite adept at using displays of emotional vulnerability and guilt induction as manipulative means of engaging the continual involvement of others in order to avoid being abandoned by the attachment figure. When these manipulative displays of vulnerability from a borderline-style parent are directed toward a child, these displays can be quite powerful in eliciting a complementary (verbal or behavioral) nurturing response from the child ("Don't worry, I won't leave you"). This relationship pattern of sad-displays by the parent and nurturing responses from the child is essentially a "call-and-response" pattern of social reciprocity. The parent emits the "call" by signaling parental sadness at separation, and the child emits the corresponding "response" of reassurance: "Don't worry, I won't leave you."

<u>Role-Reversal Exploitation of the Child</u>

The twin child displays at separation from the narcissistic/(borderline) parent of the "clinging-anxious child" and the "nurturing-reassuring child" represent the role-reversal relationship with the narcissistic/(borderline) parent in which the child being used to regulate the emotional and psychological needs of the parent. The "clinging-anxious child" display allows the narcissistic/(borderline) parent to become the "protective parent" which then serves to regulate the parent's own anxieties at separation through projective identification with the child. The narcissistic/(borderline) parent is also able to exploit the symptom display of the anxious-rejecting child to interfere with, and eventually terminate, the other parent's ability to form an affectionally bonded relationship with the child.

The "nurturing-reassuring" child role is used by the narcissistic/(borderline) parent to regulate the parent's abandonment fears at being separated from the attachment figure of the child. The sadness of the parent elicits the reassurance of the child that the child will "never leave" the parent. In the anxious-rejecting child and the nurturing-reassuring child, the child's protest at separating from the narcissistic/(borderline) parent is serving a regulatory function for the emotional and psychological state of the narcissistic/(borderline) parent.

This represents a clear display of a role-reversal relationship. In a developmentally healthy parent-child relationship, the child uses the parent as a "regulatory other" for the child's emotional and psychological state. In a role-reversal relationship, the parent uses the child to regulate the emotional and psychological state of the parent. Through the role-reversal relationship, the parent is essentially feeding off of the child's healthy self-structure development in order to support the inadequate self-regulation of the narcissistic/(borderline) personality. The damaged narcissistic/(borderline) personality structure lacks the capacity for internalized self-regulation so it is relying instead on the external regulatory support (scaffolding support) provided by the child for the regulation of the parent's emotional and psychological state. This is extremely pathological and damaging to the child's healthy development.

The regulatory responses provided by the child to the conspicuous displays of parental anxiety and sadness at separation are not expressed verbally by the child to the parent. The parent and child instead perform a coordinated dance of emotional signaling. The parent provides emotional signals to the child that then elicit corresponding behaviors and emotional signals from the child that reassure and regulate the parent's emotional and psychological state. By protesting visitation transfers of care to the targeted parent, the child is regulating the emotional and psychological state of the narcissistic/(borderline) parent through a role-reversal relationship with the pathology of the parent. The intense child protests at being separated from the narcissistic/(borderline) parent act as a behavioral communication to the parent that effectively conveys the child's desire to remain with the narcissistic/(borderline) parent, and are just as effective in conveying meaning as verbal statements.

For the narcissistic-style personality, the child's expressed reluctance and protest about being transferred to the care of targeted parent communicate:

Conveyed Meaning: "You are such a wonderful and perfect parent that I can't bear to be separated from you to be with the inadequate and awful targeted parent."

For the borderline-style personality, the child's expressed reluctance and protest about being transferred to the care of targeted parent communicate:

Conveyed Meaning: "Don't worry, I will never abandon you."

Once the child's protest behavior at separation has been elicited, the narcissistic/(borderline) parent will then actively support the child's protest displays through the passive parental acceptance for the legitimacy of the child's protest behavior. The actively tacit parental support of the narcissistic/(borderline) parent for the child's protest behavior at being with the targeted parent is evidenced in statements such as:

N/(B) Parent: "What can I do? I can't force the child go on visitations with the other parent."

N/(B) Parent: "What am I supposed to do, drag the child from my car?"

N/(B) Parent: "The child should be allowed to decide whether or not to go on visitations with the other parent."

N/(B) Parent: "The child should not be forced to go on visitations with the other parent."

This passive non-assertion by the narcissistic/(borderline) parent of normal-range parental authority to expect and require child cooperation with parental directives (and court orders) effectively communicates to the child the support of the narcissistic/(borderline) parent for the child's protest behavior. In a role-reversal relationship, the child is highly sensitized to reading parental cues regarding how to keep the parent in an organized and regulated emotional and psychological state. In typical situations, if the child were to displease the narcissistic/(borderline) parent the child is sure to receive clear and direct communications of parental displeasure from the narcissistic/(borderline) parent which would alter and correct the child's behavior. The absence of parental signals of displeasure serve as clear communications to the child that the narcissistic/(borderline) parent is NOT displeased with the child's protest behavior. The absence of parental disapproval given to the child's protest about being with the targeted parent that is provided to the child's behavior by the narcissistic/(borderline) parent clearly communicates to the child the support of the narcissistic/(borderline) parent for the child's protest behavior.

The inauthenticity of the selective parental helplessness displayed at visitation transfers can be highlighted if the narcissistic/(borderline) parent is asked if he or she has the same difficulty getting the child to do homework, go to school, or attend medical appointments. In all of these other situations the narcissistic/(borderline) parent will report that the child is fully compliant to the directives of the narcissistic/(borderline) parent. In an effort to appear as the perfect and ideal parent, the narcissistic/(borderline) parent will often make a point of saying how extraordinarily well-behaved the child is with the narcissistic/(borderline) parent, which carries the implied narcissistic reflection for how wonderful and perfect the narcissistic/(borderline) parent is as a parent.

Yet in this one select situation of transferring custody to the targeted parent, the child becomes disobedient and defiant. This is not credible. In truth, the child is also being entirely obedient to the desires of the narcissistic/(borderline) parent in this situation as well. In protesting visitation transfers the child is doing exactly what the narcissistic/(borderline) parent wants the child to do, and the child understands this. The child understands that the narcissistic/(borderline) parent is not displeased by the child's protest behavior because of the absent exercise of an effective parental authority by the narcissistic/(borderline) parent, and through the offers of support, nurture, comfort, and understanding from the narcissistic/(borderline) parent for the child's expressed reluctance to be with the targeted parent.

In the kabuki theater display of the visitation transfers, the selective display of child protest behavior only about being with the targeted parent is meant to indicate how horrible the parenting practices of the targeted parent are to be inducing in the otherwise mature and cooperative child an extreme reluctance to go on visitations with the targeted parent. This meaning, which is so clearly communicated by the child's symptoms, thereby imposes onto the targeted parent the "abusive parent" role in the trauma reenactment narrative. The role as the "abusive parent" is imposed onto the targeted parent solely through the child's induced symptom display of protest behavior. The child is presenting as obedient to the directives and desires of the narcissistic/(borderline) parent in every other situation besides the transfer of custody to the targeted parent. The implied meaning is that the only explanation for the child's selective protest is the horrible parenting of the targeted parent that is creating the child's extreme reluctance to be with the targeted parent.

In truth, however, the child is also being entirely obedient to the clearly, but subtly, communicated directives of the narcissistic/(borderline) parent to protest custody transfers to the targeted parent. In the role-reversal relationship with the narcissistic/(borderline) parent, the child has psychologically surrendered into the role of the "regulatory other" for the emotional and psychological needs of the narcissistic/(borderline) parent. In protesting visitations with the targeted parent, the child is absolutely following the implicit instructions of the narcissistic/(borderline) parent.

The implicit instructions from the narcissistic/(borderline) parent are often given to the child through their reversed form (e.g., "don't be scared" means "act scared") and through emotional signals of parental approval that are provided to the child. Parental approval for the child's protest behavior is provided either by the tacit acceptance of the child's protest or by the nurturing reassurance the child receives from the narcissistic/(borderline) parent in response to the child's supposed distress. Communication occurs across multiple channels. The mixed message communication of the narcissistic/(borderline) parent can verbally direct the child to go on visitations with the other parent while the secondary non-verbal communication channels direct the child to protest visitation transfers.

> **N/(B) Parent:** "Oh honey, I'm so sorry you have to go to be with your mother. I know how much you hate being over there. I'm going to miss you so much too. It's only for a couple of days and then you'll be able to come home."
>
> **Child:** <crying> "I don't want to go, I don't want to go!"
>
> **N/(B) Parent:** "I know, honey. I know how mom is, and I know how much you hate it over there. Give me a hug, sweetie. It's only for a

couple of days. If anything bad happens just call me and I'll try to come get you. Oh, you poor thing. I'm so sorry you have to go over there."

These displays of parental reassurance from the narcissistic/(borderline) parent clearly communicate that the child's protests at being transferred to the care of the other parent are not displeasing the narcissistic/(borderline) parent. Furthermore, the displays of parental nurture for the child's protests communicate that the child's feelings are somehow legitimate, that there is some sort of valid reason for the child's distress at being in the care of the targeted parent. The supposedly "reassuring" statements made by the narcissistic/(borderline) parent that the visit with the other parent is "only for a couple of days and then you'll be able to come home" convey that there is something legitimately terrible about being with the other parent, and that the other parent's house is not the child's "true" home. In creating the child's symptoms of attachment-based "parental alienation," the narcissistic/(borderline) parent employs a myriad of these manipulative, distorting, and inflaming implicit communications to the child that elicit, exaggerate, and maintain the child's symptomatic display.

<u>Excessive and Intrusive Contact</u>

Another type of parental retrieval behavior in attachment-based "parental alienation" involves excessive and intrusive contact by the narcissistic/(borderline) parent with the child when the child is in the custody of the other parent. This type of retrieval behavior essentially represents the parent seeking out the child (or in its reversal form the child seeking out the parent) to maintain the child's protective proximity to the supposedly "protective parent."

In this form of parental retrieval behavior display the narcissistic/(borderline) parent exchanges frequent phone calls, emails, or text communications with the child while the child is with the other parent. In its reversal form, the narcissistic/(borderline) parent elicits these behaviors from the child toward the parent. Two justifications are typically offered by the child and the narcissistic/(borderline) parent for this excessive and intrusive contact:

1) **Wonderful Parent:** This justification is that the child so loves the wonderfulness of the narcissistic/(borderline) parent that the child

simply cannot bear to be separated from such parental wonderfulness and needs the constant perfect love and nurture from the wonderfulness of the narcissistic/(borderline) parent.

2) **Protective Monitoring:** This justification is that the supposedly "abusive" parenting of the targeted parent presents some form of danger to the child (although the actual danger posed to the child is often implied by the child's reluctance to be with the targeted parent and is not specifically identified). In this justification, the narcissistic/(borderline) parent is simply displaying supposedly normal-range "protective" parental concern in monitoring the child's well-being while the child is in the dangerously inadequate, and potentially "abusive," parental care the targeted parent.

The first justification, that the child simply cannot bear to be separated from the wonderfulness of the narcissistic/(borderline) parent, represents the role-reversal use of the child as "regulatory other" for the self-inadequacy and abandonment fears of the narcissistic/(borderline) parent. Normal-range and healthy children who love their parents very much do not display this type of hyper-bonding motivation toward their parents. In secure attachments the child evidences comfort in separating from the bonded parent. High protest at separation from a parent is not an indication of secure parental attachment. Instead it is a clear symptom indicator of an insecure attachment to the parent (i.e., an insecure anxious ambivalent/preoccupied attachment).

The motivational source for the child's hyper-bonding display toward the narcissistic/(borderline) parent is not in the child, the source is in the child's role-reversal regulation of the parent's intense fear of abandonment. The narcissistic/(borderline) personality structure contains a core attachment schema for other-in-relationship that "I will be abandoned by the other person because of my inadequacy." The narcissistic/(borderline) parent is using the child's elicited displays of hyper-bonding to the narcissistic/(borderline) parent to reassure the parent's own abandonment fears triggered by separation from the "regulatory object" of the child. The narcissistic/(borderline) parent is hiding the parental pathology of abandonment fears behind the child's supposed fixation on the wonderfulness of the parent. It is supposedly the child who can't bear to be separated from the parent (because the parent is so wonderful). In truth, it is the parent who can't bear to be separated from the "regulatory object" of the child.

The role-reversal relationship incorporates the reversal theme of "It's not me; it's the child" throughout the pathological process:

> **N/(B) Parent:** "It's not me, it's the child. I tell the child to go on visitations with the other parent, but the child refuses. It's not me, it's the child."
>
> **N/(B) Parent:** "It's not me, it's the child. I tell the child to be cooperative with the other parent, but the other parent is such a horrible parent that the child simply can't get along that parent. It's not me, though, I tell the child to behave. It's the child."
>
> **N/(B) Parent:** "It's not me, it's the child. I tell the child not to call and text me so much, but what can I do? We share such a perfect love that the child can't bear to be separated from me. It's not me though, it's the child who simply can't bear to be without me."

The parent's fear of abandonment is triggered by being separated from the "regulatory other" attachment figure of the child. The narcissistic/(borderline) parent projects this abandonment fear into the child who becomes the externalized holder for the parent's abandonment fears. It is the child who supposedly cannot bear to be separated from the narcissistic/(borderline) parent. The clinical term for this process is "projective identification," in which the parent regulates his or her own emotional and psychological state by first projecting it into the child, so that the child becomes the "holder" of the parent's psychological state, and then the parent identifies with the child in taking care of the child's projected psychological state. In taking care of the psychological state of the child, the parent is actually taking care of the parent's own psychological state that is projected into the child.

The projective identification process is revealed in the reason offered for the child's inability to separate from the parent. For the narcissistic-style parent the justification is that the child simply cannot bear to be separated from the supposed "wonderfulness of the parent." This parental wonderfulness justification represents the reflection of narcissistic self-inflation of the narcissistic defense of the parent. The borderline-style explanation is that the child cannot bear to be separated from "idealized perfect love" shared between the borderline-style parent and child. This perfect love justification reflects the borderline's fear of abandonment triggered by separation from the "regulatory object" of the child. In the projective identification, however, it is the child who supposedly cannot bear to be separated from the supposedly perfect "regulating other" of the parent.

The child's supposed need for reassurance from the narcissistic/(borderline) parent simultaneously addresses both of the attachment system/personality disorder core vulnerabilities of the narcissistic/(borderline) parent. Through the child's apparent devotion, the narcissistic/(borderline) parent is defined as the all-wonderful parent and it is the child who is supposedly needing continual reassurance from the parent. The child becomes the external holder of the parent's abandonment fears. The supposed need of the child to maintain continual contact with the narcissistic/(borderline) parent during separations implicitly communicates to the narcissistic/(borderline) parent that the parent is valuable and loved, thereby addressing the fundamental inadequacies of the parent, and also reassures the parent that the child will never abandon the parent, thereby addressing the parent's fundamental fears of abandonment.

The continual contact, elicited by the parent but initiated by the child, provides the narcissistic/(borderline) parent with reassurance from the child that "Even though we are separated, I am not abandoning you." The reassurance provided to the parent is being expressed through a characteristic reversal theme of, "it's not me; it's the child." In the offered justification for the excessive parent-child contact, it is not the parent who is seeking the continual contact, it's the child. From the perspective of the narcissistic/(borderline) parent, the rationale offered for the excessive contact with the child is that the narcissistic/(borderline) does not want the child to feel abandoned to the "abusive" parenting of the targeted parent. In truth, the excessive contact is being created from the abandonment fears of the parent.

The child, in the role as the "regulatory object" for the parent, is simply being what the pathology of the narcissistic/(borderline) parent requires. It is the narcissistic/(borderline) parent who cannot tolerate separations from the "regulatory object" of the child. It is the narcissistic/(borderline) parent who seeks the excessive contact with the "regulatory object" during separations in order to regulate the parent's own self-inadequacy and abandonment fears. However, consistent with the projective externalization of emotional and psychological regulation, the narcissistic/(borderline) transfers the regulatory function onto the child. The child is used as the external "regulatory object" to regulate the parent's emotional and psychological state.

An additional regulatory function of the excessive and intrusive contact between the narcissistic/(borderline) parent and the child during the child's visitations with the targeted parent is to disrupt the ability of the targeted parent to form an affectionally bonded relationship with the child. It is essential to the regulatory function of the child for the narcissistic/(borderline) parent that the child continues to reject the targeted parent. Through the child's rejection of the targeted parent, the narcissistic/(borderline) parent is able to psychologically expel onto the targeted parent the inadequacy and abandonment fears from the narcissistic/(borderline) parent. Through the child's rejection of the targeted parent, it is the targeted parent who becomes the fundamentally inadequate and entirely abandoned parent.

The child's role as the "victimized child" is also the linchpin role in creating the trauma reenactment narrative that is essential to regulating the narcissistic/(borderline) parent's reactivated childhood trauma anxiety. If the child and targeted parent are allowed to form an affectionally bonded relationship then the child would no longer be the "victimized child" and the entire trauma reenactment narrative would dissolve. If the targeted parent and child are allowed to form an affectionally bonded relationship, then the regulatory function of the child ends. It is therefore essential to the continuing role-reversal regulatory function of the child for the emotional and psychological state of the narcissistic/(borderline) parent that the targeted parent and child not be allowed to form an affectionally bonded relationship.

Yet every time the child is on visitation with the targeted parent there is the potential that they will develop an affectionally bonded relationship. The potential loss of the regulatory function of the child's rejection of the targeted parent that would occur if the child is allowed to develop an affectional bond to the targeted parent creates intolerable anxiety for the narcissistic/(borderline) parent every time the child is in the care of the targeted parent. The intolerable anxiety of the narcissistic/(borderline) parent creates the hyper-vigilant intrusive monitoring of the child during the child's visitation with the targeted parent to ensure that the child and targeted parent do not develop an affectionally bonded relationship. By continually intruding into and disrupting the ability of the targeted parent to form an affectionally bonded relationship with the child, the narcissistic/(borderline) parent ensures that the child will continue in the role as the "victimized child" and will continue to reject a relationship with the targeted parent.

In evaluating attachment-based "parental alienation," it is imperative that treatment providers and custody evaluators understand the central and critical role played by the child's symptomatic rejection of the targeted parent for the regulation of the emotional and psychological state of the narcissistic/(borderline) parent. So crucial is the child's symptomatic rejection of the targeted parent for the regulation and stabilization of the narcissistic/(borderline) parent's psychological state that the narcissistic/(borderline) parent will spare no effort to ensure the child's continued rejection of the targeted parent. As long as the child remains under the pathogenic influence of the narcissistic/(borderline) parent's psychopathology, treatment designed to restore a normal-range and healthy relationship with the targeted parent will be **impossible**.

For the narcissistic/(borderline) parent it is a **psychological imperative** that the child continues to remain symptomatically rejecting of the targeted parent. This is in direct contrast to a normal and healthy parental attitude following divorce. Normal-range parents want their children to have an affectionate and attached relationship with the other parent following a divorce because they realize the importance to the child's healthy emotional and psychological development of having secure affectional bonds with both parents. If the other parent is problematic, then the psychologically healthy parent tries to minimize these problematic features of the other parent in order to help the child maintain a healthy affectional bond to the problematic parent. Normal-range and psychologically healthy parents encourage their children's affectional bonding to the other parent following the divorce, even if aspects of the other parent are seen as being problematic, because normal-range parents recognize the inherent importance to the child's healthy development of affectionally bonded relationships with both parents.

When the normal-range parent encourages the child's ability to form an affectionally bonded relationship with the other parent because it is important to the child's healthy emotional and psychological development, this parent is acting as a "regulatory other" for the child. In acting as a "regulatory other" for the child, the normal-range and healthy parent is putting aside his or her own animosity and experience with the other spouse in order to adopt the child's frame of reference. Children love their parents; both parents; even problematic parents. Based on an authentic parental empathy for the child's needs and experience, the psychologically healthy parent encourages the child's relationship with the other parent because it is important to the child's healthy development. Even if aspects of the other parent are seen as being problematic, the healthy parent tries to minimize the impact of these problematic parenting features in order to allow the child to form an affectionally bonded relationship with both parents. The psychologically healthy parent places the needs of the child for an affectionally bonded relationship with both parents ahead of the emotional and psychological needs of the parent.

The narcissistic/(borderline) parent, however, is incapable of authentic empathy. The central and sole psychological focus of the narcissistic/(borderline) personality is on maintaining the fragile state regulation of the narcissistic/(borderline) personality structure. Other people are used and exploited as external "regulatory objects" for the emotional and psychological needs of the narcissistic/(borderline) personality. Authentic empathy for the experience of the other person is not possible for the narcissistic/(borderline) parent.

For the narcissistic/(borderline) personality, "empathy" involves imposing the psychological self-experience of the narcissistic/(borderline) personality onto and into the beliefs of the other person. The authenticity of the other person is obliterated so that the other person becomes a regulating narcissistic refection of the state of the narcissistic/(borderline) personality. The child's authentic needs cannot be comprehended by the narcissistic/(borderline) parent. Instead, the child's needs are manipulated into being whatever the narcissistic/(borderline) parent needs. The child exists to regulate the state of the parent.

The narcissistic/(borderline) parent cannot comprehend that the child loves the other parent because the regulation of the narcissistic/(borderline) personality structure requires that the child reject the other parent. The narcissistic/(borderline) personality is entirely consumed in its self-absorption and the need to maintain the fragile regulatory organization of the narcissistic/(borderline) personality structure. The regulation of the narcissistic/(borderline) personality structure needs the child to reject the targeted parent, so the narcissistic/(borderline) parent cannot comprehend that the child loves the targeted parent. The narcissistic/(borderline) parent cannot have authentic empathy for the child because the child must be who the narcissistic/(borderline) parent needs the child to be. The child is not an autonomous person. The child is incorporated into the very fabric of the self-regulatory structure of the narcissistic/(borderline) personality.

As a result, it is beyond the psychological capacity of the narcissistic/(borderline) parent to understand the extent to which the authentic child loves his or her parents. In the mind of the narcissistic/(borderline) personality, the child is merely a narcissistic reflection of the parent, and the child is assumed to hold the same attitudes and beliefs as those held by narcissistic/(borderline) parent. If the narcissistic/(borderline) parent rejects the other parent/spouse, then the child too must reject the other parent/spouse. In the projective psychology of the narcissistic/(borderline) parent, the child's feelings and attitudes are a narcissistic reflection of what the parent needs those feelings and attitudes to be.

To maintain the state regulation of the narcissistic/(borderline) personality, the "regulatory object" of the attachment figure must maintain a continually fused psychological state with the narcissistic/(borderline) personality. The foundationally disorganized attachment schemas of the narcissistic/(borderline) personality are unable to recover from breaches to the attachment relationship. When there is a breach to the fused psychological state with the attachment figure, the fragile regulation of the narcissistic/(borderline) personality's inadequacy and abandonment fears collapse into disorganization and dysregulation. As a "regulatory object" for the narcissistic/(borderline) personality, the child must hold identical attitudes and beliefs as those of the narcissistic/(borderline) personality.

The normal-range parent is able to have empathy for the independent experience of the child. As a result of authentic parental empathy, the normal-range parent supports the child's ability to form an affectionally bonded relationship with the other parent (even when the other parent has prominent narcissistic and borderline personality traits). When the other parent displays problematic parenting, the normal-range parent will seek to minimize and compensate for potential problematic features of the other parent in order to allow the child to form an affectional bond to the other parent.

The psychopathology of the narcissistic/(borderline) personality, however, does just the opposite. The narcissistic/(borderline) parent seeks to undermine and impede the child's ability to form an affectionally bonded relationship with the other parent. The psychopathology of the narcissistic/(borderline) parent seeks to create, expand, and exploit problem areas in the child's relationship with the other parent, falsely asserting that the child severing a relationship with the other parent is in the child's best interests. Children benefit from a bonded and affectionate relationship with both parents, even if there are elements in the parenting practices of one parent that may be problematic. Only under the most extreme of circumstances (e.g., incest, severe parental violence, severe and chronic parental substance abuse) would it be in the child's best interests to sever a relationship with a parent.

The continual intrusions into the child's visitation time with the targeted parent arise from the fears of the narcissistic/(borderline) parent that the child may form an affectional bond to the targeted parent. The regulatory function of the child for the narcissistic/(borderline) parent requires that the child continues to reject a relationship with the targeted parent. The continual intrusive contacts with the child while the child is with the targeted parent are meant to disrupt and prevent the ability of the targeted parent to form of an affectional bond with the child. This intrusive contact is an expression of the narcissistic/(borderline) parent's anxiety that an affectional bond between the child and targeted parent may develop when they are together.

These continual intrusive contacts by the narcissistic/(borderline) parent communicate to the child the anxiety of the narcissistic/(borderline) parent surrounding the child's relationship with the targeted parent. In communicating parental anxiety, these intrusive parental contacts represent a form of retrieval behavior that seeks to restrict the child's exploratory behavior with the other parent because of danger[1] that is supposedly posed to the child by the inadequate and "abusive" parenting practices of the targeted parent. Parental signals of anxiety and threat perception activate the child's attachment system response to threat.

Attachment System Response to Threat

The response of the child's attachment system to parental communications of a threat to the child that is supposedly present in the child's environment is to motivate the child to flee from the parentally identified source of threat (e.g., from the predator), and to remain in the continual physical proximity of the "protective parent" (i.e., the role being adopted and conspicuously displayed to the child by the narcissistic/(borderline) parent). This attachment motivated response to parental signals of threat perception is exactly the behavior exhibited by the child in "parental alienation."

In defining the targeted parent as representing a threat to the child, the narcissistic/(borderline) parent is essentially defining the targeted parent as "the predator" relative to the functioning of the child's attachment system. The attachment system does not motivate children to bond to the predator. By defining the targeted parent as the source of threat to the child, the supposedly "protective" narcissistic/(borderline) parent is effectively turning off the normal-range functioning of the child's attachment system relative to the targeted parent.

The attachment system motivates children to flee from the source of threat identified by the parent. When the supposedly "protective" narcissistic/(borderline) parent identifies the targeted parent as a source of threat to the child (i.e., as "the predator" risk to the child), this subliminally activates the child's attachment system motivations to flee from the identified source of threat (i.e., from the targeted parent) and to

---

[1] The actual treat posed by the targeted parent is that the child will form an affectionate bond to the targeted parent and will thereby cease performing the regulatory function of the "victimized child" in the trauma reenactment narrative that defines the targeted parent as the inadequate, abusive, and abandoned parent (person).

seek to remain in the continual protective proximity of the "protective parent."

A variety of communications are provided to the child by the narcissistic/(borderline) parent regarding the parental perception of threat posed to the child by the targeted parent. These include communication exchanges with the child that define the child into the "victimized child" role relative to the "abusive parent" role created for the targeted parent, emotional signals from the narcissistic/(borderline) parent of elevated anxiety and heightened "concern" for the child when the child is with the targeted parent, and through parental retrieval behaviors in which the parent interrupts the child's exploratory activity (visitations with the targeted parent) and seeks to keep the child close to the parent (i.e., monitoring of the child's well-being).

These signals made to the child regarding the parental perception of threat to the child will subliminally activate the child's attachment system response to threat. The narcissistic/(borderline) parent turns off the child's normal-range attachment bonding motivations toward the targeted parent by designating the targeted parent as representing a source of the threat to the child (i.e., as "the predator"). The parental signals of elevated anxiety and retrieval behaviors terminate the child's motivations for exploratory behavior away from the "protective parent" and simultaneously activate the corresponding attachment motivations for the child to remain in the continual protective physical proximity of the "protective parent."

In attachment-based "parental alienation," the narcissistic/(borderline) parent adopts and then conspicuously displays to the child the role as the "protective parent" by expressing an elevated parental anxiety and heightened over-concern for the child's safety and well-being when the child is with the other parent. The narcissistic/(borderline) parent also displays the role of the supposedly nurturing and "protective parent" by responding with nurturing support to the child's elicited displays of distress at being with the targeted parent.

By co-creating the child's role as the "victimized child" relative to the supposedly "abusive" targeted parent, the narcissistic/(borderline) parent is effectively defining the targeted parent as representing a danger to the child, which to the child's attachment system represents "the predator" who is posing a threat to the child. Within the motivational directives inherent to the attachment system, when the protective parent signals the presence of a predator threatening the child, the child's attachment system activates to terminate motivations for exploratory behavior away from the protective parent, to actively avoid and flee from the parentally identified source of threat (i.e., from the predator), and to seek to remain in the continual protective proximity of the protective parent. These are inherent and overriding motivational directives of the attachment system in response to parental signals of threat perception.

The neurobiological foundations of the attachment system formed across millions of years of evolution as a result of survival pressures from the selective predation of children. The attachment system is a predator-driven primary motivational system that is highly sensitized to parental signals of threat perception. In defining the targeted parent as representing "the predator" threat to the child relative to the functioning of the child's attachment system, the narcissistic/(borderline) parent activates the child's attachment motivations to flee from the supposed threat posed by the targeted parent (by "the predator") and to seek to remain in the continual protective proximity protection of the (supposedly) "protective parent."

The child's rejection of the targeted parent evidenced in "parental alienation" essentially represents the activation by the narcissistic/(borderline) parent of the child's attachment system motivation to flee from the supposed threat posed by "the predator." The child's corresponding hyper-bonding motivation toward the narcissistic/(borderline) parent represents the activation by the narcissistic/(borderline) parent of the child's attachment system motivation to remain in the continual protective proximity of the "protective parent" when there is a parentally identified threat ("a predator") in the child's environment.

This display of the child's attachment motivation to flee from the parentally designated threat that is supposedly being posed by the parenting of the targeted parent will sometimes be overtly displayed by the child in runaway behavior from the care of the targeted parent. When this occurs, it will typically be coordinated with parental displays of retrieval behavior from the narcissistic/(borderline) parent. The retrieval of the child by the narcissistic/(borderline) parent has either been prearranged with the child or the narcissistic/(borderline) parent is contacted by the child after the runaway behavior to arrange for the pick-up of the child. These displays of runaway behavior by the child represent an overt display of the coordinated activation of the child's attachment system motivation to flee from "the predator" threat that is being identified by the anxiety of the "protective parent," and the coordinated attachment motivation of the "protective parent" to retrieve the child to the parent's sphere of protective influence and control when there is a predator threat to the child in the child's environment.

The natural attachment bonding motivations of the child toward the targeted parent are being artificially suppressed by two sources of distorted parenting practices by the narcissistic/(borderline) parent:

1. **Displays of Parental Anxiety:** The narcissistic/(borderline) parent is emitting an array of non-verbal signals of heightened threat perception that are communicating to the child that the other parent is perceived to be a parentally identified source of threat to the child.

2. **"Victimized Child"/"Abusive Parent" Roles:** The trauma reenactment role definitions of the child as being "victimized" by the "abusive" targeted parent define the targeted parent as representing "the predator" threat to the child within the child's attachment bonding motivations.

Children's attachment systems do not motivate children to bond to the predator. Instead, children are motivated to flee from the predator and to seek continual bonding protection afforded by the protective parent. The aberrant and distorted parental communications from the narcissistic/(borderline) parent distort the child's perception of the targeted parent into believing that the targeted parent represents an "abusive" threat to the child rather than being a protective and nurturing parental figure. By defining the targeted parent as representing a threat to the child, the child's natural attachment bonding motivations toward the targeted parent are turned off and the attachment system's response to parentally signaled threat are activated. This creates the distorted child attachment displays evidenced in "parental alienation" of a termination of the child's attachment bonding motivations toward one parent and the simultaneous display of a hyper-bonding motivation toward the other parent.

Attuned and Misattuned Parental Responses

Another fundamental source of distorted relational communication processes that contributes to creating the child's symptomatic rejection of the targeted parent are parentally attuned and misattuned responses by the narcissistic/(borderline) parent to the child's behavior, emotional displays, and inner psychological state that selectively amplify and dampen the parentally desired and non-desired behavior and inner psychological experiences of the child.

The constructs of "attuned" and "misattuned" parental responses originate from research on parent-child interactions during the formative period of early childhood, and are best understood by way of example:

> **Attuned Parental Responses:** If the child is hungry and the parent feeds the child, this represents an attuned parental response. If the child has a soiled diaper and the parent changes the child's diaper, this too represents an attuned parental response. These attuned parental responses are resonant matches to the child's needs and experience.
>
> **Misattuned Parental Responses:** If, on the other hand, the child is hungry and the parent changes the child's diaper, this represents a misattuned parental response. Similarly, if the child has a soiled diaper and the parent feeds the child, this also represents a misattuned parental response. These parental responses are inconsistent with the child's actual needs and psychological experience.

Parental attunement and misattunement to the child are not specific parental behaviors but rather represent how sensitive and in-tune the parental response is to the child's inner state and needs. In terms of the psychological development of the parent-child relationship, parentally attuned and misattuned responses are not made to the child's overt behavior but to the child's inner emotional and psychological experience. Parental responses that are attuned to the child's inner psychological experience augment and amplify the child's inner experience, making the experience more pronounced in the child's self-awareness. Misattuned parental responses, on the other hand, dampen and diminish the child's self-experience of the psychological state that is receiving the misattuned parental response. The analogy would be to two superimposed waveforms. If the peaks and troughs of the two waveforms are synchronized so that they reach their peaks and troughs at the same time (i.e., an attuned response), then their combined effect will be to increase the amplitude of the peaks and troughs in the combined waveform. If, on the other hand, the peaks and troughs of the two waveforms are misaligned (i.e., a misattuned response), so that a peak in one waveform occurs at the same time as a trough in the other, then the combined effect of these two waveforms would be to dampen and diminish the intensity of the peaks and troughs expressed in the combined waveform.

In parent-child communications, attuned parental responses act to amplify the child's self-experience that receives the attuned parental response, whereas misattuned parental responses will dampen and nullify the child's inner self-experience that is receiving the misattuned parental response. For example, if the child is happy about an event and the parent responds with sadness and disappointment, this would be a misattuned parental response to the child's happiness and would have the effect of dampening and nullifying the child's inner self-experience of happiness. If, on the other hand, the parent responds with an attuned emotional response of matching joy and excitement, this attuned parental response would amplify and heighten the child's self-experience of happiness.

The display of parentally attuned and misattuned responses can be quite subtle and complex, and it is not merely a case of matching the child's emotional state. If the child is mildly amused and the parent responds with an over-exaggerated display of laughter and exuberance, this would be a misattuned parental response not in the category of the emotion, but in the intensity of the emotional matching. Attuned parental responses reflect a coordinated fit with the child's inner experience. An attuned parental response to child sadness, for example, would be a parental response of comfort and nurture, and an attuned parental response to the child's experience of anxiety would be the display of calm parental confidence. Parental attunement is not necessarily the expression of an identical emotional state as that displayed by the child, but instead represents a matching coordinated state to that of the child's.

Parental attunement and misattunement to child responses are subtle but powerful relationship features that can amplify or dampen the child's inner self-experience of the child's psychological state. So, for example, suppose a child returns from a visitation with her mother and is asked by her father how the visit went. The child responds that the visit with her mother was very enjoyable and they had a great time. A normal-range and psychologically healthy parent would provide the child with an attuned verbal response of,

> **Parent:** "That's wonderful, honey. I'm glad that you and your mother had a good time together."

In addition, the emotional tone of the father would be consistent with the verbal content of approval, so the father would display a "congruent" communication of authentic approval across all channels of communication.

A misattuned parental response to the daughter's expression of joy and pleasure with her mother, on the other hand, might be expressed through verbal channels as,

> **Parent:** "I find that hard to believe, your mother is usually pretty hard to get along with."

In this example, the father's verbal message is not attuned to his daughter's expression of happiness and pleasure with her mother.

Alternatively, the father may provide an attuned verbal response but a misattuned emotional response. For example, the father may say,

> **Parent:** That's great, honey. I'm so glad that you and your mother had a good time."

yet the emotional tone of the father may be one of sarcasm and thinly veiled hostility. The verbal communication of the father would be attuned to his daughter's happiness with her mother, but the father's clearly signaled emotional response would be misattuned to the daughter's happiness and pleasure with her mother. This type of communication discrepancy between the messages conveyed in different communication channels (i.e., verbal and emotional) is referred to as "incongruent" communication involved mixed or double messages.

In attachment-based "parental alienation" the narcissistic/(borderline) parent makes skillful use of attuned and misattuned responses to selectively enlarge and augment desired child communications and psychological states and to dampen and diminish non-desired child communications and psychological states. Furthermore, this selective and differential use of attuned and misattuned parental responses to the child's psychological states occurs in the context of the child's role as the "regulatory object" for the emotional and psychological state of the parent, in which the child is actively monitoring the narcissistic/(borderline) parent for cues about how to keep the parent in a regulated emotional and psychological state. The child's active and hyper-vigilant monitoring of the narcissistic/(borderline) parent for cues about the needs of the parent allows the child to provide the proper responses that keep the narcissistic/(borderline) parent in a regulated emotional state (is the sky red, or yellow, or green?). By monitoring the parent's emotional and psychological state, the child can respond in ways that avoid the collapse of the narcissistic/(borderline) parent into chaotic and irrational emotional tirades of intense anger and hostility directed toward the child (or a collapse into tearful sadness or heightened anxiety). Within the context of the child's role as the "regulatory object" for the parent, attuned and misattuned parental responses to the child's behavior, communications, and inner psychological state provide important cues as to the regulatory needs and desires of the narcissistic/(borderline) parent.

For example, if the child responds to the query from the narcissistic/(borderline) parent,

N/(B) Parent: "How did things go at your mom's house?"

Child: "Great, we had a good time"

there are a variety of ways that the narcissistic/(borderline) parent could then respond in a misattuned way to the child's expression of bonding with the mother. For example, the narcissistic/(borderline) father might verbally negate the child's assertion of having a good time, and then offer the child an opportunity to "correct" his or her response,

N/(B) Parent: "Well I find that hard to believe. Really? Are you sure you and your mom got along well?"

The father's verbal response directly challenges the child's statement, and the father's expression of mock surprise – "Really?" –

subtly but clearly communicates to the child that the child's response is not what the father wants to hear. The child is then offered the opportunity to correct the child's response in a way that will be more pleasing to the father.

Or the father could offer a mixed message where the verbal message is attuned to the child's report of having a good experience with her mother, but the father's emotional tone is misattuned to the daughter's communication,

> **N/(B) Parent:** <sad and dejected emotional tone> "Oh. Okay. Really, you guys had a good time together?"
>
> **Child:** "Well, it wasn't all that good. I was kind of bored at times."
>
> **N/(B) Parent:** <becoming more animated and interested> "Oh, I'm so sorry you weren't happy at your mother's house. I wish she'd plan things better so you wouldn't be so bored. She's just always thinking about her own needs and never stops to consider what other people might want. Come here and give me a hug. I'm so sorry things didn't go well."

If the child insists on maintaining that she had a positive time with her mother then the child may be subjected to her father's anger and rejection (or collapse into dysregulated sadness or anxiety). The father's anger and rejection, however, may be about some secondary issue not directly tied to the daughter's relationship with her mother, such as how the daughter left her room a mess, or didn't empty the dishwasher before she left to visit her mother. Nor do the father's allegations need to be true or accurate, since the narcissistic/(borderline) parent can bend and distort truth to the needs of the moment. Yet even though the father's anger is about a topic unrelated to the daughter's relationship with her mother, the timing of the anger creates a clear communication, if the daughter displeases the father she will face his anger and retaliation.

However, children exposed to the distorted relationship dynamics of a narcissistic/(borderline) parent quickly learn to skillfully read the parent's emotional state so that they can provide the narcissistic/(borderline) parent with the parentally desired response to keep the narcissistic/(borderline) parent in a regulated emotional state. Through chaotic parental displays of irrational anger when the child missteps, and parental indulgences for the child when the child complies in surrendering into meeting the emotional needs of the parent, the child is induced into a role-reversal relationship in which the child serves as an external "regulatory other" for the narcissistic/(borderline) parent's emotional and psychological state. From the child's role as a "regulatory other" for the parent, the child will recognize the meaning conveyed by the misattuned response of her father, and she will accept his offered suggestion to correct her response in order to provide her father with a more acceptable answer,

> **Child:** "Well it wasn't all that great. She gets demanding and controlling, so I didn't have a very good time."

When the daughter reads the father's misattuned response to her communication, she backtracks and offers a different version of reality that will be more pleasing to her father. In meeting his needs, she provides her father with one of the themes for criticizing her mother that the father has previously provided to her regarding acceptable criticisms of the mother; in this case that her mother is "demanding and controlling."

The revision by the daughter is pleasing to her father, who offers an attuned parental response to the daughter's expressed displeasure with her visitation,

> **N/(B) Parent:** "Now that doesn't surprise me. I know just how she gets. I'm so sorry you didn't have a good time over there. I wish she'd be less self-centered and more concerned about what makes you happy."

Misattuned parental responses do not necessarily need to be in the verbal channel. In mixed messages, the emotionally misattuned response can actually take precedence over verbally attuned communications in conveying meaning. In responding to the child's communications, the narcissistic/(borderline) parent may offer a verbal message aligned with the child's authenticity, but an emotional message that communicates an undercurrent of anger and hostility (or sadness and dejection). These emotional signals communicate to the child in a role-reversal relationship that the emotional state of the parent is threatened with collapse, prompting the child to offer alternate communications in an effort to keep the parent in an organized and regulated state.

For example, as noted earlier, in response to the daughter's report that she enjoyed her visit with her mother, the father may provide a verbally attuned response that nevertheless misattunes emotionally to the daughter's experience,

> **N/(B) Parent:** <emotional tone of excited interest> "So, how did things go at your mother's house?"
>
> **Child:** "Great, we had a good time together."
>
> **N/(B) Parent:** <displays an abrupt drop in emotional tone from excited interest to a crestfallen, sad, and dejected emotional tone> "Oh..." <sad emotional tone> "Good. So you and your mom got along okay? You didn't have any arguments or anything?"
>
> **Child:** <reading the father's emotional cue from the misattuned parental response of sadness to her happiness> "Well, we did have one argument. She wanted me to turn off the TV and go to bed but I thought it was too early." <the daughter provides a parentally-desired response of an argument in response to the cue provided by the father>
>
> **N/(B) Parent:** <becomes more animated, displaying a heightened emotional tone of interest and nurturance> "Oh, honey. I'm so sorry you and your mom fought. You poor thing. I know how angry she can get sometimes. So she wanted you to have a bedtime that was too early? I can't believe her. You're a mature young lady, you should be able to decide when you want to go to bed. I can't believe how controlling she gets about running every little detail of people's lives."

The father's initial misattuned response of a sad and dejected emotional tone to his daughter's statement that she and her mother had a good time together communicates to the daughter that her father was not pleased with her response to his question, even though he responded verbally with "Good." The father's subsequent statement wondering about a possible argument with the mother subtly, but clearly, signals to the daughter the type of response she is to provide in order to maintain his organized and regulated state.

As a "regulatory other" for her father's emotional state, the daughter then alters her response to be more in line with the father's desires, describing a normal-range parent-child conflict surrounding bedtime. The father's shift to an attuned parental response of animated interest and nurturance communicates that she has provided him with a desired and acceptable response. The father then expands and distorts a normal-range parent-child conflict surrounding bedtime into the mother's supposed insensitivity to the daughter's needs, and he offers his daughter a narcissistic indulgence of an adult privilege in choosing her own bedtime as a "mature young lady."

Providing the child with a narcissistic indulgence of an adult privilege represents a subtle but clear reward for the child for her psychological surrender into the role as a "regulatory other" for the narcissistic/(borderline) parent. The daughter surrendered to her father's needs by providing him with the parentally desired response of criticizing her mother. When this surrender is followed by the granting of a privilege, this communicates to the child in the role-reversal relationship that the child did well.

The narcissistic-style parent will tend to offer adult privileges and material items as indulgences. These narcissistic parental indulgences of the child for the child's psychological surrender to the narcissistic-style parent can include the purchase of indulgent gifts for the child and the granting of adult-like privileges of less parental supervision. In actuality, the buying of indulgent gifts substitutes for an authentic emotional gift of love for the child (i.e., the material objects replace actual love) and the granting of adult-like privileges of less parental supervision represents a narcissistic abdication of parental involvement and responsibility. But to the immaturity of a child, being granted indulgent gifts and privileges can be a thrill, and for a daughter seeking her father's love and approval, the father's animated interest and nurture is golden, even if it has to be purchased through the daughter's criticism of her mother.

The borderline-style parent provides the child with affectional indulgences. When the child psychologically surrenders authenticity to the needs of the borderline-style parent, the child is granted hyper-affectionate displays of parental love and adoration. The borderline-style parent emphasizes the supposedly "perfect love" that the parent and child share with each other, and uses this hyper-affectionate bond to exclude the other parent as an "outsider."

Selectively attuned and misattuned parental responses are a powerful means of shaping the child's communication and self-experience into the parentally desired form. Once the "alienation" process is established and under way, parental attunement to the child's expressions of anger toward the targeted parent becomes a particularly powerful way of inflaming the child's anger into hatred.

Amplifying the child's anger into hatred involves offering an attuned parental response to the child's expression of anger at a slightly higher level of emotional intensity. If the child expresses annoyance toward the targeted parent, the narcissistic/(borderline) parent responds with an emotional tone of anger toward the "injustice" supposedly being inflicted on the child by the other parent. If the child expresses anger toward the targeted parent, the narcissistic/(borderline) parent responds with outrage toward the supposed insensitivity and selfishness of the targeted parent for the child's feelings. The attuned parental response mirrors the child's anger but slightly amplifies its intensity. Like two wave forms combining, the slightly elevated attuned parental response of emotionally resonant outrage to the child's expressed anger amplifies the child's own inner experience of anger into outrage toward the other parent.

The response of parental anger and outrage offered by the narcissistic/(borderline) to the supposedly "abusive" and unjust treatment of the child by the targeted parent can ultimately inflame the child's inner experience of anger into rage and hatred toward the supposedly "abusive" insensitivity of targeted parent. When the child then expresses a hatred for the personhood of the targeted parent, the narcissistic/(borderline) parent will provide the child with an attuned parental response of equally outraged "understanding" for the child's supposedly justified and warranted hatred of the targeted parent, followed by nurturing care and sympathetic understanding for the child's supposed "victimization." This parental response cements the parent-child bond in their shared "victimization" and anger toward the supposedly "abusive" targeted parent.

Throughout this process, the child believes that the child's anger toward the targeted parent is the child's "independent" experience toward the targeted parent, since the initial criticism of the targeted parent is being offered by the child. The distorting parental influence of the narcissistic/(borderline) parent is too subtle in its manipulation to be evident to the child. From the child's perspective, the narcissistic/(borderline) parent is simply being understanding and supportive of the child.

Hiding behind the Child

The narcissistic/(borderline) parent engages in a variety of distorted relationship and communication processes with the child that create a distorted child response to the other parent:

- **Role-Reversal Relationship:** The narcissistic/(borderline) parent induces the child into a role-reversal relationship as a "regulatory other" for the emotional and psychological needs of the narcissistic/(borderline) parent.

- **Victimized Child Role:** The narcissistic/(borderline) parent induces the child into adopting the "victimized child" role by first eliciting a criticism of the targeted parent from the child and then distorting, exaggerating, and inflaming this elicited child criticism into supposed evidence of the "abusive" parenting practices by the targeted parent.

- **Parental Emotional Signaling:** The narcissistic/(borderline) parent provides the child with subtle but clear emotional signals of parental hyper-anxious over-concern regarding the child's well-being whenever the child is in the care of the targeted parent.

- **Protective Parent Role:** The narcissistic/(borderline) parent provides the child with attachment-related signals that the narcissistic/(borderline) parent is the "protective parent" who is perceiving a threat to the child from the supposedly dangerous targeted parent.

- **Shaping Child Self-Experience:** The narcissistic/(borderline) parent subtly and continually shapes the child's inner self-experience by providing selectively attuned and misattuned parental responses to the child that cue and shape the child's communications and inner self-experience into the parentally desired form of hostility and rejection for the targeted parent.

In all of these distorted parenting practices, the narcissistic/(borderline) parent appears to the child to be the all-wonderful, understanding and nurturing "protective parent" who is merely "listening to the child." It appears to the child as if the criticism of the targeted parent is being offered by the child, and the subtle processes by which these child criticisms are being elicited and shaped by the narcissistic/(borderline) parent go unrecognized. The narcissistic/(borderline) parent is allowed to present to the child as being the nurturing "protective parent" who is merely responding to the child's expressed dissatisfaction. The pathologically manipulative relationship communications are too subtle and sophisticated for the child to recognize.

In this way, the narcissistic/(borderline) parent is able to hide the severity of his or her distorting psychopathology behind the child's belief in the "independent" origin of the child's induced symptoms. The psychopathology and the distorting parental influence on the child by the narcissistic/(borderline) parent is hidden from view within a role-reversal relationship with the child, in which the child is induced into psychologically surrendering self-authenticity to the role-reversal as a "regulatory object" for the emotional and psychological needs of the narcissistic/(borderline) parent.

In a world of ever-shifting reality, where truth is solely dependent on the arbitrary and subjective assertions of the narcissistic/(borderline) parent, and where failure to meet the ever-changing subjective needs of the parent's psychopathology can result in the collapse of the parent into chaotic and irrational onslaughts of narcissistic and borderline rage and rejection directed toward the child, the child is able to purchase a freedom from constant and intolerable anxiety by psychologically surrendering to the psychopathology of the narcissistic/(borderline) parent. The child is induced into surrendering authenticity as a requirement to meeting the needs of the parent in the child's role as an external "regulatory other" for the psychopathology of the narcissistic/(borderline) parent. In return for the child's psychological surrender to the pathology of the narcissistic/(borderline) parent, the child is granted indulgences:

- **Narcissistic-Style Indulgences:** As a reward for the child's psychological surrender to the narcissistic/(borderline) parent, the narcissistic-style parent will grant adult privileges and material gifts.
- **Borderline-Style Indulgences:** As a reward for the child's psychological surrender to the narcissistic/(borderline) parent, the borderline-style parent will provide the child with parental displays of hyper-affectionate bonding and assertions of their shared "perfect love" of complete psychological fusion into one undifferentiated state.

For the child, these indulgences provided by the narcissistic/(borderline) parent must be purchased at the price of the child's psychological surrender and sacrifice of self-authenticity. In surrendering to the emotional and psychological needs of the narcissistic/(borderline) parent, only the parent's needs exists. The child must become the perfectly reflecting "narcissistic object" used by the parent to regulate the emotional and psychological state of the parent. The child's authentic self-experience is sacrificed to meet the needs of the parent.

Part III: Attachment System Level

Chapter 7

THE TRAUMA REENACTMENT NARRATIVE

Disorganized Attachment

The foundational core of the psychological and interpersonal processes traditionally referred to as "parental alienation" are to be found in the distortions to the attachment system of the narcissistic/(borderline) parent, and in the reenactment of relationship-based attachment trauma from the childhood of the narcissistic/(borderline) parent into the current family relationships. What has traditionally been referred to as "parental alienation" involves a child's rejection of a relationship with a normal-range and affectionally available parent as a result of distorted parenting practices by the narcissistic/(borderline) parent. This set of core child symptoms of "parental alienation" essentially represent a distortion to the normal-range functioning of the child's attachment system relative to the targeted parent that is being induced by the pathology of the narcissistic/(borderline) parent.

The pathological origins of the narcissistic/(borderline) personality are also located in distortions to the internal working models of the attachment system that create the narcissistic/(borderline) personality structure. This means that the subsequent induced distortions to the child's attachment system created by the personality disorder structure of the narcissistic/(borderline) parent represent the trans-generational transmission of attachment trauma from the childhood of the narcissistic/(borderline) parent (which created the distorted personality structure) into the current parent-child relationship. The mediating parent-child process in this trans-generational transmission of pathology is the role-reversal relationship, in which the parent is using the child as a "regulatory object" for the parent's emotional and psychological state. The severity of the pathology created in attachment-based "parental alienation" through the role-reversal relationship of the child with a narcissistic/(borderline) parent warrants prominent child protection considerations.

The formation of a role-reversal relationship is associated with a disorganized parent-child attachment pattern (Lyons-Ruth, Bronfman, and Parsons, 1999). A disorganized attachment is, in turn, associated with the development of borderline personality organization (Holmes, 2004; Levy, 2005). Based on the symptom display involved in attachment-based "parental alienation," the narcissistic/(borderline) parent as a child likely had a disorganized attachment with his or her own parent which then coalesced during adolescence and young adulthood into the stable, but pathological, narcissistic/(borderline) personality traits that are currently creating the family's pathological transition from an intact family structure to a separated family structure.

If the narcissistic/(borderline) parent as a child had anxious-ambivalent attachment overtones to the primarily disorganized attachment with his or her own parent, then these anxious-ambivalent overtones will produce a more borderline-style presentation of high drama and emotionally needy displays. If, on the other hand, the narcissistic/(borderline) parent as a child had anxious-avoidant overtones to the primarily disorganized attachment, then these anxious-avoidant attachment overtones will create the more narcissistic-style personality structure of emotionally aloof judgment and dismissiveness of the inherent value of other person. The unifying feature of both personality styles is the fundamentally disorganized attachment at the core of the personality structure for both the narcissistic and borderline personality which is being expressed through the central pathology of the role-reversal relationship. Through the role-reversal relationship, the child is being incorporated into the regulatory structure of the narcissistic/(borderline) personality as an external "regulatory object" to stabilize the emotional and psychological state of the parent.

A disorganized attachment originates from a variety of distorted parenting behaviors (Lyons-Ruth, Bronfman, and Parsons, 1999) including:

Affective Errors

- Contradictory parental cues
- Nonresponsive or inappropriate parental responses

Disorientation

- The parent is confused or frightened by the child
- Disorganized or disoriented parental responding

Negative-Intrusive Behavior

- Verbal negative-intrusive parental behavior
- Physical negative-intrusive parental behavior

Role Confusion

- Role-reversal relationship
- Sexualization of the child by the parent

Withdrawal

- The parent creates physical distance
- The parent creates verbal distance

Role-reversal relationships have been identified as a causative factor in the creation of disorganized attachment. Role-reversal relationships are also transmitted across generations. Parents who experienced a role-reversal in their relationship with their own parents during childhood are more likely to subsequently engage their children in a role-reversal relationship in which the child is used to meet the parent's emotional and psychological needs.

Frightening parental behavior has also been identified as a primary pathogenic factor in the creation of disorganized attachment (Main & Hesse, 1990). Frightening parental behavior activates the threat response within the child's attachment system which motivates the child to flee from the source of threat and to seek the protective proximity of the nurturing and protective parent. However, when the protective parent is at the same time the source of threat, the child is simultaneously motivated to both flee from the parent and to seek protective bonding with the same parent, creating an incompatible set of motivational directives within the child's attachment system.

The simultaneous activation of incompatible motivations for avoidance and attachment bonding creates an intolerable and unresolvable psychological conflict for child, leading to disorganized attachment responses in which the child cannot develop a coherent strategy for establishing attachment bonds with the parent. The chronic activation of incompatible avoidance and attachment bonding motivations is eventually resolved by a complete cross-inhibition of the attachment bonding and avoidance motivation systems, manifested as the splitting dynamic. The irresolvable conflict created by the simultaneous activation of incompatible motivations is solved by turning one system entirely off when the other system is on. As a result of this intensive cross-inhibition of motivating systems, only one or the other system can be active at any one time.

This creates the splitting dynamic characteristic of narcissistic and borderline personality organizations, in which the perceptions of others are polarized into extremes of being either completely idealized as the all-wonderful and perfect other (the sole activation of the attachment bonding motivating system and complete inhibition of the avoidance system), or the relationship partner is devalued and demonized as being a an entirely malevolent and evil person (the sole activation of the avoidance motivating system and complete inhibition of attachment bonding motivations). The complete cross-inhibition of the attachment bonding and avoidance systems results in a neurological incapacity for the narcissistic/(borderline) personality to hold blended perceptions of people and relationships as having both positive and negative qualities. Ambiguity is neurologically impossible for the narcissistic/(borderline) personality structure because the neurological foundations of the spitting dynamic are created specifically to eliminate the ambiguity of complex and competing motivational directives. Ambiguity is sacrificed for clarity of motivational directive.

As a consequence of the simultaneous activation of incompatible attachment bonding and avoidance motivations during childhood, the child will develop a disorganized attachment to the parent. Faced with incompatible motivational directives, the child (i.e., the narcissistic/(borderline) parent as a child) is unable to develop a coherent strategy for establishing and maintaining a secure attachment bond to the parent, and the child is unable to repair breaches to the parent-child bond when they occur. This is the attachment structure of the narcissistic/(borderline) personality. At the core of the narcissistic/(borderline) personality structure are competing and incompatible motivations to both avoid and bond to the attachment figure. The characteristic difficulties of the narcissistic and borderline personalities in intimate relationship reflects the disorganized core of their attachment system.

In an effort to achieve motivational coherence, the neurological networks of the attachment system entirely cross-inhibit the attachment bonding and avoidance motivating systems. Singularity of motivation is achieved by activating only one or the other of these motivating systems, but never both at the same time. Yet, even in this polarization of attachment bonding and avoidance motivations, the child will nevertheless tend to favor one motivational strategy over the other. Some children will continue to strive to achieve an attachment bond to the protective-nurturing parent, while other children will respond more fully to avoiding the frightening-rejecting parent.

Children who favor continuing to try to form an attachment bond to the frightening parent will face the challenge of overcoming extreme anxiety associated with seeking an attachment bond to a frightening attachment figure. The attachment bond established to a frightening parent will always be fragile and prone to rupture. As a result, these children will develop anxious-ambivalent attachment overtones to their fundamentally disorganized attachment bond to the parent in which abandonment fears predominate (i.e., the borderline-style personality).

The immense anxiety triggered by trying to seek an attachment bond to a frightening parent will severely undermine the child's ability to coherently regulate his or her emotional state. The child's vulnerability in bonding to a parent who is a source of threat will create tremendous anxiety for the child surrounding the loss of the affectional attachment bond and the potential emergence of the frightening and abusive parent. Even when an attachment bond is formed with the parent, the bond will be fragile and the child will continually fear the potential loss of the bond to the parental attachment figure. The child with a foundationally disorganized attachment created by a frightening attachment figure, who nevertheless continues to seek an attachment bond to the frightening parent, will forever live on the edge of emotional collapse from the potential loss of the attached relationship with the frightening parent.

During adolescence and young adulthood, this foundationally disorganized attachment with anxious-ambivalent overtones will coalesce into stable, albeit pathological, borderline-style personality characteristics.

The borderline-style personality structure that coalesces from this childhood attachment trauma will have great difficulty regulating emotions and will be immensely vulnerable to fears of being abandoned by the attachment figure. The anxious-ambivalent attachment overtones to the foundationally disorganized attachment will display as a higher prevalence of active protest behavior and signaling of emotional neediness that is designed to engage the constant regulating support and involvement of the attachment figure. Yet because the attachment bond is to a fundamentally dangerous attachment figure, the emotional regulation available from this attachment pattern will be highly unstable.

Despite the threat posed by the frightening attachment figure, the anxious-ambivalent attachment style continues to try to achieve an attached bond to the frightening parent. The borderline-style personality traits that develop from these underlying attachment trauma patterns still seek the psychological safety of an idealized relationship with the perfectly attuned and regulating attachment figure. Yet these efforts at forming a bonded relationship with a frightening attachment figure are marked by the psychologically disorganizing fear of losing the fragile bond to the potentially dangerous and abusive attachment figure. This constant fear of losing the attachment bond to a frightening and dangerous attachment figure destabilizes the ability to maintain emotional regulation, even when an attachment bond has been formed, which then creates the characteristic pattern of emotional instability displayed by the borderline personality. The anxious-ambivalent overtones to the fundamentally disorganized attachment patterns of the borderline-style personality result in frequent displays of high protest behavior and signals of emotional neediness in an effort by the attachment system to continually engage the external regulating involvement of the attachment figure. This disorganized pattern of high-protest attachment creates the high-drama instability of the borderline personality style that is marked by extreme emotional instability and pronounced fears of abandonment.

On the other hand, children who favor the avoidance motivation created by the threatening attachment figure develop anxious-avoidant overtones to their foundationally disorganized attachment. These children will dismiss the importance of the attachment relationship in favor of achieving greater psychological safety by avoiding the threatening attachment figure. Children who favor the psychological safety afforded by the avoidance motivation develop an anxious-avoidant attachment style that favors psychological isolation over intimacy (i.e., the narcissistic personality style).

Children who dismiss the importance of the attachment relationship in order to achieve greater psychological safety in the context of a frightening and dangerous attachment figure will thereby avoid the challenge faced by the borderline-style personality of overcoming the excessive anxiety which is created by trying to bond to a frightening attachment figure. Dismissing and devaluing the importance of bonding to the frightening attachment figure allows the avoidant child to develop greater stability to his or her emotional state by avoiding the tremendous anxiety created by exposing psychological vulnerability to a frightening attachment figure. But the increase in psychological safety is achieved at the price of psychological intimacy and the foundational self-esteem formed in a nurturing-reflecting attachment bond to a nurturing-reflective parent.

Despite the outward appearance of emotional stability, the anxious-avoidant overtones of these children are nevertheless embedded in a fundamentally disorganized attachment system that lacks a coherent strategy for forming attachment bonds or for repairing breaches in the attachment relationship when they occur. The stability provided by the anxious-avoidant overtones to the fundamentally disorganized attachment is fragile and is achieved only by completely dismissing the importance of the attachment figure and the value of the attachment bonding motivation. For these children, emotional stability is achieved by giving primacy to the avoidance motivating system over the attachment bonding motivating system. As a result, their emotional stability is continually threatened with collapse into disorganization if they acknowledge any form of attachment-bonding motivation. During adolescence and young adulthood, the disorganized attachment of these children with anxious-avoidant overtones coalesces into a stable narcissistic-style personality structure in which intimacy is avoided and relationships are shallow and easily discarded once the other person ceases to provide narcissistic supply.

While understanding the underlying attachment system issues that created the narcissistic and borderline styles of personality traits can offer insight into their dynamics, the issue in attachment-based "parental alienation" is not the specific childhood relationship features that produced the individual personality traits of the pathogenic parent. The issue is that the narcissistic/(borderline) traits of the pathogenic parent have their origins in childhood attachment trauma. The patterns of this childhood attachment trauma subsequently coalesced into the stable narcissistic and borderline personality characteristics that are currently driving the "parental alienation" process.

Whatever particular individual variations occurred in the development of the narcissistic/(borderline) parent's attachment pathology, the development of the severe personality pathology of the narcissistic/(borderline) parent necessarily involves exposure to some form of traumatic attachment experience. As Beck and his colleagues note, the attachment trauma that creates narcissistic and borderline pathology occurs "at a very early age, notably the kind of punishing, abandoning, rejecting responses of the caretaker that led to disorganized attachment" (Beck et al, 2004. p. 191). The pathology commonly described as "parental alienation" represents the transmission of attachment trauma from the childhood of the narcissistic/(borderline) parent into the current family relationships through the coalesced personality pathology of the narcissistic/(borderline) parent that was created by the childhood attachment trauma. At its primary level, the pathology commonly described as "parental alienation" represents a trauma-related attachment disorder, reflected in and expressed through the pathology of the narcissistic/(borderline) parent.

Trans-Generational Transmission of Role-Reversal

A role-reversal relationship, in which the child is used as a "regulatory object" for the parent's emotional and psychological state, robs the child of healthy self-structure development in order to support the inadequate self-structure of the parent. When the child who is acting as a "regulatory object" for the parent grows to adulthood, this child-now-adult will then also have an inadequate self-structure that requires external regulatory support because the parent robbed this child of the developmental scaffolding needed for the formation of complex independent self-regulation. This child-now-adult will then replicate the same role-reversal attachment pattern from his or her childhood of using others as "regulatory objects" to support the adult's inadequate capacity for internalized self-regulation. In narcissistic-style personalities this is referred to as their tendency to "exploit" others, whereas with more borderline-style personalities this is referred to as their tendency to "manipulate" others.

The pathology of the role-reversal relationship is thereby passed on from one generation to the next, with each generation of parents using their children as "regulatory objects" for the regulation of the parent's emotional and psychological state. When each generation of children are robbed by their parents of healthy development, these children will then possess insufficiently developed abilities for independent self-regulation. The pathology of the role-reversal relationship is embedded into the fabric of the attachment system as a foundational parent-child relationship pattern contained in the internal working models of attachment. The child who was used as a "regulatory object" to meet the needs of the parent will then repeat this attachment pattern of the role-reversal relationship with his or her own children. In this way, the pathology of the role-reversal use of children to meet the emotional and psychological needs of the parent is repeated from one generation to the next. Research has found that "both fathers and mothers who reported role reversal in childhood with their own mother saw the pattern repeated in the next generation" (Macfie, McElwain, Houts, & Cox, 2005, p. 6). Kerig, in the Journal of Emotional Abuse, also identifies the trans-generational transmission of boundary violations from parent to children,

> "There is evidence for the intergenerational transmission of boundary dissolution within the family. Adults who experienced boundary dissolution in their relationships with their own parents are more likely to violate boundaries with their children" (Kerig, 2005, p. 22).

The role-reversal use of the child as a "regulatory object" for the parent's own emotional and psychological needs represents a profound violation of the child's psychological boundaries of self-autonomy. In using the child as a "regulatory object" for the parent's psychological state, the parent is incorporating the child into the parent's own self-regulatory structure. The child essentially becomes a regulatory component of the parent's own psychological structure. Within the pathology of the role-reversal relationship the separate individual identity and self-autonomy of the child are lost. The role-reversal relationship requires the child to sacrifice authentic self-autonomy in order to become part of the regulatory networks of the parent in meeting the emotional and psychological needs of the parent

In the role-reversal relationship, the parent essentially feeds off of the child's own self-structure development in order to support the inadequate self-regulation of the parent. By psychologically feeding off of the child's development of self-structure, the parent impoverishes the child capacity for independent self-regulation. The child's impoverished self-structure development is then passed on to the next generation of children, as their healthy development is then robbed in turn to support the parental inadequacy in self-regulation that was created in the childhood role-reversal relationships of the previous generation.

At its foundational core, the psychological and family processes traditionally referred to as "parental alienation" represent the trans-generational transmission of attachment trauma from the childhood of the narcissistic/(borderline) to the current family relationships. The role-reversal pattern for the parent-child relationship becomes embedded in the internal working models of the narcissistic/(borderline) parent's attachment system through the childhood attachment experiences of the narcissistic/(borderline) parent. The psychological processes of attachment-based "parental alienation" represent the reenactment by the narcissistic/(borderline) parent of the role-reversal attachment pattern in which the child is used as a "regulatory object" to meet the emotional and psychological needs of the parent. The current child's induced rejection of the targeted parent serves the regulatory needs of the narcissistic/(borderline) parent to stabilize the self-organization and self-regulation of the parent's fragile narcissistic/(borderline) personality structure.

The Attachment System

The patterns of attachment bonding (called "schemas" or "internal working models" of attachment) form during early childhood and are modified continually throughout childhood and into adulthood through the broad array of relationship experiences the child has with parents and caregivers. The attachment patterns formed during childhood then operate throughout the remainder of the lifespan to mediate both the formation of close emotionally bonded relationships as well as the way in which we respond to the loss of emotionally bonded relationships.

Because the basic patterns of attachment form during early childhood, some mental health professionals who are unfamiliar with the nature and operation of the attachment system may believe that the functioning of the attachment system only applies to the early childhood period. However, this is a false assumption. The internalized patterns of attachment are formed during childhood, yet these attachment patterns are then used across the lifespan to guide our behavior in intimate relationships. The internal working models of the attachment system provide the patterns by which we form later bonded relationships, such as the marital relationship and our relationship with our own children, as well as our responses to repairing breaches in intimate relationships. While the basic patterns of attachment bonding and relationship repair are formed during childhood, these patterns are used throughout the lifespan to guide both the formation of intimate relationship bonds, and also our responses to repairing these intimate relationship bonds when they are ruptured.

An analogy to how the basic patterns of attachment expectations are acquired during childhood and are then expressed throughout the lifespan would be to how we acquire language. While we acquire the basic patterns of language (i.e., the grammar of language) during early childhood, we then use language throughout the lifespan to regulate thinking and social interactions. We similarly acquire the basic patterns of attachment bonding (i.e., the "grammar" of attachment) during early childhood, but then we use these patterns of attachment across the lifespan to mediate both the formation and the loss of attachment relationships.

While the basic structural patterns of both systems (i.e., the grammar of both language and attachment) develop during early childhood relationship interactions, both systems nevertheless continue to develop across all of childhood and into adulthood, and the underlying patterns of both systems that we acquire during childhood continue to regulate social interactions throughout the lifespan. In addition, just like we can learn a second language during childhood and even into adulthood, our early attachment patterns can also be modified and changed through later experiences.

However, modifying our language patterns requires active efforts to learn a new language. Unless we make an effort to learn a new language we will tend to rely solely on our native language of origin. In a similar way, unless we make an active effort to alter our underlying attachment expectations for self- and other-in-relationship (i.e., our internal working models of attachment), then we will tend to replicate our original patterns in future relationships. Altering our fundamental attachment patterns often involves developing insight into these patterns through our intimate relationships with others (including the "therapeutic relationship" formed in psychotherapy) which leads to changes in our expectations for self- and other-in-relationship. Yet, just like we will tend to speak a second language with the accent of our native language, we will similarly tend to "speak" new attachment expectations with an "accent" from our formative attachment experiences.

In the same way that we acquire language during childhood (i.e., the grammar of language), we also acquire our basic expectations for self- and other-in-relationship during childhood (i.e., the "grammar" of attachment bonding). Since the brain expects that we will be exposed to language, it has areas of the brain pre-dedicated to acquiring language during childhood. This is called "experience-expectant" development. The brain also expects that we will develop attached relationships to our parents, so the brain also has areas that are pre-dedicated to forming attachment patterns, called "internal working models" of attachment. Brain development for both language and attachment is "experience-expectant," meaning that the brain expects and is prepared to acquire certain experiences.

Brain development is also "experience-dependent," meaning that the specific patterns of language or attachment that we acquire will be dependent on the specific experiences we have during childhood, with either the language or attachment systems. During childhood, we acquire the patterns of language which we are exposed to by our parents, such as Chinese, English, or Spanish (i.e., our language patterns are transmitted trans-generationally). Similarly, as children we acquire implicit expectations regarding attachment bonding from the specific childhood experiences we have with parents and other primary caregivers (i.e., attachment schemas are transmitted trans-generationally). Research into the attachment system has classified these attachment patterns (the "grammar" of our attachment system) into two primary categories of secure and insecure attachment, with several subcategories of insecure attachment (i.e., anxious-ambivalent, anxious-avoidant, and disorganized).

The attachment system contains the relationship patterns that govern our expectations for forming an attached bond to the parent (and later for the spouse and with our own children), and for how relationship breaches in the attachment bond are repaired. In the research conducted on attachment patterns, the classification of the various types of attachment is based on how the child *repairs* the attachment bond following a breach. Divorce represents the loss of the spousal relationship, which is an attachment-mediated relationship. The loss of the spousal relationship caused by the divorce activates the internal working models of attachment to mediate the breach in the attachment-mediated spousal relationship.

Activating Trauma Anxiety

In attachment-based "parental alienation," the breach in the spousal relationship created by the divorce activates the internal working models of attachment in the narcissistic/(borderline) parent's attachment networks to mediate the loss experience. Since the attachment patterns of the narcissistic/(borderline) parent are fundamentally disorganized with anxious-ambivalent or anxious-avoidant overtones, the response of the narcissistic/(borderline) parent to breaches in attachment relationships will be equally disorganized and distorted, and will reflect the underlying pathology contained in the narcissistic/(borderline) parent's attachment patterns.

With the divorce and loss of the intact family structure, the attachment patterns contained in the representational networks of the attachment system become active to mediate the breach that occurs in attachment bonding created by the divorce. For the narcissistic/(borderline) parent, these internal working models and representational networks for attachment relationships are highly problematic, originating from childhood attachment trauma that led to the formation of the compromised narcissistic and borderline personality structures. The basic core of the attachment patterns for the narcissistic/(borderline) personality represent a fundamentally disorganized attachment system in which the narcissistic/(borderline) parent as a child was unable to develop a coherent strategy for the formation and repair of attachment bonds. This foundationally disorganized attachment system creates a fragile self-structure that easily collapses into disorganization and dysregulation under stress.

There are a variety of distorted parenting practices that can produce the disorganized attachment of the narcissistic/(borderline) parent as a child. One of the primary means is through a frightening parental caregiver who is simultaneously a source of threat and a source of parental protection for the child. The motivational conflict created by the simultaneous activation of the child's attachment bonding and avoidance motivating systems prevents the child from developing a coherent and organized strategy for forming and repairing an attachment bond to the parent. Ultimately, this leads to the creation of narcissistic and borderline personality structures, and the splitting dynamic characteristic of these personality styles.

Within the splitting dynamic of the narcissistic/(borderline) parent's attachment networks, either the attachment bonding motivational system or the avoidance motivational system can be on at any one time, but not both. The loss of the attachment-mediated spousal relationship therefore triggers the complete termination of the narcissistic/(borderline) personality's attachment bonding motivation toward other spouse, and correspondingly triggers the complete activation of the avoidance motivational networks toward the other parent. With the divorce, the targeted parent becomes the embodiment of the threatening and abusive parent from the childhood attachment trauma of the narcissistic/(borderline) parent.

By activating the attachment trauma networks that are embedded in the internal working models of the narcissistic/(borderline) parent's attachment system, the divorce also activates the excessive childhood anxiety associated with the early childhood attachment trauma. The activation of the childhood attachment trauma reactivates for the narcissistic/(borderline) parent the immense trauma-related anxiety associated with the childhood development of disorganized attachment to a frightening attachment figure. As a result, the narcissistic/(borderline) parent needs to regulate three independent, but interrelated, sources of immense anxiety surrounding the divorce experience.

<u>Narcissistic Anxiety</u>

For the narcissistic/(borderline) parent, the attachment schema for self-in-relationship is of primal self-inadequacy. The interpersonal rejection inherent to the divorce activates the attachment schema of primal self-inadequacy which then threatens to collapse the fragile narcissistic defense of idealized self-inflation. The potential collapse of the narcissistic defense threatens to expose the primal self-inadequacy at the core of the narcissistic/(borderline) personality, both to others and also to the self-experience of the narcissistic/(borderline) parent. The threat to the narcissistic defense posed by the public exposure of the primal self-inadequacy at the core of the narcissistic/(borderline) self-structure creates tremendous anxiety for the narcissistic/(borderline) parent.

As an emotional signal, anxiety signals the presence of a threat or danger. Because the source of the narcissistic/(borderline) parent's anxiety is the interpersonal rejection associated with the divorce, the narcissistic/(borderline) parent vaguely identifies the source of the threat as being somehow related to the targeted parent. The pathology of the narcissistic/(borderline) parent lacks the insight to be able to accurately identify the meaning of the threat signaled by the anxiety. Instead of recognizing the anxiety as representing a threatened exposure of personal insecurities, the narcissistic/(borderline) parent externalizes the perception of threat and becomes convinced that the targeted parent represents an actual external danger.

The pathology of the narcissistic/(borderline) parent lacks insight and is unable to accurately interpret the meaning of the anxiety surrounding the threatened collapse of the narcissistic defense. Instead, the narcissistic/(borderline) parent misinterprets an authentic experience of intense anxiety triggered by the targeted parent (i.e., by the rejection inherent to the divorce), as representing an emotional signal that the targeted parent actually represents an authentic threat or danger. Together with the splitting dynamic that is interpreting the targeted parent as the embodiment of malevolence and danger, the narcissistic/(borderline) parent's interpretation of reality becomes highly skewed and distorted.

Borderline Anxiety

Within the internal working models of the narcissistic/(borderline) parent's attachment system, the expectation for the other person in the relationship (i.e., for the attachment figure) is of being abandoned (or rejected) by the attachment figure. The divorce represents an inherent rejection (abandonment) of the narcissistic/(borderline) parent by the attachment figure of the other spouse. The rejection (abandonment) of the narcissistic/(borderline) parent by the targeted parent which is inherent to the divorce process therefore also activates the narcissistic/(borderline) parent's primal fear of abandonment and rejection. This creates a second separate, but related, source of immense anxiety for the narcissistic/(borderline) parent that is also vaguely identified as being triggered by the targeted parent as the abandoning/rejecting attachment figure.

The interpersonal rejection inherent to divorce triggers both of the narcissistic/(borderline) parent's core attachment vulnerabilities; the threatened exposure of primal self-inadequacy and a fundamental fear of abandonment by the attachment figure.

Trauma Anxiety

The third source of anxiety for the narcissistic/(borderline) parent is the reactivation of tremendous primal anxiety surrounding the childhood attachment trauma experience itself. This anxiety was created in the childhood attachment trauma of having to form an attachment bond to a parent who was simultaneously a source of threat and the source of parental protection from threat. The intense anxiety created by this early childhood attachment trauma is embedded in the internal working models of the attachment system in the representational pattern of "abusive parent"/"victimized child"/ "protective parent." The "abusive parent" representational network reflects the split off avoidance motivations of the narcissistic/(borderline) parent as a child that were triggered by the frightening/threatening parent. The "victimized child" representational networks reflect the anxious and vulnerable self-experience of the narcissistic/(borderline) parent as a child, and the "protective parent" representational network reflects the split off attachment bonding motivations of the narcissistic/(borderline) parent as a child.

During the childhood trauma experience, the narcissistic/(borderline) parent as a child experienced intense anxiety from the complex and incompatible motivation of having to form an attachment bond with an unpredictably frightening and rejecting parent. The childhood attachment experience of the narcissistic/(borderline) parent was one of a frightened and "victimized child" who was psychologically vulnerable to an unpredictably hostile and frightening parent. The only way for the narcissistic/(borderline) parent as a child to manage the immense anxiety created by the psychological attachment trauma of disorganized attachment motivations was by splitting off the parental representation into two component parts; one representing the attachment avoidance motivations created by the frightening-rejecting parental attachment figure, and one set representing the attachment bonding motivational networks toward a hoped for idealized nurturing and "protective parent."

We know this was the experience of the narcissistic/(borderline) parent as a child because we see the effects of this childhood experience in the structures of the narcissistic and borderline personality and the splitting dynamic. The patterns of the attachment system form in response to the parenting experiences the attachment system received. Differing childhood experiences will leave differing imprints in the attachment system. Narcissistic and borderline personality structures and the splitting dynamic are created by characteristic patterns of childhood experience. In geology, if fossilized seashells are found in rocks at the top of a mountain, this represents solid evidence that these rocks were once at the bottom of a seabed because that is the only location where fossilized seashells can become embedded in rocks. Even if these rocks are currently at the top of a mountain we know that they were once under the sea because the rocks contain fossilized seashells. Similarly, if a person currently evidences narcissistic and borderline personality structures along with the splitting dynamic, then the childhood experiences necessary to produce these features are, to a large degree, understood. While there will be individual variations in the specifics, there will nevertheless be certain broad underlying childhood experiences that are necessary to produce the features in the attachment system corresponding to the creation of narcissistic and borderline personality structures and the splitting dynamic.

One of the leading figures in personality disorder dynamics, Arron Beck, draws from Young's conceptualization of borderline personality processes to describes the childhood experience responsible for the formation of borderline personality structure,

> "The conceptualization of the core pathology of BPD as stemming from a highly frightened, abused child who is left alone in a malevolent world, longing for safety and help but distrustful because of fear of further abuse and abandonment, is highly related to the model developed by Young"
>
> "Young elaborated on an idea... that some pathological states of patients with BPD are a sort of regression into intense emotional states experienced as a child. Young hypothesized that four schema modes are central to BPD: the abandoned child mode (the present author suggests to label it the abused and abandoned child); the angry/impulsive child mode; the punitive parent mode, and the detached protector mode."
>
> "The abused and abandoned child mode denotes the desperate state the patient may be in related to (threatened) abandonment and abuse the patient has experienced as a child. Typical core beliefs are that other people are malevolent, cannot be trusted, and will abandon or punish you, especially when you become intimate with them." (Beck et al, 2004, p. 199).

The childhood attachment trauma experienced by the narcissistic/(borderline) parent created a split representational network for the parental attachment figure who simultaneously triggered two incompatible motivations. Each split representation centered on the differing motivational aspects created by the parent. One set of representational networks became organized around the attachment bonding motivations for the nurturing and "protective parent," while a separate, split off, set of representational networks became organized around the attachment avoidance motivating networks created by the frightening and rejecting parental attachment figure. A single parent essentially became two separate parents, one "abusive" and one "protective."

Managing Trauma Anxiety

As a result of intensive neural cross-inhibition that creates the splitting of representational networks, only one or the other of these motivational systems can be active at any one time. This means that the psychological presence of the "protective parent" would alleviate the child's immense anxiety surrounding the potential presence of the hostile and frightening parental attachment figure, since the avoidance motivating system and its associated representational networks would be entirely cross-inhibited by the activation of the attachment bonding motivation associated with the "protective parent" representation. Only one or the other network could be active at any given time. Since the psychological presence of the "protective parent" would banish the psychological representation for the "abusive parent," the "protective parent" representational network acquired important anxiety management properties.

In the current reenactment of the childhood trauma patterns, the role of the "protective parent" becomes crucial to the management of the reactivated trauma anxiety for the narcissistic/(borderline) parent. In the trauma reenactment narrative, the targeted parent represents the "abusive parent" and the current child is enacting the role as the "victimized child." By adopting the role as the "protective parent" for the current "victimized child," the narcissistic/(borderline) parent is able to embody the anxiety management functions of the "protective parent" in the trauma reactivation and reenactment. The "protective parent" role adopted by the narcissistic/(borderline) parent plays a key role in the ability of the narcissistic/(borderline) parent to regulate the reactivated anxiety from the reawakened childhood trauma experience.

Misattribution of Anxiety

In response to the divorce and the activation of the narcissistic/(borderline) parent's attachment trauma networks, the narcissistic/(borderline) parent must regulate three separate but interrelated sources of immense anxiety,

1) **Narcissistic Anxiety:** Tremendous anxiety surrounding the threatened collapse of the narcissistic defense against the experience of primal self-inadequacy,

2) **Borderline Anxiety:** An intense anxiety surrounding an overwhelming fear of abandonment,

3) **Trauma Anxiety:** Reactivated anxiety from the childhood trauma experience, contained in the attachment system in the pattern of "victimized child"/"abusive parent"/"protective parent" representations.

The subsequent family dynamics that are traditionally referred to as "parental alienation" have their origin in the current efforts of the narcissistic/(borderline) parent to regulate these three separate, but interrelated, sources of tremendous anxiety. In order to resolve and regulate this anxiety, the narcissistic/(borderline) parent engages the current child in a role-reversal relationship as a "regulatory other" for the narcissistic/(borderline) parent's three separate sources of immense anxiety.

By inducing the child's rejection of the targeted parent, the narcissistic/(borderline) parent is able to psychologically expel the primal inadequacy and abandonment fears onto the other parent and restore the narcissistic defense as the all-wonderful idealized and perfect parent (person). By enacting the role as the "protective parent" for the supposedly "victimized child," the narcissistic/(borderline) parent is able to regulate the reactivated trauma anxiety from early childhood attachment trauma. The child's elicited and induced rejection of the targeted parent in attachment-based "parental alienation" represents the narcissistic/(borderline) parent using the child in a role-reversal relationship as a "regulatory object" to regulate the immense anxiety being experienced by the fragile narcissistic/(borderline) personality structure.

The anxiety experienced by the narcissistic/(borderline) parent is real. It is the interpretation made by the narcissistic/(borderline) parent regarding the cause of the anxiety that is false. The narcissistic/(borderline) parent is aware that this anxiety is somehow associated with, and is being triggered by, the targeted parent. In truth, the tremendous anxiety being experienced by the narcissistic/(borderline) parent is only indirectly associated with the other parent (spouse). The anxiety is simply a byproduct of the divorce and interpersonal rejection inherent to the divorce. The divorce also reawakens dormant attachment trauma networks when the attachment system of the narcissistic/(borderline) parent activates to mediate the response to the loss of the spousal relationship. As an emotional signal, anxiety signals the presence of a threat or danger. As the narcissistic/(borderline) parent tries to interpret the meaning of an authentic experience of immense anxiety triggered by the other spouse, the narcissistic/(borderline) parent misinterprets the anxiety as representing an authentic emotional signal that the targeted parent somehow poses an actual threat.

The misinterpretation by the narcissistic/(borderline) parent of an authentic experience of tremendous anxiety as representing an emotional signal of an actual threat posed by the targeted parent is further supported by the splitting dynamic of the narcissistic/(borderline) parent. With the divorce, the attachment bonding motivations toward the other parent as a spouse are completely terminated, and the complete and sole activation of the avoidance motivation system toward the other spouse (the targeted parent) is triggered. As a result of the splitting dynamic, in the mind of the narcissistic/(borderline) parent the targeted parent becomes the embodiment of malevolence and evil who represents an actual threat, and who "deserves" to be punished because of the targeted parent's inherent evil as a person.

The splitting dynamic contributes to and supports the narcissistic/(borderline) personality's misinterpretation of authentic, but misunderstood, anxiety. Together, the authentic but misunderstood anxiety and the splitting dynamic combine to lead the narcissistic/(borderline) parent to conclude that the targeted parent represents an actual threat because of the targeted parent's inherently bad and horrible qualities as a person. This false belief, born from a misinterpretation of authentic anxiety and the splitting dynamic, becomes a firmly entrenched and intransigent delusional belief system.

Consistent with the observations of Millon (2011) regarding the decompensation of the narcissistic personality into delusional beliefs, the narcissistic/(borderline) personality "reconstructs reality" into a "network of fanciful and totally invalid suspicions." In response to a misinterpreted experience of authentic anxiety and the splitting dynamic, the narcissistic/(borderline) parent begins to weave the perception of threat that is supposedly posed by targeted parent into a false narrative guided by the patterns of the attachment trauma ("abusive parent"/"victimized child"/"protective parent").

The trauma networks of the narcissistic/(borderline) parent's attachment system provide the template by which the narcissistic/(borderline) parent interprets the current relationship experience. The representational pattern of the attachment trauma contained in the narcissistic/(borderline) parent's attachment system are in the pattern of "abusive parent"/"victimized child"/"protective parent." As a result, the narcissistic/(borderline) parent interprets the threat posed by the supposedly "abusive" targeted parent within this attachment trauma pattern, as being a threat posed by the targeted parent toward the "victimized child." The remaining role, of the "protective parent," is adopted and conspicuously displayed by the narcissistic/(borderline) parent.

In the fluid psychological organization of the narcissistic/(borderline) parent, the "victimized child" represents both the current child who is believed to be at risk from the supposedly malevolent and "abusive" targeted parent, and also the narcissistic/(borderline) parent as a child, whose abusive relationship with his or her own parent remains instantiated in the traumatized representational networks of the attachment system. In the pathology of the narcissistic/(borderline) parent, the current child symbolically and psychologically represents the "victimized" narcissistic/(borderline) parent as a child. For the narcissistic/(borderline) parent, protecting "the child" becomes a central defining obsession.

In order to regulate the trauma anxiety associated with the reactivated "abusive parent"/"victimized child" representations, the narcissistic/(borderline) parent adopts the role as the all-wonderful, nurturing and "protective parent" for the child. In the childhood experience of the narcissistic/(borderline) parent, the representational network for the all-wonderful "protective parent" served to psychologically ward off (i.e., neurologically inhibit) the anxiety of the narcissistic/(borderline) parent as a child regarding the potential emergence of the "abusive parent" representation. Since "the child" representation is not simply the current child, but is also the narcissistic/(borderline) parent as a child who was the traumatized victim of the frightening-rejecting parent, "the child" being "protected" by the narcissistic/(borderline) parent is both the current child and psychologically the narcissistic/(borderline) parent as a child.

Within the pathology of the narcissistic/(borderline) mind, relationships become a fluidly organized fusion of representational networks. The "abusive parent" is both the current targeted parent and the parent of the narcissistic/(borderline) parent as a child. The "victimized child" is both the current child and the narcissistic/(borderline) parent as a child. Current relationships and past childhood trauma merge into one psychological fusion in the mind of the narcissistic/(borderline) parent. In the fusion of psychological representations, the stage is set for the reenactment of childhood trauma into and through the current family relationships.

The Trauma Reenactment Narrative

The attachment system mediates both the formation and the loss of closely bonded relationships. With the divorce, the attachment system of the narcissistic/(borderline) parent is activated to mediate the loss of the spousal relationship. Within the attachment system of the narcissistic/(borderline) parent, two different but corresponding sets of representational networks become concurrently activated; one set representing the people in the current family relationships, and one set for the attachment figures that are embedded in the internal working models of the attachment system. The representations for the attachment figures embedded in the internal working models of the attachment system are comprised of the formative attachment relationships from the childhood of the narcissistic/(borderline) parent.

The concurrent activation of two matching sets of representational networks, one from the past trauma of childhood relationships and one from the current relationships, creates an overlapping fusion of these representational networks, resulting in a psychological equivalency of these representational networks in the mind of the narcissistic/(borderline) parent. The current family relationships are seen through the psychological lens of the childhood trauma that is contained within the patterns of the internal working models of the attachment system.

The psychological equivalency that is formed between these two sets of representational networks is created through the concurrent neurological co-activation of these two separate, but matching, sets of representational networks within the attachment system of the narcissistic/(borderline) parent. The trauma patterns that are embedded within the internal working models of the narcissistic/(borderline) parent's attachment system become emotionally and psychologically overlaid with the experience of current family relationships, distorting the narcissistic/(borderline) parent's perception of the current family relationships.

The internal working models for attachment figures that are embedded in the attachment system of the narcissistic/(borderline) parent contain trauma representations for the frightening/rejecting parent of childhood and for the helpless/vulnerable child, who is fearful of the emotionally and psychologically "abusive" parent. The childhood anxiety of the helpless and vulnerable child being victimized by the dangerous and rejecting parent is re-experienced by the narcissistic/(borderline) parent with the reactivation of these trauma networks. The reactivation of trauma anxiety from childhood represents a third source of anxiety that the narcissistic/(borderline) parent must regulate in addition to the threatened collapse of the narcissistic defense against the experience of self-inadequacy and the borderline fears of abandonment and rejection.

In the internal working models of the narcissistic/(borderline) parent's attachment system, the parental representation is split into two separate networks; one for the idealized nurturing and protective attachment figure which represents the activation of the attachment bonding motivation, and the other for the dangerous and malevolent attachment figure which represents the avoidance motivating system triggered by the frightening/rejecting parent. The splitting of these representational networks (i.e., the neural cross-inhibition of these networks) is nearly total. If the representational network for the dangerous and abusive parent is active then the representational network for the nurturing and protective parent is entirely shut off. If, on the other hand, the representational network for the nurturing protective parent is active, then this entirely inhibits the activation of the representational network for the dangerous and frightening parent.

For the narcissistic/(borderline) parent as a child, the psychological presence of the nurturing and "protective parent" (i.e., the activation of these representational networks) meant that the child was protected from the frightening and dangerous parent (i.e., the activation of these representational networks). Through the splitting dynamic, the helpless and vulnerable child achieved a form of safety whenever the "protective parent" networks were active. The presence of the "protective parent" (i.e., the activation of these representational networks) thereby served to significantly reduce the child's excessive anxiety that was otherwise created by the child's experience of a dangerous and frightening parent. For the narcissistic/(borderline) parent as a child, the activated representational networks for the "protective parent" served to reduce the excessive anxiety created by a relationship with a dangerous and frightening parent.

In the current reactivation of this trauma pattern that is embedded in the attachment system of the narcissistic/(borderline) parent, the role of the "protective parent" which is adopted by the narcissistic/(borderline) parent becomes critical to the anxiety regulation of the narcissistic/(borderline) parent. The activation of the "protective parent" representational networks in the attachment system of the narcissistic/(borderline) parent are crucial to the ability of the narcissistic/(borderline) parent to regulate the reactivated trauma anxiety associated with re-experiencing of the childhood trauma. It is therefore essential to the psychological regulation of anxiety that the narcissistic/(borderline) parent enact the role of the "protective parent" for the child's corresponding role as the "victimized child" (who symbolically represents both the current child and the narcissistic/(borderline) parent as a child).

The re-experiencing and reenactment of this childhood trauma experience for the narcissistic/(borderline) parent is not a matter of conscious awareness and choice. It emerges from the simultaneous co-activation of two separate but corresponding representational networks that are neurologically embedded in the attachment system patterns of the narcissistic/(borderline) parent. Embedded within the internal working models of the narcissistic/(borderline) parent's attachment system is an unprocessed and un-metabolized trauma, instantiated in the relationship pattern of the dangerous and frightening "abusive parent," the helpless and vulnerable "victimized child" who is in need of protection from the "abusive parent," and the nurturing "protective parent" whose presence protects the child from the frightening "abusive parent."

When the attachment system of the narcissistic/(borderline) parent is activated to mediate the divorce experience (i.e., the loss of the attachment-mediated spousal relationship) the trauma pattern of "abusive parent"/"victimized child"/"protective parent" that is embedded in the attachment system of the narcissistic/(borderline) parent becomes simultaneously co-activated with the current attachment figures of the targeted parent, the child, and the narcissistic/(borderline) parent. This simultaneous co-activation of two corresponding sets of representational networks in the attachment system occurs at the neurological level, below the level of conscious awareness, and results in a neurological fusion of these representational networks into a single psychological experience. In the mind of the narcissistic/(borderline) parent, these two sets of representational networks become psychologically equivalent. In the mind of the narcissistic/(borderline) parent there is absolutely no doubt that the targeted parent is an "abusive parent," that the current child is the "victimized child," and that the narcissistic/(borderline) parent is a "protective parent" who must save the "victimized child" from the dangerous "abusive parent." These are not matters of opinion for the narcissistic/(borderline) parent, these are facts experienced by the narcissistic/(borderline) parent. The narcissistic/(borderline) parent is absolutely convinced, with neurologically imposed certainty, that the targeted parent represents an actual threat to the vulnerable and "victimized child," who, in the mind of the narcissistic/(borderline) parent, needs to be protected from the supposedly "abusive" parenting of the targeted parent.

The "Abusive" Targeted Parent

This distorted perception of the narcissistic/(borderline) parent created by the neurological co-activation of two corresponding sets of representational networks is further enhanced by the splitting dynamic that occurs in the neurological networks of the narcissistic/(borderline) parent. In the neurological networks that create the splitting dynamic only one set of motivational networks can be active at any time. The complete cross-inhibition of the attachment bonding and avoidance motivating systems creates the polarized extremes of perception characteristic of the splitting dynamic, in which other people are either completely idealized or entirely demonized. Balanced and nuanced blends of perception in which people are recognized as having both positive and negative qualities (i.e., the simultaneous activation of both networks) are neurologically impossible to achieve for the narcissistic/(borderline) personality. Either the attachment bonding motivational system is active, or the avoidance motivational system is active; but not both.

When the avoidance motivating system is the active network an extreme and polarized perception of the other person is created as representing the embodiment of pure malevolence and evil who "deserves" to be punished and rejected for this person's inherent and fundamental evil as a person. With the divorce, the other spouse shifts from being embedded within the attachment bonding system to triggering the alternative polarized extreme of the avoidance motivating system. The splitting dynamic of the narcissistic/(borderline) personality transforms the perception of the other spouse into the embodiment of malevolent and abusive inadequacy. The splitting dynamic then supports the attributions to the current family members of the trauma representations contained in the internal working models of the narcissistic/(borderline) parent's attachment networks, in which the former spouse, the targeted parent, becomes psychologically equivalent to the "abusive parent" in the attachment trauma patterns.

The neurological foundations that create this false perception of threat, both from the splitting dynamic and from the psychological equivalency of past and current representational networks through their concurrent co-activation, combines with a misinterpretation of authentically experienced anxiety to create an unshakable experiential certainty for the narcissistic/(borderline) parent that the other parent authentically represents an abusive threat to the child. For the narcissistic/(borderline) parent this false belief is not a matter of opinion, it is an experiential certainty. The narcissistic/(borderline) parent is absolutely certain, beyond all doubt, that the other parent represents an authentic threat to the child, and no amount of conflicting or contrary evidence can convince the narcissistic/(borderline) parent otherwise.

So certain is the narcissistic/(borderline) parent in his or her personal experience regarding the perceived threat posed to "the child" by the other parent, that this false belief rises to the level of a delusional fixation. The narcissistic/(borderline) parent is completely certain, beyond doubt and evidence to the contrary, that the other parent represents an actual "abusive" threat to the child. The need to "protect the child" from the supposedly "abusive" targeted parent becomes an obsession for the narcissistic/(borderline) parent. Separations from the child while the child is in the custody of the targeted parent trigger overwhelming anxiety for the narcissistic/(borderline) parent. This extreme anxiety then motivates the narcissistic/(borderline) parent to make excessive contact with the child through texts, emails, and phone calls while the child is in the care of the targeted parent.

Upon return from visitations with the targeted parent, the excessive anxiety of the narcissistic/(borderline) parent that was triggered by "the child" being with the "abusive parent" results in anxiously motivated questioning of the child regarding the child's well-being while in the care of the other parent; pulling for a report from the child that will confirm the fears and certainty of the narcissistic/(borderline) parent that the other parent represents an "abusive" threat to the child. When the child responds to the anxiously motivated questioning of the narcissistic/(borderline) parent by offering any criticism of the targeted parent, however small, then the fears and delusional certainty of the narcissistic/(borderline) parent begins to distort and inflame the child's elicited criticism into the supposed evidence that confirms the fears and delusional certainty of the narcissistic/(borderline) parent that the targeted parent represents an authentic threat to the child.

The "Victimized Child"

Simultaneously with the targeted parent becoming the "abusive parent" in the trauma reenactment narrative, the current child takes on the trauma reenactment role as the vulnerable and "victimized child." Through a variety of distorted communication exchanges with the child, the narcissistic/(borderline) parent leads the child into accepting and adopting the "victimized child" role relative to the targeted parent. Once the child adopts the "victimized child" role, this then automatically defines the targeted parent as the "abusive parent," confirming the fears and delusional certainty of the narcissistic/(borderline) parent.

As the "victimized child" in the trauma reenactment narrative, the current child occupies the same role as was held by the narcissistic/(borderline) parent as a child in the original childhood trauma of the parent. This symbolic equivalency of the current child with the narcissistic/(borderline) parent as the "victimized child" creates an obsessive fixation for the narcissistic/(borderline) parent to "protect the child," who psychologically represents for the narcissistic/(borderline) parent both the current child as well as the narcissistic/(borderline) parent as a vulnerable and "victimized child."

This fusion of psychological identities between the current child and the narcissistic/(borderline) parent as a child dissolves the psychological boundaries differentiating parent from child. The current child no longer represents a separate psychological being, but becomes fused with the psychological identity of the narcissistic/(borderline) parent. This dissolution of psychological boundaries further fuels the role-reversal relationship in which the child becomes an external "regulatory object" for the parent. To act as a "regulatory object" for the narcissistic/(borderline) parent, the child must become a reflection of the parent's own psychological needs and state. The narcissistic/(borderline) parent does not perceive the separate psychological entity of the child. For the narcissistic/(borderline) parent, parent and child become a single undifferentiated psychological entity.

The "Protective Parent"

The third role contained in the trauma networks of the narcissistic/(borderline) parent is the parental role as the all-wonderful nurturing and "protective parent." This coveted role in the trauma reenactment narrative is adopted by the narcissistic/(borderline) parent, who then conspicuously displays this role as the supposedly "protective parent" to the child and to others.

The "protective parent" role is an expression of the split-off purity of the attachment bonding motivational networks, which are completely isolated from any negative influence from the avoidance motivating networks. Just as the "abusive parent" role is the embodiment of everything bad and evil, the "protective parent" role is the embodiment of all that is good and wonderful. The role as the all-wonderful "protective parent" is the ideal role for the narcissistic/(borderline) parent to adopt and present as a means to reestablish the narcissistic defense of self-grandiosity against the experience of primal self-inadequacy. The trauma reenactment role adopted and displayed by the narcissistic/(borderline) parent as the all-wonderful, ideal, and perfect parent stands in stark contrast to the role being imposed on the targeted parent as the entirely bad, inadequate, and "abusive parent." The parental roles of the splitting dynamic are enacted in the current family relationships.

The role of the "protective parent" within the splitting dynamic is to rescue the "victimized child" from the "abusive" parenting of the malevolent and inadequate targeted parent. Since "the child" psychologically represents both the current child and the narcissistic/(borderline) parent as a child in the original trauma experience, by protecting the current child the narcissistic/(borderline) parent is symbolically also protecting himself or herself as a child. This symbolic psychological protection of the narcissistic/(borderline) parent as a child becomes a central means for the narcissistic/(borderline) parent to regulate the reactivated trauma-related anxiety.

Reenacting Trauma

The co-activation of representational networks in the attachment system of the narcissistic/(borderline) parent create a psychological equivalency of past and current representations. Once the trauma-related roles are ascribed to the current family members through the psychological equivalency of these two sets of attachment networks, a narrative structure is created for the reenactment of the childhood attachment trauma of the narcissistic/(borderline) parent into and through the current family relationships. The features of attachment-based "parental alienation" represent the reenactment in current family relationships of the childhood trauma representations contained in the attachment system of the narcissistic/(borderline) parent.

In psychoanalytic therapy, the reenactment of childhood trauma through the therapeutic relationship is referred to as the "transference," in which a patient "transfers" psychological patterns from childhood onto the relationship with the therapist. In discussing the reenactment of trauma patterns in the transference relationship, Perlman and Courtois (2005) identify four roles in the trauma reenactment narrative,

> "Reenactments of the traumatic past are common in the treatment of this population and frequently represent either explicit or coded repetitions of the unprocessed trauma in an attempt at mastery. Reenactments can be expressed psychologically, relationally, and somatically and may occur with conscious intent or with little awareness. One primary transference-countertransference

> dynamic involves reenactment of familiar roles of victim-perpetrator-rescuer-bystander in the therapy relationship. Therapist and client play out these roles, often in complementary fashion with one another, as they relive various aspects of the client's early attachment relationships" (p. 455).

The family processes traditionally described as "parental alienation" represent the reenactment of attachment trauma from the childhood of the narcissistic/(borderline) parent through the current family relationships as a means of managing the reactivated trauma anxieties, and as a means for the narcissistic/(borderline) parent to achieve a form of psychological mastery over the childhood trauma experience.

The trauma reenactment is the product of the narcissistic/(borderline) parent misinterpreting the experience of intense anxiety created by the threatened collapse of this parent's narcissistic defense against the experience of self-inadequacy, by borderline fears of abandonment and rejection, and from reactivated trauma-related anxiety, as representing an authentic emotional signal of an actual threat posed by the targeted parent. This false perception of threat is interpreted by the narcissistic/(borderline) parent within the trauma pattern embedded in the attachment system of "abusive parent"/"victimized child"/"protective parent." This trauma pattern then serves as the template for the reenactment of the childhood trauma in the current family relationships.

The narcissistic/(borderline) parent creates the reenactment of the childhood trauma by leading the child into adopting the "victimized child" role within the trauma reenactment narrative. Once the child adopts the role as the "victimized child," this automatically defines the targeted parent into the trauma reenactment role as the "abusive parent." The "abusive parent" and "victimized child" roles then allow the narcissistic/(borderline) parent to adopt, and to conspicuously display to others, the coveted role as the all-wonderful "protective parent" who rescues the child from the "abusive parent."

Corrective Changes in the Trauma Reenactment

The reenactment of trauma is an attempt to achieve psychological mastery over the childhood trauma experience as a means to regulate the excessive anxiety created by the reactivation of the childhood trauma. In order to achieve mastery over the childhood attachment trauma that is being re-experienced by the narcissistic/(borderline) parent, two important and vital changes are incorporated into the trauma reenactment narrative that alter the reenactment of the trauma from the original trauma experience. These changes to the original trauma experience serve to reduce the reactivated trauma anxiety by incorporating aspects of psychological mastery over the reenacted childhood trauma experience.

Within the trauma reenactment narrative, the current child represents the "victimized child" role that was the experience of the narcissistic/(borderline) parent as a child during the original childhood relationship trauma. In the swirling attachment representations of the narcissistic/(borderline) parent's attachment system, the current child becomes psychologically equivalent to the "victimized" narcissistic/(borderline) parent as a child. This means that changes to the reenactment narrative involving the "victimized child" role from the original childhood trauma experience of the narcissistic/(borderline) parent as a child will provide a psychologically corrective change to the original trauma experience of the narcissistic/(borderline) parent.

There are two important changes to the "victimized child" role in the trauma reenactment narrative from the original childhood trauma experience of the narcissistic/(borderline) parent that become vital to the narcissistic/(borderline) parent's ability to regulate the reactivated childhood trauma anxiety. These changes to the trauma reenactment narrative from the original childhood trauma experience of the narcissistic/(borderline) parent provide a corrective psychological experience of mastery over the childhood trauma:

1) **Active Child Agency:** In the original childhood trauma experience, the narcissistic/(borderline) parent as a child was a helpless victim of the abuse. In the current trauma reenactment, however, the current child is expressing active agency in rejecting the "abusive parent" rather than passive victimization.

2) **Real-World Protector:** In the original childhood trauma experience, the narcissistic/(borderline) parent as a child was alone and without any actual real-world protection. In the current trauma reenactment narrative, however, the current child has an actual real-world protector for "the child" from the "abusive parent" in the form of the "protective" narcissistic/(borderline) parent.

These alterations in the reenactment narrative from the original childhood trauma experience allow the narcissistic/(borderline) parent to achieve a form of psychological mastery over the childhood trauma, thereby regulating the reactivated trauma anxiety associated with re-experiencing the childhood trauma.

The Child's Active Agency

In the original trauma experience, the narcissistic/(borderline) parent as a child experienced a profound helplessness and vulnerability in the face of an unstable and unreliable affectional bond with a threatening and frightening parent. This vulnerability was a source of tremendous and unresolvable anxiety for the narcissistic/(borderline) parent as a child. When this childhood attachment trauma is reactivated by the loss of the spousal attachment figure through the divorce, the narcissistic/(borderline) parent once again re-experiences the tremendous anxiety associated with the original childhood trauma experience of childlike vulnerability and helplessness.

In the current reenactment of this trauma, however, the theme of the child's helplessness and vulnerability is altered in order to achieve mastery over the childhood trauma experience and its attendant anxiety. In the current reenactment of the childhood trauma, "the child" (who psychologically represents both the current child and the narcissistic/(borderline) parent as a child) is empowered into becoming an active agent in rejecting the supposedly "abusive" targeted parent. In the trauma reenactment "the child" is no longer helpless and vulnerable. Instead, "the child" is empowered into active agency in rejecting the bad and "abusive parent." The empowerment of the current child into actively rejecting the supposedly "abusive" targeted parent represents a significant corrective change acquired through the reenactment of the trauma to the child's helplessness and vulnerability that occurred in the original trauma experience of the narcissistic/(borderline) parent as a child.

Since the current child is psychologically equivalent to the narcissistic/(borderline) parent as a child, empowering the current child in the reenactment of the trauma provides a corrective experience of mastery for the narcissistic/(borderline) parent over the original trauma experience. The current child's empowerment and active agency in rejecting the supposedly "abusive" targeted parent represents an important and essential corrective change to the original childhood trauma experience of the narcissistic/(borderline) parent that is being provided through the trauma reenactment.

When the childhood attachment trauma is reactivated, the narcissistic/(borderline) parent re-experiences a tremendous anxiety associated with the childhood experience, and much of this anxiety is contained within the experience of being a helpless and vulnerable child. The corrective change provided by the child's empowerment reduces the anxiety being re-experienced by the narcissistic/(borderline) parent surrounding the reactivation of the attachment trauma networks. The empowerment of the current child into rejecting the "abusive parent" provides the narcissistic/(borderline) parent with a sense of psychological mastery over the childhood trauma experience and its attendant anxiety. The symbolic representation of "the child" – who psychologically represents both the current child and the narcissistic/(borderline) parent as a child – is no longer helpless and vulnerable in the reenactment of the trauma, but is instead empowered to reject the "abusive parent."

The child's active agency in rejecting the supposedly "abusive parent" requires that the child voice a complete rejection of the supposedly "abusive" targeted parent. The narcissistic/(borderline) parent actively supports the child in achieving this empowered voice. The child's voiced rejection of the targeted parent is firm and steadfast, revealing no ambivalence or uncertainty. The child's empowerment and active agency in rejecting the supposedly "abusive" targeted parent is clear and absolute. The child's voiced certainty is a key feature of empowerment that is achieved through the corrective change contained in the reenactment of the trauma. In the trauma reenactment narrative, the child's rejection of the "abusive parent" is complete, certain, and absolute.

So vital is this corrective change to the original trauma experience, that the need to empower the child can achieve a nearly obsessional focus for the narcissistic/(borderline) parent. The narcissistic/(borderline) parent will often go to great lengths to support the child's empowerment in rejecting the supposedly "abusive" targeted parent, including advocating that the child be empowered to testify in court proceedings regarding the child's desire to reject the supposedly "abusive" and inadequate targeted parent. Common themes of empowerment offered by the narcissistic/(borderline) parent are that therapists and the court should "listen to what the child wants" and that the child should be empowered to "decide whether or not to go on visitations with the other parent." The narcissistic/(borderline) parent will also often empower the child into being able to reject phone calls and visitations with the other parent.

The importance of empowering the child creates a theme of power in the narrative framing of interactions. The narcissistic/(borderline) parent interprets social relationships through a lens of power, control, and domination rather than social flexibility and cooperation. Efforts to enlist the child's cooperation are characterized by the narcissistic/(borderline) parent and child as "forcing" the child to go on visitations, "forcing" the child to accept phone calls from the targeted parent, and "forcing" the child to have a relationship with the targeted parent. This should be contrasted with an alternative and healthier characterization of these activities as the child having the "opportunity" to spend time with the targeted parent. The theme expressed by the narcissistic/(borderline) parent and the child is of either the child's empowerment or the child's "forced" submission to the power and control of others.

A typical statement offered by the narcissistic/(borderline) parent in this regard is:

> **N/(B) Parent:** "What am I supposed to do? I can't **force** the child to go on visitations with the other parent (**force** the child to be nice, **force** the child to cooperate, **force** the child to talk with, etc.)."

The typical statement from the child is,

> **Child:** "I don't want to be **forced** to have a relationship with the other parent. **I'm not ready**. Maybe I'll want a relationship with the other parent later, **when I'm ready**."

These characterizations of the child as being "forced" to have a relationship with the other parent, and the expressed desires of both the narcissistic/(borderline) parent and the child not to "force" the child to do something against the child's will because the child is "not ready" are reflections of the corrective narrative of child empowerment to the original childhood trauma experience of the narcissistic/(borderline) parent of helplessness and vulnerability. In the trauma reenactment narrative, the child must be empowered into rejecting the supposedly "abusive parent." Achieving psychological mastery over the trauma requires that the child be empowered into active agency in rejecting the attempted "domination" of the child by the "abusive parent," and by others who are seeking to "force" the child to do something against the child's will.

Characterizing the child as being "forced" to have a relationship with the other parent, rather than as offering the child a valuable "opportunity" to have a relationship with the other parent, also carries a subtly manipulative influence. Using the term "force" to characterize efforts to encourage the child's "cooperation" carries the clear implication that a relationship with the other parent is somehow negative and "abusive" of the child. If this characterization is not challenged by the other party to the conversation, then the premise contained in the word "force" that a relationship with the targeted parent is somehow "abusive" is accepted as a rational and realistic characterization. The use of the term "force" to characterize a relationship with the targeted parent assertively grabs and manipulates the framing of the child's relationship with the targeted parent.

In addition, the use of the term "force" carries the implication that we are trying to "dominate" the child rather than "respect the child's wishes." This characterization frames efforts to encourage the child's cooperation as efforts to dominate and "force" the child to do something against the child's wishes, which seems "abusive" of the child by not "respecting the child's wishes." Respecting the child's wishes, which appears to be a more noble motivation, would then act to empower the child's rejection of the targeted parent.

Therapists and attorneys who work with children are typically reluctant to "dominate children" and "force" children to do things against their wishes, especially when these children seem otherwise socially pleasant, engaged and conversant, and mature. Therapists and children's attorneys would much prefer to "respect the wishes" of the child whenever possible. By characterizing the child's "cooperation" as "forcing" the child, the manipulative communication of the narcissistic/(borderline) parent seizes control of the dialogue and enlists allies in empowering the child's active agency in rejecting the targeted parent. By using the word "force," the narcissistic/(borderline) parent and child manipulate the therapist and the child's attorney into empowering the child's rejection of the targeted parent. In response to the characterization of a relationship with the targeted parent as being "forced' to be with this parent, therapists and attorneys become reluctant to overpower the child by "forcing the child" to be with the targeted parent. Narcissistic and borderline personalities are masters at manipulative communication and exploitation.

The use of the term "force" to characterize the child's relationship with the targeted parent is a subtle but powerful manipulative communication that:

1. Mischaracterizes the child's "opportunity" to have a positive relationship with a loving and affectionately available parent as somehow being a bad thing;

2. Empowers the child within the trauma reenactment narrative into rejecting a relationship with the normal-range and affectionally available targeted parent;

3. Enlists naïve therapists and attorneys into becoming allies who inadvertently collude with the psychopathology by supporting the child's empowerment to reject the targeted parent;

4. Disempowers efforts to encourage the child's cooperation in forming a positive relationship with the targeted parent by implying that such efforts are somehow "abusive" of the child by not "respecting the child's wishes."

Whenever a child characterizes a relationship with a normal-range and affectionally available parent as being "forced" to be with this parent, therapists and attorneys working with children should immediately and clearly reframe a relationship with the other parent in a more balanced way. The child is being offered a "valuable opportunity" to form a positive relationship with both parents. The child is not being "forced," the child is "cooperating" in forming a positive relationship with a normal-range and affectionally available parent. The child is expected to show appropriate pro-social values of kindness, empathy, cooperation, and respect for authority.

The theme of empowerment adopted by both the narcissistic/(borderline) parent and the child will also be to insist that the child "should be allowed to decide" whether or not to have a relationship with the targeted parent. The empowerment theme that "the child should be allowed to decide" is often accompanied by the collateral theme that the child "shouldn't be forced to have a relationship with the other parent" in a one-two tandem of communication.

If the court continues to insist that the custody of the child be shared and that the child go on visitations with the targeted parent, then the narcissistic/(borderline) parent will often propose that the child testify in court or speak with the judge regarding the child's desire to reject the other parent. While normal-range parents and bystanders are made extremely uncomfortable at the thought of having a child testify in court about rejecting a parent, for the narcissistic/(borderline) parent this seems like a good idea because it empowers the child in the trauma reenactment narrative. The narcissistic/(borderline) parent has a complete absence of empathy for the psychological damage that can be caused to the child by being made to testify in court to reject a parent. Normal-range empathic parents will seldom, if ever, seek to have their child testify in court. The narcissistic/(borderline) parent, on the other hand, seeks it. Any parent who proposes that a child testify in court in order to empower the child into rejecting a relationship with the other parent should immediately become a strong suspect for attachment-based "parental alienation." If the child's wishes need to be heard, then the child should speak with a skilled mental health professional and the mental health professional should testify in the court proceedings.

The trauma reenactment narrative requires the corrective alteration to the original trauma experience of empowering the child into becoming an active agent in rejecting the "abusive parent." As a result, a central feature of the child's symptom display in attachment-based "parental alienation" will be the child's over-empowerment and active agency in completely rejecting with absolute certainty a relationship with the supposedly "abusive" targeted parent (who is actually a normal-range and affectionally available parent). The child's empowerment will be actively supported by the narcissistic/(borderline) parent as evidenced in statements of parental support for the child's ability to decide if the child wishes to be with the targeted parent. The origins for this empowerment symptom is in the corrective change the child's empowerment to reject the "abusive parent" provides to the original childhood trauma experience of vulnerability and helplessness experienced by the narcissistic/(borderline) parent as a child.

A Real-World Protective Parent

In the original childhood trauma experience, the narcissistic/(borderline) parent as a child was alone and unprotected in dealing with the threat posed by a frightening and rejecting parent. In response to threat, children are motivated by the attachment system to seek the protection and safety afforded by the parent. However, when the parent is both the source of protection and of threat, the child has no real-world protector from the threat posed by the frightening parent.

A parent who is simultaneously both the source of threat and of protection creates an intolerable and unresolvable conflict for the child. The child is motivated to flee from the frightening parent, and at the same time the child is motivated to seek protection from the threat with the nurturing and protective parent, who is at the same time the source of threat. This unresolvable conflict generates tremendous anxiety for the child, as the child is motivated to bond to a parent who represents a threat to the child. If the child acts on the motivation to bond to the "protective parent" then the child will be exposed to the anger and hostility of the frightening parent. If, on the other hand, the child avoids the anger and hostility of the frightening parent, then the child is alone, exposed, and without parental protection.

Faced with the unresolvable conflict created when the parent is both a source of threat and of protection, the internal working models of attachment are unable to form an organized and coherent strategy for either forming an attached relationship or for repairing a relationship with the attachment figure when it is ruptured. This disorganized attachment is at the core of the narcissistic and borderline personality structure. Over the course of time, the disorganized and incoherent patterns of attachment within the attachment system develop problematic but necessary coping responses. These problematic coping responses coalesce over time into the narcissistic and borderline personality structures and coping styles evident in adulthood.

Among the coping responses to disorganized attachment is the splitting of attachment representations for the frightening and rejecting parent that trigger avoidance motivations, from attachment representations for the nurturing and protective parent that trigger attachment bonding motivations. When faced with continual incompatible motivations to flee from the frightening parent and to seek protective safety with the protective parent, who is also the frightening rejecting parent, the motivational networks within the child's attachment system begin to increasingly cross-inhibit each other. Eventually, the cross-inhibition becomes so complete that only one or the other of these motivational networks can be active at any one time. This becomes the origins for the splitting dynamic seen in narcissistic and borderline personalities.

Splitting resolves the irreconcilable motivational directives of forming an attachment bond to a frightening attachment figure who is motivating the child's flight response to threat. Through the complete cross-inhibition of the two motivational networks, if the child is motivated to flee from the threat posed by the frightening/abusive parent then the child becomes not at all motivated to seek bonding with the parent. Only the avoidance system is active, and the attachment bonding system is entirely inhibited. If, on the other hand, the child is motivated to bond with the "protective parent," then the child becomes not at all motivated to flee from the frightening/abusive parent. Only the attachment bonding motivational system is active, and the avoidance motivating system is entirely shut down.

This intensive cross-inhibition of the attachment bonding and avoidance motivational networks resolves the child's inner conflict created by the child's efforts to form an attached relationship to a frightening and rejecting parent. The child always has a single clear motivational directive that provides some degree of organized coherence to the child's attachment patterns. However, this resolution leads to extreme perceptions of other people as being either all-bad (the complete activation of the avoidance motivation and the complete inhibition of the attachment bonding motivation), or as being idealized as being completely wonderful and perfect (the complete activation of the attachment bonding motivation and the complete inhibition of the avoidance motivating system). Since people are actually a blend of both positive and negative qualities, this splitting dynamic produces wild swings in the perception of other people, where at one moment the other person will be idealized and highly valued, and in the next moment the other person will be vilified as beneath contempt.

In trying to form an attached relationship to a frightening and rejecting parent, the child will split off (completely cross-inhibit) the networks representing the frightening/abusive parent from the networks for the nurturing/protective parent. In order to achieve some form of coherence to the attachment system, the nurturing/protective parent essentially becomes an entirely different parent from the frightening/abusive parent. Only one or the other parent is psychologically present for the child at any one time. This splitting of the representational networks for the nurturing/protective parent from the representational networks for the frightening/abusive parent eliminates the child's intolerable anxiety created by conflicting motivations to form an attachment bond to a frightening and rejecting parent. The psychological consequence is that one parent has been made into two separate parents; one entirely good, and one entirely bad.

For the narcissistic/(borderline) parent as a child, when the "protective parent" was present psychologically, the "abusive parent" was not. As a consequence of splitting, only the "good parent" or the "bad parent" could be psychologically present at any given time. So the presence of the "good parent" protected the child from the frightening/abusive parent. When the "good parent" was present the "bad parent" was not present. The splitting dynamic provided the child with a limited, yet pathological, form of purely psychological "protection" from the frightening and rejecting parent. In truth, however, the child was alone and without any real-world protection from the fear and danger created by the frightening and rejecting parent.

In the trauma reenactment narrative, however, "the child" has an actual real-world "protective parent" in the role being adopted by the narcissistic/(borderline) parent. Since the current child is psychologically equivalent to the narcissistic/(borderline) parent as a child in the original childhood attachment trauma, the presence of an actual real-world "protective parent" in the current reenactment of the trauma represents a major corrective change in the trauma experience. The role of the "protective parent" in the attachment trauma is to protect the child from the "abusive parent," which thereby eliminates the child's anxiety. By providing the current child with real-world "protection" in the trauma reenactment, not just a psychological protection, but actual real-world protection from the supposedly "abusive" targeted parent, the narcissistic/(borderline) parent is able to achieve mastery over the childhood trauma experience and its attendant anxiety.

The physical embodiment of a real-world protector in the person of the narcissistic/(borderline) parent provides an essential corrective change within the current trauma reenactment narrative from the original childhood trauma experience of the narcissistic/(borderline) parent as a child. So important is this "protective parent" role to the regulation of the reactivated trauma anxiety of the narcissistic/(borderline) parent, that the psychological need of the narcissistic/(borderline) parent to "protect the child" from the supposedly "abusive" targeted parent can achieve the level of an obsessive fixation. Protecting "the child" from the supposedly "abusive" parenting of the targeted parent becomes a psychological imperative for the narcissistic/(borderline) parent imposed by the need to regulate reactivated trauma anxiety from childhood.

In the trauma reenactment narrative, the "victimized child" role of the current child is the role of the narcissistic/(borderline) parent as a child in the original trauma experience. So in the mind of the narcissistic/(borderline) parent, the current child is psychologically equivalent to the narcissistic/(borderline) parent as a child. In protecting the current child from the supposedly "abusive" targeted parent, the narcissistic/(borderline) parent is psychologically providing protection to himself or herself as a child in the original trauma experience. Providing actual real-world protection to "the child," both the current child and psychologically to the narcissistic/(borderline) parent as a child, represents a significant corrective change to the original trauma experience.

By adopting the role of the "protective parent" the narcissistic/(borderline) parent is able to reduce the reactivated trauma anxiety from the original trauma experience. As long as the narcissistic/(borderline) parent is able to protect "the child" from the "abusive parent," the anxiety of the narcissistic/(borderline) parent is held in check. However, when the narcissistic/(borderline) parent is unable to protect "the child," such as when the child is in the care of the other parent (the supposedly "abusive" targeted parent), the anxiety of the narcissistic/(borderline) parent becomes intolerable. The excessive anxiety of the narcissistic/(borderline) parent can provoke concerns for the child's "safety" whenever the child is in the care of the targeted parent and repeated and excessive monitoring of the child through text messages, emails, and phone calls while the child on visitations with the targeted parent. Better still for the narcissistic/(borderline) parent, is to protect "the child" by preventing the child's visitations with the "abusive" targeted parent. "Protecting the child" from the supposedly "abusive" targeted parent becomes an obsessional fixation of delusional proportions for the narcissistic/(borderline) parent.

The role in the trauma reenactment narrative as the "protective parent" allows the narcissistic/(borderline) parent to manage the reactivated anxiety of the childhood trauma experience. Providing "the child" with actual real-world protection rather than merely the psychological protection of splitting that was available to the narcissistic/(borderline) parent as a child, represents a central corrective change in the trauma reenactment narrative to the original trauma experience of the narcissistic/(borderline) parent as a child. Along with the empowerment of the child to reject the "abusive parent," the real-world "protection" afforded to the child by the narcissistic/(borderline) parent allows the narcissistic/(borderline) parent to experience a sense of increased mastery and resolution of the childhood trauma experience.

Delusional Process

The divorce activates the attachment system of the narcissistic/(borderline) parent to mediate the response of the narcissistic/(borderline) parent to the loss of the spousal relationship. The activation of the attachment system reactivates attachment trauma networks that are embedded in the internal working models of the narcissistic/(borderline) parent's attachment system. This creates two simultaneously activated sets of representational networks in the attachment system of the narcissistic/(borderline) parent; one set from the past in the pattern of "abusive parent"/"victimized child"/"protective parent," and one set from the current relationships involving the targeted parent, the current child, and the self-representation of the narcissistic/(borderline) parent.

The concurrent neural activation of two sets of representational networks in the attachment system of the narcissistic/(borderline) parent creates a psychological equivalency for these two sets of networks:

- **Targeted Parent = "Abusive Parent"**

  The representational networks for the targeted parent become fused with and equivalent to the representational networks for the "abusive parent" in the internal working models of the narcissistic/(borderline) parent's attachment system.

- **Current Child = "Victimized Child"**

  The representational networks for the current child become fused with and equivalent to the representational networks for the "victimized child" in the internal working models of the narcissistic/(borderline) parent's attachment system.

- **Narcissistic/(Borderline) Parent = "Protective Parent"**

  The representational networks for the narcissistic/(borderline) parent's self-perception become fused with and equivalent to the representational networks for the "protective parent" in the internal working models of the narcissistic/(borderline) parent's attachment system.

The roles are all in place for the reenactment of the narcissistic/(borderline) parent's attachment trauma into and through the current family relationships. All that remains is to initiate the reenactment of the childhood trauma. This is accomplished by inducing the child into accepting and expressing the "victimized child" role in the trauma reenactment narrative.

The child is first induced into a role-reversal relationship with the narcissistic/(borderline) parent in which the child becomes a "regulatory object" to meet the emotional and psychological needs of the narcissistic/(borderline) parent. Next, through a series of distorted relationship and communication processes, the child is induced into adopting the role of the "victimized child" relative to the other parent. Once the child adopts the "victimized child" role, this automatically defines the targeted parent into the trauma reenactment role as the "abusive parent." The roles of "victimized child" and "abusive parent" allow the narcissistic/(borderline) parent to adopt, and conspicuously display to others, the coveted role as the wonderful and perfect "protective parent."

The trauma reenactment narrative is then played out before an audience of therapists, attorneys, family members, and school personnel. In the process, the trauma reenactment narrative defines the targeted parent as the inadequate and abandoned parent (person), thereby expelling from the narcissistic/(borderline) parent the fears of self-inadequacy and abandonment by projectively displacing them onto the targeted parent. The child's rejection of the targeted parent publicly defines the targeted parent as the inadequate and entirely abandoned and rejected parent (person), while the child's hyper-bonding display toward the narcissistic/(borderline) parent publicly defines this parent as the ideal and all-wonderful, never-to-be-abandoned, perfect parent.

But none of this constructed story is true. The targeted parent is not abusive, the child is not victimized, and the narcissistic/(borderline) parent is not a protective parent. This entire story that is created and enacted through the pathology of the narcissistic/(borderline) is merely an echo of past psychological trauma from the childhood of the narcissistic/(borderline) parent. The trauma reenactment story is not true. Yet the narcissistic/(borderline) parent is absolutely convinced that the reenactment narrative is entirely and absolutely true, and no amount of contrary evidence or rational argument can convince the narcissistic/(borderline) parent that the reenactment narrative does not reflect actual reality.

The narcissistic/(borderline) parent is no longer responding to actual people and events, but is instead reliving a trauma experience from childhood by superimposing the cast of characters from the childhood trauma onto current people and current relationships. The trauma reenactment narrative represents the core psychotic process from which the delusional beliefs of the narcissistic/(borderline) parent develop.

The disorganized attachment networks and inadequate self-structure development of the narcissistic/(borderline) parent cannot adequately regulate emotions. In response to the loss of the attachment figure, the emotional regulation of the narcissistic/(borderline) parent collapses into chaotic disorganization. This complete collapse of self-structure organization includes the collapse of cognitive structures that are responsible for the linear and rational thought used in assessing reality. For the narcissistic/(borderline) parent, if truth and reality need to be distorted and changed in order to maintain or regain a semblance of psychological organization, then truth is sacrificed and reality is distorted in whatever way is needed to meet the emotional and psychological needs of the narcissistic/(borderline) personality structure.

From the reactivation of attachment trauma networks triggered by the divorce and loss of the spousal relationship, the narcissistic/(borderline) parent authentically experiences an immense anxiety. This anxiety originates from three independent but interrelated sources. The narcissistic/(borderline) parent lacks sufficient insight and self-awareness to accurately attribute the causal meaning of the anxiety. All the narcissistic/(borderline) parent knows is that this immense anxiety is somehow being triggered by the other spouse, by the other parent.

The meaning of this authentic anxiety experience is misinterpreted by the narcissistic/(borderline) parent as representing an actual emotional signal that the targeted parent poses a threat to "the child." This authentic but misunderstood and misinterpreted experience of intense anxiety serves as the emotional foundation for the development of delusional beliefs. The trauma reenactment narrative and the splitting dynamic shape the narcissistic/(borderline) parent's interpretation of the intense experience of authentic anxiety into a narrative that the targeted parent poses an actual "abusive" threat to the current "victimized" child, who needs the "protection" of the narcissistic/(borderline) parent. But this is not true. The targeted parent is a normal-range and affectionally available parent and the child is not at risk. It is all a false drama created in the mind of the narcissistic/(borderline) parent.

The trauma reenactment narrative is at the center of creating this delusional belief system. The concurrent co-activation of two sets of representational networks in the attachment system of the narcissistic/(borderline) parent create a neurological equivalency for these representational networks. This fusion of representational networks, one from the past and one for current relationships, creates an unshakable belief in the narcissistic/(borderline) parent regarding the "truth" of the reenactment narrative. The psychological certainty in this "truth" will be maintained despite contrary evidence that the parenting practices of the targeted parent are not abusive and are entirely normal-range parenting practices, and that the child is not a victim of the inadequate parenting of the targeted parent. Actual truth and actual reality are not relevant considerations for the narcissistic/(borderline) parent. For the narcissistic/(borderline) personality, truth and reality are whatever the narcissistic/(borderline) parent needs them to be.

In the mind of the narcissistic/(borderline) parent, the other *spouse* is emotionally and psychologically "abusive" for failing to provide sufficient narcissistic supply, for failing to be the "regulatory object" needed by the narcissistic/(borderline) personality, and for ultimately abandoning and rejecting the narcissistic/(borderline) parent. The narcissistic/(borderline) parent has an experience of being psychologically "abused" by the other *spouse's* failure as a "regulatory object" and rejection/abandonment of the narcissistic/(borderline) parent.

The neurological certainty of the splitting dynamic and the attachment trauma reenactment narrative are absolute. For the narcissistic/(borderline) personality, truth and reality are defined by assertion. This self-created reality, supported by **neurologically imposed certainty**, represents the psychological foundation for the formation of the delusional beliefs regarding the "truth" of the trauma reenactment narrative. In the mind of the narcissistic/(borderline) parent, the current child is actually being emotionally and psychologically "abused" by the malevolence and fundamental parental inadequacy of the targeted parent.

Projected Dangerousness

Beneath the certainty of the narcissistic/(borderline) parent is the desire for retaliation; a malicious satisfaction in causing hurt and suffering to the targeted parent. In the mind of the narcissistic/(borderline) parent, the targeted parent "deserves" to suffer. Causing pain to the targeted parent is satisfying to the narcissistic/(borderline) parent. This represents a primitive form of empathy seeking by instilling the emotional and psychological pain of the narcissistic/(borderline) personality's self-experience into the targeted parent. By inflicting this suffering onto the targeted parent, the targeted parent now understands the primal suffering of the narcissistic/(borderline) experience of self-inadequacy and abandonment.

The narcissistic/(borderline) parent's perception that the targeted parent is abusive and represents a danger is actually a projection onto the targeted parent of the abusive dangerousness of the narcissistic/(borderline) personality. By engaging the child in a role-reversal relationship, the narcissistic/(borderline) parent is using the child as a weapon to inflict as much suffering as possible onto the targeted parent. By using the child as a weapon to inflict emotional suffering on the other parent, it is the narcissistic/(borderline) parent who is psychologically abusing the child. The perception of the targeted parent as "abusive" and dangerous is a projection onto the targeted parent of the abusive dangerousness of the narcissistic/(borderline) personality to both the child and to the targeted parent. The trauma reenactment narrative of the dangerously "abusive" targeted parent and "victimized child" in need of "protection" is not true. However, this narrative is true in reverse. It is the narcissistic/(borderline) parent who represents a danger, to the child and to the targeted parent; it is the narcissistic/(borderline) parent who is psychologically abusive of the child; and it is the targeted parent who represents the truly protective parent. The trauma reenactment narrative is a projective inversion of the actual truth.

In the satisfaction that the narcissistic/(borderline) parent takes in inflicting suffering on the targeted parent, it is the narcissistic/(borderline) parent who is dangerous. The perception of the narcissistic/(borderline) parent that it is the targeted parent who represents an abusive threat to the child because of the targeted parent's supposedly malevolent and abusive parental inadequacy is actually a projection of the narcissistic/(borderline) parent's own psychological process onto the targeted parent. By projecting onto the targeted parent the dangerous malevolence contained within the narcissistic/(borderline) parent's own psychological process, the targeted parent becomes the psychological container for the toxicity of the narcissistic/(borderline) personality. One of the leading authorities in narcissistic and borderline personality structure, Otto Kernberg, describes this projection of malevolence:

> "Patients with borderline personality organization tend to present very strong projective trends, but it is not only the quantitative predominance of projection but also the qualitative aspect of it which is characteristic. The main purpose of the projection here is to externalize the all-bad, aggressive self and object images, and the

main consequence of this need is the development of dangerous, retaliatory objects against which the patient has to defend himself" (Kernberg, 1977, p. 30).

Professional Competence

Yet many mental health and legal professionals fail to recognize the extent of the psychotic and delusional processes expressed by the narcissistic/(borderline) parent in attachment-based "parental alienation." This is because most mental health and legal professionals have only minimal experience with the collapse of narcissistic and borderline personality processes into delusional belief systems. Their lack of experience with psychotic processes may lead them to mistakenly believe that psychotic processes manifest as flamboyant displays of obviously bizarre ideation and behavior, not realizing that psychotic delusional beliefs manifest along a continuum of severity, and in many cases do not overtly appear bizarre until they are probed further for their faulty anchor to reality.

Many mental health professionals, particularly those working with children and families, have little experience with psychotic and delusional processes. For most mental health professionals, encountering delusional beliefs in clients is rare. In the vast majority of their encounters with clients, and with people generally, the other person's thought processes and perceptions are relatively grounded in a consensually agreed upon reality. The client's perceptions may be distorted, but they are not psychotically disconnected to actual reality. The thinking and perceptions for the vast majority of people can be expected to have a least a modicum of grounding in reality.

The lack of familiarity with psychotic and delusional process often leads to a misconception that psychotic processes are evidenced in a display of obviously odd and "crazy" thoughts or behavior. Inexperienced and naïve mental health professionals may interpret "psychotic" as representing the bizarre thoughts and displays of schizophrenia, not realizing that psychotic and delusional processes manifest along a continuum and are not always overtly obvious. Professional expertise in personality disorders and psychotic processes, on the other hand, recognizes that delusions do not need to be bizarre, behavior does not need to be overtly "crazy," and psychotic thinking is not always obvious.

Advanced professional expertise in assessing psychotic and delusional processes is needed to recognize the initial indicators of delusional belief systems, and to then appropriately follow-up with additional targeted assessment regarding the nature and extent of the person's delusional beliefs and psychotic distortions to reality. Since delusional and psychotic distortions are commonly associated with the expression of narcissistic and borderline personality processes, professional expertise regarding the interplay of personality disorders with delusional and psychotic decompensation is required for professional competence when diagnosing and treating family processes that contain a narcissistic or borderline personality parent.

Since most mental health and legal professionals do not expect to encounter psychotic and delusional processes, and have little familiarity in recognizing psychotic and delusional beliefs, they naturally default to the expectation that the reports of the other person have at least some basis in reality. Furthermore, mental health and legal professionals are more likely to make this error when the reports they are relying on come from two separate sources; from the allied and seemingly favored parent and from the child. The assumption made by the mental health professional or attorney is that a report that is corroborated by two persons must have some basis in reality.

While this may be a reasonable expectation in a vast majority of cases, it is not a valid expectation when encountering a narcissistic or borderline personality. The chances of encountering delusional processes with a narcissistic or borderline personality are extremely high, and the expectation surrounding a narcissistic or borderline personality should be to expect to encounter psychotic distortions to reality, rather than the other way around. All assertions made by a narcissistic or borderline personality require <u>independent</u> validation, and the child does <u>not</u> represent independent. It is critical that mental health professionals and children's attorneys have an advanced understanding for narcissistic and borderline personality disorders when dealing with the psychological and family processes associated with attachment-based "parental alienation" and the formation of delusional beliefs. Mental health professionals and children's attorneys dealing with attachment-based "parental alienation" <u>must</u> be able to assess and recognize the psychotic and delusional distortions to reality that emerge from narcissistic and borderline personality processes.

The recognition of psychotic and delusional distortions to reality becomes even more difficult because of the superficially engaging and seductive presentations of the narcissistic and borderline styles of personality. Both the narcissistic and borderline personality styles can be highly skilled at the social manipulation of others, at least in superficial encounters. Their skill at social manipulation and exploitation is derived from the same childhood experiences with a frightening and rejecting parent that created the underlying distortions to their personality structure. In a dangerous interpersonal environment, the narcissistic/(borderline) parent as a child learns to superficially present in ways that make other people "safe." This means becoming superficially charming and enlisting other people as allies. The narcissistic-style personality achieves this by developing socially manipulative approaches that are designed to achieve control over others by acquiring their admiration and submission. The borderline-style personality achieves social safety by developing manipulative approaches that control others through emotional seduction into providing nurture and protection.

With the narcissistic-style personality, the extent of their delusional processes is hidden behind a superficial veneer of assertive self-confidence. The narcissistic-style personality presents as calm and reasonable, and displays a social presentation designed to elicit our admiration. This social presentation of calm self-assurance is directly counter to the general assumption of what a "crazy" psychotic presentation looks like, so the inexperienced and naïve mental health professional or attorney does not expect to encounter a delusional distortion to reality in the reports of the narcissistic-style personality. However, delusional beliefs and a psychotic level of distortion to reality is exactly what is encountered with a narcissistic-style personality (Millon, 2011).

The borderline-style personality is highly skilled at eliciting protective allies and nurturing support from others. The borderline-style personality presents as being very charming and socially engaging (emotionally seductive). The characteristic presentation of the borderline-style personality is as the victim in need of protection. The victim presentation is highly manipulative because it naturally elicits a nurturing and protective response from others. Once the borderline-style presentation of victimization succeeds in eliciting a protective and nurturing response from the other person, the borderline-style personality responds by making the new ally feel wonderful for "protecting" the "helpless vulnerability" of the borderline-style personality. The borderline-style personality is socially "seductive." By presenting as a victim, the borderline-style personality is able to seduce the other person into becoming a protective ally, thereby making the other person safe. Yet the borderline personality is, by definition, on the "borderline" of psychotic disorganization,[2] making the assertions of the borderline personality of alleged victimization highly suspect without additional confirming evidence.

The degree of psychopathology in attachment-based "parental alienation" is severe. That mental health professionals would miss recognizing the psychotic delusional processes, the highly destructive role-reversal relationship, the personality pathology, and the trauma reenactment is professionally inexcusable. It is the professional responsibility and central professional task of mental health professionals to recognize psychopathology. To diagnostically miss the level of pathology involved in attachment-based "parental alienation" can only be explained by professional ignorance that results in professional incompetence.

The confluence of family system dynamics, personality pathology, psychotic delusional processes, trauma reenactment, role-reversal parent-child relationships, and significant attachment system pathology warrant the designation of this group of children and families as representing a "special population" requiring specialized professional knowledge, experience, and expertise to appropriately and accurately assess, diagnose, and treat. Failure to possess the necessary professional knowledge, experience, and expertise required to appropriately and accurately assess, diagnose, and treat this special population of children and families likely represents practice beyond the boundaries of professional competence.

Failure to possess the requisite knowledge and professional expertise necessary to accurately diagnose and appropriately treat this special population of children and families will likely result in the mental

[2] "The diagnosis of "borderline" was introduced in the 1930s to label patients with problems that seemed to fall somewhere in between neurosis and psychosis" (Beck et al., 2004, p. 189).

health professional colluding with and supporting the pathological processes within the family. When, as a result of professional ignorance and practice beyond the boundaries of professional competence, the mental health professional colludes with and supports the psychopathology in the family, the incompetence of the mental health professional will result in significant psychological and developmental harm to the child and emotional and psychological harm to the targeted parent. Practice beyond the boundaries of professional competence that inflicts harm to the client would represent a violation of professional practice standards, and may warrant professional or legal sanctions.

The Bystander Role

Perlman and Courtois (2005) identify four characteristic roles in the reenactment of trauma; the "roles of victim-perpetrator-rescuer-bystander." The three primary roles in the trauma reenactment of attachment-based "parental alienation" are:

- The "abusive parent" role, corresponding to the "perpetrator" role identified by Perlman and Courtois,
- The "victimized child" role, corresponding to the "victim" role identified by Perlman and Courtois
- The "protective parent" role, which corresponds to the "rescuer" role of Perlman and Courtois.

In addition to these three primary trauma reenactment roles, the "bystander" role identified by Perlman and Courtois also plays an important part in the trauma reenactment narrative of attachment-based "parental alienation." The role of the "bystander" in attachment-based "parental alienation" is filled by all the various therapists, attorneys, judges, teachers, and extended family members. These "bystanders" serve three separate functions in the trauma reenactment narrative of attachment-based "parental alienation." The role of the "bystander" is first to legitimize the "truth" of the reenactment narrative. The second role of the "bystander" in the trauma reenactment narrative is to publically shame the targeted parent. The "bystander" role also acts to provide "narcissistic supply" by legitimizing the wonderful-parent presentation of the narcissistic-(borderline) parent.

Legitimize the Reenactment Narrative

By accepting the reenactment narrative as being true, the "bystanders" validate the legitimacy and authenticity of the reenactment narrative. The trauma reenactment narrative of attachment-based "parental alienation" actually represents a false drama created by the narcissistic/(borderline) parent. In truth, the targeted parent is not abusive, the child is not a victim, and the narcissistic/(borderline) parent is not protecting the child. In truth, the targeted parent is a normal-range and affectionally available parent, the child is a normal-range child who loves both parents, and the narcissistic/(borderline) parent is using the child as a weapon to inflict suffering on the targeted parent. The reenactment narrative created by the narcissistic/(borderline) parent is a delusion.

Yet when the "bystander" therapists and attorneys accept the trauma reenactment narrative as being a reasonable explanation for the child's rejection of the targeted parent, they are allowing their power and authority in their role as therapist or attorney to be used by the pathology of the narcissistic/(borderline) parent to confirm the legitimacy of the trauma reenactment narrative. Their acceptance of the reenactment narrative legitimizes the truth of the reenactment narrative. The reenactment narrative of "abusive parent"/"victimized child"/"protective parent" becomes true because the "bystanders" in the trauma reenactment narrative accept it as being true. The role of the "bystander" in attachment-based "parental alienation" is to validate the truth of the trauma reenactment narrative.

When therapists and children's attorneys accept the validity of the false drama created by the pathology of the narcissistic/(borderline) parent in attachment-based "parental alienation," they are inadvertently fulfilling their "bystander" roles within the trauma reenactment narrative. By conferring legitimacy to the delusional construction of the narcissistic/(borderline) parent, these "bystander" mental health professionals and attorneys are actively colluding with the psychopathology. Through their ignorance regarding the psychopathology involved in attachment-based "parental alienation," these "bystander" mental health professionals and attorneys are allowing their professional standing to be exploited by the psychopathology of the narcissistic/(borderline) parent to confer legitimacy to a delusional belief and false drama that ultimately destroys the lives of both the child and the targeted parent.

Shaming of the Targeted Parent

The "bystander" role in the trauma reenactment narrative of attachment-based "parental alienation" also serves to confer public shaming onto the targeted parent. The "bystanders" bear public witness to the exposed parental (personal) inadequacy of the targeted parent. The "bystanders" provide the audience for the public humiliation of the targeted parent, who is being rejected by the child for being an "abusive" and inadequate parent (person).

The divorce represents a narcissistic injury in which the inadequacy of the narcissistic/(borderline) parent as a *spouse* is publicly exposed. The narcissistic/(borderline) parent is being publicly rejected as a spouse by the targeted parent because of the inadequacy of the narcissistic/(borderline) personality. This public exposure of the inadequacy of the narcissistic/(borderline) parent threatens to collapse the narcissistic defense against the experience of primal self-inadequacy. The processes of attachment-based "parental alienation" represent the efforts of the narcissistic/(borderline) parent to restore the narcissistic defense by projectively displacing onto the targeted parent the fears of inadequacy and abandonment. The child's rejection of the targeted parent defines the targeted parent as being the inadequate and rejected parent (person).

The role of the "bystander" is to provide social validation for the inadequacy and abandonment of the targeted parent. Within the reenactment narrative, the fundamental inadequacy and "abusive" parenting of the targeted parent is being publicly exposed to the social community, represented by the "bystanders" in the trauma reenactment narrative. The public display to the "bystanders" through the trauma reenactment narrative of the child's rejection of the targeted parent represents a public shaming of the targeted parent for his or her primal inadequacy as a parent (person).

The "bystanders" act as the social community for this public shaming of the targeted parent. By publicly exposing the fundamental inadequacy and abandonment of the targeted parent to the social community represented by the "bystanders," the narcissistic/(borderline) parent is able to counteract and repair the public exposure of his or her own inadequacy as a spouse that was triggered by the targeted parent through the divorce.

Witness to Narcissistic Grandiosity

The "bystanders" in the trauma reenactment narrative also serve as public witness to the displayed magnificence of the narcissistic/(borderline) parent as the wonderfully nurturing and "protective parent." In choosing to reject the "abusive" and inadequate targeted parent in favor of being with the narcissistic/(borderline) parent, the child is used to validate to the "bystanders" the magnificence of the narcissistic/(borderline) parent as being the ideal and wonderful parent. The possession of the narcissistic object of the child represents a symbol of the narcissistic/(borderline) parent's superiority and victory over the targeted parent. It is the targeted parent who is rejected as the inadequate parent (person) by the child. The narcissistic/(borderline) parent is the all-wonderful and perfect parent (person) who is being selected by the child.

The narcissistic/(borderline) parent is secure in the child's well-rehearsed criticisms of the targeted parent:

- The child hates being with the targeted parent because of some past parental failure or inadequacy. This past parental failure by the targeted parent is simply too heinous to be forgiven.

- The child is afraid of the targeted parent, having panic attacks and stress at simply the thought of being with the targeted parent, or at having the targeted parent attend the child's event or activity.

- The targeted parent never spent enough special time with the child in the past, and is too involved with the new spouse.

- The targeted parent is too controlling and never listens to what the child wants. The targeted parent is too insensitive to the child's feelings.

- The child wants to be allowed to "decide" which parent the child wants to be with, and maybe, if the targeted parent "respects the child's wishes" and allows the child to be completely with the allied and supposedly favored narcissistic/(borderline) parent, then maybe the child might want to spend time with the targeted parent sometime in the future (maybe).

Confident in the child's oft-rehearsed criticisms of the targeted parent, the narcissistic/(borderline) parent will eagerly present the child to the "bystanders" of therapists and attorneys, which allows the narcissistic/(borderline) parent to conspicuously display for the "bystanders" the coveted role as the wonderfully nurturing and understanding "protective parent."

Having psychologically surrendered to the will of the narcissistic/(borderline) parent, the child eagerly embraces the "victimized child" role by offering to the "bystander" therapists and attorneys a litany of well-rehearsed criticisms of the targeted parent, both as a parent and also as a person. The child fully expects that these criticisms will be met with the same understanding support from the "bystander" as they received from the narcissistic/(borderline) parent. If, perchance, the "bystander" somehow challenges the legitimacy of the child's rehearsed criticisms, the child will become confused and disoriented, and the reporting of criticism begins to break down.

If a "bystander" therapist fails to validate the reenactment narrative and challenges the legitimacy of the child's criticisms, then the narcissistic/(borderline) parent will quickly seek to have this therapist removed from treatment. For the narcissistic/(borderline) parent, the purpose of therapy is not to have the child get better and restore a relationship with the targeted parent. For the narcissistic/(borderline) parent, the purpose of therapy is for the "bystander" therapist to validate the legitimacy of the trauma reenactment narrative of "abusive parent"/"victimized child"/"protective parent." If the therapist fails in their "bystander" role in the trauma reenactment narrative, then the narcissistic/(borderline) parent will replace this "bystander" therapist with one who will validate the legitimacy of the reenactment narrative.

There are two ways that the narcissistic/(borderline) parent can remove a non-cooperative "bystander" therapist from treatment. The first way is to simply withdraw parental consent for treatment with the non-cooperative "bystander" therapist. The most effective way of ensuring that the therapist fulfills the "bystander" role in the reenactment narrative is for the narcissistic/(borderline) parent to only consent to the child's treatment with providers who legitimize the trauma reenactment narrative.

If withdrawing parental consent for treatment with the non-cooperative "bystander therapist" is not possible as a means to remove a non-cooperative "bystander" therapist, then the narcissistic/(borderline) parent will employ a tried-and-true method of achieving power and control; i.e., inducing and then exploiting child symptoms. Following a therapy session, the narcissistic/(borderline) parent will elicit a child criticism of the therapist, typically that the therapist is not sufficiently "understanding" of the child's feelings (meaning that the therapist does not accept the legitimacy of the trauma reenactment narrative). The narcissistic/(borderline) parent then uses this child complaint to petition the court for a change in therapists to one who is more "understanding" of the child, and with whom the child feels more "comfortable." In this way, the child is empowered to select a therapist who does not challenge the child's presentation as a "victim" of the supposedly "abusive" parental inadequacy of the targeted parent.

Together, the narcissistic/(borderline) parent and the child put on their show of the reenactment narrative for the audience of "bystanders," with the child in the leadership position of offering a well-rehearsed set of criticisms of the targeted parent around select themes that were previously provided to the child by the narcissistic/(borderline) parent during the induction process. Meanwhile, the narcissistic/(borderline) parent takes the opportunity to make a full display to the "bystanders" of being the perfectly nurturing and concerned "protective parent." The role of the "bystander" therapists and attorneys is to accept and thereby validate the legitimacy of the reenactment narrative; that the targeted parent is the "abusive" and inadequate parent who is being rejected by the child for being a fundamentally inadequate parent (person).

The failure of mental health and legal professionals to recognize the extreme degree of psychopathology involved with attachment-based "parental alienation" will result in their seduction by the psychopathology into adopting their collusive role as the legitimizing "bystander" in the trauma reenactment narrative. In this "bystander" role, therapists and attorneys will wind up actively supporting and colluding with the psychopathology in the family, to the psychological and developmental harm of the child and the emotional and psychological harm of the targeted parent.

Attachment-based "parental alienation" is not a child custody issue, it is a child protection issue. Mental health professionals and legal professionals assigned to represent the child's interests must possess the level of professional competence necessary to serve the best interests of the child. Failure to recognize the extraordinary severity of the pathology involved in attachment-based "parental alienation," and failure to protect the child from the profound psychological and development harm associated with attachment-based "parental alienation," is to collude with the pathology and psychological abuse of the child.

Chapter 8

THE CHILD'S EXPERIENCE

The Goal-Corrected Attachment System

The attachment system is a primary motivational system that evolved from the selective predation of children. The attachment system strongly motivates children's bonding to parents in order to acquire parental protection from predators and other environmental dangers. As a primary motivational system embedded in the neurological networks of the brain, the attachment system functions and dysfunctions in characteristic ways that have received considerable research focus and identification.

The attachment system is a "goal-corrected" motivating system, meaning that it always maintains as its goal the formation of an affectionally attached bond to the parent. Problematic parenting produces an insecure attachment bond to the parent that increases the child's exposure to predators and other environmental dangers. Children who rejected parents lost parental protection from predators and other environmental dangers, and their genes were selectively removed from the collective gene pool. On the other hand, children who became more strongly motivated to bond to problematic parents were better able to continue to receive parental protection. These children survived at higher rates and their genes increased in the collective gene pool.

Problematic parenting creates an insecure attachment bond which increases the child's motivation to seek an attachment bond with the problematic parent. The approach the child develops to forming an attachment bond to a problematic parent represent the patterns of insecure attachment. When the child is confronted with problematic parenting, the attachment system motivates the child to make adjustments *to the way* in which the child seeks to form an attachment bond to the parent, yet the attachment system always maintains the goal of forming an attachment bond to the parent. This is what is meant by the attachment system being a "goal-corrected" motivational system. It always maintains the goal of forming an attached relationship to the parent, and in response to problematic parenting it adjusts (corrects) the child's behavior in characteristic ways that maximize the available attachment bond to the parent to the fullest extent possible. Under no circumstances does the attachment system seek to sever the parent-child bond. Severing the parent-child would expose the child to increased predation and other environmental dangers, so that genes that allowed children to sever the parent-child attachment bond were selectively removed from the collective gene pool

Because the attachment system is a goal-corrected motivational system that always seeks to form an attachment bond to the parent, the type of problematic parenting the child has been exposed to will be evident in the type of adjustments the attachment system makes to the child's behavior in an effort to maximize the attachment bond to the problematic parenting. In response to problematic parenting that creates inconsistent parental availability, the child develops an "anxious-ambivalent" attachment response (sometimes called a "preoccupied" attachment) in which the child displays increased protest behavior that elicits increased parental involvement and demands continual parental attention (commonly referred to as seeking "negative attention"). Sometimes the child with anxious-ambivalent attachment will display increased anger and defiance that elicit greater parental involvement and attention. At other times the child may demand increased parental involvement through displays of emotional neediness and dependency. The characteristic behavior of children with insecure anxious-ambivalent attachment is to seek increased parental involvement through displays of increased child protest behavior (such as child defiance, angry outbursts, tantrums, anxiety displays, etc.). These characteristic responses of the child to problematic parenting have the goal of eliciting greater parental involvement from an inconsistently available parent.

In response to problematic parenting in which the parent becomes rejecting or withdraws further from the child's demands for involvement, such as a depressed or chronically angry parent, the child develops an "anxious-avoidant" attachment response of being low-demand and overly self-reliant. In an anxious-avoidant attachment response the child becomes withdrawn and overly self-reliant so as to avoid provoking the parent's further rejection or withdrawal. When the child is confronted with a parent who becomes rejecting or withdraws further when the child displays protest and needy behaviors, the child develops a response of being low-demand as a means to maximize the amount of parental involvement that is available by not provoking further withdrawal from the parent by being demanding or needy.

In authentic parent-child conflict, the child's behavior always has the goal of forming an attachment bond to the parent. The anxious-ambivalent child emits a high frequency of protest behaviors that create parent-child conflict in order to elicit the continual focus of the parent on the child, whereas the anxious-avoidant child learns to become low-demand and overly self-reliant to avoid provoking the parent's further withdrawal or rejection. In both cases, however, the goal is always to form an attachment bond to the parent to the greatest extent possible.

The goal of the attachment system is <u>always</u> to form a parent-child attachment bond. When parent-child conflict is created by problematic parenting, the child still <u>wants</u> to form an attached relationship with the parent. However, the child's attachment bonding motivations are being frustrated by the problematic parenting practices of the parent. In response, the child will emit increased protest behavior designed to elicit greater parental involvement in hopes to be able to establish or restore the parent-child attachment bond. When authentic parent-child conflict arises from problematic parenting practices, the child's increased protest behavior is a product of the child's frustrated desire to form an affectionally attached relationship with the parent.

The attachment system is a primary motivational system embedded in the neurological networks of the brain. The attachment system evolved in the context of the selective predation of children because it confers significant survival advantage to children. It is a very strong and resilient system that does not dysfunction easily. The attachment system strongly motivates children's affectional bonding to parents. The attachment system is a "goal-corrected" motivational system that always maintains the goal of establishing an affectional bond to the parent. Problematic parenting alters *the approach* that the child uses to form an attachment bond, but problematic parenting does not alter the primary goal of the attachment system to form an attachment bond to the parent.

Under no circumstances is the normal-range response of the attachment system to sever the parent-child bond. Children never evidence "detachment" behavior toward a parent because "detachment" behavior would expose children to increased risks of predation and other environmental dangers. Under some circumstances, children may become discouraged in forming an affectionally attached relationship with a parent, but they always want an affectionally attached relationship with the parent. The attachment system is a primary motivational system that always motivates the child toward the goal of forming an affectionally attached relationship with a parent.

There are only four circumstances involving severely pathogenic parenting that can induce a termination of the child's attachment bonding motivation toward a parent:

1) **Incest:** Sexual abuse of the child by a parent will immediately terminate the child's attachment bonding motivation toward the parent. Incest represents a profound boundary violation involving a narcissistic parent who is using the child in a role-reversal relationship to meet the parent's highly aberrant and distorted sexual-psychological needs. In incest, the parent essentially becomes a sexual "predator." The attachment system does not motivate children to bond to the predator. Instead, the attachment system motivates children to flee the predator and seek the protection of the protective parent. Incest will immediately terminate the child's attachment bonding motivations toward the parent.

2) **Extreme Parental Violence:** Years of severe parental violence, expressed as either physical child abuse or severe domestic violence, can in some cases terminate the child's attachment bonding motivation toward the violent parent. The violent parent essentially becomes the violent "predator" who presents a safety risk to the child or to the parent with whom the child shares an attachment bond.

As a predator driven system, the child's attachment system is a very strong and resilient primary motivational system embedded in the neural networks of the brain. It is extremely hard to induce a termination of the child's attachment bonding motivations toward a parent. In order for parental violence to terminate the primary motivational system of attachment bonding toward a parent, the parental violence needs to be severe and the child's exposure to the parental violence needs to be chronic and long-lasting. In cases of less severe forms of parental violence, the parental violence will tend to create an insecure attachment bond to the parent in which the child becomes MORE strongly motivated to bond to the aggressive-hostile parent. In an insecure attachment relationship with a violent-aggressive parent, the child displays timid and submissive behavior of being low-demand (i.e., anxious-avoidant attachment) as a means to establish and maintain, to the extent possible, the attachment bond to the hostile-aggressive parent.

A bad parent, even a severely bad parent, is always preferable to the predator. Children who rejected a bad parent were either eaten by predators or fell prey to other environment dangers. Rejecting a parent selectively removed these children's genes from the collective gene pool. Children who responded to bad parenting with a <u>stronger</u> motivation to bond to the problematic parent (i.e., who developed an insecure attachment) were better able to receive continued parental protection from predators and other environmental dangers. As a result of the selective survival advantage provided to children by an attached relationship with their parents, even to bad parents, genes motivating <u>increased</u> bonding to bad parents increased in the collective gene pool.

In their study on the neurological foundations for children's stronger motivations to bond to abusive parents, Raineki, Moriceau, and Sullivan (2010) concluded,

> "A potential evolutionary explanation suggests selection pressures supported infants that remained attached because it increased the probability of survival. From an adaptive point of view, perhaps it is better for an altricial animal to remain attached to an abusive caregiver than receive no care" (p. 1143).

John Bowlby who first described the functioning of the attachment system, observed,

"The paradoxical finding that the more punishment a juvenile receives the stronger becomes its attachment to the punishing figure, very difficult to explain in any other theory, is compatible with the view that the function of attachment behavior is protection from predators" (Bowlby, 1969, p. 227).

3) **Chronic Parental Neglect:** Decades of severely neglectful parenting, such as might occur with severe and chronic parental substance abuse, can sometimes terminate a child's attachment bonding motivation toward the parent.

The termination of the attachment bonding motivation under these circumstances tends to reflect profound child discouragement in the ability to form an affectionally attached bond to the parent, rather than an outright termination of the attachment bonding motivation itself. Since this represents discouragement rather than an actual termination of the attachment bonding motivation, if the problematic parent subsequently recovers and becomes available for attachment bonding with the child then the child's normal-range attachment bonding motivations often reappear.

More often, however, in response to severe parental incapacity such as occurs in chronic parental substance abuse, the child will develop a "parentified" role-reversal relationship with the parent. In a parentified role-reversal relationship, the child adopts the "parent role" of providing care toward the incapacitated parent, who adopts the "child role" of dependency.

4) **Role-Reversal with a Narcissistic/(Borderline) Parent:** The formation of a role-reversal relationship with a narcissistic/(borderline) parent can induce an artificial suppression of the child's attachment bonding motivations toward the **other parent**.

In this induced artificial suppression of the child's attachment bonding motivations, the narcissistic/(borderline) parent co-creates with the child a definition of the other parent as representing an "abusive" threat to the child. By defining the **other parent** as representing a threat to the child, the narcissistic/(borderline) parent essentially creates a definition of the other parent as being the dangerous "predator" relative to the child's attachment bonding motivations. When one parent defines the other parent as representing a threat to the child (i.e., as "the predator"), this effectively suppresses the normal-range attachment bonding motivations of the child toward the supposedly dangerous "predator," who is now represented by the other parent.

The survival advantage provided by the attachment system is so strong that the child's attachment bonding motivations can only be terminated in these extreme cases of narcissistic parenting. In other cases of poor and problematic parenting, the effect on the child's goal-corrected attachment motivations is to produce an insecure attachment bond to the parent. An insecure attachment will distort the child's behavior toward the problematic parent in characteristic ways that are designed to maximize the parent's involvement with the child.

Children do not reject parents, even bad parents. Instead, under all but the most extreme circumstances, children show an insecure attachment toward a problematic or bad parent. An insecure attachment is evidenced by an increase in the child's attachment bonding motivation toward the problematic parent. The response of the attachment system to problematic parenting behavior is to distort the child's responses to the parent in characteristic ways as the child's attachment system tries to establish and maintain an attached bond to the problematic parent.

Specificity of Attachment Bonding

Children's attachment bonding motivations are very specific to the parent. In the evolution of the attachment system, children who fled from the predator and sought protection from any adult in the social group might not receive protection from other, non-parental adults. While children might sometimes receive protection from other adults in the social group, especially from extended family, there would nevertheless be a small but important survival advantage provided to children from flight to the *specific* person of a parent, rather than to any member of the social group. Over the course of millions of years of evolution of the attachment system, this small but significant survival advantage provided by flight to a specific parental attachment figure created a prominent bias in the attachment system toward bonding to specific individuals, the child's parents, over other members in the social group.

The specificity of attachment motivation creates one of its characteristic features, the distinctive feelings of possessive ownership of the other person in an attached relationship. This feeling of possessive ownership can achieve an almost property ownership quality; **my** mother, **my** father, **my** son, **my** daughter, **my** husband, **my** wife. That other person "belongs" to me, and I "belong" to that person.

Relative to our attachment motivations, people are not interchangeable. The child can form additional attachment bonds to additional people, but a primary attachment bond will always exist to the specific person of the child's mother and father. This specificity of the attachment bond to a parent is not interchangeable or replaceable by any other additional attachment bond that may form to any other person. Additional attachments to grandparents, aunts, uncles, cousins, coaches, teachers, and step-parents, can all form in addition to the attachment bond the child has for the specific parental attachment figures, but none of these supplemental attachment figures can *replace* the specificity of the child's primary attachment bond to "**my** mother" and "**my** father."

However, in attachment-based "parental alienation" the child may sometimes assert that a relationship with the new spouse of the narcissistic/(borderline) parent, or with an extended family member of the narcissistic/(borderline) parent, serves as a "replacement" attachment bond to the one the child has with the targeted-rejected parent. In some of these cases, the child may discontinue expressing possessive ownership of the targeted parent. The child will begin calling the targeted parent by this parent's first name, rather than using the possessive appellation of "mom," or "dad," or "my" mother or "my" father. In these cases, the child may begin calling the new step-parent (i.e., the spouse of the narcissistic/(borderline) parent) "mom" or "dad." This transfer of possessive ownership to the step-parent spouse of the narcissistic/(borderline) parent is typically supported by the narcissistic/(borderline) parent, who uses the child's transfer of possessive ownership of the parent to the step-parent as supposed evidence that the child no longer needs the targeted-rejected parent.

This transfer of possessive ownership, however, is not authentic to how the attachment system actually functions. Primary attachment relationships are not interchangeable or replaceable. Indications that the child is replacing a primary attachment bond to a parent with one to a step-parent represents the unequivocal product of the distorting parental influence of the narcissistic/(borderline) parent on the child. The child can form additional attachment bonds, but the child will not replace a parent with a new attachment figure.

The assertion that the child's attachment bond to the targeted parent has been *replaced by the child's new relationship* with the (step-parent) spouse of the narcissistic/(borderline) parent is not authentic to how the attachment system functions. Indications of the child's *termination of possessive ownership* of the targeted parent are also foundationally inconsistent with the normal-range functioning of an authentic attachment system. Both of these circumstances would represent clear diagnostic evidence for an induced distortion to the child's attachment system by a narcissistic/(borderline) allied and supposedly favored parent.

The replacibility of people is a distinctive characteristic of the narcissistic personality. For the narcissistic personality, people become expendable once they cease to provide narcissistic supply. According to Kernberg,

> "Underneath the feelings of insecurity, self-criticism, and inferiority that patients with borderline personality organization present, one can frequently find grandiose and omnipotent trends. These very often take the form of a strong unconscious conviction that they have the right to expect gratification and homage from others, to be treated as privileged, special persons. The devaluation of external objects is part of a corollary of the omnipotence; if an external object can provide no further gratification or protection, it is dropped and dismissed because there was no real capacity for love of this object in the first place" (Kernberg, 1975, p. 33).

For the narcissistic/(borderline) parent, the attachment figure becomes expendable, to be "dropped and dismissed," when they no longer provide "further gratification" to the narcissistic/(borderline) personality. The child who is dismissing possessive ownership of a parent, or who is replacing a parent with the step-parent spouse of the allied and supposedly favored parent, is evidencing this characteristic narcissistic/(borderline) trait of distorted attachment bonding. The termination of the child's possessive ownership of the targeted parent is foundationally inconsistent with the authentic functioning of the child's attachment system. The child's termination of possessive ownership of the targeted parent represents a diagnostically distinctive feature indicating the influence on the child by a narcissistic/(borderline) parent. For the narcissistic/(borderline) parent, the premise that the targeted parent would be "dropped and dismissed" by the child when the targeted parent no longer provides the child with "further gratification" is accepted as a reasonable and normal occurrence. In truth, however, it is far from reasonable and far from normal.

The Grief Response

As a primary motivational system, the attachment system functions in characteristic ways, and it dysfunctions in characteristic ways. One of the leading experts in the attachment system, Mary Ainsworth, describes the formation of affectional bonds and the characteristic functioning of the attachment system,

> "I define an 'affectional bond' as a relatively long-enduring tie in which the partner is important as a unique individual and is interchangeable with none other. In an affectional bond, there is a desire to maintain closeness to the partner. In older children and adults, that closeness may to some extent be sustained over time and distance and during absences, but nevertheless there is at least an intermittent desire to reestablish proximity and interaction, and pleasure – often joy – upon reunion. Inexplicable separation tends to cause distress, and permanent loss would cause grief."
>
> "An 'attachment' is an affectional bond, and hence an attachment figure is never wholly interchangeable with or replaceable by another, even though there may be others to whom one is also attached. In attachments, as in other affectional bonds, there is a need to maintain proximity, distress upon inexplicable separation, pleasure and joy upon reunion, and grief at loss" (Ainsworth, 1989, p. 711).

The attachment system is a primary motivational system embedded in the neurological networks of the brain as a result of millions of years of selective evolutionary pressures. As a primary motivational system, the attachment system is analogous to the other primary motivational systems for eating and reproduction. When we do not eat for an extended period of time we experience hunger. The experience of hunger at the loss of food is a natural result of the primary motivational system for eating. Similarly, when an attachment bond is lost the attachment system creates a grief response. Grief is the natural and consistently produced response of the attachment system to the loss of an affectional bond to an attachment figure.

When family bonds are disrupted by the divorce, the child will naturally feel sadness over the loss of the intact family structure and the separation from family members. In attachment-based "parental alienation," this seed of grief at the loss of the intact family, which is a natural product of the child's attachment system, is then distorted and inflamed under the pathological influence of the narcissistic/(borderline) parent into the child's anger and rejection of the other parent. Through the distorting influence of the narcissistic/(borderline) parent, the child is led into misinterpreting the meaning of this authentic and natural grief response as instead representing something "bad" that the targeted parent is doing to produce the child's sadness. The narcissistic/(borderline) parent leads the child into believing that the child is being made sad by the supposedly "abusive" parenting practices of the targeted parent.

In the absence of an alternative explanation to that offered by the narcissistic/(borderline) parent for the child's sadness and hurt (i.e., for the natural grief response to the loss of the intact family) that the other parent is doing something bad to hurt the child, the child accepts the false interpretation offered by the narcissistic/(borderline) parent. When people do bad things to us, it hurts. The child hurts. So this must mean that someone is doing something bad to make the child hurt.

Parents are supposed to help children understand and make sense of their feelings and experiences. However, the narcissistic/(borderline) parent is incapable of helping the child understand and process the child's sadness and grief surrounding the divorce because the narcissistic/(borderline) parent is incapable of processing sadness and loss themselves. The inability to process sadness is an inherent characterological deficit of the narcissistic/(borderline) parent. As noted earlier, Kernberg (1975) describes this deficiency of the narcissistic personality,

> "They are especially deficient in genuine feelings of sadness and mournful longing; their incapacity for experiencing depressive

> reactions is a basic feature of their personalities. When abandoned or disappointed by other people they may show what on the surface looks like depression, but which on further examination emerges as anger and resentment, loaded with revengeful wishes, rather than real sadness for the loss of a person whom they appreciated" (p. 229).

Since the narcissistic/(borderline) cannot adequately experience and process sadness and grief, this parent cannot help the child correctly interpret and process the child's own authentic experience of sadness and loss surrounding the divorce and the changing family structure. In the child's fused psychological relationship with the narcissistic/(borderline) parent in which the child is being used as a "regulatory object" for the narcissistic/(borderline) parent, the child must share the same attitudes and beliefs as the narcissistic/(borderline) parent. The narcissistic/(borderline) parent therefore leads the child into a similar interpretation of the child's sadness as that of the parent, as "anger and resentment, loaded with revengeful wishes" directed toward the other parent (spouse).

From the child's perspective, the child has an authentic experience of sadness surrounding the loss of the intact family. Yet the child's interpretation of this feeling is under the distorting influence of the narcissistic/(borderline) parent. As the child becomes the external "regulatory object" for the narcissistic/(borderline) parent, the child becomes a mere reflection of the psychological state and attitudes of the narcissistic/(borderline) parent. The narcissistic/(borderline) parent then leads the child into an identical interpretation of the child's natural and authentic sadness and grief as being "anger and resentment, loaded with revengeful wishes" directed toward the other parent. The narcissistic/(borderline) parent leads the child into a distorted interpretation of the child's authentic sadness that it is something "bad" and "abusive" about the other parent that is creating the child's sadness, rather than the child's natural and normal experience of grief and sadness at the break-up of the family.

Blaming the Other Parent

One of the easiest methods of twisting the child's sadness into anger and resentment directed toward the targeted parent is to blame the targeted parent for the divorce and breakup of the family. The narcissistic/(borderline) personality is highly skilled at manipulative communications and can use a variety of subtle communications that blame the other parent for the divorce. One of the surest manipulative methods for blaming the targeted parent for the breakup of the family is for the narcissistic/(borderline) parent to present as the victim of the targeted parent. Presenting as the victim has the advantage of allowing the narcissistic/(borderline) parent to create a bond of "shared victimization" with the child concerning the "abusive" targeted parent.

In describing the breakup of the family, the narcissistic/(borderline) parent will subtly use the plural pronouns of "us" and "our" to refer to the child and the narcissistic/(borderline) parent. The subtle use of these plural pronouns is a manipulative communication that creates a shared bond with the child that excludes the targeted parent.

> **N/(B) Parent:** "Your mother decided to leave **our** family to pursue her own selfish interests. She doesn't care about what happens to **us**."

> **N/(B) Parent:** "I don't know how **we**'re going to make ends meet financially now that your father has left **us**."'

The manipulative use of plural pronouns by the narcissistic/(borderline) parent makes it seem like the other parent is rejecting and abandoning the child too. The targeted parent is not divorcing the *child*, the targeted parent is divorcing the *spouse*. The child is still an equal and integral part of the separated family structure with the targeted parent. The targeted parent is not leaving or abandoning the child. Furthermore, the targeted parent is still financially supporting the child. It is the financial support being provided to the former spouse that may be affecting the former spouse.

However, by using plural pronouns that include the child into an association with the narcissistic/(borderline) parent, the child is subtly led into believing that the actions of the targeted parent toward the narcissistic/(borderline) parent as a spouse are directed toward the child as well. This distorted triangulation of the child into the spousal conflict reflects the narcissistic/(borderline) parent's loss of psychological boundaries between the child's and parent's experience. In the mind of the narcissistic/(borderline) parent, the child and parent are one fused entity reflecting the experience of the narcissistic/(borderline) parent.

A more accurate, corrected version of these statements to the child would be:

> **N/(B) Parent:** "Your mother decided to leave **me** to pursue her own interests without me. She no longer cares about **me**."
>
> **N/(B) Parent:** "I don't know how **I'm** going to make ends meet financially now that your father is no longer supporting **me** with his salary. He will still take care of you; it's me that will be affected financially."

The meaning conveyed to the child in these corrected statements is very different from what was conveyed to the child in the original statements. Through the manipulative use of plural pronouns, the narcissistic/(borderline) parent turns a purely spousal conflict into the targeted parent's seeming rejection and abandonment of the child as well in order to inflame the child's hurt and anger toward the targeted parent.

During these communications to the child, the borderline-style parent will often present to the child with an emotional tone of tearful and anxious vulnerability which will elicit the child's desire to nurture the borderline-style parent as the "regulatory other" for the emotional and psychological state of the parent. The narcissistic-style parent, on the other hand, will typically present to the child as being the aggrieved victim of cruel injustice inflicted by the targeted parent. This presentation as an aggrieved victim of cruel ("abusive") injustice will be used to instigate and then inflame the child's "righteous outrage" at the targeted parent.

The distortion to the child's interpretation of a natural feeling of sadness and "mournful longing" surrounding the breakup of the family is inflamed by the narcissistic/(borderline) parent through subtly manipulative statements made to the child. The child is hurt by the breakup of the family. If the targeted parent can be blamed for the breakup of the family, then the targeted parent can be blamed for causing the child's hurt. By using plural pronouns of "our" and "us" that include the child into the parent's experience, the narcissistic/(borderline) parent creates a shared bond with the child that excludes the targeted parent from "our family."

The narcissistic/(borderline) parent begins to alter the child's sadness by subtly (or not so subtly) placing blame on the targeted parent for causing the divorce and the loss of the intact family. By placing blame for the divorce onto the targeted parent, the narcissistic/(borderline) parent is placing blame onto the targeted parent for causing the child's sadness and grief over the loss of the intact family. Blaming of the other parent for the divorce begins to twist the child's sadness over the loss of the intact family into "anger and resentment" directed toward the other parent for supposedly causing the child's sadness (i.e., for supposedly causing the divorce). In addition, by extending the targeted parent's rejection of the narcissistic/(borderline) *spouse* to also be rejection of the child through the manipulative use of plural pronouns, the narcissistic/(borderline) is able to imply that the targeted parent is rejecting and abandoning the child (e.g., the divorce is presented to the child not as the father leaving the marriage, but as the father leaving "our family" – meaning the narcissistic/(borderline) parent and the child). The narcissistic/(borderline) parent doesn't need to make these statements explicitly to the child. The meaning is manipulatively implied in subtle communications.

These manipulative statements of blame can be exceedingly subtle, yet incredibly sophisticated. For example, the narcissistic/(borderline) parent may overtly present to the child as wanting to retain the intact family, which then implies that the targeted parent is responsible for the breakup of the family. Presenting to the child as wanting to "hold the family together" is seemingly a noble motivation which is in alignment with the child's desire to maintain the family, as so joints with the child in a nascent coalition to "keep the family together" against the targeted parent who is seemingly seeking to "break up our family." The child and narcissistic/(borderline) parent now have a shared bond of wanting to hold the family together, and it is the (selfish) targeted parent who wants to break up "our" family. At a very subtle level, when the narcissistic/(borderline) parent joins with the child in a shared desire to "hold our family together," the targeted parent's rejection of the narcissistic/(borderline) parent as a spouse is expanded into rejecting the child as well. Both the narcissistic/(borderline) parent and the child want to hold the family together, but not the targeted parent who is "rejecting us" in "our desire" to maintain the family.

In truth, however, the family is not ending, only the spousal relationship is ending. The family itself is simply transitioning from an intact family structure united by the marriage to a separated family united by the child. Because of the child, the family will always be present. The child acts as a unifying force through the continuing parental roles with the child and through the mutual affectional bonds that each parent shares with the child. The family isn't ending, just the marriage. But by equating the end of the marriage to the end of "our family," and then joining with the child in a shared bond of wanting to maintain "our family," the narcissistic/(borderline) parent is able to extend the spousal rejection of the divorce into an implied rejection of the child as well.

Example of Manipulative Communication

The manipulative communications of the narcissistic/(borderline) parent can be contained in very short statements that carry complex and sophisticated manipulative overtones. For example, the narcissistic/(borderline) parent might make the following type of manipulative statement to the child:

> **N/(B) Parent:** "When you see your mother, tell her I still love her, that I forgive her and that I just want our family back the way it was."

The surface features of this statement appear to present the father as a loving spouse, who is simply communicating to the child that he still holds the mother in esteem and would like to restore the family. Yet this statement is extremely manipulative. First, it directly triangulates the child into the spousal conflict. The mother in this situation has decided to divorce the narcissistically self-involved father after years of enduring his emotional neglect, his chronic failures of empathy, and his dismissive and contemptuous treatment of her. The father has been an atrocious husband. Yet this statement by the father to the child places the blame for the divorce entirely onto the mother, since it appears that the father is seeking to maintain "our family." The implied meaning contained in the father's wanting to restore "our family back the way it was" is that it is the mother who is breaking up "our family," rather than the years of the father's emotionally neglectful and inadequate treatment of the mother.

When the child then follows through on the father's request in hopes of keeping the intact family together, this places the mother in an untenable position. When the child says to the mother,

Child: "Dad says he still loves you, and that he forgives you and wants the family back the way it was."

the mother will be manipulatively placed in the position of seeming to be uncaring about maintaining the family. In response to the father's seeming offer to restore the family "back the way it was," the mother's continued insistence on divorcing the father will appear to be unreasonably intransigent. The father wants to keep "our family" together, so in the eyes of the child the mother appears to become the cause of the divorce rather than the years that the mother had to endure the father's neglect, emotional abandonment, devaluation, open contempt, and absence of empathy.

If, however, the mother tries to avoid being blamed for breaking up the family by providing her reasons for divorcing the father to the child, then this only further triangulates the child into the spousal conflict and would cause additional psychological injury to the child. It is not in the child's best interests to be drawn into the spousal conflict by being given the reasons for the divorce. Yet the manipulative communication of the father has already drawn the child into the spousal conflict, so the mother is now placed in a bind. If she explains to the child the reasons she is divorcing the father, then this just further triangulates the child into the spousal conflict. If, on the other hand, the mother chooses not to defend her decision to divorce the father, then she will be characterized as being to blame for the divorce because of her intransigence and "selfishness."

The mother is being placed into an unresolvable conflict. In order not to seem rigid in her rejection of the father's seemingly magnanimous offer to restore the family "back the way it was" (which the father manipulatively directed to the mother through the child), the mother will need to explain to the child all the reasons for her decision to divorce the father that justify her decision; reasons which she may have withheld from the child during the marriage in order to protect the child from the spousal conflict. Yet if the mother now explains to the child why she is declining the father's seeming overture of supposed love for her, and his offer to restore "our family," the mother will only further triangulate the child into the spousal conflict by making the child the judge of the parents in their spousal conflict.

Furthermore, if the mother tries to explain to the child why she is refusing the father's offer of supposed love and reconciliation by describing to the child her reasons for divorcing the father, she will then be accused of saying negative things about the father to the child. In his (manipulative) communication to the child the father appears to be saying positive things about the mother; that he loves and forgives her (the implication being that he forgives her for her supposed faults and "abusive" treatment of him). If, however, the mother defends her decision to divorce the father by describing her reasons to the child, then she will appear to be saying negative things to the child about the father.

The father presents to the child as being the wonderfully loving and forgiving parent, and his communication carries the clear implication that it is the mother who is to blame for breaking up "our family." The manipulative communication by the father to the child sets up the mother either to accept blame for the breakup of the family or to be the one who further triangulates the child into the spousal conflict by making derogatory statements about the seemingly wonderful (loving and forgiving) narcissistic/(borderline) parent.

If the mother tries to avoid further triangulating the child into the spousal conflict by not exposing the father's spousal inadequacies to the child, then the mother is prevented from explaining to the child why she is declining the father's offer of love, forgiveness, and reconciliation. If, on the other hand, she chooses to defend her decision to divorce the father, then she is further harming the child and will appear to be denigrating the wonderfully loving and forgiving father in front of the child. The mother is completely trapped by the father's manipulative triangulation of the child into the spousal conflict. She cannot defend herself, nor can she not defend herself. Either way, she's trapped.

Suppose the mother elects to do the right thing by not further triangulating the child into the spousal conflict, what then? The mother will respond to the child by deflecting the child's intrusion into the marital relationship with a vague response that the issue raised by the child is between the mother and father. However, if she chooses this approach and so does not explain to the child why she is divorcing the father, then the child is left with the impression that it is the mother who is being unreasonably rigid, arbitrary, and selfish in deciding to break-up the family. The father is clearly expressing love and forgiveness for the mother. The father clearly said that he wants to keep the family "the way it was," just like the child does. If the mother deflects the child's intrusion into the spousal conflict then it will appear to the child that the mother is arbitrarily and unilaterally deciding to divorce the seemingly loving and forgiving father, who wants to keep "our family" together; just like the child does.

In wanting to keep "our family" together, the father and the child are on the same "side." This is the early nascent form of the cross-generational coalition of side-taking that will become more prominent later in the "alienation" process. In this early joining of the child with the narcissistic/(borderline) parent in their shared desire to keep "our family" together, the mother is also being placed on the outside of "our family." She doesn't care about what "we" want, she doesn't care about "our family," she only cares about what she wants.

The impression of the mother that is given to the child by the father's manipulative communication will then be exploited by the father in later characterizations of the mother made to the child. In these characterizations of the mother, the father will blame her for the break-up of the family because of her supposed "selfishness." He wanted to keep the family together but she was self-centered, thinking only of herself. She didn't consider his feelings or those of the child when she unilaterally decided to break up the family. She doesn't care about "us."

Again, in truth, the mother doesn't care about the father anymore. That is why they are getting divorced. She still loves the child very much. She still very much cares about the child. But by joining with the child in their supposedly shared desire to keep "out family" together, the father is able to extend the mother's rejection of him into an implied rejection of the child as well, which creates an in-group of the father and child, and an out-group of the mother.

In these communications, the father will portray himself as aligned with the child in their shared desire to maintain "our family." It is the mother who arbitrarily and unilaterally decided to break-up "our family" because of her own "selfish" needs. The implication of this characterization is that the mother does not care about (i.e., does not love) "us" (i.e., the father; and by implication the child). According to the narrative being constructed about the mother, she only cares about herself. This characterization of the mother as "selfish" and self-centered (a projection of the father's narcissistic characteristics) is then used by the narcissistic father to blame the mother for the breakup of the family, which transforms the child's sadness and grief at the loss of the intact family into blame and anger directed toward the mother for arbitrarily and unilaterally causing this loss because "she does not love us" (i.e., you; the child).

So the mother is caught in an unresolvable dilemma by this manipulative communication from the father. She cannot explain to the child why she is divorcing the father because then she will be triangulating the child further into the spousal conflict and she will appear to be denigrating the "wonderful and loving" narcissistic/(borderline) parent. But neither can she not explain to the child why she is divorcing the father, because if she does not explain her reasons to the child then she will be blamed for causing the divorce because of her own selfish motivations. In blaming the mother for the breakup of the family, the narcissistic/(borderline) parent is able to twist the child's sadness over the loss of the intact family into "anger and resentment" directed toward the mother for her supposedly selfish and self-centered decision to break-up the family because she does not love "us" (i.e., the child). If the mother does not offer to the child her reasons for divorcing the father, then the father will frame her reasons as her "not caring about the feelings or needs of other people." This characterization carries the implication that the mother doesn't care about (i.e., doesn't love) the child.

In addition, because of these prior manipulative communications of the father, when he later overtly places blame on the mother for the breakup of the family, thereby openly twisting the child's sadness into anger toward the mother for "abandoning our family," the child will seemingly have direct experiential evidence for the truth of the father's assertion. In the direct experience of the child the mother dismissed without consideration the father's seemingly generous offer of love and "forgiveness" to restore "our family." Based on the evidence of the child's direct experience, the mother was "selfish and self-centered." She "only cared about what she wanted" and she didn't care about what anyone else wanted (including the child).

The communication by the father of continuing love for the mother, which is being directed to the mother through the child, also contains a second insidiously manipulative communication. The father also offers to forgive the mother for her (implied) inadequacies and (implied) "abusive" treatment of him. The father's offer of "forgiveness" seemingly represents a magnanimous gesture intended to maintain the family just "the way it was." On the surface, as perceived by the child, this communication presents the father as being a wonderful person who is willing to graciously forgive the mother's inadequacies and prior "abusive" treatment of him in order to keep the family together. However, underneath this communication is the clear implication that the mother did something that needs the father's forgiveness.

In actuality, the mother did nothing requiring the father's "forgiveness." She is divorcing the narcissistic father after years of enduring his emotional neglect, his chronic empathic failures, and his narcissistic anger and contemptuous treatment of her. Yet from the perspective of the narcissistic father, the mother failed to provide him with the required "narcissistic supply" of her continuing submission and her adoration of his wonderfulness. She failed as his narcissistic "regulatory object." In his arrogance and grandiosity, the father is "magnanimously" willing to "forgive" the mother for her failure and inadequacies as the "regulatory object" for his needs.

By offering to forgive the mother for her (implied) inadequacies and prior "abusive" treatment of him, the narcissistic father manages to adopt the appearance of being a wonderfully magnanimous person who is willing to graciously forgive the mother's inadequacy in order to maintain "our family," (ostensibly because the father supposedly places the "needs of the children" ahead of his own needs - unlike the storyline being created about the mother). At the same time, the father also communicates his own supposed "victimization" from the (implied) "abuse" of the mother, who apparently did something horrible to him that needs his forgiveness. The father's offer of "forgiveness" is a masterfully manipulative communication, both subtle and complex.

The statement made to the child "When you see you mother, tell her I still love her, that I forgive her and that I just want our family back the way it was" is a sophisticated manipulative communication that also invites the child to try to convince the mother to restore the family,

> **Child:** "Come on mom, why not? Dad says he's willing to forgive you, why can't you forgive him?"

How can the mother counter the father's manipulative use of the child? If she tries responding to the child that she did not do anything that needs the father's forgiveness, then it appears as if she's not accepting responsibility for her failures in the marriage. After all, haven't we all done things that we could have handled better, particularly in a marriage? Why can't the mother simply "take responsibility" for her role in the marital conflict (i.e., for her failures as a martial partner)? Why can't the mother simply accept the father's forgiveness, and forgive him in return?

Yet if she ignores or deflects the father's supposed offer of forgiveness then the implication that she did something wrong that needs the father's forgiveness is left to stand unchallenged. The implied assertion of the father is that he was somehow "victimized" by the mother's "abusive treatment" of him which now requires the father's forgiveness of her. This narrative storyline regarding the father's "victimization" by the "abusive" mother has now been provided to the child by the father's offer of forgiveness of the mother. The mother must challenge this implied allegation or else it is left to stand within the narrative storyline being created about her.

The father's communication of "love" and "forgiveness" is magnificently manipulative. Not only does the narcissistic father look like a wonderfully loving and magnanimous person, the mother must also accept blame for causing the marital conflict and the breakup of the family because of her inadequacies and her "abusive" treatment of the poor "victimized" father. Furthermore, if only she would "accept responsibility" for her failures and inadequacies then the wonderful father would forgive her and accept her back because such is the magnificence of his wonderful love. But, according to the constructed narrative, the mother is too selfish and self-centered to accept responsibility for her faults, and so she is not worthy of the father's wonderful love. She doesn't care about the family (or the child). She only cares about her own selfish needs. So she "deserves" to be rejected because of her faults and failures, and for rejecting the father (and by implication the child through their coalition).

What an elegantly complex manipulative communication to deliver in just one sentence to the child. What's more, the ability of the narcissistic/(borderline) personality to deliver these subtle and magnificently manipulative communications is without limit. The communications of a narcissistic/(borderline) parent to the child can be filled with these manipulative communications that will then exploited by the narcissistic/(borderline) parent to transform the child's authentic feelings of sadness and grief into a twisted "anger and resentment, loaded with revengeful wishes" directed toward the targeted parent.

The targeted parent is trapped by the manipulative communications of the narcissistic/(borderline) parent to the child. The double-bind of the father's manipulative communication effectively prevents the mother from defending herself. If she tries, the child will not want to be further triangulated into the spousal conflict, and so will not want to hear the mother's criticisms of the father, and it will appear to the child that the mother is simply being a malicious and vindictive person who is denigrating the wonderfully loving father. The mother's apparent denigration of the father will contrast with the father's presentation to the child as being the all-wonderful "forgiving" parent. The mother is made defenseless.

However, neither can she not defend herself. If she does not defend herself then the implications of the father's manipulative communication are left unchallenged. The child joins with the father in their shared desire to hold "our family" together, and the mother is placed on the outside of "our family." This represents the early formation of the cross-generational coalition of the narcissistic/(borderline) parent and child against the targeted parent that will later be inflamed into the child's rejection of the targeted parent.

If the father's implied assertions are not challenged, then a storyline is created about the mother that she is to blame for breaking up "our family" because she is selfish and self-centered, that she doesn't care about what the child wants, that she was an inadequate and "abusive" spouse (later to be transformed into an inadequate and "abusive" parent), and that she refuses to take responsibility for her failures and inadequacies. The mother can neither defend herself against the implied allegations of the father, nor can she afford not to defend herself and simply allow the implied allegations to stand unchallenged. She is trapped.

All of this is accomplished in a single sentence delivered by the narcissistic/(borderline) parent to the child, and the variety of these types of manipulative communications available to the narcissistic/(borderline) parent are nearly limitless. In placing an implied blame on the targeted parent for the breakup of the family, the narcissistic/(borderline) parent begins to distort the child's personal experience of authentic sadness surrounding the loss of the intact family into "anger and resentment" directed toward the targeted parent. The communications of the narcissistic/(borderline) parent to the child are filled with these types of masterfully subtle and complex manipulative communications. The single sentence offered by the father in this example is just one illustration of the variety of these types of complex and sophisticated manipulative communications by which the narcissistic/(borderline) parent can influence the child's interpretation of sadness surrounding the loss of the intact family as instead being "anger and resentment" directed toward some supposed inadequacy or failure of the targeted parent.

Once a breach is created in the child's attachment bonding to the targeted parent, the child's authentic experience of sadness and grief is amplified exponentially by the loss of a relationship with the beloved-but-now-rejected targeted parent. The amplification in the child's grief can then be further distorted by the narcissistic/(borderline) parent into increasingly inflamed anger and rejection directed toward the supposed failures and inadequacies of the targeted parent.

Misinterpretation of the Grief Response

The narcissistic/(borderline) parent employs a variety of distorted and manipulative communication practices with the child as a means for terminating the child's attachment bonding motivations toward the other parent, and ultimately inducing the child's rejection of the targeted parent. The primary distortion created by the narcissistic/(borderline) parent is to lead the child into misinterpreting an authentic experience of sadness and grief as meaning that the targeted parent is doing something bad to create the child's authentic, but uncomprehended, emotional pain. Initially, the child's sadness and grief is over the loss of the intact family, but once the child begins to lose an affectionally bonded relationship with the authentically loved, but now rejected, targeted parent, the child's grief increases a thousand-fold as a result of the lost attachment bond to the targeted parent.

However, the child is unable to understand what the source of the child's authentic hurt is relative to the targeted parent, who is actually not doing anything that would account for the severity of the child's emotional pain. Under the distorting influence of the themes for criticizing the targeted parent that are provided to the child by the narcissistic/(borderline) parent, the child comes to misinterpret his or her authentic emotional pain that is created by an uncomprehended and misunderstood grief response (triggered first by the loss of the intact family and then amplified exponentially by the loss of an affectionally bonded relationship with the beloved-but-now-rejected targeted parent) as due to some fundamental inadequacy in the "personhood" of the targeted parent as being the cause of the child's pain.

The typical themes offered to the child by the narcissistic/(borderline) parent are that the targeted parent is selfish and self-centered, inconsiderate of the needs of others, lacks sensitivity and empathy for the child, is overly angry and demanding, doesn't accept responsibility for his or her faults, did not or does not pay enough attention to the child, or is somehow vaguely inadequate as a person. Sometimes an alleged past failure of the targeted parent in some specific incident is identified which then serves as a supposedly "unforgivable act" perpetrated by the targeted parent that the child then uses to justify all subsequent rejection.

All of the supposed justifications represent constructed false reasons for the actual source of the child's authentic pain associated with the targeted parent; i.e., the child's misunderstood and unprocessed sadness and grief, first about the loss of the intact family and later about the loss of an affectionally attached relationship with the beloved-but-now-rejected targeted parent. This child misunderstanding and misinterpretation of an authentic "mournful longing" and grief is created and fostered by the distorted parenting practices of the narcissistic/(borderline) parent who leads the child into an interpretation of the child's sadness in the same way that the narcissistic/(borderline) personality processes sadness, as "anger and resentment, loaded with revengeful wishes."

In the psychological processes of the narcissistic/(borderline) personality, the other spouse "deserves" to be punished for their failures as a spouse. This belief system is then redirected and channeled through the child, who expresses it as the targeted parent "deserves" to be punished (by the child) for past failures as a parent. The child is a narcissistic reflection of the narcissistic/(borderline) parent. The authentic child feels sadness and grief over the loss of the intact family and the loss of an affectionally attached relationship with the beloved-but-now-rejected targeted parent. But this authentic sadness and grief experienced by the child is being twisted and mangled by the distorted parenting practices of the narcissistic/(borderline) parent into an unrecognizable hostility and rejection of the targeted parent in which the targeted parent "deserves" to be rejected by the child for the supposed parental inadequacies of the targeted parent that are causing the child's emotional pain.

The child's belief in the authenticity of the false interpretation for the child's emotional pain as being caused by something bad about the targeted parent is supported by objective empirical evidence available to the child from the child's own personal experience. Whenever the child is with the targeted parent the child experiences more emotional pain, whereas whenever the child is away from the targeted parent and is with the narcissistic/(borderline) parent the child hurts less. This differential rise and fall in emotional pain related to the presence or absence of the targeted parent is interpreted by the child as clear empirical evidence that something about the targeted parent is creating the child's suffering. This distorted explanation for the child's authentic emotional pain associated with the targeted parent is being actively supported by the false interpretations about the targeted parent that are being provided to the child by the narcissistic/(borderline) parent. In the absence of any other alternative explanations, the child comes to believe the explanation being provided by the narcissistic/(borderline) parent that the cause of the child's authentic experience of emotional pain associated with the targeted parent is the result of "abusive" parenting practices by the targeted parent.

In actuality, the authentically experienced differential rise and fall in the child's emotional pain based on the presence or absence of the targeted-rejected parent simply represents the normal-range functioning of the child's attachment system. When the child is with the targeted-rejected parent the child's attachment system motivates the child to form an affectionally attached bond to the targeted parent. But because the child is withholding affectional bonding with the targeted parent, the uncompleted attachment motivation for affectional bonding produces an increased grief response. The presence of the targeted parent increases the child's attachment bonding motivations toward the targeted parent, which then increases the child's grief response when the child does not complete this motivational press. Therefore, the child hurts more (i.e., more grief at the lost affectional bond) in the presence of the targeted parent.

On the other hand, when the child is away from the targeted parent and in the custody of the narcissistic/(borderline) parent, the physical absence of the targeted parent reduces the motivation of the attachment system for bonding to the targeted parent, thereby lessening the child's grief response from an unfulfilled attachment bond to the targeted parent. When the child's attachment bonding motivation decreases because the targeted parent is not physically available for bonding, then the corresponding grief response decreases. The child hurts less (a less active grief response) when the child is away from the targeted parent.

The differential rise and fall of the child's emotional hurt associated with the presence or absence of the targeted parent (i.e., the availability of the targeted parent for attachment bonding) is simply a normal-range response of the attachment system and the grief response at the loss of an affectionally attached relationship with the beloved-but-now-rejected targeted parent. If the child were simply encouraged and allowed to form an affectionally bonded attachment relationship with the targeted parent then the child's grief response would automatically resolve and the child would no longer feel any emotional pain with the targeted parent.

In addition, if the child were allowed to form an affectionally bonded relationship with the targeted parent then the child would also acquire an accurate interpretation for the child's grief and sadness as representing the loss of an affectionally attached relationship to the targeted parent. Once the child is allowed to form an attached relationship with the targeted parent, then the child's distorted misinterpretations of an authentically experienced sadness and pain as being created by some aspect of the "personhood" of the targeted parent's fundamental inadequacy as a parent would immediately be resolved.

The child's misunderstanding and misinterpretation of the emotional pain surrounding an authentic grief response at the loss of an affectionally bonded relationship with the beloved-but-now-rejected targeted parent creates the symptom identified by Gardner as the "independent thinker phenomenon," in which the child strongly asserts that the motivation for rejecting the targeted parent is the sole authentic feeling of the child and is not being induced or influenced by the allied and supposedly favored narcissistic/(borderline) parent. From the child's perspective, the child authentically feels a differential rise and fall in emotional pain associated with the presence or absence of the targeted parent (i.e., the availability of the targeted parent for attachment bonding). The child's authentic rise and fall in hurt surrounding visitations with the targeted parent convince the child that there is actually something that the targeted parent is doing that is creating the child's emotional pain, since this pain increases when the child is with the targeted parent (i.e., when the targeted parent is physically available for attachment bonding) and decreases when the child is away from the targeted parent (i.e., when the targeted parent is physically unavailable for attachment bonding).

Eventually, the only avenue open to the child for resolving the misunderstood grief response for the beloved-but-now-rejected targeted parent is for the child to terminate all contact with the targeted parent. As long as the targeted parent is available for bonding but the child is not completing the attachment motivation for affectional bonding, then the child will continually experience an immense but misunderstood grief and sadness over the lost relationship with the targeted parent. In normal-range grieving, the parent dies and the child grieves. In attachment-based "parental alienation" this is reversed. In attachment-based "parental alienation," the child is grieving and so must "psychologically kill" the parent in the child's life in order to resolve the grief response. In actuality, however, all the child needs to do to resolve the grief response is to allow affectionate bonding to occur with the beloved targeted parent. The moment the child allows an affectionate bond to develop with the beloved targeted parent, the child's grief response and emotional pain will immediately resolve.

It is critical that mental health professionals who are assessing the family processes of attachment-based "parental alienation" recognize the authentic origins of the child's hurt in the child's misunderstood and misinterpreted grief and sadness surrounding the changes in the family structure and the loss of an affectionally bonded relationship with the beloved-but-now-rejected targeted parent. Helping the child develop an accurate interpretation regarding an authentic grief response at the loss of an affectionally bonded relationship with the beloved-but-rejected targeted parent is foundational to resolving the child's induced symptom display in attachment-based "parental alienation."

However, the narcissistic/(borderline) parent will actively resist and undermine efforts to restore the child's affectionally bonded relationship with the targeted parent from an obsessive and delusional need to protect "the child." The need to protect "the child" represents an important corrective healing change to the attachment trauma of the narcissistic/(borderline) parent, so that this parent will relentlessly seek to maintain the child's "victimized child" role in order to allow the narcissistic/(borderline) parent to adopt the role as the "protective parent" for "the child" (who psychologically represents both the current child and the narcissistic/(borderline) parent as a child in the original trauma experience).

The psychological state of the narcissistic/(borderline) parent is lost in a delusional obsession, formed within a reenactment narrative of childhood attachment trauma. In the distorted psychopathology of the narcissistic/(borderline) parent, the current child and targeted parent are psychologically equivalent to the "victimized child" and "abusive parent" of the attachment trauma. In order to regulate the immense trauma-related anxiety embedded within the internal working models of the attachment system, the narcissistic/(borderline) must fulfill the role as the "protective parent" in the trauma reenactment, and the child must be empowered into active agency in rejecting the supposedly "abusive parent" in order to provide the corrective changes to the childhood trauma experience necessary to regulate the immense anxiety of the narcissistic/(borderline) parent and achieve psychological mastery over the childhood trauma experience.

In the psychopathology of the narcissistic/(borderline) parent, it becomes a psychological imperative that the child continues in the role as the "victimized child" who is actively rejecting a relationship with the targeted parent. The full measure of distorted and manipulative strategies available to the narcissistic/(borderline) parent will therefore be directed toward disrupting the child's ability to form an affectionally bonded relationship with the targeted parent. Under no circumstances will the narcissistic/(borderline) parent allow the child to form a bonded relationship with the targeted parent. The fragile psychological stability of the narcissistic/(borderline) parent is entirely dependent on the "regulatory other" function of the child's rejection of the targeted parent, so that the active resistance of the narcissistic/(borderline) parent to the child's formation of an affectionally bonded relationship with the targeted parent will achieve obsessive and delusional proportions.

In some cases, the narcissistic/(borderline) parent may create false allegations of child abuse supposedly inflicted on the child by the targeted parent, although to the pathology of the narcissistic/(borderline) parent these allegations are not false since truth and accuracy are subjectively determined and the narcissistic/(borderline) parent is absolutely convinced with neurologically imposed certainty that the targeted parent represents an "abusive" risk to the child. When these delusional allegations of child abuse occur, the false beliefs of the narcissistic/(borderline) parent will be steadfastly maintained, and the narcissistic/(borderline) parent will remain un-reassured, despite repeated investigative failures to confirm child abuse.

<u>False Allegations of Abuse</u>

The issues of false allegations of child abuse are complex. Child-initiated reports of abuse should always be taken very seriously and investigated thoroughly. In addition, narcissistic "<u>targeted</u>" parents who are authentically abusive parents will use an allegation of "parental alienation" against a normal-range and authentically protective parent as a means to deflect and externalize blame for the parent-child conflict the child is having with the narcissistic and authentically abusive "<u>targeted</u>" parent. False allegations of "parental alienation" by an authentically abusive parent represent a cynical defense by a narcissistic and abusive parent to deflect blame away from the child's allegations of child abuse that are actually true. On the other hand, there are <u>also</u> narcissistic and borderline personality parents who are enacting attachment-based "parental alienation" and who will make false allegations of child abuse from a delusional perception of threat emanating from their re-experiencing of childhood trauma, and its psychological reenactment in current relationships. Both psychological processes exist.

When child abuse allegations are made, a variety of differential diagnoses need to be considered, preeminent of which is authentic child abuse. If authentic child abuse is not confirmed by thorough investigation, then consideration of alternative diagnostic possibilities may be warranted based on the circumstances.

Protecting the Child during Therapy

When a role-reversal relationship associated with attachment-based "parental alienation" is creating the child's symptomatic rejection of a normal-range and affectionally available parent, treatment efforts to restore the child's healthy and normal-range development will be <u>actively</u> resisted by the narcissistic/(borderline) parent's need to keep the child symptomatic. The active resistance of the narcissistic/(borderline) parent to the goals of therapy will turn the child into a "psychological battleground" between the therapeutic efforts to restore the child's normal-range and healthy development and the unrelenting efforts of the narcissistic/(borderline) parent to keep the child symptomatic. Turning the child who is caught in the pathology of attachment-based "parental alienation" into a "psychological battleground" can be emotionally and psychologically damaging for the child. Before treatment efforts are initiated, the child's psychological protection from the delusional pathology of the narcissistic/(borderline) parent needs to be ensured.

PART IV: Professional Issues

Chapter 9

DIAGNOSIS

Diagnostic Indicators

Attachment-based "parental alienation" can be reliably diagnosed by the presence in the child's symptom display of three characteristic and definitive diagnostic indicators. Each diagnostic indicator rests within a surrounding psychopathology that serves as the theoretical foundation for the diagnostic indicator.

The first diagnostic indicator of attachment-based "parental alienation" is the complete suppression of the child's attachment bonding motivations toward a normal-range and affectionally available parent. The suppression of the child's attachment system is indicative of the attachment origins of the pathology and is the product of the trans-generational transmission of attachment trauma from the childhood of the narcissistic/(borderline) parent to the current functioning of the child's attachment system. The source of the pathology being expressed in attachment-based "parental alienation" is the distortion to the attachment system of the narcissistic/(borderline) parent that is being transmitted to the child's attachment system by the pathogenic parenting practices of the narcissistic/(borderline) parent.

The second diagnostic indicator for attachment-based "parental alienation" is a specific set of five narcissistic/(borderline) personality disorder traits that are displayed by the child toward the targeted-rejected parent. This diagnostic indicator in the child's symptom display is a product of the pathogenic parental influence on the child by a narcissistic/(borderline) parent.

In some cases, these personality symptoms will be replaced or augmented by severe child anxiety displays that meet DSM-5 diagnostic criteria for a specific phobia, but the type of phobia will be a bizarre and unrealistic "father phobia" or "mother phobia." The child's severe anxiety displays represent the transfer of delusional parental anxiety from the narcissistic/(borderline) parent to the child through pathogenic parenting practices.

The third diagnostic indicator of attachment-based "parental alienation" is an intransigently held, fixed and false belief evidenced by the child regarding the fundamental inadequacy of the targeted-rejected parent. In this diagnostic indicator, the child typically characterizes the parenting of the targeted-rejected parent as being somehow "abusive" of the child. This symptom is the result of the child's role as the "victimized child" within the trauma reenactment narrative. The trauma reenactment narrative of the narcissistic/(borderline) parent is a false drama created by the delusional pathology of the narcissistic/(borderline) parent. Since the trauma reenactment narrative is a false drama, the child's role as a supposedly "victimized child" as part of this trauma reenactment narrative is also false. The origins of this false belief system is in the psychological collapse of the narcissistic/(borderline) parent into delusional beliefs regarding the other parent. The delusional beliefs of the narcissistic/(borderline) parent are then transferred to the child though the role-reversal relationship with the child, in which the child serves as a "regulatory other" for the pathological beliefs of the narcissistic/(borderline) parent.

The presence in the child's symptom display of this specific set of three diagnostic indicators represents definitive clinical evidence for the presence of pathogenic parenting by the allied and supposedly favored parent associated with an attachment-based model for the construct of "parental alienation." No other psychological or interpersonal process besides an attachment-based model of "parental alienation" can result in this specific set of three diagnostic indicators in the child's symptom display. When this specific set of three diagnostic indictors are present in the child's symptom display, the only possible explanation for the presence of this specific set of three diagnostic indicators is an attachment-based model for the construct of "parental alienation."

Diagnostic Indicator 1: Attachment System Suppression

A. The child's symptom display evidences a selective and targeted suppression of the normal-range functioning of the child's attachment bonding motivations toward one parent, in which the child seeks to entirely terminate a relationship with this parent (i.e., a child-initiated cutoff in the child's relationship with a normal-range and affectionally available parent).

B. A clinical assessment of the parenting practices of the rejected parent provides no evidence for severely dysfunctional parenting (such as parental sexual abuse of the child, parental violence, or chronic parental substance abuse) that would reasonably account for the child's desire to sever the parent-child bond.

C. The parenting of the targeted-rejected parent is assessed to be broadly normal-range, with due consideration given to the wide spectrum of acceptable parenting practices typically displayed in normal-range families, and with due consideration given to the legitimate exercise of parental prerogatives in establishing family values, including parental prerogatives in the exercise of normal-range parental authority, leadership, and discipline within the parent-child relationship.

The attachment system is a "goal corrected" primary motivational system (Bowlby, 1969), meaning that the goal of the attachment system to form an affectionally bonded relationship with a parent is maintained even when presented with problematic parenting that interferes with the goal. In response to problematic parenting, children's behavior is distorted in characteristic ways, but always with the goal of establishing an attachment bond to the parent.

Problematic parenting often creates an anxious-ambivalent (preoccupied) attachment pattern in the child. In response to problematic parenting that creates inconsistent parental availability, children respond by presenting increased demands and protest behaviors (i.e., parent-child conflict) that require continual parental involvement. On the other hand, parents who are overly disengaged or rejecting create an anxious-avoidant attachment pattern in the child in which the child becomes low-demand and overly self-reliant. Parenting that is disorienting or frightening for the child produces a disorganized attachment response from the child in which the child's attachment system is unable to develop an organized or coherent pattern for acquiring and maintaining an attachment bond to the parent. Disorganized attachment will produce highly oppositional and defiant children, as well as severe mood swings, depression, and anxiety. But in all cases, the attachment system maintains as its primary motivational goal the formation of an affectional attachment bond to the parent. Only in a limited number of extreme circumstances can the attachment system be induced into terminating its goal of forming an affectional bond to the parent.

Terminating the Attachment System

As a goal-corrected motivational system, when presented with problematic parenting practices the attachment system adjusts how it achieves its goal of forming an attached bond to the parent but it does not terminate its goal of seeking an affectional bond to the parent. There are only a limited set of severely problematic and pathogenic parenting practices that can lead to the termination of the child's attachment bonding motivations toward a parent:

1. **Incest:** Sexual abuse of the child by the parent will immediately terminate the child's attachment bonding motivations toward the parent.

2. **Hostile-Violent Parenting:** Years of chronic exposure to hostile and violent parenting practices or severe domestic violence can eventually terminate the child's attachment bonding motivations toward the parent in some, but not necessarily all, cases.

3. **Neglect:** Chronic exposure of the child to parental neglect, such as might occur with chronic parental substance abuse, can sometimes result in the termination of the child's attachment bonding motivations toward the severely and chronically neglectful parent. However, the more typical child response to chronic parental incapacity, such as occurs with severe parental substance abuse, is more often for the child to adopt a "parentified" role of becoming a caretaker for the chronically incapacitated parent.

4. **Role-Reversal Use of the Child:** In a role-reversal relationship with a narcissistic/(borderline) parent the child is serving as an external "regulatory object" for the pathology of the narcissistic/(borderline) parent. Under these circumstances, the child can be induced by the regulatory needs of the narcissistic/(borderline) parent into rejecting a relationship with the other, normal-range parent. The artificial suppression of the child's attachment bonding motivations toward the targeted-rejected parent is created through a variety of distorted parenting practices by the narcissistic/(borderline) parent. This form of pathogenic parenting by a narcissistic/(borderline) parent, that induces the artificial suppression of the child's attachment bonding motivations toward a normal-range and affectionally available parent, represents an attachment-based model for the construct of "parental alienation."

Chronic exposure to less severe forms of hostile-aggressive or neglectful parenting can lead children to become discouraged in their expectations to form an attachment bond to the parent. Under these circumstances, the discouraged child may no longer display attachment motivations toward the parent. However, this suppression of attachment bonding motivation reflects the child's discouragement in achieving the goal of an attached relationship rather than the termination of the attachment motivation itself. In response to discouragement, some children will display increased protest behaviors such as acting out at school or delinquency (i.e., an anxious-ambivalent pattern of high protest behavior to elicit <u>increased</u> parental/adult involvement), while other children will withdraw into depression and possible substance abuse (i.e., an anxious-avoidant pattern of withdrawal into low-demand displays of their needs). If, however, the parent subsequently becomes available for affectional bonding, then the child's discouragement can be resolved and the child's normal-range attachment motivations will recover their overt expression.

In attachment-based "parental alienation," however, the targeted-rejected parent is affectionally available to the child for attachment bonding. The child's behavior toward the targeted parent is, therefore, not a product of child discouragement but instead represents a motivated "detachment behavior" designed to actively sever the parent-child bond. There are no normal-range circumstances that will produce child <u>detachment</u> behavior. Detachment behavior can only be produced by the severely problematic parenting of incest, chronic exposure to severely hostile-aggressive parenting, chronic exposure to severe parental incapacity and neglect, or a role-reversal relationship with a pathological parent that is inducing the artificial suppression of the child's attachment bonding motivations toward the other parent in order to meet the emotional and psychological needs of the allied parent. These are the only circumstances that produce child detachment from the parent.

In all other cases of problematic parenting, children will evidence characteristic goal-corrected responses of distortions to their behavior that retain the goal of forming an affectionally attached bond to the parent to the greatest extent possible. Authentic parent-child conflict in response to problematic parenting emerges from a child's efforts to form an affectional bond to the parent that are being frustrated by the problematic parenting. The child's protest behavior represents the child's frustrated efforts to form an attachment bond to the parent. The attachment system is a primary motivational system that always has as its goal the formation of an attachment bond to the parent. Children do not display detachment behavior except under a very limited set of severely pathogenic parenting.

Diagnostic Indicator 1 for an attachment-based model of "parental alienation" captures the characteristic distortion created in the child's attachment system from the pathology of a role-reversal relationship with a narcissistic/(borderline) parent. This pathology essentially involves the trans-generational transmission to the child of the distortions in the narcissistic/(borderline) parent's own attachment networks. This trans-generational transmission of attachment trauma is mediated through the pathogenic parenting practices of the narcissistic/(borderline) parent. The pathogenic parenting of the narcissistic/(borderline) parent involves the role-reversal use of the child as an external "regulatory object" for regulating the parent's own emotional and psychological state.

By inducing the child's rejection of the other parent the narcissistic/(borderline) parent is able to recreate in the current family relationships the attachment trauma patterns of "abusive parent"/"victimized child"/"protective parent" from the childhood of the narcissistic/(borderline) parent, with the additional corrective additions of the child's empowerment into active agency in rejecting the supposedly "abusive parent," and the real-world "protection" afforded by the narcissistic/(borderline) parent to the current child, which was not available to the narcissistic/(borderline) parent in the original trauma experience of childhood. The reenactment of childhood trauma into and through the current family relationships allows the narcissistic/(borderline) parent to achieve a form of psychological mastery over the activated trauma anxiety contained within the attachment trauma networks of the narcissistic/(borderline) personality structure.

The symptomatic display of the child's "detachment behavior" (i.e., the display of an inauthentic attachment system) in attachment-based "parental alienation" is so distinctive and characteristic that an advanced professional understanding for the functioning of the attachment system during childhood would allow for the clinical diagnosis of attachment-based "parental alienation" based solely on Diagnostic Indicator 1 and the surrounding clinical features of the trauma reenactment narrative. However, the addition of the two supplementary diagnostic indicators of attachment-based "parental alienation" allows for the definitive confirmation of the diagnosis because no other psychological or interpersonal process besides attachment-based "parental alienation" could produce <u>all three</u> diagnostic indicators in the child's symptom display.

Diagnostic Indicator 2: Narcissistic Personality Symptoms

A. The child's symptom display toward the targeted-rejected parent evidences a specific set of five narcissistic and borderline personality disorder traits that are diagnostically indicative of parental influence on the child by a parent who has these narcissistic and borderline personality traits. The specific set of narcissistic and borderline personality disorder symptoms displayed by the child toward the targeted-rejected parent are:

Grandiosity: The child displays a grandiose self-perception of occupying an inappropriately elevated status in the family hierarchy above that of the targeted-rejected parent. From this grandiose position of elevated status, the child feels empowered to sit in judgment of the targeted-rejected parent as both a parent and as a person (DSM-5 Narcissistic Personality Disorder criterion 1).

Entitlement: The child displays an over-empowered sense of entitlement. The child expects that his or her desires will be met by the targeted-rejected parent to the child's satisfaction, and if the rejected parent fails to meet the child's entitled expectations to the child's satisfaction then the child feels entitled to enact a retaliatory punishment on the rejected parent for the child's judgment of parental failures (DSM-5 Narcissistic Personality Disorder criterion 5).

Absence of Empathy: The child displays a complete absence of empathy for the emotional pain being inflicted on the targeted-rejected parent by the child's hostility and rejection of this parent (DSM-5 Narcissistic Personality Disorder criterion 7).

Haughty and Arrogant Attitude: The child displays an attitude of haughty arrogance and contemptuous disdain for the targeted-rejected parent (DSM-5 Narcissistic Personality Disorder criterion 9).

Splitting: The child evidences the psychological process of splitting involving polarized extremes of attitude. Splitting is expressed in the child's symptom display as the differential polarized attitudes that the child holds toward his or her parents in which the supposedly "favored" parent is idealized as the all-good and nurturing parent while the rejected parent is entirely devalued as the all-bad and entirely inadequate parent (DSM-5 Borderline Personality Disorder criterion 2).

Anxiety Variant

Some children may display extreme and excessive anxiety symptoms toward the targeted-rejected parent rather than narcissistic and borderline personality disorder traits, or in addition to the personality disorder traits. In the anxiety variant of attachment-based "parental alienation" the child's anxiety symptoms will meet DSM-5 diagnostic criteria for a specific phobia.

Persistent Unwarranted Fear: The child will display a persistent and unwarranted fear of the targeted-rejected parent that is cued by either by the presence of the targeted parent or in anticipation of being in the presence of the targeted parent (DSM-5 Phobia criterion A).

Severe Anxiety Response: The presence of the targeted parent almost invariably provokes an anxiety response which can reach the levels of a situationally provoked panic attack (DSM-5 Phobia criterion B).

Avoidance of Parent: The child seeks to avoid exposure to the targeted parent due to the situationally provoked anxiety or else endures the presence of the targeted parent with great distress (DSM-5 Phobia criterion C).

Since the focus of the child's phobic response is a parent, the type of phobia displayed by the child is a bizarre and unrealistic "father type" or "mother type." Children never develop a specific phobia toward a parent. The primary motivational networks of the attachment system would prevent the emergence of a phobic anxiety response toward a parent.

The presence of a DSM-5 specific phobia that targets a parent as its triggering stimulus is evidence of the influence on the child by the distorted parenting practices of the allied and supposedly favored parent who is inducing the child's bizarre phobic response to the other parent. The formation of the child's phobic response to the targeted parent is the product of the narcissistic/(borderline) parent's communications to the child regarding the threat supposedly posed to the child by the targeted parent. This distorted perception of threat has its origins in the intense anxiety experience of the narcissistic/(borderline) parent that reflects:

1. **Narcissistic Anxiety:** The activation of narcissistic anxieties surrounding the threatened collapse of the narcissistic defense against the experience of primal self-inadequacy. The public rejection of the narcissistic/(borderline) parent by the targeted parent surrounding the divorce represents a narcissistic injury that threatens to collapse the narcissistic/(borderline) parent's fragile narcissistic defense against the experience of primal self-inadequacy.

2. **Borderline Anxiety:** The activation of intense abandonment fears that are triggered by the divorce, in which the narcissistic/(borderline) parent is being rejected and abandoned by the primary attachment figure of the other spouse. If the child is allowed to form a bonded relationship with the targeted parent, the

narcissistic/(borderline) parent is afraid that the child will also abandon the narcissistic/(borderline) parent.

3. **Trauma Anxiety:** The divorce triggers the activation of the narcissistic/(borderline) parent's attachment system to mediate the loss of the spousal relationship. The activation of the attachment system also activates the embedded trauma networks of the attachment patterns of the narcissistic/(borderline) parent. The reactivation of the narcissistic/(borderline) parent's childhood attachment trauma reactivates the trauma-related anxiety from childhood that is contained in these trauma networks.

These sources of authentically experienced anxiety are misinterpreted by the narcissistic/(borderline) parent as representing authentic emotional cues regarding an actual threat posed by the other spouse/(parent). The nature of this supposed threat becomes interpreted within the attachment trauma patterns of "victimized child"/"abusive parent"/"protective parent" that are contained within the internal working models of the narcissistic/(borderline) parent's attachment networks. This misattribution regarding an authentic experience of anxiety creates the delusional belief of the narcissistic/(borderline) parent that the targeted parent represents an "abusive" threat to the "victimized child." The distorted parental perception of threat regarding the targeted parent is then transferred to the child's belief system through the distorted parenting practices of the narcissistic/(borderline) parent.

The unstable emotional state and unpredictably hostile and rejecting parenting of the narcissistic/(borderline) parent, in which truth and reality shift based on the subjective needs of the narcissistic/(borderline) parent, induce the child into a role-reversal relationship of becoming an external "regulatory object" for the psychological state of the narcissistic/(borderline) parent. In order for the child to keep the narcissistic/(borderline) parent in a regulated state, the parent requires that the child maintain a continual correspondence of psychological attitudes, states, and beliefs as are held by the narcissistic/(borderline) parent. If the child fails to serve as a narcissistic reflection of the psychological state and attitudes of the narcissistic/(borderline) parent, then this state-discrepancy can lead to the collapse in the emotional and psychological regulation and organization of the narcissistic parent. The child quickly learns that to keep the narcissistic/(borderline) parent in an organized and regulated psychological state requires that the child reflect the same opinions, attitudes, and beliefs as the parent.

Acting as the "regulatory other" for the narcissistic/(borderline) parent requires that the child surrender to the shifting truth and reality which is subjectively defined by the narcissistic/(borderline) parent. If the parent asserts that the sky is red, the child agrees. If a little while later the parent asserts that the sky is yellow, the child agrees. If the child fails to surrender to the ever-changing subjective reality as defined by the narcissistic/(borderline) parent, then this failure to act as a "regulatory object" for the parent can result in the emotional and psychological collapse of the narcissistic/(borderline) parent into displays of irrational anger and hostile rejection (or immense sadness and depressive dysregulation). The child only needs to experience this parental collapse into psychological and emotional dysregulation on a few occasions before the child becomes highly motivated to be or do whatever is needed to keep the parent in a regulated state and so avoid the emotional collapse of the narcissistic/(borderline) parent into irrational tantrums and verbal assaults.

Once the child surrenders into being who and what the narcissistic/(borderline) parent needs the child to be (i.e., once the child becomes the "regulatory object" for the parent) then the parent-child relationship takes on the superficial appearance of a bonded relationship because, in truth, there is only one person present in the relationship; the narcissistic/(borderline) parent. The child simply becomes a regulatory reflection of the parent.

In their shared psychological state and the child's role as the "regulatory object" for the narcissistic/(borderline) parent, the child adopts the same delusional threat perception regarding the targeted parent as is held by the narcissistic/(borderline) parent. The child's display of a phobic anxiety toward the targeted parent represents the delusional anxiety and threat perception of the narcissistic/(borderline) parent transferred to the child. Through a variety of distorted communication processes, including emotional signaling of parental anxiety and supportive parental responses to displays by the child of supposed anxiety directed toward being with the targeted parent, the distorted parental perception of threat and its associated anxiety are transferred to the child's symptom display.

The child's display of phobic anxiety represents a symptomatic manifestation of the severe anxiety and the distorted threat perception of the narcissistic/(borderline) parent that is being symptomatically expressed by the "regulatory object" of the child. Through the child's overt display of anxiety, the child becomes the symbolic "holding container" for the narcissistic/(borderline) parent's own excessive anxiety. Because the child's expressions of anxiety are acting as the "holding container" for the parent's own anxiety, the "protective" response of the narcissistic/(borderline) parent for the "anxious child" becomes a means for the narcissistic/(borderline) parent to regulate the parent's own anxieties by providing "protective" care to the external "regulatory object" of the child who is the "holding" the anxiety for the parent.

The allied and supposedly favored parent typically offers an explanation for the child's phobic anxiety symptoms toward the targeted parent as reflecting the child's understandable and justified response to some prior incident of problematic parenting by the targeted parent. This explanation essentially frames the child's phobic anxiety as a post-traumatic response to a prior frightening experience that the child supposedly had with the targeted-rejected parent.

When this post-traumatic explanation for the child's phobic anxiety symptoms is offered, then the child's anxiety presentation needs to be evaluated as a symptom of a Post-Traumatic Stress Disorder (PTSD). The first step in this assessment of possible PTSD is a specific clinical focus on evaluating the severity of the precipitating stressor that supposedly triggered the "trauma" experience for the child. Under closer clinical scrutiny, the originating stressor for the supposedly post-traumatic anxiety of the child (i.e., criterion A for a DSM-5 diagnosis of PTSD) will typically fall far short of the severity needed to actually produce an authentic PTSD response.

In the anxiety variant of attachment-based "parental alienation," the child's anxiety symptoms will present as an inauthentic "father type" or "mother type" of specific phobia, and the explanation typically offered by the child and the narcissistic/(borderline) parent regarding the cause of the child's phobic anxiety toward the targeted parent is that it represents a symptom of a Post-Traumatic Stress Disorder. However, the supporting clinical data for a PTSD diagnosis will not be credible because the child was not exposed to any stressor capable of producing a PTSD response (i.e., DSM-5 criterion A for PTSD).

Professional experience and expertise in childhood trauma, particularly developmental trauma involving abusive parent-child relationship experiences during childhood (e.g., van der Kolk, 2005), is essential for the professional assessment of the child's display of excessive anxiety symptoms associated with attachment-based "parental alienation." When a trauma related explanation for the child's excessive anxiety is offered by the child or narcissistic/(borderline) parent, professional expertise and experience in the assessment of developmental trauma is a requirement of professional competence in the diagnosis of the family's dysfunction. Mental health professionals assessing this anxiety symptom display must possess the level of professional expertise in developmental trauma necessary to differentiate authentic trauma-anxiety displays from inauthentic displays created in a role-reversal relationship with a parent who has anxiety symptoms. Mental health professionals who lack the necessary clinical experience and expertise in assessing developmental trauma may not be able to appropriately assess the child's anxiety symptom display in attachment-based "parental alienation," and a referral to a more competent mental health professional should be strongly considered. Professional experience and expertise in the assessment of developmental trauma is a vital component of professional competence for the clinical assessment and diagnosis of this special population of children and families.

Diagnostic Indicator 3: Delusional Belief System

A. The child's symptoms display an intransigently held, fixed and false belief (i.e., a delusion) regarding the fundamental parental inadequacy of the targeted-rejected parent in which the child characterizes a relationship with the targeted-rejected parent as being somehow emotionally or psychologically "abusive" of the child. While the child may not explicitly use the term "abusive," the implication of emotional or psychological abuse is contained within the child's belief system.

B. The child may use this fixed and false belief regarding the supposedly "abusive" inadequacy of the targeted parent to justify the child's rejection the targeted parent. The justification offered by the child for rejecting the targeted parent carries the judgmental theme that the targeted parent "deserves" to be rejected because of the supposedly "abusive" parental inadequacy of this parent.

Deserves to be Rejected

The child's belief that the targeted parent deserves to be rejected because of supposedly "abusive" parenting practices, or for some personal inadequacy of the targeted-rejected parent, is often present and is a particularly characteristic feature of the child's justifications for rejecting the targeted parent in attachment-based "parental alienation." The child's belief that the targeted parent deserves to be rejected is a manifestation of the child's role-reversal relationship with the narcissistic/(borderline) parent. The child has acquired this belief from the attitude of the narcissistic/(borderline) parent toward the targeted parent. In the role-reversal relationship the child has with the narcissistic/(borderline) parent, the child serves as a narcissistic reflection of the pathological beliefs of the parent. The actual source of the child's belief that the targeted parent deserves to be punished for supposed parental inadequacy is in the pathological beliefs of the narcissistic/(borderline) parent toward the other *spouse*. The narcissistic/(borderline) parent holds the belief that the other spouse deserves to be punished for failing to provide the narcissistic/(borderline) parent with the required "narcissistic supply" during their marriage, and for rejecting (abandoning) the narcissistic/(borderline) parent through the divorce.

The theme of "deserving to be punished" is an attitude of the narcissistic/(borderline) parent toward the other spouse, that the child then acquires through the child's reflective role-reversal relationship with the narcissistic/(borderline) parent. According to Beck et al., (2004),

> "If others fail to satisfy the narcissist's "needs," including the need to look good, or be free from inconvenience, then others 'deserve to be punished'... Even when punishing others out of intolerance or entitlement, the narcissist sees this as 'a lesson they need, for their own good" (p. 252).

As an external "regulatory object" for the psychological state of the narcissistic/(borderline) parent, the child becomes a mere reflection for the narcissistic beliefs and attitudes of the parent, including the parental belief that the other parent (spouse) deserves to be punished for the past failures of this parent (spouse). According to Beck et al., (2004), a central cognitive schema of the narcissistic personality is, "if others don't recognize my special status, they should be punished" (p. 44). This cognitive schema of the narcissistic/(borderline) parent is transferred into the child's symptom display toward the targeted parent.

The theme expressed by the child's attitude that the targeted parent "deserves to be punished" by the child's rejection is a narcissistic personality theme acquired by the child through the role-reversal relationship the child has as the "regulatory other" for the narcissistic/(borderline) parent. In psychologically surrendering to the role as a "regulatory object" for the psychological state of the narcissistic/(borderline) parent, the child adopts and reflects the attitudes and psychological state of the narcissistic/(borderline) parent, including the belief that the other parent (spouse) "deserves to be punished" (rejected) for supposed parental (spousal) inadequacies and failures.

<u>The Child's Delusional Belief</u>

The child's delusional belief regarding the supposedly "abusive" parental inadequacy of the targeted parent represents the child's role as the "victimized child" in the trauma reenactment narrative of the narcissistic/(borderline) parent. The roles in the trauma reenactment narrative of the "abusive parent"/"victimized child"/"protective parent" represent a false drama created from the reactivated attachment trauma patterns of the psychologically decompensating narcissistic/(borderline) parent. This false trauma reenactment narrative is recreated in the current family relationships by inducing the child into adopting the "victimized child" role in the reenactment narrative, which then defines the targeted parent into the "abusive parent" role, and allows the narcissistic/(borderline) parent to adopt and conspicuously display to others as being the supposedly "protective parent."

The delusional belief of the child that serves as the third diagnostic indicator of attachment-based "parental alienation" represents the child's display as the "victimized child" in the false trauma reenactment narrative created by the pathology of the narcissistic/(borderline) parent. This false trauma reenactment display by the child as the "victimized child" is often accompanied by the child's inauthentic display of the supposed PTSD trauma anxiety discussed earlier, in which the child reports being afraid of the supposedly "abusive parent" in the absence of a precipitating stressor of sufficient severity to produce the child's excessive display of anxiety.

The delusional belief of the child in attachment-based "parental alienation" is a reflection of the delusional belief of the psychologically decompensating narcissistic/(borderline) parent. The source of the child's delusional belief is in the psychopathology of the narcissistic/(borderline) parent. The child is acquiring this delusional belief through a role-reversal relationship in which the child is acting as the external "regulatory object" for the psychological state of the narcissistic/(borderline) parent. In the child's role as the "regulatory object" for the psychological state of the narcissistic/(borderline) parent, the child's attitudes and beliefs represent a stabilizing reflection of narcissistic/(borderline) parent's attitudes and beliefs. The child's false beliefs in the "abusive" parental inadequacy of the targeted parent are a reflection of the narcissistic/(borderline) parent's delusional beliefs in the "abusive" parental inadequacy of the targeted parent. In creating the trauma reenactment narrative through the child's false role as the "victimized child," the narcissistic/(borderline) parent and the child co-create and manifest a shared delusional belief.

The presence of all three diagnostic indicators in the child's symptom display represents definitive diagnostic evidence for the presence of severely pathogenic parenting emanating from the allied and supposedly favored parent that is responsible for producing significant developmental (i.e., attachment system suppression), personality (i.e., narcissistic and borderline symptoms in the child's symptom display), and psychiatric (i.e., a delusional belief in the child) pathology in the child. The specific nature of the child's symptom pathology can only be created by the severely pathogenic parenting associated with attachment-based "parental alienation." No other causal agent other than the processes of attachment-based "parental alienation" can produce this specific set of child symptoms. The presence in the child's symptom display of the three diagnostic indicators of attachment-based "parental alienation" therefore represent definitive clinical evidence that the pathogenic parenting practices of the allied and supposedly favored parent are the direct and responsible causal agent in creating the child's pathology as expressed in the termination of the child's attachment bonding motivations toward the other parent.

Sub-Threshold Diagnoses

All three diagnostic indicators must be present to make a clinical diagnosis of attachment-based "parental alienation." Other types of family and parent-child issues can produce some of the diagnostic features, but no other psychological or interpersonal process can produce all three diagnostic indicators other than an attachment-based model of "parental alienation."

If all three diagnostic indicators are not present in the child's symptom display, or if these diagnostic features are sub-threshold for a clear clinical diagnosis of attachment-based "parental alienation," then a three- to six-month Response-to-Intervention (RTI) trial can be initiated to clarify the diagnosis. Two forms of RTI trial can be initiated based on whether the diagnostic indicators suggest possible attachment-based "parental alienation" or more normal-range parent-child conflict between the child and the targeted parent.

Single-Case ABAB Response-to-Intervention

If attachment-based "parental alienation" is suspected but not confirmed by the presence of the three characteristic diagnostic indicators of attachment-based "parental alienation," then a three- to six month single-case ABAB design RTI trial which treats the family dynamics as if they represented attachment-based "parental alienation" can be initiated to clarify the diagnosis. A description of an ABAB single-case assessment protocol is beyond the scope of this current book and will be reserved for a more complete description in a different format.

Essentially, an ABAB single-case assessment protocol employs a Response-to-Intervention trial involving data collection through four distinct phases of a single-case ABAB reversal design as an RTI approach to clinical assessment.

A_1 - Initial Baseline Phase: During this phase, initial baseline data is collected on the severity of the child's rejection of the targeted parent.

B_1 - Initial Intervention Phase: The intervention phase begins with the child's protective separation from the allied and supposedly favored parent during the active phase of the child's recovery of normal-range behavior. An intensive four-day intervention for attachment-based "parental alienation" is initiated, followed by a structured behavior program in which completion of the protective separation period is made contingent upon the child's display of appropriate pro-social behavior. With the child's active participation, the protective separation can be as little as four to six weeks. Continued child symptomatology would extend the period of the protective separation. Data on the child's behavior is collected daily during the intervention period and the implementation of the structured intervention program is monitored by a supervising therapist to ensure the integrity of the intervention.

A_2 - Second Baseline Phase: Once the child demonstrates the required period of appropriate pro-social behavior, the protective separation is ended and the child's relationship with the allied parent is restored under the custody and visitation orders deemed appropriate by the court. Data on the child's symptoms continues to be collected. If the child's symptoms do not return during the Second Baseline period, then the problem is resolved. If, on the other hand, the child's symptoms reemerge upon reintroducing the pathogenic parenting practices of the allied and supposedly favored parent, then this would represent an empirically based diagnostic indicator that the pathogenic parenting of the allied and supposedly favored parent is producing the child's symptoms, since the child's symptoms are resolved when separated from the pathogenic parenting of the allied and supposedly favored parent and return when the pathogenic parenting of the allied and supposedly favored parent is reintroduced.

B_2 - Second Intervention Phase: If the child's symptoms return upon reintroduction of the pathogenic parenting of the allied and supposedly favored parent, then a Second Intervention Phase is initiated involving a second protective separation of the child from the pathogenic parenting of the allied and supposedly favored parent. During the Second Intervention Phase, additional intervention for attachment-based "parental alienation" is initiated and follow-up therapy is provided to the targeted parent and child to stabilize the child's recovery of normal-range functioning before the child is once again reintroduced the pathogenic parenting of the allied parent.

In an ABAB single-case assessment protocol, when the child's normal-range functioning is achieved for a second time during the Second Intervention Phase, this would represent extremely strong empirically based evidence that the pathogenic parenting of the allied and supposedly favored parent is responsible for the child's symptoms. The implementation of the single-case ABAB assessment protocol would be monitored by a supervising therapist who would ensure the integrity of the protocol's implementation.

The overall duration of ABAB single-case assessment protocol is designed to be from three- to six-months for all four phases, the exact duration is variable since the initial period of the child's protective separation (B_1) is within the child's power to control. If the child actively participates in the intervention protocol, then the duration of the initial protective separation can be as little as four- to six-weeks. The child's non-cooperation, however, can extend the duration of the protective separation period under the monitoring of the supervising therapist until the child achieves an appropriate display of normal-range pro-social behavior.

Standard-of-Care Response to Intervention

An alternative Response-to-Intervention trial would be to address the family dynamics as representing normal-range parent-child conflict between the child and the targeted parent. This approach would employ a standard-of-care RTI trail of a three- to six-month period of traditional parent-child relationship therapy to assess the child's symptom display and restore a normal-range parent-child relationship with the targeted parent.

In clinical presentations in which the diagnostic indicators are present but sub-threshold for a clinical diagnosis of attachment-based "parental alienation," a six-month RTI trial of traditional parent-child psychotherapy can be used to clarify the diagnostic features surrounding the child's symptom display. During this standard-of-care treatment period, the parenting practices of the targeted parent can be more fully assessed as can the symptom display presented by the child.

Assessing Parenting

In general, healthy child development expects that children will adapt to the parenting practices of the parent. Normal-range parenting extends across a broad range of corrective and nurturing parenting practices, from lax and permissive parenting to more structured and firm approaches to parenting. If parenting practices were placed on a continuum ranging from 0 to 100, with the lower range of the spectrum representing lax and permissive parenting styles and the higher range representing more firm and structured approaches to parenting, then normal-range parenting would be in the range of 20-80. Only the extremes of severely neglectful and uninvolved parenting (0-20) and severely restrictive and inflexible parenting (80-100) would represent significantly problematic parenting. Between the range of 20-80, children are expected to cooperatively adapt to parental values, parental guidance, and parental leadership of the family.

Research in child development suggests that a flexible blend of parenting approaches that is more in the mid-range between lax and permissive parenting and firm and structured parenting (in the range of 40-60 on the informal parenting scale) tends to produce the healthiest children with the least amount of parent-child conflict. As a result of established psychological theory and research regarding healthy child development, professional psychology tends to recommend a parenting approach that balances discipline and clear family structure with flexible negotiation and respectful dialogue (consistent with the age and developmental level of the child; younger children tend to benefit from increased structure, adolescents tend to benefit from increased dialogue and respect).

As parenting extends more toward the extremes of either structured and firm or lax and permissive parenting (60-80; or 20-40), greater parent-child conflict and increasingly problematic child behavior will tend to emerge. Parenting approaches that emphasize parentally imposed structure tend to foster increased maturation, but at the expense of positive family relationships. More lax and permissive parenting styles tend to foster improved relationships, but at the expense of child maturation.

In general, decisions regarding parenting will be influenced both by cultural and personal values, and the value system of parents should receive considerable deference and respect from mental health professionals. As long as parenting remains within broadly normal-range parenting practices (20-80), parents should be granted broad latitude in the exercise of their legitimate parental rights to define family values within their family, and children should be expected to cooperatively conform and adapt to the parent's expectations and values. If there are problematic parental approaches to communication, discipline, or child guidance that are creating problematic child behavior and increased parent-child conflict, then parenting therapy can address these issues.

When parent-child conflict is the product of authentic parent-child interactions, then changes to the parent's approach to parenting and communication should produce a corresponding change in the child's responses. If the child's problematic behavior and attitude continues unchanged despite therapist recommended changes to the parenting practices of the parent, then this would represent evidence for a potential cross-generational coalition of the child with the allied and supposedly favored parent that is maintaining the child's problematic behavior toward the targeted parent irrespective of the actual parenting delivered by the targeted parent. In authentic parent-child conflict, changes to the parenting practices of the parent produce corresponding changes in the child's behavior.

If the child's symptoms are the product of issues other than attachment-based "parental alienation," then three to six months of standard-of-care treatment should substantially reduce or entirely resolve the child's symptoms. The failure of a six-month standard-of-care RTI trail to resolve, or substantially reduce, the child's symptoms would represent a strong clinical indicator that the child's symptoms are <u>not</u> the product of authentic parent-child conflict but are more likely the result of a cross-generational coalition of the child with the allied and supposedly favored parent that is directed against the targeted parent.

The additional presence of associated clinical signs of attachment-based "parental alienation" can also help confirm a diagnosis of an attachment-based model of "parental alienation" when the three definitive diagnostic indicators are present but may be sub-threshold for a clear diagnosis of attachment-based "parental alienation." The identification and discussion of these associated clinical signs is beyond the scope of this current book and will be reserved for later discussion.

DSM-5 Diagnosis

The child's display of the three characteristic diagnostic indicators of attachment-based "parental alienation" represent clear and definitive clinical evidence for the presence of the psychological and interpersonal processes that comprise an attachment-based model of "parental alienation." The presence of severely pathological processes in the child's symptoms warrant the following DSM-5 diagnosis for the child:

DSM-5 Diagnosis

309.4 Adjustment Disorder with mixed disturbance of emotions and conduct

V61.20 Parent-Child Relational Problem

V61.29 Child Affected by Parental Relationship Distress

V995.51 Child Psychological Abuse, Confirmed

Child Psychological Abuse

The DSM-5 diagnosis of Child Psychological Abuse, Confirmed is warranted by the presence in the child's symptom display of three separate domains of significant pathology represented by the three diagnostic indicators of attachment-based "parental alienation," that are the product of pathogenic parenting:

1. **Induced Developmental Psychopathology:** The induced suppression of the normal-range functioning of the child's attachment system, a primary motivational system, as the result of extremely distorted pathogenic parenting practices by a narcissistic/(borderline) parent who is using the child in a role-reversal relationship as a "regulatory object" for the pathology of the parent.

2. **Induced Personality Psychopathology:** The presence of five distinctive narcissistic and borderline personality disorder traits in the child's symptom display that are being created by the highly distorted pathogenic parenting practices of a narcissistic/(borderline) parent (or an induced phobic anxiety toward a normal-range and affectionally available parent).

3. **Induced Psychiatric Psychopathology:** The presence in the child's symptom display of an induced delusional belief created by the severely pathogenic parenting practices of a narcissistic/(borderline) parent.

The parent is the primary case for the delusional belief system, and pathogenic parenting practices are the origin of the child's delusional belief. This induced delusional belief in the child, created by the highly distorted pathogenic parenting practices of a narcissistic/(borderline) parent, is resulting in the child's expressed desire to terminate a relationship with a normal-range and affectionally available parent who could otherwise act as a protective psychological buffer to the pathogenic psychopathology of the narcissistic/(borderline) parent.

The creation of significant developmental, personality, and psychiatric psychopathology in the child through highly aberrant and distorted parenting practices as a means for the parent to then exploit the induced child psychopathology to regulate the parent's own psychopathology warrants the DSM-5 diagnosis of V995.51 Child Psychological Abuse, Confirmed. The form of the child psychological abuse is a role-reversal relationship in which the child's induced psychopathology is used to regulate the psychological state of the parent. The psychological child abuse is confirmed by the presence in the child's symptom display of the three definitive diagnostic indicators of attachment-based "parental alienation." When the three diagnostic indicators of attachment-based "parental alienation" are present, the DSM-5 diagnosis of V995.51 Child Psychological Abuse, Confirmed is warranted because of the highly destructive developmental impact on the child that is created through the child's role-reversal relationship with the narcissistic/(borderline) parent.

The nature, severity, and developmental impact of the parentally induced psychopathology displayed by the child in attachment-based "parental alienation" elevates the clinical concerns from those of child custody and visitation to prominent child protection considerations.

Chapter 10

THERAPY

Models of Treatment

There are currently two primary and foundationally different approaches to treatment,

1) **Reunification Therapy:** This represents a more traditional psychotherapeutic approach that seeks to resolve the child's symptoms through weekly therapy sessions with a mental health professional.

2) **Family Reunification Protocols:** This approach involves an intensive psychoeducational intervention that seeks to resolve the child's symptoms through non-therapy approaches that systematically realign the child's distorted functioning into a normal-range relationship with the targeted parent.

As a clinical psychologist, I am most familiar with a traditional psychotherapeutic approach to healing the dysfunctional family relationships created by the pathology of a narcissistic/(borderline) parent within the family. The alternative approaches currently being developed and used with "parental alienation" that involve intensive psychoeducational family reunification protocols, such as the *Family Bridges* protocol developed by Randy Rand and Richard Warshak, the *Family Reflections Reunification Program* developed by Kathleen Reay, the *Overcoming Barriers* program developed by Matthew Sullivan, Peggie

Ward, and Robin Deutsch, and the *High Road to Family Reunification* protocol developed by Dorcy Pruter, are currently protected by their developers as proprietary trade secrets, so that the exact nature of these protocols has not been publicly described in the clinical literature. The proprietary protection of these protocols prevents a more complete professional review and analysis regarding how these protocols function to achieve their results.

Since the content of these family reunification protocols has not been described in the clinical literature, I will defer an analysis of these intensive psychoeducational models to a later time, and will limit my current discussion of treatment models to the application of more traditional psychotherapy principles to the psychological and family dynamics surrounding an attachment-based model of "parental alienation." However, before leaving a discussion of these intensive family reunification protocols I wish to offer at least a preliminary assessment of their potential benefit.

Through professional collaborations with Dorcy Pruter, I have been allowed to review her *High Road to Family Reunification* protocol. Ms. Pruter has agreed to allow me to offer a broad review of her protocol approach, as long as I protect the specific content of the protocol. Her desire to protect the protocol content is based on the need to protect the integrity of the intervention structure, which after my review of her approach is both warranted and justified.

Based on my review of the *High Road to Family Reunification* protocol, I understand how her intensive family reunification protocol achieves the success it does in resolving the child's symptoms of attachment-based "parental alienation." Ms. Pruter indicates that a successful resolution of the child's symptoms can be achieved within days, and based on my review of her protocol I believe this represents a reasonable expectation. The *High Road* protocol uses a structured series of catalytic steps for restoring the normal-range psychological and emotional processes of the child. The use of catalytic change requires both the proper catalytic interventions and their proper sequencing. Again, based on my review of the *High Road* protocol, Ms. Pruter has identified both the proper catalytic interventions and has them aligned in the proper sequence, and I believe that achieving an initial resolution of the child's symptoms within days is a reasonable expectation for her protocol.

A catalytic approach represents a foundationally different methodology than is employed in traditional psychotherapy. Traditional approaches to psychotherapy employ synthesizing interventions that integrate prior experiences and expectations into current functioning. Catalytic interventions, on the other hand, move the brain state through a series of structured steps to achieve the desired end state. An example of a catalytic intervention would be the 12-Step program of Alcoholics Anonymous. The catalytic interventions developed by Pruter are <u>not</u> a 12-Step program. The catalytic interventions employed in the *High Road* protocol are uniquely developed for the issues of parent-child conflict in "parental alienation," but the underlying approach of using catalytic rather than synthesizing interventions is similar.

Through a structured series of catalytic steps, the *High Road* protocol of Pruter moves the child through a sequence of psychological states that deactivate the child's anxiety, restore the normal-range functioning of the child's empathy and attachment systems, and deactivate the child's inflamed anger. As the child moves through these psychological states the child's natural attachment bonding motivations toward the targeted parent reactivate. Once the child is able to affectionally re-bond with targeted parent, the child's grief response resolves and the child is returned to normal-range functioning. The *High Road* protocol also provides a series of structured steps and family activities across four days of intervention that restore normal-range parent-child dialogue, respect, and family discipline.

I raise the issue of these intensive family reunification protocols to highlight the fact that there are alternative models to traditional psychotherapy that hold significant promise for the rapid resolution of the child's symptoms of attachment-based "parental alienation. Of note is that the *High Road* protocol still requires a period of the child's protective separation from the pathology of the narcissistic/(borderline) parent during the child's recovery and stabilization. Re-exposing the child too quickly to the pathogenic parenting of the narcissistic/(borderline) parent can reverse the gains made from the intervention protocol. Additional follow-up supportive psychotherapy is recommended within the protocol to stabilize the child's recovery prior to re-exposing the child to the pathogenic parenting of the narcissistic/(borderline) parent.

Based on my review of the *High Road to Family Reunification Protocol* developed by Pruter, I am optimistic that these alternative approaches to family reunification may represent an even better approach to resolving the child's symptoms of attachment-based "parental alienation" than is offered by more traditional psychotherapy approaches. These intensive family reunification protocols may be able to achieve an initial resolution to the child symptoms of attachment-based "parental alienation" in a matter of days once the child is provided with a period of protective separation from the ongoing pathogenic parental influence of the narcissistic/(borderline) parent.

A critical feature of any approach to treatment is to first protect the child from the pathogenic parenting of the narcissistic/(borderline) parent. Treatment efforts should not be initiated prior to establishing the child's protective separation from the psychopathology of the narcissistic/(borderline) parent. We cannot ask the child to expose his or her authenticity unless we are first able to protect the child from the psychopathology and pathogenic parenting practices of the narcissistic/(borderline) parent.

Achieving this protective separation of the child from the psychopathology and pathogenic parenting of the narcissistic/(borderline) parent will require obtaining the cooperation of the court with the treatment efforts. Without the cooperation of the court in establishing the necessary conditions needed for treatment, the severe psychopathology of attachment-based "parental alienation" cannot be resolved. As long as the child remains under the active influence of the psychopathology of the narcissistic/(borderline) parent, no amount or nature of child or family therapy will resolve the child's symptoms.

Recovery of the child's healthy development will be impossible unless we first protect the child from the pathogenic influence of the narcissistic/(borderline) parent. Unless we protectively separate the child from the ongoing pathogenic influence of the narcissistic/(borderline) parent during the treatment period, we will essentially be abandoning the child to the narcissistic and borderline psychopathology of the parent. Effective treatment **requires** a period of protective separation of the child from the pathogenic influence of the narcissistic/(borderline) parent.

With a court-ordered period of protective separation of the child from the severely pathogenic parenting of the narcissistic/(borderline) parent, effective treatment can be initiated to resolve the child's symptoms and recover the child's healthy development, potentially within a matter of days, with continuing supportive therapeutic follow-up to stabilize the child's recovery.

Reunification Therapy

The treatment of "parental alienation" is often referred to as "reunification therapy" and therapists may sometimes even assert that they conduct "reunification therapy." Unfortunately, there is no current model for what reunification therapy entails. The term "reunification therapy" currently lacks any defined clinical meaning. Since there is no model for what "reunification therapy" entails, there is no such thing as "reunification therapy." There are defined forms of psychoanalytic therapy, there are defined types of humanistic/existential therapy, there are defined family systems therapies, there are defined forms of cognitive-behavioral therapy, and there are defined forms of post-modern therapy, but there is no current definition for what constitutes "reunification therapy." Nowhere in the professional literature is there a defined model for what "reunification therapy" entails.

The structure being offered here for a description of the required therapeutic interventions needed with attachment-based "parental alienation" therefore serves as the nascent organizational core for a professional description of what constitutes "reunification therapy." The focus of this model for therapy is on treating the child's symptomatic display. The personality disorder dynamics of the "alienating" narcissistic/(borderline) parent are likely to be intractable and highly treatment resistant, so no focus is made toward altering the processes of the "alienating" narcissistic/(borderline) parent within an attachment-based model of therapy. While recognizing that the cause of attachment-based "parental alienation" lay in the distorted and pathogenic parenting practices of the narcissistic/(borderline) parent, the treatment focus for this model of attachment-based reunification therapy is solely focused on restoring the child's healthy development and the child's relationship with the targeted-rejected parent.

Courts may order the narcissistic/(borderline) parent's participation in collateral therapy to support the recovery of the child's relationship with the targeted parent, however these orders for the participation of the narcissistic/(borderline) parent in collateral therapy are not likely to be followed by the narcissistic/(borderline) parent, nor is treatment for the narcissistic/(borderline) parent likely to be effective. The pathology of the narcissistic/(borderline) parent is at the level of a delusional obsession to "protect the child" that originates from a reenactment narrative born in childhood trauma. A delusional belief is not likely to be amenable to change from any form of psychotherapy. That is what makes it a delusion. If the belief was amenable to change, then it would not be delusional.

Because the parent's delusional belief is originating from personality disorder and trauma pathology, it may be possible to reduce the overt manifestation of the delusional belief by reducing the pressure of the personality and trauma processes in the current situation. If therapy could reduce the narcissistic/(borderline) personality's activated anxiety from the narcissistic, borderline, and trauma processes, then some relief from the delusionally obsessive fixation of the narcissistic/(borderline) parent on enacting the childhood trauma narrative might be achieved. If collateral therapy is sought for the narcissistic/(borderline) parent, then a variant of Schema Therapy (Young, Klosko, & Weishaar, 2002) might represent a possible foundation for the narcissistic/(borderline) parent's own therapeutic involvement in the reunification therapy process of the child with the targeted parent.

Protective Separation

In order to accomplish the treatment goal of restoring the child's healthy relationship with the targeted parent, which has been so severely damaged by the pathology of the narcissistic/(borderline) parent, it is vital that the child first be protectively separated from the ongoing pathogenic influence of the narcissistic/(borderline) parent. The treatment-related need for the child's protective separation from the psychopathology of the narcissistic/(borderline) parent during the child's treatment and recovery is necessary for two independent and equally valid reasons:

1) **Child Protection Concerns:** As a required response to child protection concerns arising from the pathogenic parenting of the

narcissistic/(borderline) parent that is inducing significant developmental, personality, and psychiatric symptoms in the child.

2) **Psychological Battleground:** As a treatment-related need to psychologically protect the child during therapy from being turned into a "psychological battleground" between the efforts of therapy to restore the child's normal-range and healthy development and the ongoing efforts of the narcissistic/(borderline) parent to induce and maintain the child's symptomatic rejection of the targeted parent.

Response to Psychological Child Abuse

In healthy child development, the child uses the parent as a "regulatory other" for the child's emotional and psychological state. When the child faces a developmental challenge that the child cannot independently master, the child emits increasingly disorganized and dysregulated behavior that elicits the involvement of the parent, who then helps the child regain an emotionally and psychologically organized and regulated state. The parent acts as an external "regulatory other" for the child, and in doing so the parent "scaffolds" the canalization of the child's own internal networks for self-regulation.

With brain networks, we build what we use. Every time we use a brain system or network, structural and chemical changes take place along the neural pathways that were used that make the connections stronger, more sensitive, and more efficient. In healthy child development, every time the parent acts as a "regulatory other" for the child by scaffolding the child's state transition from a disorganized and dysregulated brain state (as manifested in disorganized and dysregulated behavior) back into an organized and well-regulated brain state (as manifested by calm and cooperative behavior) all of the brain networks and brain systems that were used in this transition process become stronger, more sensitive, and more efficient. We build what we use.

Over multiple repetitions of these state transitions, the child's own brain networks for making these transitions become stronger, more sensitive, and more efficient so that the child develops the internalized capacity for "self-regulation" without the need for the scaffolding support of the "regulatory other" of the parent. This overall developmental process of building the integrated brain networks for self-regulation is called the child's development of "self-structure."

The parent's role as a "regulatory other" for the child is extremely important for the child's healthy development. In fact, it is the **central role** of parenting beyond providing for the child's basic needs for food, shelter, and safety. By acting as a "regulatory other" for the child, the parent scaffolds the child's internal neurological development of healthy "self-structure" organization that is necessary for the child's independent self-regulation of emotions and behavior.

However, in a role-reversal relationship, the developmental roles for the parent and child are reversed. In a role-reversal relationship, it is the parent who uses the child as a "regulatory other" to regulate the parent's emotional and psychological state. This is extremely destructive to the child's emotional and psychological development. Through a role-reversal relationship, the parent essentially robs the child of the developmental experiences necessary for the child's own self-structure development. Through a role-reversal relationship, the pathology of the parent uses the child to support the parent's own inadequate self-structure and self-regulation. The parent's own inadequate self-structure is essentially feeding off of the child's healthy self-structure development as a means to keep the parent in an organized and regulated psychological state.

This extremely unhealthy role-reversal relationship will cause deep psychological damage to the child's capacity for independent self-regulation, which will then subsequently affect this child's later parenting relationships with his or her own children. The pathology of the role-reversal relationship is passed on from one generation to the next. The child in a role-reversal relationship has his or her own self-structure development robbed by the parent to support the parent's inadequate self-regulation. When this child then grows up, the child-now-adult will have inadequate self-structure formation because it was robbed in its healthy development during childhood in order to feed the parent's inadequate self-structure. So this child, now an adult, will then repeat this process of using the next generation child in a role-reversal relationship as a "regulatory object" for the new parent's emotional and psychological state. The role-reversal relationship is thus passed on across generations, with each generation of parents psychologically feeding off of the children's self-structure development in order to support the parents' incapacity to self-regulate their own emotional and psychological state.

In healthy parent-child relationships, the child uses the parent to meet the child's emotional and psychological needs. In the pathology of the role-reversal relationship, the parent is using the child to meet the parent's emotional and psychological needs.

While a role-reversal relationship is extremely pathological, to all external appearances it will appear as if the child is in a highly bonded relationship with the (pathological) parent. The child and the (pathological) parent share a fused psychological state designed to meet the parent's needs, yet superficially this role-reversal relationship appears as if it is a bonded relationship. However, to a trained clinical eye familiar with healthy parent-child development, the role-reversal relationship is clearly evident in a variety of distorted parent-child relationship features. It is vital to assessing the psychological and developmental needs of children that mental health professionals understand the neuro-biological foundations of the parent's role as the "regulatory other" in the healthy development of the child. The role-reversal relationship, in which the parent uses the child as a "regulatory other" for the parent's own emotional and psychological state, is one of the most psychologically destructive forms of parent-child relationship.

A protective separation of the child during the period of the child's treatment and recovery stabilization is a warranted child protection response to the severely pathogenic role-reversal relationship created in attachment-based "parental alienation." The highly distorted pathogenic parenting practices of the narcissistic/(borderline) parent are robbing the child of healthy child development and a healthy relationship with the normal-range and affectionally available targeted-rejected parent. The period of childhood is fleeting and irreplaceable. Once developmental periods of childhood are lost, they cannot be recovered. The severity of the role-reversal pathology in attachment-based "parental alienation" is of the highest magnitude, and the psychological damage being inflicted on the child's development by the pathogenic parenting of the narcissistic/(borderline) parent is profound.

The pathogenic parenting practices of the narcissistic/(borderline) parent are creating overt psychopathology in the child. This overt psychopathology is evidenced in the child's symptom display of severe developmental pathology (Diagnostic Indicator 1), severe personality pathology (Diagnostic Indicator 2), and severe psychiatric pathology (Diagnostic Indicator 3). This severe child psychopathology is the direct result of the psychopathology and pathogenic parenting practices of the narcissistic/(borderline) parent. Protectively separating the child from the pathogenic parenting of the narcissistic/(borderline) parent represents an appropriate child protection response. Once the child's healthy psychological and developmental functioning has been restored and stabilized, then the pathology of the narcissistic/(borderline) parent can be reintroduced.

Attachment-based "parental alienation" is a child protection issue. When the three definitive diagnostic indicators of attachment-based "parental alienation" are present, providing an immediate protective separation for the child from the severely distorting pathogenic parenting practices of the narcissistic/(borderline) parent represents both a warranted and a necessary child protection response to the severity of the role-reversal pathology.

When the three diagnostic indicators of attachment-based "parental alienation" are present in the child's symptom display, child custody and visitation issues recede as primary considerations and the goal of protecting the child's healthy development becomes the sole and preeminent consideration. In attachment-based 'parental alienation," parental rights become secondary considerations to child protection concerns. In order to protect the child's healthy development, the child must be protectively separated from the psychologically abusive pathogenic parenting practices of the role-reversal relationship created by the narcissistic/(borderline) parent that is inducing severe psychopathology in the child. The nature and severity of the child's symptom display in attachment-based "parental alienation" warrant an immediate child protection response.

<u>Psychological Battleground</u>

Attempting to restore the child's normal-range and healthy development while the narcissistic/(borderline) parent continues to apply psychological pressure on the child to remain symptomatic will have the effect of turning the child into a "psychological battleground" between the efforts of therapy to restore normal-range and healthy child development and the relentless pathogenic efforts of the narcissistic/(borderline) parent to keep the child's in a symptomatic state.

As long as the child is in a relationship with the narcissistic/(borderline) parent, the child will be compelled through the role-reversal relationship to act as a "regulatory object" for the parent's psychopathology. The narcissistic/(borderline) parent will use the role-reversal relationship with the child in a relentless effort to undermine the efforts of therapy designed to restore the child's normal-range and healthy relationship with the targeted parent. It is essential to regulating the psychopathology of the narcissistic/(borderline) parent that the child remain symptomatically rejecting of the targeted parent.

Turning the child into a psychological battleground between the efforts of therapy to restore the child's healthy functioning and the relentless efforts of the narcissistic/(borderline) parent to keep the child pathological runs the considerable risk of harming the child psychologically and developmentally. As long as the child remains under the pathogenic influence of the narcissistic/(borderline) parent, therapy cannot seek to restore the child's normal and healthy development without turning the child into a psychological battleground because of the continuing efforts of the narcissistic/(borderline) parent to maintain the child's pathology. In order to protect the child's emotional and psychological development, ethical and professionally responsible therapy requires that the child first be protectively separated from the pathology of the narcissistic/(borderline) parent during the active phase of the child's treatment and recovery stabilization.

Standard 3.04 of the Ethical Principles of Psychologists and Code of Conduct of the American Psychological Association requires that "psychologists take reasonable steps to avoid harming their clients/patients... and to minimize harm where it is foreseeable and unavoidable." Protectively separating the child from the severely distorted and pathogenic parenting practices of the narcissistic-borderline parent during the active phase of the child's treatment and recovery stabilization represents a reasonable step that is needed to "minimize harm where it is foreseeable and unavoidable" as required by professional practice standards.

Reunification therapy to restore the child's healthy relationship with the targeted parent should not be attempted prior to achieving the child's protective separation from the pathogenic parenting of the narcissistic/(borderline) parent. The protective separation of the child is a necessary precondition of therapy which is needed to protect the child from the potential harm of being turned into a "psychological battleground" by the relentless efforts of the narcissistic/(borderline) parent to maintain the child's pathology while therapy is simultaneously seeking the opposite goal of restoring the child's healthy functioning.

Once a protective separation of the child from the pathogenic parenting of the narcissistic/(borderline) parent is achieved, then therapy can be initiated to restore the normal-range and healthy development of the child without the risk of turning the child into a "psychological battleground" as a result of the contrary efforts of the narcissistic/(borderline) parent to maintain the child's induced psychopathology. When therapy has successfully recovered and stabilized the child's healthy and normal-range development, then the pathogenic parenting of the narcissistic/(borderline) parent can be reintroduced with appropriate treatment-related monitoring to ensure that reintroduction of the pathogenic parenting of the narcissistic/(borderline) parent does not recreate the child's pathology.

When the three definitive diagnostic indicators of attachment-based "parental alienation" are present in the child's symptom display, then child protection and treatment concerns take precedence over typical child custody considerations. The pathology being evidenced by the child in attachment-based "parental alienation" is of such severity and of such deep clinical concern that the first and foremost consideration should be establishing the necessary conditions needed for the successful treatment and recovery of the child's healthy development. Child custody considerations regarding shared visitation and parental rights return once the child's evident psychopathology has been treated and resolved.

When the pathology of the narcissistic/(borderline) parent is reintroduced, the child's relationship with the formerly targeted-rejected parent should be closely monitored by the treating family therapist in order to ensure the stability of the child's treatment gains. Reintroducing the pathology and pathogenic parenting of the narcissistic/(borderline) parent runs the considerable risk of once again creating pathology in the child. If symptoms of attachment-based "parental alienation" reemerge upon reintroducing the pathogenic parenting of the narcissistic/(borderline) parent, then another cycle of protective separation from the personality disordered parent, or restricting the narcissistic/(borderline) parent to monitored visitations, may be necessary to ensure the continuation of the child's healthy emotional and psychological development.

Resolving the Grief Response

The central focus of treatment is on reorienting the child to the child's authentic experience of grief, sadness, and loss regarding the divorce and the subsequent loss of an affectionally bonded relationship with the targeted parent. The fundamental issue in recovering an authentic child is resolving the child's misattribution of a natural grief response that occurred in response to the divorce and family's dissolution. The child's initial grief and sadness at the loss of the intact family increased exponentially when the child lost an affectionally bonded relationship with the beloved-but-now-rejected targeted parent. At its foundational core, reunification therapy represents helping the child to accurately understand, process, and resolve the experience of normal-range grief and sadness at the losses surrounding the divorce.

The goal of reunification therapy is to help the family successfully transition to a separated family structure that is united by the continuing parental roles with the child. In order to accomplish this goal, the feelings of grief and sadness over losses needs to be understood, processed, and resolved by the family members. The attachment and personality pathology of the narcissistic/(borderline) parent is unlikely to allow this processing of sadness and loss, so continued pathological expressions of disordered grief and mourning should be expected from the narcissistic/(borderline) parent. Reunification therapy with attachment-based "parental alienation" focuses on helping the child to understand and process the normal-range experience of sadness and loss in healthy ways of seeking affectional bonding and comfort.

The core issue in reunification therapy therefore becomes helping the child effectively understand and process the child's experience of sadness, grief, and loss. These feelings are metabolized through our affectional bonding and the comforting we receive from loved ones. For example, when a loved one dies we come together to grieve at the funeral. We cry, we hug, and we receive and offer emotional support in our sadness. Through the social acknowledgement and sharing of grief we are able to release our sadness and move forward. Our grief and sadness is processed through affectional bonding with others, particularly with our loved ones. This is essentially what needs to happen with the child in the resolution of attachment-based "parental alienation." The child needs to have his or her sadness and grief acknowledged, and the child needs to receive and share affectional comfort from his or her parents for the child's experience of loss and sadness.

In a healthy parent-child relationship, the parent serves as a "regulatory other" for the child. In a healthy resolution of the grief response that allows the child to make a successful transition from the intact family structure to a new separated family structure, the child uses the regulatory scaffolding support provided by an empathically attuned and responsive parent. In a healthy family transition, the child uses parental guidance and support for understanding the meaning of the divorce and the family's transition from an intact family structure united by the marriage, to a separated family structure united by the continuing parental relationships with the child. Empathically attuned parenting acknowledges the child's sadness, and provides comfort and nurture for the authentic experience of sadness and loss while also supporting the child's affectional bonding to both parents.

Under the distorting influence of the narcissistic/(borderline) parent, however, the child's sadness was twisted into anger and resentment directed toward the targeted parent following the divorce. The narcissistic/(borderline) parent used the child's induced anger and rejection of the targeted parent to regulate the psychological state of the narcissistic/(borderline) parent. Therapy therefore involves correcting the effects of this role-reversal use of the child by the narcissistic/(borderline) parent. Therapy needs to establish a healthy parent-child relationship with the targeted parent in which the child is led into an accurate understanding for the meaning of the child's experience of sadness surrounding the family's transition to a separated family structure. Therapy for attachment-based "parental alienation" involves restoring the targeted parent into the developmentally healthy parent role as the "regulatory other" for the child to assist the child in processing sadness and loss, which will then allow the family to transition into a new separated family structure in a developmentally healthy way.

Attachment-based "parental alienation" occurs when one parent, the narcissistic/(borderline) parent, transforms the child's natural feelings of sadness and grief into anger and blaming directed toward the other spouse – "it's your fault this happened, you deserve to be punished, you deserve to suffer." The pathology of the narcissistic/(borderline) parent leads the child into a similar interpretation of the child's own natural grief response as that of the narcissistic/(borderline) parent; as blame and anger directed toward the targeted parent/spouse.

Assigning blame for the divorce is not productive generally, but when it does occur it should always remain contained within the spousal relationship and it should never be allowed to slip into and infect either of the parent-child relationships. The reasons why the divorce occurred is a spousal issue. The fact that a divorce occurred is a family issue. All family members will need to process their sadness at the loss. Even if the marriage was problematic, there will still be sadness and feelings of loss at an ending of the intact family structure. The therapist needs to help the child release blame, acknowledge the sadness, and process the sadness through affectional bonding with the targeted-rejected parent in order to resolve the grieving and loss experience for the child.

In addition, under the distorting influence of the role-reversal relationship with the narcissistic/(borderline) parent, the child has learned to become a "regulatory object" for the other person in the relationship. As a result, the child has lost the capacity for authentic self-experience. The therapist needs to reorient the child to the child's own authentic self-experience surrounding sadness and loss, including the child's own authentic bonding motivations for the targeted parent (the sky isn't blue because we say it's blue; the sky is blue because we see it's blue).

The goal of reunification therapy is to help the child recover the child's own capacity for self-authentic experience. The therapist accomplishes this by providing the child with attuned therapist resonance for expressions of child authenticity, and with misattuned therapist responses for expressions of the pathology acquired from the enmeshed relationship with the narcissistic/(borderline) parent. All children love their parents and want to be loved by their parents in return. This is authentic. The child is fundamentally a kind and cooperative child. This is authentic. The child's display of rude and contemptuous hostility toward the targeted parent, or of phobic levels of anxiety, are not an authentic expression of the child's genuine kindness and love for the targeted parent but are instead the acquired product of the distorted pathogenic parenting the child has received from the narcissistic/(borderline) parent.

Once the child can acknowledge his or her authentic affectionate bonding motivations toward the targeted parent, and allow this affectional bonding to achieve completion, the grief response will resolve. Once the child's grief at the loss of an affectionally bonded relationship with the targeted parent is resolved, then the child will no longer feel the anger, resentment, and blame toward the targeted parent that is part of attachment-based "parental alienation." The child will recover his or her self-authenticity once more.

Over time, there will be naturally occurring parent-child conflicts with the targeted parent because some degree of parent-child conflict is entirely normal in healthy parent-child relationships. When these occur, as they inevitably will, the therapist can help the parent and child resolve these conflicts in healthy ways that support the continued deepening of the parent-child bond.

Phases of Reunification Therapy

Treatment of the *special population* of children and families evidencing attachment-based "parental alienation" involves four component phases:

1) Rescue of the Child – Protective Separation

Professionally responsible standards of practice require that the child be protectively separated from the pathogenic parenting practices of the narcissistic/(borderline) parent during the active phase of the child's treatment and recovery stabilization. Therapy cannot ask the child to expose his or her psychological authenticity by expressing the child's authentic bonding motivations toward the targeted parent until the child is protected from retaliation by the narcissistic/(borderline) parent for the child's bonding to the targeted parent. Reunification therapy with the child should not be engaged as long as the child remains under the pathogenic influence of the narcissistic/(borderline) parent because of the risks to the child from being turned into a "psychological battleground" as the result of the ongoing efforts of the narcissistic/(borderline) parent to maintain the child's psychopathology while therapy is simultaneously seeking to resolve the child's pathology.

2) Recovery of the Child's Self-Authenticity

The recovery of the child's self-authenticity involves several component processes. The child needs to be reoriented to the authentic experience of grief, sadness, and loss, along with a restoration of the child's normal range capacity for empathy that has been suppressed by the child's enmeshed psychological relationship with the narcissistic/(borderline) parent. The therapist also needs to eliminate the child's expression of narcissistic and borderline psychopathology that the child has acquired from the pathogenic parenting practices of the narcissistic/(borderline) parent. This is accomplished by providing the child with misattuned therapist responses to child displays of narcissistic and borderline psychopathology, and with attuned therapist responses to child displays of normal-range and healthy development.

The therapist's support for the child's normal-range development also includes recognizing and acknowledging that normal-range parent-child conflicts occur and are developmentally healthy. These normal-range parent-child conflicts are called "breach-and-repair" sequences, and they are vital components of healthy child development. The therapist's role is to help the targeted parent and child successfully navigate these normal-range "breach-and-repair" sequences with mutual respect and affection.

The disorganized attachment of the narcissistic/(borderline) parent is unable to repair breaches to the relationship when they occur. As a result, the narcissistic/(borderline) parent requires that the relationship partner (i.e., the "regulatory other" of the attachment figure) remains in a continually fused psychological state with the narcissistic/(borderline) parent in order to prevent breaches to the relationship that would undermine the regulation of the narcissistic/(borderline) parent's emotional and psychological state. Under the distorting influence of the narcissistic/(borderline) parent, the child is being taught to respond to relationship problems by cutting off the relationship with the other person (with the attachment figure). Restoring healthy child development requires that the targeted parent and therapist help the child develop normal-range and healthy ways of restoring affectional relationship bonds when they become ruptured.

Empathic failures occur naturally within the parent-child relationship and are normal and healthy parent-child experiences within the individuation process of the child's developing self-autonomy. The goal in child therapy is not to obtain an obedient child, the goal of therapy is to achieve an emotionally and psychologically healthy child. Normal-range parent-child conflict is expectable and developmentally healthy. The issue for therapy becomes successfully managing and resolving these normal "breach-and-repair" sequences.

The therapist in reunification therapy for attachment-based "parental alienation" needs to both misattune with child expressions of pathology, while also offering attuned and supportive therapist responses to authentic child expressions of normal-range self-autonomy, even when this may create breaches with the parent's wishes and attitudes. The goal of therapy is not simply to replace the psychological control of the child by the narcissistic/(borderline) parent with psychological control of the child by the targeted parent (with therapist support). The goal of therapy is to achieve a healthy and self-autonomous child and a healthy and affectionally bonded parent-child relationship.

3) Restoration of Attachment Bonding Motivations

The pathology of attachment-based "parental alienation" has nullified the targeted parent as a protective and nurturing parent. Instead, the targeted parent has been falsely cast into the trauma reenactment role as being the dangerous and "abusive parent." The nullification of the targeted parent as a protective parent, and the redefinition of the targeted parent as supposedly being "abusive" of the child (i.e., as "the predator" relative to the functioning of the child's attachment system), has artificially suppressed the child's normal-range attachment bonding motivations toward the targeted parent. The restoration of the child's healthy development requires restoring the targeted parent as a protective and nurturing parent in order to allow the child's natural attachment bonding motivations to reactivate and achieve completion.

The restoration of the targeted parent to the developmentally healthy role as a nurturing and protective parent requires verbal and non-verbal communications by the therapist directly to the child, and to the targeted parent in the presence of the child, that act to re-validate the targeted parent as a caring, compassionate, and nurturing protective parent. The therapist should also invalidate the child's false assertions and beliefs that the parenting of the targeted parent is inadequate and "abusive" by providing the child with direct communication and socio-emotional cues for social referencing by the child regarding what normal-range parenting entails. Restoring the targeted parent as a nurturing and protective parent allows the child's natural attachment bonding motivations toward the targeted parent to become active once more and to then be supported in achieving their completion, thereby resolving the child's grief response at the loss of an attached relationship with the targeted parent.

4) Reintroduction of the Pathogenic Parent

Once the child's symptomatic rejection of the targeted parent has been resolved, and the child's recovery of self-authenticity has been stabilized, the pathogenic parenting of the narcissistic/(borderline) parent can be reintroduced. When the child's protective separation from the pathology of the narcissistic/(borderline) parent is ended, there is a considerable risk that the reintroduction of the pathogenic parenting of the narcissistic/(borderline) parent will once more create a role-reversal relationship with the child that induces child pathology. Prior to reintroducing the child to the pathology of the narcissistic/(borderline) parent, steps should be taken in therapy to inoculate the child against once again being induced into entering the role-reversal relationship with the narcissistic/(borderline) parent.

Coping Strategies: Before reintroducing the child to the pathogenic parenting of the narcissistic/(borderline) parent, the child can be provided with cognitive and behavioral coping strategies for managing the expectable pathological expressions of the narcissistic/(borderline) parent. Particularly important will be strategies to help the child avoid being induced into becoming a "regulatory object" for the pathology of the narcissistic/(borderline) parent to stabilize the emotional and psychological functioning of the parent.

In addition, if it is made abundantly clear to the narcissistic/(borderline) parent that a return of child symptoms will result in another round of protective separation, this might potentially discourage the narcissistic/(borderline) parent from using the child as a "regulatory object" once the protective separation is lifted. Narcissistic and borderline personalities are highly exploitative and manipulative. Managing the pathology of the narcissistic and borderline personality benefits from establishing and enforcing clear expectations, structure, and boundaries.

Monitoring Treatment Stability: Protecting healthy child development is of paramount concern. The active monitoring of child symptomatology by the guiding family therapist will be necessary to ensure that the reintroduction of the pathological parenting of the narcissistic/(borderline) parent does not once again create pathology in the child through the formation of a role-reversal relationship of the child acting as the "regulatory object" for the pathology of the narcissistic/(borderline) parent.

Treating Relapse: If child symptoms reemerge upon the reintroduction of the pathogenic parenting of the narcissistic/(borderline) parent, then another round of protective separation, or limiting the narcissistic/(borderline) parent to supervised visitation, becomes warranted to protect the child's healthy development. Ongoing therapeutic monitoring and restrictions placed on the narcissistic/(borderline) parent for supervised visitation may be required until the child has achieved sufficient developmental maturity to independently resist the psychological pressures placed on the child by the narcissistic/(borderline) parent to form a role-reversal relationship with this parent.

Coordinating Therapies

The core of the family processes associated with an attachment-based model of "parental alienation" is a disorganized attachment of the narcissistic/(borderline) parent that is then reflected in disorganized and chaotic family processes. The therapeutic response to disorganization is to provide clearly defined structure. Treatment for the generalized family disorganization surrounding attachment-based "parental alienation" needs to provide a structured and organized coherence to the treatment process. The involvement of multiple therapists would threaten to fragment the organized coherence of the treatment's focus and should be avoided if at all possible. A capable family therapist should be able to effectively manage all components of the therapy process, including individual sessions with parents and children as necessary. Coordinating therapy through a single family therapist will prevent the fragmentation of the therapy process by allowing all components of therapy to be managed through a single family therapist. Coordinating therapy through a single family therapist also allows for the effective integration of material covered in individual sessions with material covered in family sessions.

This single coordinating family therapist should also be empowered to discuss all aspects of treatment and the child's treatment-related needs with the court to ensure an effective therapeutic collaboration with the court that meets the needs of the child. Periodic written treatment updates can be provided to the court to ensure ongoing oversight of the child's treatment needs.

While a single family therapist will provide an organized coherence to treatment, many therapists are not comfortable assuming the multiple roles inherent to a family therapist. For this reason, therapy is sometimes separated into component parts involving a conjoint family therapist for the parent-child relationship and individual therapists for the children. This structure for the therapeutic team runs a considerable risk of fragmenting treatment efforts, including the potential for "staff splitting" associated with treating borderline personality processes. Marsha Linehan, one of the premier mental health professionals treating borderline personality processes, describes the potential for "staff-splitting" when treating borderline personality disorder dynamics,

> "Staff splitting, as mentioned earlier, is a much-discussed phenomenon in which professionals treating borderline patients begin arguing and fighting about a patient, the treatment plan, or the behavior of the other professionals with the patient... Arguments among staff members and differences in points of view, traditionally associated with staff splitting, are seen as failures in synthesis and interpersonal process among the staff rather than as a patient's problem... Therapist disagreements over a patient are treated as potentially equally valid poles of a dialectic. Thus, the starting point for dialogue is the recognition that a polarity has arisen, together with an implicit (if not explicit) assumption that resolution will require working toward synthesis" (Linehan, 1993, p. 432).

If a decision is made to divide therapy between a conjoint family therapist for the parent-child relationship and individual child therapists, then additional consideration needs to be taken for ongoing consultation within the treatment team to coordinate treatment interventions and prevent staff splitting. If individual child therapists are added, then it becomes vital that the individual therapists work from the same treatment model for reunification therapy as the family therapist, meaning the full recognition of an attachment-based model for "parental alienation." The individual therapists <u>should not</u> work from a humanistic model of "validating the child's feelings" as this would be contra-indicated for the treatment of a role-reversal relationship involving induced child symptoms, in which the child's authenticity has been nullified.

If possible a single family therapist coordinating all aspects of therapy would be preferable to dividing therapy among multiple therapists, and a single treating therapist is recommended. If treatment is separated into component parts, then the family therapist should be empowered to provide leadership within the treatment team and should be sufficiently empowered to select, and if need be change, individual therapists.

Chapter 11

PROFESSIONAL COMPETENCE

Professional Knowledge of Child Development

Childhood is a period of profound and extensive developmental change. The formative experiences of childhood will have a significant and enduring impact on the future of the child as a person, as a spouse, and as a parent. The formative experiences of childhood are crucial to the later development of emotional and psychological health. There is no other time period as important for the psychological development of the person as the period of childhood.

The formative processes occurring during childhood are also incredibly complex. Not only do the developmental challenges change continually across childhood, from early childhood, to the school-age years, to early adolescence, to later adolescence and emerging young adulthood, but within each phase the impact and importance of different developmental and relationship experiences varies. The processes of child development are profoundly complex.

Because of both the incredible importance and the incredible complexity of child development, mental health professionals who work with children and families should be among the best-trained and most expert of all mental health professionals. Not only should childhood mental health professionals have expert training in adult models of mental health and therapy, they should also receive extensive advanced training in the neuro-development of the brain across the multiple developmental periods of childhood, as well as the processes involved in the healthy developmental integration of the variety of brain systems relevant to childhood maturation.

Instead of being our best trained and most skilled mental health professionals, therapists treating children and families are often among the most poorly trained professionals. In many cases, child therapists lack a fundamental understanding for the basic principles of socially mediated brain development during childhood. This is because the focus of most educational models for mental health professionals is on providing training in research methodology and in adult psychotherapy and psychopathology, with child therapy being an add-on rather than primary component of training. Instruction in child development is typically offered in only one or two courses on development, and these courses typically cover development across the entire lifespan.

The period of childhood is so complex and so important to future emotional and psychological health, that the educational curriculum for child and family therapists should require at least ten separate core courses in child development and therapy:

1. **Overview of Lifespan Development:** A broad survey of development across the lifespan, linking the navigation of earlier developmental challenges to later developmental expressions.

2. **Early Childhood Mental Health:** A particular focus on the socially mediated neuro-development of the brain and emerging integration of brain systems during the first five years of development.

3. **Middle Childhood and Adolescence:** A core focus on the developing brain from middle childhood, through puberty, and into young adult organization.

4. **Child Therapy Models:** Education and training in relationship-based, neuro-developmental, behavioral systems, and parent-facilitated models of child therapy, applied to the multiple stages of child development; early childhood, middle childhood, pre-adolescence, adolescence, and emerging young adulthood.

5. **Family Systems Models:** Education and training in the primary family systems theorists and models of family therapy.

6. **Fundamentals of Child Assessment:** An introduction to standardized testing and assessment of children.

7. **Advanced Child Assessment:** Principles of advanced behavioral analysis (applied and functional), play-based assessment, and developmental assessment with children.

8. **Developmental Trauma:** The neuro-developmental impact of developmental trauma, child abuse, and domestic violence and its treatment.

9. **Specialty Focus I:** Additional education and training in the area of the therapist's specialty focus, such as autism-spectrum disorders, ADHD and school-related issues, infancy assessment and treatment, trauma and foster care, forensic child custody evaluation, etc. Based on the desired comprehensiveness of the training, multiple specialty training courses can be required.

10. **Specialty Focus II:** Additional advanced education and training in the area of specialty focus is recommended for professional expertise.

Given the breadth and depth of education and training required for professional competence in child and family therapy, doctoral graduate programs in clinical psychology should strongly consider offering a separate specialty focus doctoral degree in clinical child therapy (Ph.D.-Child.; Psy.D.-Child). Professional organizations, such as the American Psychological Association, should also strongly consider whether the current depth and breadth of scientific research regarding child development is becoming so extensive and complex as to require a specialized professional focus in education and training for professional competence in child and family therapy, rather than simply representing an add-on to general doctoral education and training.

The current education of doctoral-level mental health professionals, however, typically falls far short of providing this level of professional training and expertise. The education of doctoral level child therapists typically focuses on providing training in adult mental health models for diagnosis and treatment, with child development and child therapy representing a supplemental consideration. The typical doctoral program provides students with training in the diagnostic categories of the DSM diagnostic system, in techniques of clinical interviewing and a few select models of psychotherapy (often only client-centered therapy and cognitive-behavior therapy), in assessment techniques and the use of testing instruments, in procedures of scientific research, a course in legal and ethical issues, a course in multicultural sensitivity, and usually just one class regarding development across the lifespan. The course in lifespan development typically covers all of the periods from prenatal development to old age. One course covering the entire lifespan allows little opportunity for a more in-depth and sophisticated education regarding the complexity of child development, particularly regarding the socially mediated neuro-development of the brain during childhood.

In terms of instruction in models of psychotherapy, doctoral students are typically first taught the "client-centered" approach of Carl Rogers which provides a foundation for their therapy work with clients. In the client-centered model, the therapist is taught to validate the patient's feelings and experiences by providing the client with unconditional acceptance and empathy. The central premise of the client-centered approach is that affording the client with the non-judgmental unconditional acceptance and empathy of the therapist will create the necessary relationship context for the client's personal growth and "self-actualization."

Once the student is taught the basic client-centered therapeutic principles of validating the client's feelings through non-judgmental acceptance of the client, the doctoral student is then usually instructed in the cognitive-behavioral model of psychotherapy next. Cognitive-behavioral therapy (CBT) offers the student a structured intervention model for directive therapy. Until the student-therapist learns more sophisticated and complex models of psychotherapy, such as psychoanalytic or family systems models, providing the student-therapist with a highly structured model of psychotherapy provides the new therapist with structured guidance that restricts the flexibility granted to the new therapist, and thus limits their potential for causing harm to the client.

This is typically the content of doctoral level instruction. Additional instruction in the more advanced models of psychoanalytic, family systems, and post-modern therapies are generally deferred to the therapist's own post-graduate study and initiative. A fledgling student therapist interested in child therapy might take an additional elective course in play therapy or behavioral therapy with children. Advanced training in the neurodevelopment of the brain during childhood, however, is not typically part of the educational curriculum. This level of advanced expertise in brain neuro-development is usually only acquired if the therapist seeks additional post-doctoral training in early childhood mental health, which is a limited area of sub-specialty practice.

This is the typical academic curriculum for a four-year doctoral program of study (with variations). A two-year master's level curriculum is further truncated, although some marriage and family therapy (MFT) programs may include an additional focus on models of family systems therapy rather than the scientific research methodology courses provided to doctoral level students.

Professional expertise in childhood development and child therapy is typically acquired during practicum and internship placements of the therapist in clinics offering child therapy. The typical models of child therapy taught are play therapy and behavior therapy. Play therapy is derived from a theoretical foundation proposed during the 1950s and 60s by Anna Freud (the daughter of Sigmund Freud) regarding the application of her father's approach of psychoanalysis to children. The play therapy model was extended in the 1960s by Virginia Axline who proposed a humanistic model of child play therapy that emphasizes non-directive child play in which the child is provided with unconditional acceptance in order to achieve the child's supposed "self-actualization" of authenticity. The play therapy model was further extended by Violet Oaklander into Gestalt therapy approaches to working with art therapy.

Behavioral therapy is derived from laboratory research conducted primarily in the 1940s and 50s regarding modifying the behavior of lab rats using various principles of operant and classical conditioning. As most commonly employed, behavior therapy with children involves modifying the contingencies of reward and punishment that children receive for their behavior. Modifying reward and punishment contingencies for behavior is an effort to influence the child's behavioral expressions into those desired by parents and teachers, and limiting the child's expression of behaviors that are not desired by parents and teachers.

Both of these child therapy approaches are archaic and foundationally primitive. The theoretical underpinnings for both approaches have been greatly superseded by the revolutionary advances in research on brain development and child development that have occurred within the past 50 years. But none of the wealth of information regarding brain and child development that has occurred during the past 50 years has been incorporated into our current approaches to educating and training child therapists, or into our models for child therapy. Professional models of child therapy are continuing to rely on outdated and archaic models developed during the early days of psychotherapy in the 1950s and 60s.

Gradually, ever so gradually, the revolutionary information acquired by science is starting to be incorporated into training and therapy, but this process is glacial at best. Most child therapists have little to no training in advanced principles of child development and neuro-relational child therapy. Rather than representing our best trained and most expert therapists, child therapists are often our least trained and most under-educated therapists.

Where current scientific evidence on brain and child development is most impacting training and therapy is in early childhood mental health. Mental health professionals who obtain sub-specialty training in early childhood mental health must acquire a professional level of expertise regarding the neuro-development of the brain during childhood, the various brain systems involved, and the implications for therapy. This information is so crucial to understanding child development generally that all mental health professionals working with children should possess extensive expertise in early childhood mental health as the foundation of their professional competence in working with children generally, irrespective of the age of the clients that the mental health professional then goes on to treat. Even adolescent mental health professionals need to have expertise in the socially mediated development of the brain in early childhood in order to understand the organizational core and fundamental processes of the brain systems they are treating in adolescence. Similarly, therapists treating school-age children should also possess a professional expertise in early childhood mental health in order to understand the foundations of the socially-mediated brain neuro-development during the childhood period that they are treating.

The period of childhood is so centrally important to both the child's development and to the person the child will eventually become, and the neuro-social processes of child development are so incredibly complex, that all mental health professionals working with children of any age should receive the highest level of training and should possess the highest level of expertise possible. This includes an expert level of understanding for the current scientific evidence related to the socially mediated neuro-development of the brain during childhood.

Yet almost no child therapists outside of the early childhood specialty are trained in or understand the current scientific research on the socially mediated neuro-development of the brain during childhood. Instead, most childhood mental health professionals employ only a superficial understanding of child development and use antiquated models from the 1950s and 60s for treatment that are not applicable to our current understanding of brain development during childhood. Outside of the field of early childhood mental health, our current approaches to child therapy do not incorporate the current scientific evidence regarding the factors creating healthy emotional and psychological development of children. In my view, this is unconscionable.

Mental health professionals working with children should be the most expert of all mental health professionals. Less than outstanding professional expertise regarding the foundational and elaborated aspects of childhood development is unacceptable given the crucial importance and complexity of childhood.

Domains of Professional Competence

The children and families evidencing attachment-based "parental alienation" represent a *special population* requiring specialized professional knowledge, training, and expertise to appropriately and competently diagnose and treat. Failure to possess the necessary specialized knowledge, training, and professional expertise needed to appropriately assess, diagnose, and treat this special population of children and families likely represents practice beyond the boundaries of professional competence in possible violation of professional practice standards. To the extent that professional ignorance and practice beyond the boundaries of professional competence then causes harm to the child client and to the targeted parent, the mental health professional may become vulnerable to professional or legal sanctions.

Given the domains of psychological processes involved in attachment-based "parental alienation," three areas of professional expertise are required for professional competence in assessing, diagnosing, and treating this *special population* of children and families.

1) Attachment Theory

A child's rejection of a relationship with a normal-range and affectionally available parent represents a foundational distortion to the functioning of the child's attachment system. The attachment system is a socially-mediated goal-corrected primary motivational system that directs the formation of attachment bonds, the response of the person to the loss of attachment bonds, and the approach used by the person to repair breaches in attachment bonds. The internalized and acquired patterns for attachment bonding are transmitted trans-generationally from parents to children, so that the attachment patterns of parents affect the parenting responses they provide to the child.

Mental health professionals who are diagnosing and treating a disorder that centrally involves the child's attachment system must possess professional expertise in the nature and functioning of the attachment system, both foundationally and as expressed at differing developmental periods, including adulthood, as well as trans-generationally.

The attachment system also functions and dysfunctions in characteristic ways, so that mental health professionals diagnosing and treating distortions to the functioning of the child's attachment system must possess professional expertise in the characteristic patterns of functioning and dysfunctioning displayed by the attachment system under differing parental contexts. In particular, mental health professionals working with the special population of children and families evidencing attachment-based "parental alienation" must possess professional expertise in the nature, origin, and expression of disorganized attachment, with a special focus on the formation of a role-reversal relationship in which the child is used by the parent as a "regulatory object" for the parent's emotional and psychological functioning.

The formation of a disorganized attachment (representing the attachment pattern of the narcissistic/(borderline) parent) is the product of developmental trauma. In addition, the child in attachment-based "parental alienation" often presents with an excessive phobic anxiety display falsely attributed to a post-traumatic response to a prior parent-child incident. As a result of these factors associated with attachment-based "parental alienation," a professional expertise in the causes, nature, and expression of developmental trauma, including its trans-generational impact on attachment bonding, is also necessary for the professionally competent assessment, diagnosis, and treatment of this special population of children and families.

Professional competence in diagnosing and treating family processes involving the trans-generational transmission of attachment trauma associated with attachment-based "parental alienation" requires a thorough professional understanding for and expertise in the functioning and dysfunctioning of the attachment system.

Attachment Content Domains of Knowledge

Recommendations for professional literature of vital importance for the development of professional expertise in this area would include:

Bowlby, J. (1969). Attachment and Loss: Vol. 1. Attachment. NY: Basic Books.

Bowlby, J. (1973). Attachment and Loss: Vol. 2. Separation: Anxiety and Anger. NY: Basic Books.

Bowlby, J. (1980). Attachment and Loss: Vol. 3. Loss: Sadness and Depression. NY: Basic Books.

Fonagy, P., Target, M., Gergely, G., Allen, J.G., and Bateman, A. W. (2003). The developmental roots of Borderline Personality Disorder in early attachment relationships: A theory and some evidence. Psychoanalytic Inquiry, 23, 412-459.

Fonagy P. and Target M. (2005). Bridging the transmission gap: An end to an important mystery in attachment research? Attachment and Human Development, 7, 333-343.

Fonagy, P., Luyten, P., and Strathearn, L. (2011). Borderline personality disorder, mentalization, and the neurobiology of attachment. Infant Mental Health Journal, 32, 47-69.

Lyons-Ruth, K., Bronfman, E. and Parsons, E. (1999). Maternal frightened, frightening, or atypical behavior and disorganized infant attachment patterns. In J. Vondra & D. Barnett (Eds.) Atypical patterns of infant attachment: Theory, research, and current directions. Monographs of the Society for Research in Child Development, 64, (3, Serial No. 258).

Main, M. and Hesse, E. (1990). Parents' unresolved traumatic experiences are related to infant disorganized attachment status: Is frightened and/or frightening parental behavior the linking mechanism? In M.T. Greenberg, D. Cicchetti, & E.M. Cummings (Eds.), Attachment in the preschool years: Theory, research, and intervention (pp. 161–182). Chicago: University of Chicago Press.

van IJzendoorn, M.H., Schuengel, C., and Bakermans-Kranenburg, M.J. (1999). Disorganized attachment in early childhood: Meta-analysis of precursors, concomitants, and sequelae. Development and Psychopathology, 11, 225–249.

Kerig, P.K. (2005). Revisiting the construct of boundary dissolution: A multidimensional perspective. Journal of Emotional Abuse, 5, 5-42.

Macfie, J. Fitzpatrick, K.L., Rivas, E.M. and Cox, M.J. (2008). Independent influences upon mother-toddler role-reversal: Infant-mother attachment disorganization and role reversal in mother's childhood. Attachment and Human Development, 10, 29-39

Macfie, J., McElwain, N.L., Houts, R.M., and Cox, M.J. (2005) Intergenerational transmission of role reversal between parent and child: Dyadic and family systems internal working models. Attachment & Human Development, 7, 51-65.

Pearlman, C.A. and Courtois, C.A. (2005). Clinical applications of the attachment framework: Relational treatment of complex trauma. Journal of Traumatic Stress, 18, 449-459.

Prager, J. (2003). Lost childhood, lost generations: the intergenerational transmission of trauma. Journal of Human Rights, 2, 173-181.

Shaffer, A., and Sroufe, L. A. (2005). The developmental and adaptational implications of generational boundary dissolution: Findings from a prospective, longitudinal study. Journal of Emotional Abuse. 5(2/3), 67-84.

Sroufe, L. A. (2005). Attachment and development: A prospective, longitudinal study from birth to adulthood, Attachment and Human Development, 7, 349-367.

Bacciagaluppi, M. (1985). Inversion of parent-child relationships: A contribution to attachment theory. British Journal of Medical Psychology, 58, 369-373.

Benoit, D. and Parker, K.C.H. (1994). Stability and transmission of attachment across three generations. Child Development, 65, 1444-1456

Brennan, K.A. and Shaver, P.R. (1998). Attachment styles and personality disorders: Their connections to each other and to parental divorce, parental death, and perceptions of parental caregiving. Journal of Personality 66, 835-878.

Bretherton, I. (1990). Communication patterns, internal working models, and the intergenerational transmission of attachment relationships. Infant Mental Health Journal, 11, 237-252.

Sable, P. (1997). Attachment, detachment and borderline personality disorder. Psychotherapy: Theory, Research, Practice, Training, 34(2), 171-181.

Cassidy, J., and Berlin, L. J. (1994). The insecure/ambivalent pattern of attachment: Theory and research. Child Development, 65, 971–991.

Mikulincer, M., Gillath, O., and Shaver, P.R. (2002). Activation of the attachment system in adulthood: Threat-related primes increase the accessibility of mental representations of attachment figures. Journal of Personality and Social Psychology, 83, 881-895.

Tronick, E.Z. (2003). Of course all relationships are unique: How co-creative processes generate unique mother-infant and patient-therapist relationships and change other relationships. Psychoanalytic Inquiry, 23, 473-491.

van der Kolk, B.A. (1987). The separation cry and the trauma response: Developmental issues in the psychobiology of attachment and separation. In B.A. van der Kolk (Ed.) Psychological Trauma (31-62). Washington, D.C.: American Psychiatric Press, Inc.

van der Kolk, B.A. (1989). The compulsion to repeat the trauma: Re-enactment, revictimization, and masochism. Psychiatric Clinics of North America, 12, 389-411

van Ijzendoorn, M.H. (1992) Intergenerational transmission of parenting: A review of studies in nonclinical populations. Developmental Review, 12, 76-99

Holmes, J. (2004). Disorganized attachment and borderline personality disorder: a clinical perspective. Attachment & Human Development, 6(2), 181-190.

Lopez, F. G., Fuendeling, J., Thomas, K., and Sagula, D. (1997). An attachment-theoretical perspective on the use of splitting defenses. Counseling Psychology Quarterly, 10, 461-472.

Raineki, C., Moriceau, S., and Sullivan, R.M. (2010). Developing a neurobehavioral animal model of infant attachment to an abusive caregiver. Biological Psychiatry, 67, 1137-1145.

Cozolino, L. (2006): The neuroscience of human relationships: Attachment and the developing social brain. WW Norton & Company, New York.

Siegel, D. (1999). The developing mind: Toward a neurobiology of interpersonal experience (New York: Guilford Press, 1999)

Iacoboni, M., Molnar-Szakacs, I., Gallese, V., Buccino, G., Mazziotta, J., and Rizzolatti, G. (2005). Grasping the intentions of others with one's own mirror neuron system. Plos Biology, 3(3), e79.

Kaplan, J. T., and Iacoboni, M. (2006). Getting a grip on other minds: Mirror neurons, intention understanding, and cognitive empathy. Social Neuroscience, 1(3/4), 175-183.

Fraiberg, S., Adelson, E., and Shapiro, V. (1975). Ghosts in the nursery. Journal of the American Academy of Child and Adolescent Psychiatry, 14, 387–421.

All mental health professionals treating this special population of children and families should have read the literature above in order to attain professional competence. To argue that mental health professionals should not have read the information above in order to competently understand and treat the attachment system distortions related to an attachment-based model of "parental alienation" is to argue in favor of professional ignorance as an acceptable standard of practice. If a mental health professional wishes to practice with a special population of children and families, it is incumbent upon the mental health professional to acquire the professional expertise necessary for competent professional practice. Professional ignorance and incompetence is not acceptable when working with children.

If professional ignorance and practice beyond the boundaries of professional competence is responsible for harm to the child client or targeted parent, the mental health professional may be vulnerable to professional or legal sanctions.

2. Narcissistic and Borderline Personality Disorders

The family processes surrounding attachment-based "parental alienation" prominently express the distorting influence of narcissistic and borderline personality processes on family relationships. Professional competence in the diagnosis and treatment of attachment-based "parental alienation" therefore also requires professional expertise in the core processes of narcissistic and borderline personalities, their formative dynamics, their characteristic expressions, and the characteristic features of their presentation in clinical interviews. A particular focus on the development and expression of the splitting dynamic and on the psychological decompensation of narcissistic and borderline personalities into delusional processes is necessary for competent professional diagnosis and treatment of the children and families expressing attachment-based "parental alienation."

Personality Disorder Content Domains of Knowledge

Recommendations for professional literature of vital importance for the development of professional expertise in this area would include:

Millon. T. (2011). Disorders of personality: introducing a DSM/ICD spectrum from normal to abnormal. Hoboken: Wiley.

Beck, A.T., Freeman, A., Davis, D.D., and Associates (2004). Cognitive therapy of personality disorders. (2nd edition). New York: Guilford.

Kernberg, O.F. (1975). Borderline conditions and pathological narcissism. New York: Aronson.

Moor, A. and Silvern, L. (2006). Identifying pathways linking child abuse to psychological outcome: The mediating role of perceived parental failure of empathy. Journal of Emotional Abuse, 6, 91-112.

Trippany, R.L., Helm, H.M. and Simpson, L. (2006). Trauma reenactment: Rethinking borderline personality disorder when diagnosing sexual abuse survivors. Journal of Mental Health Counseling, 28, 95-110.

Rappoport, A. (2005). Co-narcissism: How we accommodate to narcissistic parents. The Therapist.

Carlson, E.A., Edgeland, B., and Sroufe, L.A. (2009). A prospective investigation of the development of borderline personality symptoms. Development and Psychopathology, 21, 1311-1334.

Juni, S. (1995). Triangulation as splitting in the service of ambivalence. Current Psychology: Research and Reviews, 14, 91-111.

Barnow, S. Aldinger, M., Arens, E.A., Ulrich, I., Spitzer, C., Grabe, H., Stopsack, M. (2013). Maternal transmission of borderline personality disorder symptoms in the community-based Griefswald Family Study. Journal of Personality Disorders, 27, 806-819,

Dutton, D. G., Denny-Keys, M. K., and Sells, J. R. (2011). Parental personality disorder and its effects on children: A review of current literature. Journal of Child Custody, 8, 268-283.

Fruzzetti, A.E., Shenk, C. and Hoffman, P. (2005). Family interaction and the development of borderline personality disorder: A transactional model. Development and Psychopathology, 17, 1007-1030.

Garety, P. A. and Freeman D. (1999) Cognitive approaches to delusions: A critical review of theories and evidence. The British Journal of Clinical Psychology; 38, 113-154.

Hodges, S. (2003). Borderline personality disorder and posttraumatic stress disorder: Time for integration? Journal of Counseling and Development, 81, 409-417.

Levy, K.N. (2005). The implications of attachment theory and research for understanding borderline personality disorder. Development and Psychopathology, 17, p. 959-986

Stepp, S. D., Whalen, D. J., Pilkonis, P. A., Hipwell, A. E., and Levine, M. D. (2011). Children of mothers with Borderline Personality Disorder: Identifying parenting behaviors as potential targets for intervention. Personality Disorders: Theory, Research, and Treatment. 1-16.

Svrakic, D.M. (1990). Functional dynamics of the narcissistic personality. American Journal of Psychiatry. 44, 189-203.

Widiger, T.A. and Trull, T.J. (2007). Plate tectonics in the classification of personality disorder: Shifting to a dimensional model. American Psychologist, 62, 71-83.

Again, to argue that mental health professionals who are involved in diagnosing and treating family processes involving narcissistic and borderline personality dynamics should not be required to possess professional knowledge of narcissistic and borderline personality dynamics is to argue for the acceptability of professional ignorance. Treating family processes involving a narcissistic/(borderline) personality parent requires professional expertise in narcissistic and borderline personality processes, particularly as expressed in family relationship dynamics.

3. Family Systems Theory

Mental health professionals who are diagnosing and treating problematic family relationships need to possess foundational professional expertise in family relationship dynamics, which means family systems theory. Professional ignorance when diagnosing and treating children should not be acceptable professional practice.

The principle family systems model is Structural family systems theory articulated by Salvador Minuchin. Familiarity with additional family systems models, such as the works of Satir, Haley, Bowen, Madanes, and Boszormenyi-Nagy would greatly improve the expertise and clinical competence of the mental health professional working with children and families. Diagnosing and treating complex family relationship dynamics requires professional knowledge and expertise in recognizing and treating family processes. A recommended starting point would be the work of Salvador Minuchin:

Minuchin, S. (1974). Families and family therapy. Harvard University Press.

Special Population

Children and families evidencing attachment-based "parental alienation" represent a *special population* requiring specialized professional knowledge, training, and expertise to appropriately diagnose and treat.

If mental health professionals do not want to expend the effort needed to acquire the specialized professional knowledge, training, and expertise to appropriately and competently assess, diagnose, and treat children and families within this special population, then these mental health professionals should simply refrain from working with this special population of children and families and refer these children and families to mental health professionals who possess the needed professional knowledge and expertise. Mental health professionals who lack the necessary knowledge required for professional competence are not required to diagnose and treat this special population of children and family issues, and they should refrain from doing so.

It is unacceptable professional practice to remain ignorant and yet nevertheless continue to work with children and families who require a specialized professional knowledge and expertise to appropriately and competently assess, diagnose, and treat. The period of childhood is too important and crucial to the future development of the person, and to the future of children yet unborn who will be the recipients of this current child's future parenting, to allow the childhood of these children to be sacrificed to professional incompetence that is born of professional ignorance.

If a mental health professional wants to work with this special population of children and families, it is incumbent upon the mental health professional to acquire the necessary knowledge and expertise needed to appropriately assess, diagnose, and treat this special population of children and families. Professional competence is not a suggested professional practice, it is a professional obligation. Otherwise, the mental health professional should refer the client child and family to someone who does possesses the necessary knowledge and professional expertise necessary to competently assess, diagnose, and treat this special population of children and families.

Chapter 12

CONCLUSION

Integration

An attachment-based model of "parental alienation" provides an integrated and cohesive description of the psychological and family processes within each of three separate levels of analysis.

1. **Family Systems Level:** At the level of the family system, attachment-based "parental alienation" represents the triangulation of the child into the spousal conflict through the formation of a cross-generational coalition of the child with the allied and supposedly favored narcissistic/(borderline) parent against the other parent. The purpose of this cross-generational coalition is to stabilize the functional inability of the narcissistic/(borderline) parent to adaptively transition from an intact family structure united by the marriage to a separated family structure united by the child.

2. **Personality Disorder Level:** At the personality disorder level, attachment-based "parental alienation" represents the projective displacement of core self-inadequacy and abandonment fears onto the other parent by means of a role-reversal relationship with the child in which the child is induced into rejecting the other parent for alleged parental inadequacy. The child's induced rejection of the targeted parent is used by the narcissistic/(borderline) parent to regulate the emotional and psychological state of the parent.

3. **Attachment System Level:** At the level of the attachment system, attachment-based "parental alienation" represents the concurrent activation of two sets of attachment representations, one from the childhood of the narcissistic/(borderline) parent and one involving the current family members, which creates a psychological fusion of representations from past and present that leads the narcissistic/(borderline) parent to reenact past attachment trauma into and through current family relationships in an effort to achieve psychological mastery over the childhood trauma experience and its attendant anxiety.

An attachment-based model of "parental alienation" also provides a coherent description of the psychological and family processes that is integrated across the three separate levels of analysis:

1. **Family Systems Integration:** The difficulty in the family's ability to transition from an intact family structure to a separated family structure is the result of problems at the personality disorder level. The personality structure of the allied and supposedly favored narcissistic/(borderline) parent is characterologically unable to process sadness and grief, and instead translates these emotions into "anger and resentment, loaded with revengeful wishes" (Kernberg, 1975). The characterological inability of the narcissistic/(borderline) parent to process sadness prevents this parent from emotionally processing the losses surrounding the divorce, which then prevents the family's adaptive transition to a separated family structure. In addition, the splitting dynamic associated with narcissistic and borderline pathology makes the experience of ambiguity neurologically impossible. The neurological inability of the narcissistic/(borderline) personality structure to experience ambiguity in relationships requires that the ex-husband or ex-wife also become the ex-father or ex-mother as well.

2. **Personality Disorder Integration:** The pathology at the personality disorder level has its origins in attachment trauma from the childhood of the narcissistic/(borderline) parent that created internal working models of self-in-relationship as, "I am fundamentally inadequate as a person," and expectations for the attachment figure in relationship as, "I will be rejected and abandoned by the attachment figure because of my fundamental

inadequacy." The divorce activates these core attachment vulnerabilities, which leads to a defensive response of psychologically expelling these attachment vulnerabilities onto the other parent by means of the child's induced rejection of the targeted parent ("I'm not the inadequate and abandoned parent; you are"). Through the child's induced rejection of the targeted parent, it becomes the targeted parent who is the inadequate person (parent) who is being rejected (abandoned) by the child because of this fundamental personal (parental) inadequacy.

3. **Attachment Disorder Integration:** The attachment trauma in the childhood of the narcissistic/(borderline) parent created a disorganized attachment that coalesced during adolescence and young adulthood into stable, but pathological, narcissistic/(borderline) personality traits. The underlying disorganized attachment of the narcissistic/(borderline) parent is unable to effectively restore breaches to the relationship and so requires a constantly fused psychological state with the external "regulating object" of the attachment figure. The divorce collapses the fragile personality structure of the narcissistic/(borderline) parent into disorganized attachment networks that engage the external "regulatory object" of the child to stabilize and prevent the psychological collapse of the narcissistic/(borderline) parent into primal psychological disorganization.

An attachment-based model of "parental alienation" provides a cohesive and integrated description of the complex pathology across the full range and specificity of clinical features. For a theoretical model to provide such an integrated and cohesive description of a clinical phenomenon from within each of three separate levels of analysis, and also across all three of these separate levels of analysis, it must reflect an accurate description of the psychological and family processes involved. An attachment-based model of "parental alienation" represents an accurate description of the clinical phenomenon traditionally referred to as "parental alienation."

From this theoretical formulation, an attachment-based model of "parental alienation" provides a set of three definitive diagnostic indicators in the child's symptom display that will accurately identify the induced pathology evidenced in the child's symptom display of pathogenic parenting by a narcissistic/(borderline) parent. This set of three diagnostic indicators will accurately identify cases of attachment-based "parental alienation, and will reliably differentiate cases of attachment-based "parental alienation" from all other possible causes of post-divorce parent-child conflict. The three definitive diagnostic indicators for attachment-based "parental alienation" are:

1. **Attachment System Suppression:** A suppression of the child's attachment bonding motivations as evidenced by a child-initiated cutoff in the child's relationship with a normal-range and affectionally available parent.

2. **Personality Disorder Symptoms:** The child's symptoms will evidence a specific set of five a-priori predicted narcissistic/borderline personality traits directed toward the targeted-rejected parent, reflecting the child's role-reversal use as a "regulatory object" by a narcissistic/(borderline) allied and supposedly favored parent. In the anxiety variant, the child's symptoms will evidence an excessive anxiety surrounding the targeted-rejected parent that will meet DSM-5 criteria for a specific phobia, but the type of phobia will be a bizarre and unrealistic "mother type" or "father type."

3. **Delusional Belief System:** The child's symptoms will evidence an intransigently held, fixed and false belief (i.e., a delusion) regarding the supposedly "abusive" parenting practices of a normal-range and affectionally available parent. This delusional belief held by the child is the result of the child's induced role in a trauma reenactment of the narcissistic/(borderline) parent expressed in the pattern of "abusive parent"/"victimized child"/"protective parent."

Processes of "Parental Alienation"

Attachment-based "parental alienation" involves the following set of psychological and family systems dynamics:

- The child is triangulated into the spousal conflict through the formation of a cross-generational role-reversal relationship of the child with a narcissistic/(borderline) parent in which the child is used by the narcissistic/(borderline) parent as a "regulatory object" to stabilize the emotional and psychological state of the parent.

- The splitting dynamic of the narcissistic/(borderline) personality is neurologically incapable of accommodating to ambiguity, so that the addition of parental narcissistic and borderline pathology to a cross-generational coalition with the child transmutes the pathology of the cross-generational coalition into a particularly malignant and virulent form of pathology that seeks to entirely terminate the other parent's attachment bond to the child (i.e.. the ex-spouse must become an ex-parent as well).

- The activation of excessive anxiety within the personality structure of the narcissistic/(borderline) parent results in the psychological decompensation of the narcissistic/(borderline) personality structure into a delusional belief system regarding the threat potential posed by the targeted parent.

- The narcissistic/(borderline) parent projectively displaces onto the targeted parent the core self-inadequacy and abandonment fears of the narcissistic/(borderline) parent through the child's induced rejection of the targeted parent.

- The delusional beliefs of the narcissistic/(borderline) parent are transferred to the child's interpretation of relationship dynamics through the child's role-reversal relationship as a "regulatory object" for the narcissistic/(borderline) parent, and through a series of manipulative and distorted communications and parenting practices by the narcissistic/(borderline) parent.

- A psychological equivalence of current family members with prior trauma patterns contained within the attachment system of the narcissistic/(borderline) parent is created by the concurrent co-activation of two sets of representational networks in the narcissistic/(borderline) parent's attachment system, one set representing the instantiated trauma representations of "abusive parent"/"victimized child"/"protective parent" that are contained in the internal working models of the attachment system, and the other set representing the current family members of the targeted parent, the current child, and the self-representation for the narcissistic/(borderline) parent.

- The child is induced into adopting the "victimized child" role in a trauma reenactment narrative of the narcissistic/(borderline) parent, which then automatically defines the other two roles in the trauma reenactment, of the "abusive parent" as being the targeted parent and the "protective parent" as being the allied narcissistic/(borderline) parent.

- The two corrective changes to the original childhood trauma experience of child empowerment and the availability of a real-world protector for the "victimized child" through the "protective parent" role adopted by the narcissistic/(borderline) parent provide key anxiety management functions for the narcissistic/(borderline) parent in achieving psychological mastery over the childhood trauma experience.

- The termination of the child's attachment bonding motivations toward the targeted-rejected parent essentially represents the trans-generational transmission of attachment trauma from the childhood of the narcissistic/(borderline) parent into the current family relationships through the reenactment of childhood attachment trauma in the current family relationships.

The complicated and interwoven pathology of attachment-based "parental alienation" represents sufficiently unique and complex domains of professional expertise as to warrant the designation of children and families expressing the psychological dynamics of attachment-based "parental alienation" as being a *special population* who require specialized professional knowledge, training, and expertise to appropriately and accurately assess, diagnose, and treat.

A professional level of competence in specific content areas of knowledge related to the attachment system, narcissistic and borderline personality dynamics, childhood developmental trauma, and family systems theory are all necessary for the accurate assessment, diagnosis, and treatment of this special population of children and families. Failure to possess the requisite knowledge, training, and professional expertise in the domains of knowledge needed for professional competence may represent practice beyond the boundaries of professional competence, in possible violation of professional practice standards. To the extent that harm then accrues to the child and targeted parent as a consequence of practice beyond the boundaries of professional competence in assessing, diagnosing, and treating this special population of children and families, the mental health professional may become exposed to professional and legal sanctions.

The role-reversal relationship of the child with a narcissistic/(borderline) parent in which the child is used as a "regulatory object" by the parent to regulate the parent's own pathology is extremely destructive to the normal-range and healthy development of the child. Not only will the child's role-reversal relationship with the narcissistic/(borderline) parent impoverish the child's development of autonomous self-structure, the child will also lose an affectionally bonded relationship with a normal-range, loving, and affectionally available parent across important periods of child development. Once lost, these developmental periods of affectional bonding with a parent cannot be recovered. Children love their parents, both parents, and the loss of an affectionally bonded relationship with a loving parent is highly damaging to the internal working models of the child's attachment system. The psychological damage within the child's attachment system becomes especially pronounced when the child is made to be the agent that causes the loss of the relationship with the loving and affectionally available parent.

What superficially appears to be the child's bonded relationship with the narcissistic/(borderline) parent, is not. It is actually a severely pathological role-reversal relationship. The narcissistic/(borderline) parent is essentially feeding off of the child's self-structure development to support the inadequate self-regulation of the narcissistic/(borderline) parent. The role-reversal use of the child as a "regulatory object" for the parent's emotional and psychological regulation is extremely destructive to the child's healthy development. Attachment-based "parental alienation" is not a child custody issue, it is a child protection issue.

The first step in restoring the child's healthy and normal-range development is to protectively separate the child from the ongoing pathogenic influence of the narcissistic/(borderline) parent. The child's protective separation from the pathology of the narcissistic/(borderline) parent during the active phase of the child's treatment and recovery represents an appropriate child protection response to the pathogenic parenting of the narcissistic/(borderline) parent, and it protects the child from being turned into a psychological battleground between the efforts of therapy to restore normal-range and healthy child development and the unrelenting efforts of the narcissistic/(borderline) parent to maintain the child's pathology. Once the child is psychologically protected, therapy can be initiated to restore the child's self-authenticity and normal-range affectionally bonded relationship with the beloved but currently rejected targeted parent.

The family processes of attachment-based "parental alienation" represent the child's entanglement into the spousal conflict of his or her parents. Children deserve a childhood that is free from the stress of their parents' spousal conflict, and they deserve to love and be loved by both parents. Both parents also deserve to love and be loved by their children. The professional controversy surrounding the construct of "parental alienation" needs to be brought to a close so that children who are caught in their parents' spousal conflict can be granted a normal and healthy childhood of loving their parents, both parents, and of being loved by both parents in return.

References

Ainsworth, M.D.S. (1989). Attachments beyond infancy. American Psychologist, 44, 709-716.

Beck, A.T., Freeman, A., Davis, D.D., & Associates (2004). Cognitive therapy of personality disorders. (2nd edition). New York: Guilford.

Bowlby, J. (1969). Attachment and Loss: Vol. 1. Attachment. NY: Basic Books.

Bowlby, J. (1973). Attachment and Loss: Vol. 2. Separation: Anxiety and Anger. NY: Basic.

Fonagy, P., Luyten, P., and Strathearn, L. (2011). Borderline personality disorder, mentalization, and the neurobiology of attachment. Infant Mental Health Journal, 32, 47-69.

Fruzzetti, A.E., Shenk, C. and Hoffman, P. (2005). Family interaction and the development of borderline personality disorder: A transactional model. Development and Psychopathology, 17, 1007-1030.

Haley, J. (1977). Toward a theory of pathological systems. In P. Watzlawick & J. Weakland (Eds.), The interactional view (pp. 31-48). New York: Norton.

Holmes, J. (2004). Disorganized attachment and borderline personality disorder: a clinical perspective. Attachment & Human Development, 6(2), 181-190.

Kernberg, O.F. (1975). Borderline conditions and pathological narcissism.. New York: Aronson.

Kerig, P.K. (2005). Revisiting the construct of boundary dissolution: A multidimensional perspective. Journal of Emotional Abuse, 5, 5-42.

Kohut, H. (1971). The analysis of the self. New York: International University Press.

Levy, K.N. (2005). The implications of attachment theory and research for understanding borderline personality disorder. Development and Psychopathology, 17, p. 959-986

Linehan, M. M. (1993). Cognitive-behavioral treatment of borderline personality disorder. New York, NY: Guilford

Linehan, M. M. & Koerner, K. (1993). Behavioral theory of borderline personality disorder. In J. Paris (Ed.), Borderline Personality Disorder: Etiology and Treatment. Washington, D.C.: American Psychiatric Press, 103-21.

Lyons-Ruth, K., Bronfman, E. & Parsons, E. (1999). Maternal frightened, frightening, or atypical behavior and disorganized infant attachment patterns. In J. Vondra & D. Barnett (Eds.) Atypical patterns of infant attachment: Theory, research, and current directions. Monographs of the Society for Research in Child Development, 64, (3, Serial No. 258).

Macfie, J., McElwain, N.L., Houts, R.M., and Cox, M.J. (2005) Intergenerational transmission of role reversal between parent and child: Dyadic and family systems internal working models. Attachment & Human Development, 7, 51-65.

Main, M., & Hesse, E. (1990). Parents' unresolved traumatic experiences are related to infant disorganized attachment status: Is frightened and/or frightening parental behavior the linking mechanism? In M.T. Greenberg, D. Cicchetti, & E.M. Cummings (Eds.), Attachment in the preschool years: Theory, research, and intervention (pp. 161–182). Chicago: University of Chicago Press.

"syndrome." (2015). In Merriam-Webster.com Retrieved March 3, 2015, from http://www.merriam-webster.com/dictionary/syndrome

Millon. T. (2011). Disorders of personality: introducing a DSM/ICD spectrum from normal to abnormal. Hoboken: Wiley.

Mineka, S., Davidson, M., Cook, M. and Keir, R. (1984). Observational conditioning of snake fear in rhesus monkeys. Journal of Abnormal Psychology, 93, 355-372.

Minuchin, S. (1974). Families and family therapy. Harvard University Press.

Pearlman, C.A., Courtois, C.A. (2005). Clinical applications of the attachment framework: Relational treatment of complex trauma. Journal of Traumatic Stress, 18, 449-459.

Raineki, C., Moriceau, S., Sullivan, R.M. (2010). Developing a neurobehavioral animal model of infant attachment to an abusive caregiver. Biological Psychiatry, 67, 1137-1145.

Rappoport, A. (2005). Co-narcissism: How we accommodate to narcissistic parents. The Therapist.

Sroufe, L.A. (2000). Early relationships and the development of children. Infant Mental Health Journal, 21(1-2), 67-74.

Shaffer, A., & Sroufe, L. A. (2005). The Developmental and adaptational implications of generational boundary dissolution: Findings from a prospective, longitudinal study. Journal of Emotional Abuse. 5(2/3), 67-84.

Trevarthen, C. (2001). The neurobiology of early communication: Intersubjective regulations in human brain development. In Kalverboer, A.F. and Gramsbergen, A. (Eds) Handbook of Brain and Behaviour in Human Development. London: Kluwer Academic Publishers

Tronick, E.Z. (2003). Of course all relationships are unique: How co-creative processes generate unique mother-infant and patient-therapist relationships and change other relationships. Psychoanalytic Inquiry, **23**, 473-491.

van der Kolk, B.A. (2005). Developmental trauma disorder. Psychiatric Annals, 35(5), 401-408.

Young, J. E, Klosko, J. S., and Weishaar, M.E (2003). Schema therapy: a practitioner's guide. New York: Guilford Press.

ABOUT THE AUTHOR

Dr. Childress is a licensed clinical psychologist currently in private practice in Pasadena, California. He teaches graduate level courses in Models of Psychotherapy, Assessment and Treatment Planning, Diagnosis and Psychopathology, Research Methods, and Child Development. Prior to entering private practice, Dr. Childress served as the Clinical Director for an early childhood assessment and treatment center primarily working with children in the foster care system. The clinical focus of Dr. Childress is child and family therapy, the treatment of Attention Deficit Hyperactivity Disorder (ADHD), angry and oppositional children, parent-child conflicts, parenting, and marital problems. He also has an additional clinical expertise in early childhood mental health, with a focus on the neurodevelopment of the brain during childhood.